SOCIAL WORK: THEMES, ISSUES AND CRITICAL DEBATES

Co-edited title by the editors:
Critical Practice in Social Work

Other titles by Robert Adams:

A Measure of Diversion? Case Studies in IT (co-author)
Prison Riots in Britain and the USA (2nd edition)
Problem-solving with Self-help Groups (co-author)
Protests by Pupils: Empowerment, Schooling and the State
Quality Social Work
Self-help, Social Work and Empowerment
Skilled Work with People
Social Policy for Social Work
Social Work and Empowerment (2nd edition)
Social Work With and Within Groups (co-author)
The Abuses of Punishment
The Personal Social Services: Clients, Consumers or Citizens?

Other titles by Lena Dominelli:

Beyond Racial Divides: Ethnicities in Social Work (co-author)
Feminist Social Work Theory and Practice (Palgrave)
Community Action and Organising Marginalised Groups
Women in Focus, Community Service Orders and Female Offenders
Love and Wages: The Impact of Imperialism, State Intervention and Women's
  Domestic Labour on Workers Control in Algeria
Anti-racist Social Work (2nd edition)
Feminist Social Work (co-author)
Women and Community Action
Women Across Continents: Feminist Comparative Social Policy
Gender, Sex Offenders and Probation Practice
Getting Advice in Urdu
International Directory of Social Work
Anti-racist Perspectives in Social Work (co-author)
Anti-racist Probation Practice (co-author)
Sociology for Social Work
Beyond Racial Divides: Ethnicities in Social Work (co-author)
Feminist Social Work Theory and Practice

Other titles by Malcolm Payne:

Teamwork in Multiprofessional Care
What is Professional Social Work?
Social Work and Community Care
Linkages: Effective Networking in Social Care
Modern Social Work Theory (2nd edition)
Writing for Publication in Social Services Journals (2nd edition)
Social Care in the Community
Working in Teams
Power, Authority and Responsibility in Social Services: Social Work in Area Teams

Social Work: Themes, Issues and Critical Debates

Second Edition

Edited by

Robert Adams, Lena Dominelli and Malcolm Payne

Consultant editor: Jo Campling

palgrave in association with The Open University

First edition 1998
Reprinted five times
Second edition 2002

Published by
PALGRAVE
Houndmills, Basingstoke, Hampshire RG21 6XS and
175 Fifth Avenue, New York, N.Y. 10010
Companies and representatives throughout the world

PALGRAVE is the new global academic imprint of
St. Martin's Press LLC Scholarly and Reference Division and
Palgrave Publishers Ltd (formerly Macmillan Press Ltd).

ISBN 0–333–98593–1 paperback   07370

This book is printed on paper suitable for recycling and
made from fully managed and sustained forest sources.

A catalogue record for this book is available
from the British Library.

Editing and origination by
Aardvark Editorial, Mendham, Suffolk

10 9 8 7 6 5 4 3 2 1
11 10 09 08 07 06 05 04 03 02

Printed in Great Britain by
Creative Print & Design (Wales), Ebbw Vale

Contents

List of Figures and Tables

Figures

Tables

Notes on the Contributors

Robert Adams is a qualified social worker who worked in the penal system for several years, latterly as Deputy Governor of a young offenders' institution, before running a community-based social work project for Barnardo's. He has written extensively about youth and criminal justice, social work and the personal social services, and protest and empowerment. He is Professor of Human Services Development attached to the Policy Studies Research Centre at the University of Lincoln and Visiting Professor in the School of Health, University of Teesside.

Suzy Braye is a Reader in Social Work in the Department of Sociology, Social Policy and Social Work Studies at the University of Liverpool. She has a range of professional experience in practice, education, staff development and management, with professional interests in children's services and mental health. She is joint author, with Michael Preston-Shoot, of *Practising Social Work Law*, 2nd edn (1997) and *Empowering Practice in Social Care* (1995). Since 1990, they have published articles exploring partnership, empowerment, anti-oppressive practice and social work law.

Beverley Burke is Senior Lecturer on the DipSW course at Liverpool John Moores University. Her current work includes teaching and training on anti-oppressive practice to students and practitioners. Trained as a generic social worker, her main practice has been largely in the area of child protection. She has recently been involved in therapeutic work with women survivors of sexual abuse.

Katy Cigno PhD until recently worked as Senior Lecturer at the University of Hull. She is still a Specialist Practice Teacher for Wakefield Community and Social Services Department. She was a founder member of the Cognitive Behavioural Social Work Group, which she currently chairs.

Helen Cosis Brown is the Course Director for the Masters in Social Work at South Bank University. She was a social worker and team leader for ten years in an inner London borough. She has continued to offer training in the field of fostering and adoption and has a number of publications relating to social work practice with lesbians and gay men.

Viviene E. Cree is a lecturer in the Department of Social Work and Associate Dean (Admissions) of the Faculty of Social Sciences at the University of Edinburgh. Before this, she worked for sixteen years as a social work practitioner and practice teacher, in both statutory and voluntary organisations. She has conducted research on social work history and social work education, and her current research is on children with a parent or carer with HIV.

Mark Doel is Professor of Social Work and Head of the School of Social Work and RNIB Rehabilitation Studies at the University of Central England in Birmingham. He trained as a task-centred practitioner in 1981 and has used the task-centred method extensively in his practice, teaching, writing and research. Since 1994, he has been developing task-centred programmes at post-qualifying level with colleagues at Sheffield University and Wakefield Social Services Department.

Lena Dominelli is Professor of Social and Community Development in the Department of Social Work Studies at the University of Southampton where she is the Director of the Centre for International Social and Community Development. She is also currently the President of the International Association of Schools of Social Work. Besides being an educator and researcher, she has had practice experience as a social worker, probation officer and community worker. She has a vast array of publications to her name. Her most significant publications include *Feminist Social Work Theory and Practice* (2002), *Anti-racist Social Work*, 2nd edn (1997) and *Sociology for Social Work* (1997).

Angela Everitt is an Honorary Research Fellow at the University of Durham and runs 'Reading Lasses', a second-hand radical bookshop in Wigtown, Scotland's Book Town, specialising in women's studies and social studies. For a number of years, she worked in social work education and social research, undertaking research and evaluation studies with a wide variety of statutory and voluntary organisations and community groups.

Philomena Harrison is Senior Lecturer on the DipSW course at Liverpool John Moores University. Her current work includes teaching and training on anti-oppressive practice to students and practitioners. Trained as a psychiatric social worker, her main practice experience has been with children and families. She is currently undertaking direct work around issues of identity with black children who are using personal social services.

David Howe is Professor of Social Work at the University of East Anglia, Norwich. His research and writing interests include child maltreatment, family support, attachment theory and adoption. He is the editor of the journal *Child and Family Social Work*. His two most recent books are *Attachment Theory for Social Work Practice* (1995) and *Patterns of Adoption* (1998).

Chris Jones is Professor of Social Policy and Social Work at the University of Liverpool, and Head of the Department of Sociology, Social Policy and Social Work Studies. He is a Marxist academic whose recent publications have been concerned with current developments in Britain's social work policy and education.

Mary Langan is Senior Lecturer in Applied Social Sciences at the Open University. In the early 1970s, she was an inner-city social worker and an active participant in the radical social work movement. She has written extensively on social policy, social work and health in *Crises in the British State 1830–1930* (1985, with Bill Scharz), *Radical Social Work Today* (1989, with Phil Lee), *Women, Oppression and Social Work* (1992, with Lesley Day), *Criminological Perspectives – a Reader* (1996, with John Muncie) and *Welfare Needs, Rights and Risks* (1998). She is also general editor of the Routledge social policy series, The State of Welfare.

Michael Leadbetter is Director of Social Services for Essex and President of the Association of Directors of Social Services. He is the longest serving director in England and Wales and takes a particular interest in childcare and service user empowerment.

Joyce Lishman is Professor and Head of the School of Applied Social Studies at the Robert Gordon University, Aberdeen. Her practice experience was with children and adolescents, including children with cancer and leukaemia, and their families. She has taught on social work courses at non-graduate, degree and postgraduate levels. She was lead assessor in the quality assessment of social work in Scotland in 1995. Her research has been primarily in client perceptions and the analysis of social work interviews, and more recently on the role of volunteers within the social services. She is general editor of the Research Highlights in Social Work series.

Janice McGhee is Lecturer in the Department of Social Work in the University of Edinburgh, with responsibility for teaching law and human development on the Master of Social Work course. She qualified as a social worker in 1979 and has worked in a local authority social work team and a social work department emergency duty team providing an out-of-hours service. Much of her career has involved direct work with children and families, although she has also been employed as a senor social worker in a large London teaching hospital.

Marjorie Mayo is a Reader in Community Development in Professional and Community Education at Goldsmiths College, University of London. She has taught, carried out research and written about community participation and community development and she has also worked in a variety of practice settings.

Audrey Mullender is Professor in Social Work at the University of Warwick and an elected Academician of the Academy of Learned Societies for the Social Sciences. She was, for four years until the end of 1999, editor of the *British Journal of Social Work* and has herself produced well over a hundred publications in the social work field, including ten books. She has recently jointly authored studies of children's perspectives on living with domestic violence, women's voices in domestic violence services, groups for domestic violence perpetrators and mapping family support services in domestic violence across the UK.

Joan Orme is Professor of Social Work at the University of Glasgow. She has researched workload measurement from the perspective of both trade unions and management and is firmly committed to the need to ensure that workload issues are considered as part of effective practice for the protection of both service users and workers.

Nigel Parton is Professor in Child Care and Director of the Centre for Applied Childhood Studies at the University of Huddersfield. A qualified social worker, he has a particular interest in child welfare and child protection, and social theory and social work. He has published numerous papers on the general theme of postmodernity and social work. He is the author (with Patrick O'Byrne) of *Constructive Social Work: Towards a New Practice* (2000), and is currently working on a new book (with Julie Boffa and Andrew Turnell) entitled *Constructive Social Work in Child Protection*, to be published in 2003.

Malcolm Payne is Professor of Applied Community Studies, Manchester Metropolitan University, having previously worked in probation, social services departments and the national and local voluntary sector. He is author most recently of *Social Work and Community Care* (1995), *What is Professional Social Work?* (1996), *Modern Social Work Theory*, 2nd edn (1997) and *Teamwork in Multiprofessional Care* (1998).

Stella Perrott is a Social Work Services Inspector with the Scottish Office. She was previously an Assistant Chief Probation Officer and part-time Lecturer in Management. Her publications include 'Working with men who abuse women and children' in Lupton, C. and Gillespie, T. (eds) *Working with Violence* (1994).

Michael Preston-Shoot is Professor of Social Work and Social Care at Liverpool John Moores University. He has a background in social work and family therapy, and has recently completed research on user and carer views of community care services and on equal opportunities in education and training. He is currently undertaking research on practice teachers and social work law. He is joint author, with Suzy Braye, of *Practising Social Work Law*, 2nd edn (1997) and *Empowering*

Practice in Social Care (1995). Since 1990, they have published articles exploring partnership, empowerment, anti-oppressive practice and social work law.

Lena Robinson is Lecturer in Psychology at the University of Birmingham and has been in social work education for many years. She is the author of *Psychology for Social Workers: Black Perspectives* (1995) and *Race, Communication, and the Caring Professions* (in press) and has researched on issues related to racial identity and children in care.

Steven M. Shardlow is Professor of Social Work at the University of Salford, England and editor-in-chief of the *Journal of Social Work*. Previously he has worked as a social work practitioner and manager in both field and residential work. He has been involved in international social work, particularly in Europe, through development work, consultancy and research. Current research and teaching interests are in the following areas: professional ethics; comparative social practice in the social professions; professional social work education and practice – especially practice learning. He has published widely in these fields and his work has been translated into several languages.

Neil Thompson is a Director of Avenue Consulting Ltd (www.avenuecon-sulting.co.uk) and a Visiting Professor at the University of Liverpool. He is the author of several books, including *Promoting Equality* (1998), *Stress Matters* (Pepar, 1999), *Tackling Bullying and Harassment in the Workplace* (2000), *Anti-Discriminatory Practice*, 3rd edn (2001) and *People Skills*, 2nd edn (2002).

Alan Walker is Professor of Social Policy in the Department of Sociological Studies at the University of Sheffield. He has researched and written extensively on the fields of poverty, inequality, social exclusion, disability, ageing and European social policy.

Carol Walker is Professor of Social Policy in the School of Health and Community Studies at Sheffield Hallam University. She has researched and published widely in the fields of poverty and social security, and services for people with learning difficulties.

Dave Ward is Professor of Social and Community Studies at De Montfort University, Leicester. The Centre for Social Action at De Montfort University promotes and undertakes practice, training and research within the principles of the anti-oppressive groupwork advocated in his chapter.

Lorraine Waterhouse is Professor in the Department of Social Work at the University of Edinburgh with responsibility for childcare teaching. She qualified as a social worker in 1972. She has worked in child and family psychiatry and is currently on the Parole Board of Scotland.

Introduction

Robert Adams, Lena Dominelli and Malcolm Payne

The fact that a second edition of this book about social work theories, approaches and practice is necessary within five years of its first publication is recognition of the significant changes occurring since we first prepared this text. We are reminded that when the first edition was being planned and prepared in 1996 and 1997, many of the changes in the laws, policies and the wider social and political context were not envisaged. Concern about human rights issues in Britain, the European Union and elsewhere have led to many initiatives, including the enactment of the Human Rights Act 1998 in the UK. Two successive Labour governments elected in landslide victories in the UK have generated massive swathes of legislation, much of which affects the health and social services as well as criminal justice. Devolution of the UK has gathered momentum, in the form of differing arrangements for governing England, Northern Ireland, Scotland and Wales (Payne and Shardlow, 2002). Remarkably perhaps, the climate of major debates about social work approaches and practice remain unaltered, although their local weather changes. Social work remains highly visible and makes an increasingly important contribution to almost all aspects of social policy and practice – including community care, work with children and families, employment and unemployment issues, health care, housing practice, criminal and youth justice, schooling, and work with people on social security and experiencing poverty. Social work is as essential as ever, in the UK as in other countries. Social problems of conflict and poverty come to our attention more readily through the enhanced power of the mass media and long-distance satellite, electronic and telecommunications. Many of the social problems shared by people in different countries have parallels in the difficulties and uncertainties which individuals and families face in their relationships through the life course. Social workers practise at those points in people's lives where risks and uncertainties are often greatest and at the junctions with many other services, including health care, education, employment and unemployment, mental health and social security. Often, social work involves taking decisions in circumstances where there is no single preferred or ideal solution and in continuing, subsequent work with people.

Although the complexities of the problems people face in their lives create many challenges for social workers, in determining how to respond they can refer to an extensive body of literature which engages with different theories and approaches to practice. Of course, these theories and approaches change as social conditions, policies and laws change and in the process are subject to debate, often arising from different experiences and perspectives. So, the second edition of this book is still unfinished, as befits the constantly changing nature of social work.

This book introduces the main currents of theory, research and practice in social work, but it does not provide only a single and preliminary summary of the important features of social work. The book is introductory, in the sense of being an invitation: we invite the reader into the territory of social work contexts, values, approaches and practices. We introduce into this territory some of the ideas that participate in current debates in social work. Readers should feel free to be swept into these debates. You should apply your mind and experience to understand, evaluate and criticise the positions taken. In this way, you are introducing yourself into social work and introducing social work into your thinking and action.

We have provided chapters which are more than pure expositions of each topic, based simply on asking experts to summarise their research or their major book in their specialism. Each chapter offers an 'insider' perspective on its particular topic, but also adopts a critical 'outsider' position. This makes it possible to examine issues, engage in debates with other aspects and sustain throughout the book the spirit of what Lena Dominelli (Chapter 1) calls 'dialogue over controversies'.

While some readers of this book will be new to social work, no one should regard themselves as a beginner. The backgrounds of all readers will impinge on its contents. Students will bring their life experiences and academic and personal preparations for social work to bear on the book's coverage of essential aspects of social work; practitioners will be able to illuminate its analysis of current debates with their own experiences; and general readers from other disciplines and professions, with an interest in social work, will find easy access to its subject matter to chart against their own perspectives. In every case, readers bring themselves to the book and can examine the effect of reading it on their understanding and practice.

Many edited collections of essays achieve a degree of integration through the selection of contributors from a single network or a shared, unifying perspective. This book, in contrast, arises from Palgrave Macmillan bringing together three editors of different experience and stance, who have in their turn recruited a group of 28 authors from diverse backgrounds and traditions, and who have enabled this diversity of experience and perspective to interact and, on occasions, bite on each other.

We are living and working in a period when, in the UK at any rate, the monolithic social services department is about to disappear. It is more realistic to participate in continuing debates about the future of social work than to invest in the fallacy that the structures and organisations which sustain it will continue for ever. However, irrespective of how the personal social services are labelled, and how their staff are designated, social work will not disappear. This book contributes to the affirmation of the centrality of knowledge and values of social work, irrespective of such changes as the deconstruction of social services departments.

In the way we have set about creating this book, it occurs to us in retrospect that we have put into practice several core values of social work: respecting other people's views; active listening and not competing with someone else over their point of view; and rejecting conflict and anger, while valuing difference and diversity. Such values have a quality which in our view transcends some postmodern perspectives, asserting the fragmentation of all realities. We are doubtful of the view that all reality is ephemeral. We believe that in social work, to say nothing of other aspects of life and work, people share their dreams, visions, ideals and continuities, for example in the personal and professional values they espouse. To be human is to go beyond the ultimate fragmentation of individualism and competition, by collectively creating and ordering responses to the world. Social work, as a socially constructed project aiming to tackle oppression, is in this sense a perpetually changing and unfinished project. It faces enduring divisions and inequalities in societies throughout the world, where problems such as poverty and a lack of access to other resources such as education affect people's ability to fulfil themselves and others. Poor people, for example, cannot get a purchase on participation, no matter how professionals go on about empowerment. We give these ideas about poverty – from an historical perspective (Chapter 4) and informed by contemporary research (Chapter 5) – due prominence in Part I of the book, but these are not matters for academic debate alone. They are aspects of widespread human need which require challenging in ways not always recognised adequately from the vantage point of a postmodern perspective.

Therefore, we believe that social justice is a theme woven into everything we do, as a way of approaching social work, not as part of a hierarchy of knowledges and objects 'out there', or a reductionist set of ideas, but as a perspective which informs our thoughts and feelings. For justice to be done to the ideas and experiences addressed in this book, practitioners' passions as well as their intellectual attentions are likely to be engaged. Authors' views also interact with their feelings about their subjects. There should be no segregation either between academic and practitioner perspectives. Viewing knowledge in a broader sense, as crossing personal, professional and disciplinary among many other boundaries, is difficult but worthwhile, since in the process intellectual and experiential knowledge – academic and practice wisdom – interact, sometimes very creatively. Where appropriate, we have deliberately encouraged the authors to display their commitment and, by implication, their individuality through the strength of the cases they advance for their viewpoint on their topics. This is also a feature of social work: the capacity to allow individuals to express their diversity and their uniqueness, the quality of their ideas and experiences, through their work.

All three of us believe in academic discourse being essential. None of us can describe the nature of social work in a simple way, but we are convinced of its existence being shaped and influenced continually by a number of key debates. During the process of developing the book, we have met and engaged in such debates. The purpose of this book is to create wider opportunities to share in and extend those debates. This book sets out to provide more than a 'reader' of someone else's ideas, by involving you and us in the issues and debates within it. Such debates are open-ended, since they are ongoing, with no starting or finishing point. They do not converge on a set of guidelines on what social work is and how to do it. They involve a continual journey, whose outcome will never be complete understanding or a finished project. This is an anxiety-provoking reality, but it is also exciting, because, like work with clients, it offers people practising social work the reality of engaging in a profession which is in the ferment of continual change and continually in the process of considering, and sometimes taking, new directions. Some subject matter crops up in more than one place in the book. This reflects the reality that we can approach some aspects of social work from more than one direction, and that more than one view of them exists. We have cross-referenced – in the text and through the index – many of the places where this occurs, rather than artificially attempting to edit out the differences and discontinuities which result. Having set the diversity of social work themes and debates going in this book, it is unsurprising that we offer no neat conclusions in the last chapter. This mirrors the reality that social work offers no global solutions in work with people, and reflexively – holding the mirror up to our own practice – no final answer to the question of what social work consists of.

The authors of all the chapters in this book have been invited to revise, update and where necessary extend their original contributions. In addition, we have added three new chapters – one in each Part. In Part I, Viviene Cree (Chapter 2) introduces the contexts of global, European and UK-wide changes. In Part II, Michael Leadbetter (Chapter 20) surveys advocacy and empowerment approaches and issues. In Part III, we as editors round off the book (Chapter 27) by surveying social work – in retrospect and with regard to future prospects.

The structure of the book reflects our view that we draw on social work approaches in our practice, in a societal context which affects us at every turn. Thus, Parts I, II and III deal respectively with social work contexts, approaches and practice. Part I offers a number of major topics which interact to a greater or lesser degree with anti-oppressive practice (Chapter 1), which provides its linking theme. Part II sets against the linking theme of encouraging reflectiveness on theory in practice (Chapter 11) a selection of those social work approaches we view as generating debates and controversies. Part III considers social work with the major client groups – children and families, adults and offenders – against the backcloth of unfinished debates on social work processes (Chapter 23). Thus, the structure of the book offers the reader the opportunity to use the introductory chapters to the three parts in dialogue with the other chapters in them.

We have prepared a second, companion book, *Critical Practice in Social Work* (Adams et al., 2002), which is designed to complement the material in this book. It starts from practice in the way this book starts from contexts and approaches. We hope the opportunity to dip in and out of both books will enhance the contribution of this second edition to critical reflection and practice.

Social Work in Context

1

Anti-oppressive Practice in Context

Lena Dominelli

Anti-oppressive practice: an old–new paradigm

The role and purpose of social work has been hotly contested since its inception. The diverse answers which have been provided can be categorised as follows into roughly three types:

- therapeutic helping approaches;
- 'maintenance' approaches;
- emancipatory approaches.

Therapeutic approaches to social work are best exemplified by counselling theories, of which Carl Roger's work stands paramount (Rogers, 1980). In these, the 'client'[1] is assisted by the counsellor to better understand him/herself and his/her relationships with others, particularly close relatives and friends, and move on to a more effective way of dealing with their situation. Yet its long history and wide currency means that it is most readily understood by readers as 'those people with whom social workers work'. Therapeutic approaches focus on individuals and their psychological functioning as the basis of intervention. The role of the counsellor as helper is to listen actively to what is being said and facilitate a process of exploration which enables people better to address their life circumstances. Any change which takes place is in the individual who is being counselled as they either learn or develop more effective strategies for dealing with the problems they encounter.

The 'maintenance' approach is best explicated by Martin Davies (1994) in his book, *The Essential Social Worker*. In this, he argues that the social worker's main preoccupation is that of ensuring that people can cope or deal adequately with their lives. Under this approach, social workers do not adopt a therapeutic helping role. Their interventions are much more pragmatic – usually passing on information about resources and possibilities. They are guided in their interventions by 'practice wisdoms' or the accumulated experience of 'what works'. Probing deeply into the individual's psyche does not, therefore, form part of the concerns of those following this approach. The 'maintenance' approach relies on the expert practitioner adopting a largely neutral attitude towards 'clients', although this may involve the use of authority that may be resisted by the 'clients', as for example when the social worker receives a child into care or a probation officer recommends custody for an offender. Engaging in political issues, particularly those which challenge the existing social order, falls outside the remit of the 'maintenance' practitioner, who views society as being basically benign.

Those endorsing an emancipatory approach to social work have an explicit commitment to social justice and engage in overt challenges to the welfare system if it is seen to thwart this goal. While some see service users as 'victims' of unjust social relations (for example, Bailey and Brake, 1975), others focus on their strengths (for example, Collins, 1990). However, both schools of thought aim to empower those with whom they work by helping them to understand their situation, make connections between their personal plight and that of others, examine power relations and their impact on the specifics of their daily routines and acquire the knowledge and skills for taking control of their lives. Many of these activities draw on the consciousness-raising techniques advocated by Freire (1972).

Social change at both the individual and societal levels lies at the heart of an emancipatory approach. Practitioners may adopt an openly political stance which can create complications between the social workers' professional roles and their activities as social change agents. In this context, gaining the support of sympathetic others outside the social work remit is an important facet of the job undertaken by practitioners endorsing emancipatory forms of social work. In recent times, women, black activists, disabled people, gay men, lesbian women and older people have worked to develop forms of social work practice which seek to empower users and enable them to participate in their own emancipation when in receipt of official assistance. Anti-oppressive practice, with its value commitment to the realisation of social justice, is one variant of a range of emancipatory approaches to social work.

Social justice has provided a thread of historical continuity running through social work practice. The modern variant of a concern with its implementation has been expressed by appealing to 'social work's value base' and through the range of progressive social work paradigms. These began with radical social work in the 1970s, moving on to feminist social work and anti-racist social work in the 1980s and to anti-oppressive practice in the 1990s. The development of anti-oppressive practice has been a fragmented and highly contentious affair as different groups jockey to define and influence its meaning.

The supporters of anti-oppressive practice – white women, black men and women, lesbian women, gay men, disabled people, older people and others –

have sought to articulate their questions about its place in and relevance to social work as well as shape the replies proffered by practitioners. They have argued that its role is one of highlighting social injustice and finding ways of eradicating at least those forms of it which are reproduced in and through social work practice (see Corrigan and Leonard, 1978; Dominelli, 1988; Dominelli and McLeod, 1989; Ahmad, 1990). Securing social change that is in keeping with this goal is, therefore, the aim of anti-oppressive practice.

Its opponents have endeavoured to trivialise its stances and undermine its achievements (see Phillips, 1993, 1994). A large part of their argument is based on claims that those endorsing anti-oppressive practice have exaggerated the extent to which social inequality pervades society. In addition, they believe that anti-oppressive practice has been imposed through draconian measures upon unwilling victims (see Appleyard, 1993; Phillips, 1993; Pinker, 1993), thereby conflating good anti-oppressive practice with poor practice, which should not be condoned regardless of what it purports to be doing.

This chapter focuses on anti-oppressive practice because this book is committed to providing readers with an understanding of the knowledge base and tools that social workers use to engage in progressive practice which takes the side of people who have been subjugated by structural inequalities such as poverty, sexism and racism and seeks to assist them in their desire to reverse the position they are in, that is, to move in emancipatory directions. It is one paradigm for practice among others which vie for the practitioners' attention. Practising in accordance with the principles of anti-oppressive practice requires a commitment to doing so. It can also be very hard work. Given social work's age old concern with the underdog, anti-oppressive practice is an old–new paradigm for practitioners and academics to follow. Its spread has been marked by a problematic reception brought about by the mode of its introduction into training and the barriers that impede its growth. These hurdles include the resistance which has ironically been engendered through the successes that anti-oppressive practice has achieved in the field. I also argue that these obstacles have to be transcended for anti-oppressive practice to become firmly embedded in practice.

Anti-oppressive practice, insofar as it is preoccupied with the implementation of social justice, is intimately bound up with notions of improving the quality of life or well-being of individuals, groups and communities. This concern lends it a holistic mantle which encompasses all aspects of social life – culture, institutions, legal framework, political system, socio-economic infrastructure and interpersonal relationships which both create and are created by social reality. In its early days, anti-oppressive practice highlighted specific social divisions, that is, personal attributes such as 'race',[2] class, age, gender and sexual orientation, that acquire specific social meanings which are rooted in unequal power relations based on the creation of oppositional pairs in which one part is dominant over the other, as in the case, for example, of men over women. This concern gave rise to particular practice paradigms aimed at addressing these social divisions: class in radical social work (Corrigan and Leonard, 1978), women in feminist social work (Brook and Davis, 1985; Hanmer and Statham, 1988; Dominelli and McLeod, 1989) and 'black people'[3] in anti-racist social work (Cheetham et al., 1986; Dominelli, 1988; Ahmad, 1990) among others.

More recently, the realisation that individual identity and social existence are more complex than can be dealt with by focusing on a single social division expressed as a dichotomous pair, and the need to prevent the nihilistic fragmentation of social life, has led black women, white women, people in the disability movement, older people, gay men, lesbian women and those in the ecology movement to look for bonds of solidarity which acknowledge the different starting points held by groups of people working towards a common aim (Collins, 1990; Dominelli, 1997a). These principles have been extended globally now that feminists, black activists and environmentalists have acknowledged the interdependency of the peoples living on this planet (Basu, 1997). Their shared objective of securing social relations which endorse social justice can be articulated as one of sustaining a people-oriented social environment which allows each person, community or group to develop their full potential while cherishing their cultural traditions and respecting the rights and dignity of others. Moreover, there is a refusal to endorse a hierarchy of oppressions and a commitment to recognising diverse identities as being on an equal footing (Collins, 1990).

As a result of its all-encompassing orientation, anti-oppressive practice is concerned with inputs, outputs and processes (Dominelli, 1996). Indeed, its holistic approach to practice can become a barrier to its implementation because individual practitioners can feel overwhelmed by the multiple dimensions of reality which they need to engage with at any one time. However, overcoming this problem does not have to be undertaken by a single individual. Teamwork and working collectively with others to cover its various aspects in the course of delivering an anti-oppressive service are more realistic solutions to this dilemma. I will now turn to defining anti-oppressive practice.

Defining anti-oppressive practice

Dominelli has defined anti-oppressive practice as:

> a form of social work practice which addresses social divisions and structural inequalities in the work that is done with 'clients' (users) or workers. Anti-oppressive practice aims to provide more appropriate and sensitive services by responding to people's needs regardless of their social status. Anti-oppressive practice embodies a person-centered philosophy, an egalitarian value system concerned with reducing the deleterious effects of structural inequalities upon people's lives; a methodology focusing on both process and outcome; and a way of structuring relationships between individuals that aims to empower users by reducing the negative effects of hierarchy in their immediate interaction and the work they do together. (1993: 24)

Thus, there is a pervasiveness about anti-oppressive practice which permeates all aspects of social work policy and practice. It impacts on service delivery, 'client'/worker relationships, employer/employee relationships, relationships between employees, agency culture and the social context. In defining anti-oppressive practice in liberationist terms, Dominelli (1993) has firmly located anti-oppressive practice within the longstanding tradition of humanism with which social workers are familiar. In drawing upon these antecedents, anti-oppressive practice forms part of an old practice paradigm.

The emphasis of anti-oppressive practice on a holistic approach to social work intervention has directed it towards the development of a new practice paradigm which guides practitioners beyond the traditional goal of controlling 'clients' for the purposes of helping them to adjust to existing power relations or, as a 'maintenance' practitioner might put it, to 'cope' with life as they find it. Based on egalitarian principles, the moral and ethical positions of anti-oppressive practice are those which ask social workers to both understand and engage with the harsh realities within which they work and their 'clients' live, and to seek to change them. Because anti-oppressive practice has to facilitate both coping and change strategies, I argue that anti-oppressive practice constitutes an old–new practice paradigm.

Being able to operate effectively in this milieu requires practitioners working in anti-oppressive ways to be both experiential and research-led. Being rooted in peoples' lived-in reality ensures that anti-oppressive practice responds to the issues and questions which are identified by oppressed groups themselves. This approach is important if anti-oppressive practice is not to be imposed on reluctant service users. Moreover, this concern with validating the significance of everyday experience as a legitimate source of information in designing services endorses experiential knowledge as an important source of data. Anti-oppressive practice's capacity also to draw upon a more traditional research base in the social sciences will lend an empirical aura to experiential reality, thereby enabling well-informed 'client'-led social work practice to take place more readily.

'Client'-centeredness forms the basis on which anti-oppressive practice offers a paradigm for practice that is highly relevant to practitioners working in contexts in which political hostility to marginalised groups is the norm. Having clearly established empirical or 'hard' facts on which to base service provision also facilitates a more thorough refutation of the arguments posed by the critics of anti-oppressive practice and empowers social workers to advocate more forcefully alongside their 'clients'. In addition, research can, as Everitt shows in Chapter 10, contribute to the development of a reflective practitioner who uses research as an integral element of improving their practice and monitoring its compliance with anti-oppressive practice principles.

Working in ways that are consistent with anti-oppressive practice has implications not only for service provision, but also for the professionals engaged in delivering an anti-oppressive service. To begin with, anti-oppressive practice calls for a redefinition of professionalism, with expertise being rooted in more power-sharing egalitarian directions and making explicit the value system to which the professional subscribes. Hence, anti-oppressive practice challenges traditional or 'maintenance'-oriented views of professionalism in which a neutral expert is required to exercise power over the 'client' and other workers lower down the labour hierarchy through rules which endorse deferential responses to those in 'superior' positions.

Under the auspices of anti-oppressive practice, 'client'-centeredness acquires a different meaning, that is, one based on power-sharing and an empathy which has the 'client's' position as its starting point. A 'client'-centered approach which seeks to reverse inegalitarian relations between the 'client' and worker facilitates the practitioner's ability to work with the messy realities that 'clients' bring with them in more sensitive and relevant ways. It also uses relationship-building to secure change and places the practice value system under the spotlight to reveal the room for ambiguity contained in seemingly straightforward statements about social work's value base and ethical stances. However, as Shardlow demonstrates in Chapter 3, this complexity in value positioning can be a strength which social workers can use constantly to engage in revisiting their own values and how they use them in their practice.

Understanding social relations, and how power operates within them through the relationships they establish with their 'clients', enables practitioners more readily to apply the principles of egalitarianism which are both explicitly and implicitly expounded in anti-oppressive practice. Living up to this expectation in practice is immensely difficult, given the competing discourses identified by Parton in Chapter 22, and calls for an open acknowledgement of the constraints which hinder its implementation. This may mean that securing egalitarian relations in a pure form is an unreachable goal and that the best that can be achieved is a constant lowering of the power imbalance through a continual process of identifying the sources of power differentials and eliminating as many of these obstacles as possible. The tensions that social workers seeking to implement this approach have to deal with are explored throughout Part I of this book. Their impact in 'client'/worker relationships is, however, most clearly evident in Chapter 17, where Doel considers task-centred social work. Here, he indicates that there is more to power than meets the eye. Nonetheless, social workers have the duty of exploring these difficulties in an open and frank manner with their 'clients', so that, together, they may move forward in partnerships that the 'clients' feel they can own.

Processual considerations or questions of how relationships are conducted, and on whose terms, are also crucial to the realisation of anti-oppressive practice. Furthermore, process provides the means whereby the experience of anti-oppressive practice or its absence will be confirmed. This is in contrast to traditional understandings of 'client'/worker relationships in which ethics focus more on the ends to be achieved than on the mechanisms whereby these are to be reached.

The emphasis on outcomes in the current competency-based approaches to social work is consistent with an ethical standpoint that ignores process. This is a position which practitioners following anti-oppressive practice would eschew. For them, substance and form are integral parts of one whole, process providing the link between them. For this reason, the adding-on of 'social work's value base' to a competence-based approach is deemed to be incapable of delivering anti-oppressive practice, despite its avowed intention of doing so (Dominelli, 1996). The collaring of social work education and training at the qualifying level by the Diploma in Social Work (DipSW), which encapsulates the competence-based approach, therefore puts the two on a collision course except at the most tokenistic level in which form stands for substance. The issue of competency in doing a professional job well is another, albeit related, matter. Working in anti-oppressive ways requires skills and expertise. Practitioners must know what they are doing and why they adopt one course of action over another and consistently reflect on how they can improve the services that they are making available to others.

Those advocating anti-oppressive practice have a responsibility to develop theories and concepts which reflect its principles in practice. As Burke and Harrison demonstrate in Chapter 21, this requires academics to move beyond dualistic thinking and approach their study in a holistic manner. Theorising anti-oppressive practice is an important aspect through which the integration of theory and practice is retained. Social work, uniquely among the social science disciplines, is compelled to maintain the link between theory and practice. Moreover, working in one area of anti-oppressive practice can lead to innovation and theory-building in others. For example, feminist work with women has contributed to a rethinking of masculinity (Bowl, 1985; Connell, 1995), black and anti-racist perspectives have had implications for the way in which white identity and whiteness is understood (Roediger, 1991), and disabled people have contributed new understandings to the meaning of 'expert' knowledges and sought to affirm their own experiential ones (Wendell, 1996).

Practising equality requires the practitioner to value 'difference' in lifestyles and identities instead of settling for a clone of oneself as expressed by demanding a uniform conformity in others. Valuing 'difference' is one dimension of the complexities of life to be addressed explicitly by practitioners subscribing to anti-oppressive practice. For, as Lorde (1984) says, unless individuals follow this path, their reaction to 'difference' is not to value it, but to do one of three things – exercise the wish to control or dominate it, copy it or exterminate it.

Thus, valuing 'difference' goes against common-sense socialisation which portrays difference as 'inferior' or deems it in pathological terms as a 'deficit'. The casting of people different from oneself in a subordinate status is central to the process of 'othering' them (de Beauvoir, 1974; Rutherford, 1992). The 'othering' of individuals or groups withdraws them from the circle of humanity and facilitates the denial of their human, social and political rights. Central to this approach is the idea of oppressed people as passive victims who are unable to act on their own behalf. Such views permit their being treated as dependent beings who can have others (that is, those who are 'superior' to them) take decisions on their behalf, allegedly for their own good, and authorise their being able to act in this manner without having to justify it. 'Othering' people is, therefore, inimical to anti-oppressive practice.

Transcending common-sense attitudes about 'difference' requires the exercise of an empathy which goes beyond placing oneself in another's shoes by daring to put these on and wear them for a while to develop a deep understanding of the other person's position while at the same time reflecting on the privileged nature of one's own. The importance of knowing oneself in order to engage effectively with others who are different is, as Lishman reveals in Chapter 9, essential to carrying out anti-oppressive practice but immensely difficult to do. Challenging inequality transforming social relations is an integral part of anti-oppressive practice. Kn oneself better equips an individual for undertaking this task. Self-knowle central component of the repertoire of skills held by a reflective p (Schön, 1983; see Chapter 11). Moreover, reflexivity and social cha bedrock upon which anti-oppressive practitioners build their interv

The commitment to social justice and its capacity to challenge existing social relations of inequality are key features of anti-oppressive practice. From these two elements stems the capacity of anti-oppressive practice to affect profoundly social work practice and the society in which it is conducted. As Jones demonstrates in Chapter 4, poverty is a principal manifestation of the structural inequalities that social workers encounter. And, poverty is being exacerbated under globalisation.

Challenging this state of affairs through anti-oppressive practice antagonises social workers' paymasters within the local state and can lead them to lose their jobs, as the Community Development Project (CDP) workers discovered, for example (Loney, 1983; Dominelli, 1990, 1997a). Nonetheless, anti-oppressive practice's focus on social divisions and its aim to reduce inequality through the delivery of the personal social services contributes to social workers' capacity to address the issue of poverty in their work. Their doing so is also linked to anti-oppressive practice's potential to transform society and empower those at the bottom of socio-economic hierarchies. Anti-oppressive practice aims to enable those included in the 'underclass' to acquire hope in changing their situation and take action on their own behalf. Although lending credibility to grass-roots-oriented social workers, this commitment is a major source of fear for those who oppose the spread of anti-oppressive practice.

For those individuals who lack allegiance to anti-oppressive principles, this fear is rooted in a loss of taken-for-granted privileges accorded to them through an inegalitarian social order (Rutherford, 1992). With this fear comes their desire to obliterate or destroy anti-oppressive practice rather than witness the realisation of its threat to realign the status quo. The backlash to anti-oppressive practice stems from resistance to the transformation of social relations demanded by oppressed people on the part of those who can see their assumed privileges vanish were such change to be implemented. For they know that the benefits they have enjoyed thus far have been possible because others who have been oppressed by them have been excluded from legitimating their claim to material resources and collectively distributed forms of power. In other words, the backlash is a struggle aimed at preserving the privileges of those accustomed to having them.

The struggle over anti-oppressive practice – an old–new controversy

Anti-oppressive practice began in the late 1960s/early 1970s as a critique of ... in social work practice as practitioners, particularly those in ...gan to challenge class-based privileges within the ambit of ... Corrigan and Leonard, 1978; Loney, 1983). This critique ...s/early 1980s to encompass women (Brook and Davis, ...Dominelli, 1988). The recent media emphasis, however, ... was happening with 'race', the field in which black ... more generally since the 1960s. The spread of anti-... ...ic social work circles was slow, although it achieved ... ate 1980s just as the Central Council for Education ...k (CCETSW) published its *Paper 30*. *Paper 30* itself ...ce', the area in which black and white practitioners had been organising to redress CCETSW's neglect of the topic since the late 1970s. Opposition to these developments ran alongside these initiatives (see Pinker, 1993; Davies, 1994). The impetus for expansion in this area of anti-oppressive practice was threefold. One of these was the activities of the 'new social movements', particularly those involving women and black people. Another force was *Paper 30*. The third was the policies on equal opportunities and the legislation around their implementation. These began with the Race Relations Act 1968 (amended in 1975 and 2000) and later encompassed the Sex Equality Act 1975 and Disability Discrimination Act 1995 as these spread into social work agencies under the aegis of equal opportunities policies. The opposition's arguments against anti-oppressive practice in social work have consistently been based on the notion that social workers as professional beings have no right to engage in political action which challenges the existing social order in the way that anti-oppressive practice purports to do by demanding egalitarian social relations (Davies, 1994; Phillips, 1994).

The struggle between the adherents of anti-oppressive practice and those seeking to eliminate it from the domain of social work is a contest about the role of social work in society and the tasks that caring professionals should undertake. As such, it constitutes an old refrain in a new guise. In earlier times, it might have been depicted as the 'maintenance' school of social work against those arguing for social change through social work (see Davies, 1994). The new version of this debate has been framed in the language of 'political correctness' over what rightly characterises the heart and soul of the profession. The backdrop against which the current debate is taking place is one in which social work is feeling the impact of globalisation (Dominelli and Hoogvelt, 1996), the privatisation of the welfare state including the personal social services (Oakley and Williams, 1994), and a deepening polarisation in the social structure of British society as indicated by an increasing gap in wealth between rich and poor (Oakley and Williams, 1994; *Social Trends*, 1996).

Moreover, the British government is using social policy and legislative instruments to restructure the context within which social work has to operate. The Children Act 1989, the National Health Service and Community Care Act 1990 and the Criminal Justice Act 1991 have fundamentally altered the statutory environment within which practitioners operate. In giving more choice to consumers and casting these in terms of citizens' rights, these developments have provided a supportive backdrop for anti-oppressive practice (Braye and Preston-Shoot, 1995). However, these initiatives have been promoted at a time which has coincided with severe cutbacks in public expenditures in the welfare state, including the personal social services, and a significant expansion in the implementation of privatisation measures driven by 'contract government' (Greer, 1994). These have meant that the progressive thrust of the legislative forces has been undermined by a more conservative one which has placed economic rather than social priorities at the top of the political agenda. In seeking to reverse this trend in the field through their practice, the supporters of anti-oppressive practice have been caught in the crossfire between the two opposing sides.

Social policy has a crucial role to play in either endorsing or rejecting the development of anti-oppressive practice. Moreover, as Carol and Alan Walker argue in Chapter 5, social policy can assist social work to make a major contribution in reducing the 'growing divide' between the rich and poor people of this country. It can identify the plight of poor people, pinpoint their skills in devising survival strategies for coping in bleak social circumstances and provide the research material for strengthening their case for securing social justice. In supporting such efforts, social policy can make a substantial contribution to putting anti-oppressive practice on a firmer footing and embedding it in the political arena. Anti-oppressive practice can achieve more rapid progress if there is political support from those currently controlling society's political and economic resources.

Moreover, the *structural* changes being brought about by powerful economic and political forces provide the context which gives this old debate a new potency. For there is more at stake than the provision of services for needy people. At the heart of the matter lies the question of how the post-war welfare state can be transformed to provide a fertile breeding ground for entrepreneurs who can ensure that capitalist relations enter a hitherto sacrosanct area to promote capital accumulation under new conditions in new arenas (Dominelli and Hoogvelt, 1996; Delgado, 2000). Alongside this issue is another one which draws on the anti-intellectual tendencies apparent in popular consciousness (Jones, 1994). This is tied to the question of how professionals can be made to comply with government diktat rather than promote the interests of society's most marginalised groups as they see fit. That poor people lose out as a result of this struggle is an unfortunate consequence, possibly even unintended at the ideological level, of the developments which flow from the restructuring of the welfare state which is being progressed by free-market advocates.

In this context, the perpetuation of anti-oppressive principles and practice as discussed in terms of poor people taking control of their lives, and using their right to fulfil their welfare needs as a basis for challenging existing inegalitarian social relations, is not something that power-holders would wish to encourage. Bureaucratised forms of empowerment through the appeals and complaints procedures, which can be activated once a service which has been delivered is shown to have failed to live up to expectations, are excluded from the attack being mounted against anti-oppressive practice. Indeed, bureaucratic forms of involvement are actively being fostered by the state. The apparatus for processing customer complaints has been rapidly put into place as agencies seek to comply with provisions outlined in the National Health Service and Community Care Act 1990 and the demands of the various citizens' charters originally promoted by the Conservative government headed by John Major.

These mechanisms have been exempted from the attacks being mounted against anti-oppressive practice because they are consistent with top-down forms of control exercised by those in power. Moreover, they are neither intended to nor do they challenge the present order of things. Law, as Braye and Preston-Shoot suggest in Chapter 6, has a similar form of ambiguity. It can be very useful in challenging unlawful inequality but, at the same time, can be used to restructure social relations only to a limited extent. Its tendency to individualise collective problems can only mean that redistributive justice remains beyond its scope. Yet it is precisely this form of justice which black activists, women and other oppressed groups are demanding. Additionally, it has provided the base for bureaucratising rights as is indicated in the various citizens' charters which proceduralise empowerment in consumer rather than social justice terms (Dominelli, 2000). Free-market ideologies which enhance consumerism and promote the citizen as consumer (Clarke and Newman, 1997) are likely to intensify this trend.

The 'backlash' – a rejection of anti-oppressive practice by its opponents

The backlash against anti-oppressive practice, led by government ministers at the highest levels, reached its height in the summer of 1993 (see Appleyard, 1993; Pinker, 1993; Phillips, 1993, 1994). Their attack has to be understood as a rejection of anti-oppressive practice because it is inconsistent with using the welfare state to meet economic rather than social needs. For a social needs-based welfare state would have to encourage the bonds of solidarity encompassed in the pooling of risks to ensure that all members requiring services receive them free at the time of need. This collective strategy for welfare, however, is anathema to privatisation initiatives (Gilder, 1984; Murray, 1984, 1990, 1994) and the consolidation of market principles through the purchaser–provider split. Limited to a market economy, anti-oppressive practice can be no more than the promotion of bureaucratic procedures and not of empowering social relations.

Market-led approaches to welfare can only allow those with money a real choice about what personal social services they can call upon when they need them. The economic relations underpinning these developments are camouflaged under an ideological cloak which focuses attention on the value system of those supporting anti-oppressive practice. Moreover, because language and access to the mass media have provided the terrain upon which the struggle surrounding the aims of social work is being conducted, it has been easier for traditional power-holders and media pundits to define the terms under which the encounter between the two opposing groups is being carried out. In it, given their greater hold on formal power and control over the media, the traditionalists opposing anti-oppressive practice seem to have gained the upper hand.

This appearance, however, to some extent belies reality in the field. Anti-oppressive practice has gained a strong foothold in the agencies in the form of equal opportunities policies which expanded across the whole of the welfare sector during the 1980s. A greater awareness of the existence of oppressed peoples and their demands for justice have followed this. The theory and practice of anti-oppressive practice also has generalised support among academics who see the value of confronting structural inequalities in and through social work.

Thus, those at the vanguard of the backlash cannot count on things going completely their way. Indeed, some of them were astonished at the amount of support that anti-oppressive practice received among mainstream academics, policy-holders and practitioners when the issue hit the popular media in a big way in 1993. Rather than see the complete demise of anti-oppressive practice, these opponents had to content themselves with a restructuring of the mechanisms of CCETSW, which they had identified as being the culprits promoting the most obvious form of anti-oppressive practice – anti-racist practice. This they achieved by replacing the academic head of CCETSW's governing council with a lawyer, abolishing the Black Perspectives Committee which had spearheaded CCETSW's anti-racist initiatives and getting rid of a paragraph stating that racism is endemic in British society. This latter statement was contained in Annex 5 of Paper 30, which regulated the requirements for the DipSW. Paper 30 has now also been revised to expunge anti-racist ideology from its midst (Black Assessors, 1994). In the probation service, an area of social work practice which had taken anti-oppressive practice to heart in a fairly positive way and over which the government had financial control, the relevant ministers decided to withdraw its training programme from the university setting despite almost unanimous resistance to its proposed plan of action (Sone, 1995). Thus, within a short period of time, anti-oppressive practice was deemed to have been effaced from social work training and, in consequence, from practice.

Reality is, of course, more complicated. What the opponents of anti-oppressive practice ignored is that anti-oppressive practice did not achieve popularity because a few academics and practitioners wrote texts which identified what it was and proposed guidelines for practice. Anti-oppressive practice caught the imagination of academics, practitioners and policy-makers alike because it responded to the needs of oppressed people who objected to the failure of state services to meet their needs as they defined them. In short, anti-oppressive practice represented a small attempt made by social work academics and practitioners to respond to the agendas for practice being set in the field by members of the 'new social movements' led by women and black people. Oppressed people had created these organisational entities for themselves to challenge the inadequate services being meted out to them under the prevailing system.

These 'new social movements' and their demands for relevant services will not go away just because the government decrees that they should, nor will they die just because professionals fail to support their demands through anti-oppressive practice. They will continue with action that will produce oppositional forms of practice regardless of what happens within the mainstream system. And, regardless of the outcome of this struggle, they will continue to put pressure on mainstream policy-makers and professionals to respond to their agendas.

A good current example of this trend is the disability movement. Its adherents are asking practitioners to step aside if they cannot support their demands on their terms (Oliver, 1990). For unless they do so, these professionals are deemed to be working against them and they wish to have nothing to do with them. At the same time, disabled activists maintain their prerogative to criticise constantly whatever professionals do or claim to do on their behalf. As Mayo demonstrates in Chapter 14, community organisers have a long history of working collectively to challenge the status quo by subjecting professional practice to public scrutiny. Their activity is not diminishing simply because anti-oppressive practice is being challenged by the establishment. During the next decade, anti-oppressive practice in Britain will have to counter the authoritarian populism begun by Margaret Thatcher and endorsed under subsequent administrations including Tony Blair's. This is unlikely to endear its proponents to government and they may have to prepare themselves for another twist in the attack against their principles.

Structural constraints limiting the spread of anti-oppressive practice

Despite the continuing struggle over anti-oppressive practice and its place in social work practice, its spread is limited by structural constraints which would exist irrespective of the ideological attack on it. Many of these have to do with the resourcing levels necessary to ensure that anti-oppressive practice permeates the whole of an organisation's workforce, culture and structures. To begin with, workers need to be trained in anti-oppressive practice. They will not acquire it from the air through osmosis. It needs to be learned, thought about, debated and absorbed into one's practice. Teaching anti-oppressive practice in a thorough and reflective manner requires highly skilled specialists who know their material to teach it to others in a way that engages with their fears about working in accordance with its principles as well as their aspirations for better practice.

Making these resources available will cost money. Anti-oppressive practice cannot be taught on the cheap. Yet CCETSW sought to introduce anti-oppressive practice in the DipSW without appropriate training being provided for either practitioners or academics teaching this subject. The net result of this policy was a patchy and inadequate outcome as poorly prepared academics and practice teachers tried to teach students and assess them on something that many were incapable of delivering, even when they had the desire to do so. Consequently, much inappropriate learning occurred as people grasped the form without knowing the substance, thereby endorsing tokenism of the worst kind. Those who had been antagonistic to the whole enterprise had their hostility confirmed.

Thus, no real dialogue over the issues involved ensued. Yet, a dialogue about anti-oppressive practice is essential for carrying the hearts and minds of those committed to it and to engage those opposed to it in confronting and reflecting upon its content. For anti-oppressive practice requires practitioners to integrate their understanding on three levels:

● intellectually – to grasp its central principles and methods of working;

● emotionally – to feel secure about and confident in working in anti-oppressive ways, or at least to be able to own up to and learn from the mistakes they make when reality falls short of their ambition to work in this way; and

● practically – to be able to implement the principles they have learnt and feel they own in their practice.

This is a tall order, which needs to be met in total rather than being skimped upon by focusing solely on the mind in the manner that has been evident in CCETSW's past endeavours on the anti-racist front. Worthy as the texts which have come out of the Northern Curriculum Development Project's efforts have been, they have, on their own, been insufficient. Anti-oppressive practice is a specialism with specialist knowledge which, as in other specialisms, must be learnt fully. But it differs from other specialisms in that everyone needs to know about it and how to use it in their practice in a way that infuses the whole of their work with anti-oppressive principles, regardless of the 'client' group. Moreover, it requires a commitment to it from the individual at the emotional and intellectual level as well as the abilities for implementing it in practice. Since these needs on the training front have yet to be met, these constraints will continue to impede the progress of anti-oppressive practice in the field.

The feasibility of such resourcing becoming available is unlikely given the current political context. Hence, new ways of approaching the problem will have to be invented. One way of doing this could be a system of secondments whereby those academics and practitioners with the requisite skills could help to train their colleagues in anti-oppressive practice. Another could be the active exchange of models of best practice, not as exemplars, but as models for discussion with an eye to constant improvement for those who have developed them. Such exchanges should be coupled with the possibility of seeing how to adapt them to meet the specific circumstances of those who are struggling to develop them. Forging collaborative partnerships of this nature within hard-pressed agencies and universities is asking a lot in today's climate. The pressures of the private market in both the field and the academy will exact a toll which discourages their formation.

Agencies will have to take on such responsibilities knowing that obtaining additional resources to arrange cover is improbable, regardless of the training needs they can demonstrate. Social work academics will still have to produce the goods that count alongside their other colleagues when teaching quality assessment and research assessment exercise forms are completed. In other words, the busy work of getting through each day is a substantial barrier that those wishing to develop anti-oppressive practice and live up to its principles have to overcome. Moreover, the time in which to contemplate their next move is also at an all-time low.

Then, there is the business of engaging in organisational change both within the agencies and the universities, if an anti-oppressive working environment is to prevail. Organisational change favouring anti-oppressive practice will make demands of everyone within the institution regardless of rank. As Mullender and Perrott argue in Chapter 7, changing the inegalitarian culture of an organisation is also an important structural constraint to be transcended if anti-oppressive practice is to be realised in the workplace. This goal is a particularly problematic one to achieve as it does not rely solely on having the resources necessary for its implementation. It also requires management and workers to move in new directions, including a rethinking of how people relate to one another on both the individual and collective levels to promote egalitarian relations as the norm. Achieving this state of affairs also requires the transformation of the existing organisational value system, which tends to devalue 'difference' and perpetuates structural inequalities of various kinds.

Finally, changing organisational structures is also more than a matter of acquiring additional material resources, although having these to hand helps. It is also about promoting a different vision about what an organisation stands for and how it can be (re)organised to accomplish its new aims successfully. In this sense, changing the organisational structure also draws upon changes in the organisation's value orientation and culture (Broadbent et al., 1993). Changing management and the accompanying managerial structures is central to securing this change.

Management relations, workplace relations among employees and relationships between workers and their 'clients' have to incorporate more egalitarian ways of working with each other. In other words, there is a flattening of hierarchies followed by the ultimate goal of reducing them to the lowest possible level so that egalitarian relations can flourish as a source of creative energy and innovation in developing better and more relevant services for those who need them. Service users also have to be brought on board as equal participants in the enterprise. Anti-oppressive practice, therefore, relies on teamwork in the best sense of the word and is hard work. Being aware of the obstacles that have to be overcome can also block those who think that embarking upon anti-oppressive practice is an easy option.

The future of anti-oppressive practice

Anti-oppressive practice has yet to fulfil its potential in social work. What lies in store for it in the current bleak climate? Will anti-oppressive practice survive into the new millennium, despite the pessimistic prognosis being advocated by its opponents? I am cautiously optimistic for its future because it is rooted in the needs of oppressed people and their visions for alternatives to mainstream services. But the future of anti-oppressive practice will not be assured without a struggle. The forces seeking to undermine it are ideologically, socially, economically and politically powerful. In this context, it is important that those favouring anti-oppressive practice take a leaf from this text and engage in what I call a dialogue over controversies about its meaning and substance. This will require its proponents to undertake a number of initiatives to transform social relations and publicly present their case for anti-oppressive practice, thereby winning new adherents to the cause. These initiatives are outlined below.

To begin with, the supporters of anti-oppressive practice must form stronger alliances between the professionals who advocate anti-oppressive practice and the activists involved in the 'new social movements' so that they can know very clearly what their critiques of existing services are and what ideas they have for improving them. Anti-oppressive services should in a very real sense belong to them as the users. This will require anti-oppressive practitioners to be accountable to the users for their professional behaviour in a way that has not been practised very well in the past. Because of this, it may take a while for anti-oppressive practitioners to establish their credibility with users, for it will have to be earned. User involvement only becomes empowerment when there is a level playing field between the professionals and the service users. Thus, professional relationships with users should model the anti-oppressive practice being sought. Anti-oppressive practice should be seen as a normal part of citizenship entitlements. People requiring access to the personal social services should not feel that they are charity cases begging from the bowl of mercy. They should have their welfare needs met as a right and should be assured that they will be responded to with dignity and respect. Moreover, they should also know that the services they receive will be appropriate to their needs. Their requests for assistance should not become further barriers which disenfranchise them from their rights as citizens. Academics and practitioners will need to present the arguments necessary for this state of affairs to become reality.

Achieving this objective would be much easier if anti-oppressive practitioners and educators could establish better relationships with the media. Having supporters located within them would facilitate the proactive publicising of progressive social work activities, promote knowledge of existing good practice in this area and encourage the debate to be conducted on terms advocated by anti-oppressive practitioners and not just those of the opposition. Anti-oppressive social workers will also have to engage in anti-oppressive practice in many more areas than is currently the case. The anti-oppressive cause can be strengthened if its adherents can become more involved in research and theory-building to develop a theoretical base that emanates from anti-oppressive practice carried out in the field. This can become suited to enhancing the status of social work theory and practice in its own right. Social work practitioners acting as social anthropologists who have a strong research orientation can amass the data for arguing in defence of an anti-oppressive practice which responds to the needs of service users as they see them. Were they to succeed in this, social workers acting in the role of intermediaries between policy-makers and 'clients' could more powerfully serve the needs of the disenfranchised groups they purport to represent.

On the training front, anti-oppressive practitioners will have to perform more effectively than they have done to date. Courses which have established good practice in this area should be encouraged to share their models with other courses that are struggling to implement anti-oppressive practice without the resources and knowledge base that this requires. Such exchanges can assist the process of learning from the mistakes that others have made without having to revisit them in their own practice. Dialogue between courses can also enrich the models of good practice in those places which originated them. For complacency acts as a barrier to reflexivity in practice and the constant improvement in ways of working that anti-oppressive practice demands.

Finally, anti-oppressive practitioners need to develop a coherent professional organisation for social work. It will have to have the support of the profession as a whole and be able to defend its interests in the political arena. To do this effectively, it will have to be independent from government and encompass the academics, policy-makers, practitioners and service users who endorse its activities. A continuous dialogue with others about the role and purpose of social work in society ought to feature constantly on its agenda. Such an organisation could play a crucial role in promoting anti-oppressive practice and advocating its adoption in the field as well as monitoring its achievements on a regular basis.

CONCLUSION

Anti-oppressive practice is occurring in a controversial context and continues to develop despite the hostile climate that has surrounded it. However, its continued growth depends on much more work being carried out to constantly ensure that it meets the needs of those whom it is intended to serve and extends its remit so that it can be adopted more widely. Only in this way can its long-term future be assured. Thus, it is important that its supporters find ways of raising its profile and increasing the number of people committed to it being followed as a model of good social work practice.

The chapters which follow in this book continue the dialogue begun here by focusing on specific issues, dilemmas and controversies. Those which comprise Part 1 demonstrate how the contexts within which anti-oppressive practice is developed and practised are constantly shifting in response to external forces generated through the activities of services users and policy-makers, and the aspirations of practitioners and academics within the profession. Readers are invited to contribute to this process by reflecting upon their own life experiences in relation to what is being said through the written word. To give you maximum space, there is no predetermined order in which to read the chapters that follow. Your choice in what to read first will prevail. Hence, I have resisted describing the structure of this section in sequential order, preferring instead to outline the content of a particular chapter as an element within an organic whole at the point at which a particular topic is being explored. This way of proceeding also means that chapters from other sections of the book can be brought in without erecting artificial boundaries between one part and another. Through this means, I also hope to encourage you to make links between the different chapters in the book for yourself.

Notes

1   I use the word 'client' here in quotation marks to denote the problematic usage of this term.
2   I use 'race' in quotation marks to highlight the social construction of racial and ethnic attributes.
3   The term 'black people' is used in a political sense and should not be taken to mean a homogeneous and ungendered category.

FURTHER READING

Braye, S. and Preston-Shoot, M. (1995) *Empowering Practice in Social Care* (Buckingham, Open University Press). This text is primarily about community care. However, it focuses on issues of empowerment and working in anti-oppressive ways within this context.

Dalrymple, J. and Burke, B. (1995) *Anti-Oppressive Practice: Social Care and the Law* (Buckingham, Open University Press). Although this book focuses largely on using the law as a tool for progressive practice, it threads the principles of anti-oppressive practice and the empowerment of service users throughout the discussion. Thus, it can be used by readers to deepen their knowledge and understanding of anti-oppressive practice in a particular area of practice.

Dominelli, L. (1997) *Sociology for Social Work* (London, Macmillan – now Palgrave Macmillan). This text explores the theoretical underpinnings of anti-oppressive practice, examines the struggle over policy developments favouring its spread, provides case study examples of how anti-oppressive practice is used in holistic ways to address a range of different oppressions which exist in any one intervention and integrates theory and practice within it. The author examines further the themes of this text in a forthcoming book, *Anti-Oppressive Social Work* (London, Palgrave Macmillan).

CHAPTER 2

The Changing Nature of Social Work

Viviene E. Cree

Introduction

Social work has changed beyond recognition, and is changing still. The jobs which social work students trained for twenty years ago have all but gone; the agencies which employ them have been transformed. Widespread regional differences have emerged in policy and practice in social work; what countries share in common is a new insistence on the monitoring, regulation and control of social workers and social work. Social workers are quitting the profession in vast numbers (DoH, 2001b); those who are left behind experience disillusionment and public censure (Jones, 2001). But the idea that social work is 'in crisis' may be overstating the case (Clarke, 1993). There are opportunities as well as constraints in the new world of social work. And continuities remain, demonstrating that the central function and purpose of social work have not changed.[1] By charting some of the key developments which are taking place, it is possible to foresee a social work service in the future which may be located in different places to that of twenty years ago, but is still built on fundamental social work skills and values.

This chapter will focus on changes taking place in social work in the UK, while setting these in the context of European and global developments. I will argue that change is taking place across three broad fronts, political, organisational and individual.[2] Threading through these changes are a particular set of discourses – ideas and practices – which determine what social work is and should be, and what society is and should be. These are not, of course, peculiarly UK discourses. Similar debates are taking place within social work in the United States and Europe, and here similar – and sometimes different – resolutions have been found.

Political changes

Political changes have transformed Europe in recent years, as the former Soviet Union and Eastern bloc have broken down, to be replaced by new alliances and the formation of new nation states. In the UK, political change has been expressed in the drive for a form of devolution within the current constitutional settlement. On 6 May 1999, the first elections to a Scottish parliament and to the National Assembly for Wales were held, marking a culmination of years of campaigning for some kind of constitutional change in Scotland and Wales. It was asserted that the new Scottish parliament and Welsh Assembly would bring decision-making 'nearer to the people'. Policy and resources would be targeted better to meet specific needs and conditions; there would be 'Scottish solutions for Scottish problems', in the rhetoric of the day. For Scotland, there was an added dimension. 'The great opportunity under the Scottish parliament is to do what we're in the business to do and promote social welfare' (George Irving, Scotland's new president of the Association of Directors of Social Work, interviewed in *Community Care*, 29 April 1999). Devolution would thus allow Scotland to fulfil the promise that had been made in the Social Work (Scotland) Act of 1968 that each local authority should 'promote social welfare, by making available advice, guidance and assistance on such a scale as may be appropriate for their area' (Social Work (Scotland) Act 1968, section 12(1) pp. 7–8). Devolution was not, then, simply an exercise in administration. It was charged with a mission, to bring about real changes in Scottish society. And social work was to be at the heart of those changes.

The actual management of the new constitutional settlement suggests something rather less ambitious in scope. Some matters which have great signif-icance for social work and society (notably social security and employment) are 'reserved' ones: they apply to the UK as a whole and are dealt with by the UK government based at Westminster. The UK parliament continues to have power over the constitution, foreign policy, defence, the UK fiscal and economic system, common markets, employment legislation, social security, transport safety and regulation and other areas which are subject to regulation by the UK or Great Britain. Some matters are devolved issues. The Scottish parliament today has powers to make primary legislation on a wide range of devolved matters including social work, health, education, housing, criminal law, prisons, police and fire services, food standards, sport, arts and local government. It has tax-raising powers of 3p in the pound and a budget of more than £14 billion, but made an election pledge not to use its tax-raising powers in its first term of government. The Welsh Assembly, in contrast, controls a budget of more than £7 million but does not have tax-raising powers and does not have full law-making powers. It does, however, handle around 400 pieces of secondary legislation a year.

The new constitutional arrangements have been the subject of much debate. Critics point out that devolution took place within the context of strong, central-ising government, and was only ever intended to be partial. Devolution was principally an exercise in regulation; it was 'a way of ensuring that local authorities perform up to the centre's standards' (Jordan, 2000: 68). But, writing as someone who has lived through the changes in Scotland, I believe that the impact of devolution has been more than this. The creation of a new parliament brought with it a new confidence in the idea that Scotland might develop its own approaches. The advent of a degree of proportional representation in the new structures has led to the arrival of new voices within the devolved structures, including the voices of more women. Decision-making has become more transparent by the introduction of committees with 'lay' (non-politician) representatives, and politicians from all sides of the political spectrum have demonstrated commitment to consultation and participation. Devolution in government has led to devolution of power in other areas, so that large UK voluntary organisations such as Barnardo's have followed the lead of the UK government in introducing greater autonomy for their Welsh and Scottish offices. Two key developments demonstrate the extent within the new constitutional settlement for regional solutions, and for creating pressure, simultaneously, on central government: the appointment of a Children's Commissioner in Wales[3] and the controversy that has arisen in the UK over Scotland's plans to meet the personal, as well as the nursing care needs of older people.[4]

I have suggested that the new constitutional arrangements in the UK have led to the possibility of a greater diversity of approaches towards social care. There are, however, developments taking place on a global scale which are more likely to lead to convergence, not just within the UK, but within industrialised countries as a whole. The impact of economic organisation on an international scale has been that individual countries can no longer function as closed societies, if this was ever truly possible. Decisions taken at the international level govern the capacity of individual countries to act in all spheres of life, political, economic and social. This can have positive spin-offs for countries and individuals within them. For example, the adoption of the UN Convention on the Rights of the Child in 1989 has led to important changes in legislation and childcare practice in all the member states which have signed the declaration.[5] Similarly, the European Convention on Human Rights has led to major realignments within the organisation of social and legal affairs in the UK, as demonstrated by the enforcement in October 2000 of the Human Rights Act 1998.[6]

But the effects of globalisation are not always experienced as benign. The benefits of globalisation increasingly flow directly into the global market and no longer serve to create jobs or augment tax revenue in the countries where the activities originated (Adams, 2000). In consequence, even within the European community, members compete with one another 'as global, economic and technical rivals'; globalisation generates 'new opportunities for both competition and harmonisation across increasingly fragile national boundaries' (Adams, 2000: 1). In consequence, globalisation has been accompanied by attempts across advanced industrialised societies to cut public expenditure and introduce new ways of managing welfare (Wilson, 1998: 51).

Organisational changes

Changes at an organisational level in the UK reflect the changes that have been taking place across Europe. The mechanism of the market – familiar in US social services for many years – has been introduced throughout public sector agencies: social services, transport, higher education and the health service. Statutory social work agencies have seen the creation of a split between purchaser and provider roles, and the introduction of charges for services, the contracting out of services and the promotion of competition between the statutory, voluntary and private sectors (Pinkney, 1998: 263). The Labour government which came to power in May 1997 began with an agenda for change: for what was described as 'modern', 'joined up' government, with national strategies for combating issues such as social exclusion and unemployment. But for all the rhetoric of change, the government has continued the previous Conservative administration's strategies of ever-tighter control of public spending, increasing involvement of the private sector in public services, and intensifying regulation, inspection and centralised control of social work and social workers. And it is legislation which has proved to be the mechanism through which changes in policy and practice have been managed, as the government has introduced a whole programme of legislation affecting work with adults, children and families and offenders.

The third way for social care

The government White Paper, *Modernising Social Services* (DoH, 1998b), sets the scene for the future direction of social work and social services in the UK. The stated driving force behind the White Paper was the urgent need for change; social services are accused of 'failing to provide the support that people should expect' (1998b: 5). The recommendation is for a 'third way for social care': one which would promote independence, improve consistency, ensure equality of opportunity to children (especially in relation to education), protect adults and children from abuse or neglect in the care system, improve standards in the workforce, and improve delivery and efficiency. Few would disagree with such sentiments, but how this is to be achieved remains the subject of much disquiet. The government's answer has lain principally in the reorganisation of social work services and greater scrutiny and control of social work and social workers.

Modernising services

A key priority of government has been to seek to break down the organisational barriers which exist between services and create 'new shared ways of delivering services that are individually tailored, accessible and more joined up' (DoH, 2000c: 30). New partnerships have been encouraged, with users and carers, between health and social care, across the local authority (between housing and education), and with private and voluntary sector agencies. Health and social care services are primary targets for change, as outlined in the Health Act 1999 and taken forward in the Health and Social Care Act 2001.

Scotland provides a clear illustration of the impact of 'joined up' thinking on the organisation of social work services (Scottish Office, 1999). One of first steps taken by the new Scottish Executive after devolution was to break up the Social Work Services Group, which had held responsibility for social work services across

Scotland. Social services were split between the new ministries of children and education, health and community care, and justice. The phrase 'social work' all but disappeared from official Scottish Executive business. There is now no minister or department with overall responsibility for social work, and instead seven ministers across five departments share social work portfolios. Changes at ministerial level have been reflected in changes at regional level. Distinct social work departments have been disappearing, as a growing number of councils have abolished social work departments by joining social work up with education, housing, and even with health services. There is disagreement about the eventual outcome of these changes. Some commentators foresee the end of social work – the profession will simply be swallowed up by its larger and more powerful partners in the fields of health and education. Others suggest that the organisational changes may benefit service users, if there is more multidisciplinary working and greater coordination of service delivery (Bywaters and McLeod, 2001).

But joined up thinking is not envisaged solely at the level of statutory services. The call for change is also for new partnerships between statutory, voluntary and private sectors, as well as between agencies, service users and their carers. The voluntary sector in the UK has always been a key provider of social work services, and more recently, the private sector has made a major contribution to services particularly for older people and those with mental health problems (Lewis, 1996). What is envisaged now is somewhat different. New multi-agency groupings are being formed to manage services (such as the new Care Trusts for health and social care). Perhaps even more significantly, the private sector is being invited to fund key statutory services, including aspects of education and health services. The implications are again unknown at this stage, but it seems likely that the priorities of a private agency (with its responsibility to its shareholders) may be at variance with those of public sector organisations. Critics assert that corporate cultures are the very antithesis of conceptions of 'public service' (Clarke, 1998: 248). The experience of social work in the US would suggest this may be likely, as the public sector has been increasingly coopted by the private sector, through the managed health care movement (Meinert et al., 2000).

Modernising is, of course, about more than joined up services. Modern social work also means the increasing use of information technology for managing information and service user data, and for controlling the workforce; for communication and for web-based enquiries. Social workers in the future are likely to be using computers for a wide range of service-related activities, from accessing research databases to inputting service user details. Again, this development is not without consequences, both positive and negative. While bringing the possibility of easier communication and the creation of new social networks, information technology has also brought with it the capacity for surveillance and control to a degree unthinkable in the past. Networked computer systems, electronic 'tagging' and DNA screening bring ever-more sophisticated ways in which the 'disciplinary society' can 'police' its members (Foucault, 1977). More fundamentally, Meinert et al. argue that the increasingly elaborate forms of micro-technologies available to ever-larger numbers of human professionals have 'eroded the centrality of face-to-face conduct' (2000: 62).

Regulation and inspection

Concerns about inconsistent standards of service delivery have led to an explosion of different ways of measuring and controlling standards in social work and social care. These developments have been targeted at both services and service providers.

Performance indicators have been worked out for an increasing number of social service functions, and new service frameworks and targets for measuring Best Value outcomes have been introduced as well as new ways of managing the inspection and regulation of services. The Best Value regime, introduced in April 2000, replaced compulsory competitive tendering in local government, compelling social services to scrutinise the services they provide and justify their effectiveness and efficiency. Local authorities have pointed out that while Best Value assumes that it is possible to compare services, that comparison is not currently readily available. The establishment of the Social Care Institute for Excellence (SCIE) is expected to go some way towards meeting this need. SCIE will disseminate what works best in social care, and so inform practice, regulation, training, inspection and review. Local councils will be held to account for the implementation of SCIE's guidelines (see DoH, 2000c.)

In April 2002, inspection and regulation units previously run by local authorities will transfer to new non-departmental public bodies answerable directly to central government. The National Care Standards Commission (NCSC) will inspect and regulate almost all forms of residential and domiciliary care in England, including care homes, children's homes, nursing agencies, schools, adoption and fostering agencies, and private and voluntary hospitals. Similar arrangements are in place in Scotland, with the Scottish Commission for the Regulation of Care (SCRCC) and in Wales, with the Commission for Care Standards (CCS). New arrangements are also being put in place for the regulation of service providers – social workers and social care personnel – and social work training. Four new bodies will be in place by 2002: the General Social Care Council in England (GSCC), accountable to the Secretary of State for Health; the Scottish Social Services Council (SSSC), accountable to the Scottish parliament; the Cyngor Gofal Cymru/Care Council for Wales (CGC/CCW), accountable to the National Assembly for Wales; and the Northern Ireland Social Care Council (NISCC). Social workers will be registered through these bodies, and social work education regulated.

It is clear that all the above developments may have positive outcomes for social service delivery. Standards in the workforce may improve, as social workers develop methods and systems which are based on good practice, rather than local custom. The so-called 'postcode lottery' may be less apparent, as those using services become more aware of the services they should expect, and as services become more standardised across the UK. Again, those using services may feel some reassurance that those working with them are trained and registered to do the job. But there is an undercurrent running beneath these developments which suggests that a more circumspect approach should be taken. The increasing regulation and inspection is very 'top-down'; the centralised monopoly of power may have a detrimental effect on local autonomy and accountability. It also implies more surveillance and external control of social workers and social work education. This is, in large measure, a response to the 'risk society' (Beck, 1992). The realities of risk and uncertainty are managed by the introduction of new systems for organising professional practice and new mechanisms for predicting future risks and their potential negative outcomes. The end result is that the social work task becomes increasingly broken down into discrete units which can be measured and controlled. The push within social work towards 'evidence-based' practice similarly seeks to provide answers in a world which is increasingly complex and uncertain (Webb, 2001).

Individual changes

Just as social work has been transformed by constitutional and organisational changes, so there have been important changes at the individual level, at the level of service users and service providers.

Social work 'clients' have become 'customers', and the introduction of direct payments has given service users much more power over the nature of the services they receive, transforming the role of social worker to that of adviser and facilitator. Many social workers have become budget-holders: they work as care managers, assessing need and arranging packages of care; a small number have become inspectors regulating standards in care. This process has been referred to as the 'McDonaldisation' of welfare (Powell, 2001). The settings in which social workers are located have also changed. They are as likely to be working in a GP surgery, school or hospital, as in a local authority social work or social service department, and their colleagues in the future will be nurses, health visitors, occupational therapists and teachers as well as social workers. Some social workers have 'jumped ship' altogether, leaving the statutory sector to become care providers in the voluntary or private sectors. Interestingly, this plurality of identity is much closer to a European model, where social workers are more likely to be scattered among a range of central and local government agencies and civil society organisations (Lorenz, 1994).

Social workers have experienced the changes in a variety of ways. Some have described feeling high levels of anxiety and pressure, as they strive to maintain the social work role in the face of challenges from other care professionals, such as occupational therapists, district nurses and community psychiatric nurses. Others have complained that they can no longer use their social work skills as they would wish. There are simply too many forms to complete; and there is little scope for individual discretion or for creativity in the work (Rickford, 2001). Jones' study of social workers working in local authority social services departments suggests that the manifestations of stress and unhappiness were 'various, serious and pervasive', with the greatest source of stress coming from above – from the agency – and not from the clients (2001: 551). Social workers describe their relationship with clients as highly regulated and much more mundane and routinised – not social work, 'at least in the terms that they understood it' (2001: 552). Jones concludes that social work has become like a factory through which people are processed; yet at the same time, the gap between rich and poor people has widened.

While social workers feel increasingly pressurised in their work, there are ever-more managers to direct their output. A recent report recorded that while the number of social services staff in England fell by 7 per cent between 1995 and 2000, the number of directors and senior staff rose by nearly 50 per cent over the same period (DoH, 2001b). This reflects a general trend towards managerialism in social welfare. Managerialism is about more than simply a head-count of those in management posts. Instead, it is a whole discourse which has pervaded social work, turning social workers into 'managers' who must take into account the 'realities and responsibilities' of budgetary management and proclaiming the faith of good management as the answer to all problems (Clarke, 1998: 244).

Some jobs have ceased to be social work jobs altogether. From 1997, it was no longer a requirement that probation officers in England and Wales held a social work qualification. Since then, new, employer-led probation training has been developed, accompanied by changes in service delivery towards a focus on changing offending behaviour through cognitive-behavioural means and what is now called 'restorative justice' (May and Anniston, 1998).

CONCLUSION

'We live in a society defined by risk, polarisation, global markets, chronic change and fragmentation' (Powell, 2001: 14). Social work, situated as it is between the individual and society, inevitably reflects the wider society within which it is located (Cree, 2002). It is therefore not surprising that social work in this late modern (postmodern?) age should be undergoing major change and reformation. But there is more to consider here. Social work demonstrates a compromise solution – a compromise between liberal ideas of freedom and personal autonomy and the need for the state to safeguard the functioning of society as a whole (Parton, 1996). As this compromise solution is always being challenged and modified, so social work itself has a contingency about its being, its task and direction by no means self-evident (Cree, 1995).

Looking ahead, it seems likely that we will see increasing convergence and diversity in the nature of social work across Europe and the United States. Global economic forces and information technologies mean that there will be an increasing transfer of resources, personnel and information in the years ahead, leading to some standardisation of practices and systems. But at the same time, new boundaries continue to be drawn up across Europe, and new alliances formed, suggesting that there will continue to be different kinds of solution to shared problems such as immigration and refugees, poverty and social exclusion, humanitarian disasters and wars. Social work in the UK is at the crossroads (Lymbery, 2001). It can either continue to fight to hold onto its nascent professional status, in the face of the encroachment of other professional groupings and the steady march of managerialism, or it can take a step back and try to recover its purpose and its expertise. Social work has a strong tradition of working alongside people, valuing difference and having concern for social justice and inequality. These are the aspects of social work that we must build on in the future, wherever social work is located.

Notes

1 In 2001, the International Association of Schools of Social Work and the International Federation of Social Work agreed the following definition of social work: 'The social work profession promotes social change, problem-solving in human relationships, and the empowerment and liberation of people to enhance well-being. Utilising theories of human behaviour and social systems, social work intervenes at points where people interact with their environments. Principles of human rights and social justice are fundamental to social work.'

2 Change is taking place across so many areas in social work that it has been necessary to make choices about what will be discussed in this chapter. In consequence, some issues have either had to be left out, or touched on only in passing. This says as much about the diverse and complex nature of social work as it does about my selection.

3 As one of its first priorities, the Welsh Assembly instituted a programme of policies aimed at increasing the participation and inclusion of children and young people in Wales. The legislation creating the new position of Children's Commissioner for Wales passed through parliament in May 2001. The UK government expects similar posts to be created in England, Scotland and Northern Ireland in the future, but what is most significant, in this instance, is that the impetus for change, and the way that change has been conceived, lies firmly with Wales and the National Assembly for Wales.

4 In 1999, the Royal Commission on Long Term Care for the Elderly reported. It proposed that the care needs of older people, both personal and nursing care, should be met by the state, and that taxes should be raised to pay for this. The response in Scotland, after persistent lobbying and campaigning inside and outside the Scottish parliament, was to seek to support this broad recommendation. The response in England and Wales, however, was to agree to pay for nursing care, while means testing personal care (Health and Social Care Act 2001). Legislation introducing free care for older people in Scotland was passed in February 2002, and will be implemented on 1 July 2002 (Community Care and Health (Scotland) Act). This creates major anomalies and inconsistencies of treatment across the UK.

5 Two articles in the UN Convention have proved particularly influential to policy-makers, practitioners and researchers in the UK: article 12, the right of children to express an opinion and to have that opinion taken into account, and article 13, the right to information and freedom of expression. Both the 1989 Children Act in England and Wales and the Children (Scotland) Act of 1995 demonstrate this new concern for children's views being heard and being taken into account in social work and legal decision-making processes, as does the Children (Northern Ireland) Order 1995.

6 The Human Rights Act 1998 makes it unlawful for a 'public authority' to behave in any way that is not compatible with the provisions of the European Convention on Human Rights. The 'public authority' includes all courts and tribunals, central and local government, the National Health Service and any organisation whose functions are of a public nature – likely to include voluntary and independent, as well as statutory, social work agencies.

FURTHER READING

Adams, A., Erath, P. and Shardlow, S. (eds) (2000) *Fundamentals of Social Work in Selected European Countries* (Lyme Regis, Russell House Publishing). This offers an introduction to social work across Europe.

British Journal of Social Work (2001) **31**(4) August. This special issue is a collection of articles about social work in the UK during the first term of the New Labour government.

Cree, V.E. (2002) 'Social work and society', in Davies, M. (ed.) *Blackwell Companion to Social Work*, 2nd edn (Oxford, Blackwell). This examines the relationship between social work and society historically and in the present day.

Meinert, R., Pardeck, J.T. and Kreuger, L. (2000) *Social Work. Seeking Relevancy in the Twenty-First Century* (New York, Haworth Press). This provides an analysis of choices facing social work in the United States.

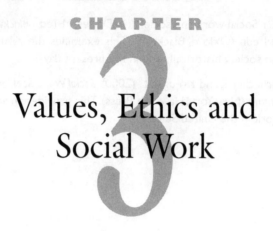

CHAPTER 3

Values, Ethics and Social Work

Steven M. Shardlow

Introduction and context

Getting to grips with social work values and ethics is rather like picking up a live, large and very wet fish from a running stream. Even if you are lucky enough to grab a fish, the chances are that just when you think you have caught it, the fish will vigorously slither out of your hands and jump back in the stream. Values and ethics similarly slither through our fingers for a variety of reasons: we don't try hard enough to catch them, preferring the practical business of doing social work; the subject matter, if we really investigate it, may sometimes seem complex, hard to grapple with and possibly obscure;[1] there is a lack of conceptual clarity about many of the terms used that form part of the lexicon of 'social work values and ethics'; the boundaries of 'social work values and ethics' are imprecise and ill-defined, so the notion of what should constitute 'social work values and ethics' is itself part of a discussion about the nature of social work values. No doubt there are other reasons for not picking up this particular fish! Yet despite these difficulties in picking up the 'fish', there is something that intuitively suggests that social work is bound up with values and ethics. Is not ethics, according to the *Oxford English Dictionary*, 'the science of morals in human conduct', and is not social work about human relationships and behaviour? This conjunction is suggestive of a duty upon social workers to understand both ethics and social work, not least because social work practice contains a terrible potential for the misuse of power (Payne and Littlechild, 2000).

This chapter considers both the nature of current debates about values and also reviews the context of those debates. It is grounded on the presumption that no consensus exists about value questions in social work. Evidence of the contested nature can be seen by looking at longstanding debates, for example over the nature of contracts between clients and social workers, and the extent to which they do or do not empower clients (Cordon, 1980; Cordon and Preston-Shoot, 1987, 1988; Rojek and Collins, 1987, 1988); the extent to which social work is grounded in Kantian ethics (Downie, 1989; Webb and McBeath, 1989, 1990; Gould, 1990); the significance of ideology and knowledge in social work (Dominelli, 1990–91; Webb, 1990–91a, 1990–91b; Smith, 1992), part of which was summarised by Shardlow (1992); and the extent to which a social worker is responsible or accountable when something goes wrong (Hollis and Howe, 1987, 1990; Macdonald, 1990a, 1990b). These debates are inevitably open-ended where social work itself is intrinsically political, controversial and contested, and where the nature of practice is subject to constant change, for example through the emergence of 'care in the community' (see Chapter 25) or the restructuring of work with children and families after the passing of the Children Act 1989 and the ever-changing moral agendas in children's welfare (King, 1999) (see Chapter 24).

The scope of 'social work values'

If, as suggested, the boundaries of the subject 'social work values and ethics' are themselves subject to different interpretations, understanding the scope of such interpretations may be the first step to 'netting' the 'fish'. A narrow or 'restricted description' of the scope of social work 'values and ethics' might focus on:

- social workers' behaviour with clients (that is, professional ethics).

A 'mid-range description' would add to the above:

- the nature of social work as a professional activity (that is, the sociology of professions);
- the function of social work in society – (that is, political philosophy and political sociology) (see Chapter 4);
- the interface between social work and the law (see Chapter 6);
- the characteristics of social work organisations and their influence on the behaviour of individual social workers (that is, managerial and organisational theory) (see Chapter 7).

A 'broad definition' might further add:

- the construction of social work as a social activity (that is, social theory, for example: postmodernism);
- the relationship of social work to religious belief systems (that is, theology);
- the nature and form of social work knowledge – what knowledge do we possess about social work and with what degree of certainty do we hold that knowledge (that is, epistemology).[2]

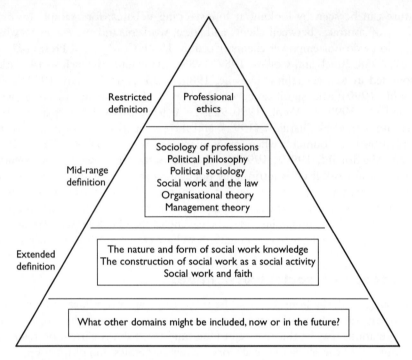

This figure illustrates the different domains of social work ethics and values: each section represents a different conceptualisation of the scope of social work ethics and values, from the most restricted to the most extended. You, the reader, might like to speculate upon these conceptualisations: are they sufficiently comprehensive, do they concur with your perceptions and how might these domains expand in the future?

Figure 3.1 The scope of social work values

This delineation of three different interpretations of the scope of 'social work values and ethics', illustrated in Figure 3.1, is indicative of a broad range of notions and disciplines that might legitimately fall within the rubric of 'social work ethics and values'.

It can also be seen that this conceptualisation is itself potentially fluid and subject to possible future modification and debate. From these interpretations (some of which have received much greater analysis than others), it is evident that the subject matter of 'social work values' is frequently, although not exclusively, defined by the interaction of different domains of knowledge (in particular those reliant upon philosophical forms of thinking) and social work practice.

Understanding values and ethics

Philosophy is about asking questions and is concerned as much with finding the best questions as with providing complete or incontrovertible answers. Likewise, in trying to understand values and ethics in social work, we should be as much concerned with the questions we ask, as the answers we might find – not perhaps a satisfying position for the busy practitioner in search of help in dealing with a particular client. Over time, the questions that philosophers ask have changed: similarly, for social work values – a dynamic and evolving subdiscipline with the broader field of social work itself. In the rest of this chapter, three central themes in social work values and ethics will be examined; space precludes the exploration of all the different domains:

● work with service users;
● the role of social work in society;
● newly emerging professional values.

These themes define core elements within social work values and illustrate current concerns where social work practice and values intersect.

Ethics and work with service users

The first question to ask ourselves might be framed in words such as:

How should social workers behave towards their clients?

This is obviously a useful question and one that social work practitioners need to answer for their everyday practice. So, 'What are the boundaries of acceptable behaviour, either for themselves or their clients?'; for example, is it acceptable for a male social worker to touch and provide comfort to a female client in distress (see, for example, Doel and Shardlow, 1998: 33)?; to what extent does an older person, who is not caring for themselves, have the right to live as they choose (see, for example, Horne, 1999: 39)?; should a child be removed from a carer who is a drug addict (Clark, 2000: 14)?

Yet, such apparently simple and straightforward questions immediately spawn a whole raft of other more problematic questions. Is the language in which these questions are framed sufficiently neutral or are terms used, which have powerful emotional connotations, prejudicial implications for individuals or groups, highly contested meanings and so on (see, for example Webb, 1994)? If any of these factors apply, it becomes even more difficult to think carefully about how to answer questions about how to behave with clients or when to intervene in clients' lives. In this example, the word 'clients' is problematic and other terms such as 'service user' or 'customer' might perhaps be preferred by some. The problem about using *any* of these words – 'client', 'service user' or 'customer' – is that they all carry implications about how people should be treated in everyday discourse. For example, 'customers' have certain legal rights and expectations about treatment when receiving services – increasingly, social work is, rightly or wrongly, being defined by legal requirements. Assuming that we can frame questions about how social workers should behave towards their 'clients', both in respect of personal interactions and more broadly about when to intervene in people's lives, in ways that do not presuppose answers on account of commonly held understandings of the terms used, then other definitional problems arise, for example, who are the clients: is it people who are receiving help from social workers, clients' families, those who might receive help and so on? Thus, to make sense of the original question, we need to be able to define carefully the situations and people to whom the question refers. Despite the apparent prevarication about meaning and not wanting to wallow in difficulties, we can turn our attention to how others have sought to answer these questions concerning how social workers ought to behave towards their clients (using 'clients' as a generic term to refer to all who do or who might use social work services) by examining three of the most important types of response: the 'traditional list' of values, the professional code of ethics and the 'principle' approaches.

Lists of values

Biestek, a Catholic priest, stands as the originator of a set of values that seek to define how social workers ought to behave with their clients. His list, a set of values, included individualisation, the purposeful expression of feelings, controlled emotional involvement, acceptance, a non-judgmental attitude, client self-determination and confidentiality (Biestek, 1961). Each of these terms refers to a principle describing how social workers ought to behave. Therefore, the list lays down a moral code that is determinate, apparently absolute and grounded in Christian theology. The list approach to social work values has been extensively criticised by Timms on the grounds that as the various lists contain different values (Timms, 1983), how can they therefore claim universality for the social work profession as an entirety? Similarly, how can the list be justified? Does it represent anything more than one individual's beliefs – a personal view of what social work values ought to be? Despite the difficulties in justifying 'lists of values', they have had and continue to exert considerable influence on practice. Some of the values contained within the 'lists', such as 'confidentiality' or 'self-determination', chime persistent chords within the social work profession.

Professional codes of ethics

A development from the 'list' approach is to be found in the professional codes of ethics adopted by many national professional associations, for example Australia (AASW, 2000), UK (BASW, 1996),[3] US (NASW, 1996) and the International Federation of Social Workers, (IFSW, 1994). These codes of ethics are broader in scope than the 'list of values'. They represent a consensus among the organisation's membership to define the nature and purpose of social work, to positively espouse some features of expected behaviour by professional social workers and prohibit others. For example, the BASW code of ethics is typical in requiring that social workers:

> will respect their clients as individuals and will seek to ensure that their dignity, individuality, rights and responsibility shall be safeguarded. (BASW, 1996)

Equally, according to the NASW code of ethics, social workers are required not to 'exploit professional relationships for personal gain' (NASW, 1996).

Such statements are typical of the content of professional codes of ethics (see, for example, Banks, 2001 who compares the contents of 15 national professional codes of social work ethics). As can be seen from these examples, and more particularly the codes themselves, the contents of the codes of practice are highly general and do not in themselves provide much help to the social worker, or client for that matter, who wants to know how social workers ought to behave towards clients. For example, the codes do not provide any immediate answer to questions such as 'Is it a social worker's duty to inform the police if they discover that a client has committed a crime?' The statements in the codes of ethics seem to prompt other questions, such as '*How* do I respect clients as individuals?' Codes of practice have as much to do with the establishment of a sense of professional identity for national or international professional social work organisations as providing answers to questions such as '*How* ought social workers behave towards their clients?' Yet the codes purport to provide such help! They do offer some guidance, but at a very general level. Whatever the extent of the contribution that professional codes of ethics make towards enabling good professional practice, they can only be truly effective if they are an integrated part of the structural arrangements of a fully regulated profession: that is, there must be sanctions if the code is broken. To date, such enforceable codes of ethics have not existed in most countries. Following an extended debate in the UK (see, for example, Parker, 1990; NISW, 1992; Guy, 1994), in 2001 the government set up the General Social Care Council (GSCC) which now has the function of regulating the social work profession in the broader context of regulating the occupational field of social care (DoH, 2000c). It is anticipated that in the next few years a code of ethics for social work will be developed.[4]

Fundamental moral principles

A third approach to answering questions surrounding how social workers ought to behave towards their clients is to be found in the use of a fundamental moral principle to determine desired behaviour. Within professional social work practice, 'respect for persons' is the most frequently employed such principle. This moral notion was fully explored by Downie and Telfer (1969). As a moral principle, 'respect for persons' is derived from Kant's moral principle of the *categorical imperative*. This is variously written, but among the best-known formulations are:

> I ought never to act except in such a way that I can also will that my maxim should become a universal law. (Kant, 1785, in Paton, 1948: 67)

> Act in such a way that you always treat humanity whether in your own person or in the person of any other, never simply as a means but always at the same time as an end. (Kant, 1785, in Paton, 1948: 91)

Through following these two principles, social workers are 'respecting persons'. Rather than having a set of prescribed or proscribed actions, this approach requires that if social workers wish to know how they ought to behave with their clients, they should consider the proposed action in the light of these two moral principles. This type of approach requires that social workers are fully able to engage in moral reasoning to determine how they ought to behave with their clients. The application of Kantian approaches in caring professions has been fully developed by Downie and Telfer (1980) and more recently in respect of social work by Reamer (1990).

Having explored three different examples as ways of approaching the question, we may legitimately ask whether we are any nearer to being able to answer the question 'How should social workers behave with their clients?' The answer is yes we are; we now know some of the different ways in which the question has been approached. What we do not have is much of an answer about what a social worker should do in any particular situation – which is just answer the practitioner needs. Answers may also be found by looking to clients themselves, who have defined their expectations of social workers as evidenced in a long series of research studies dating back to the seminal work by Mayer and Timms (1970). (For recent summaries, see, for example, DoH, 1995a; Lindow and Morris, 1995.) One can also look to legal or procedural guidance provided by the government, as exemplified in the fields of care management (DoH, 1991a; SSI, 1991a, 1991b), child protection (DoH, 1991b) and childcare (DoH, 1993). Some of these governmental statements tend to reduce professional autonomy and restrict the arena for independent professional decision-making and might, therefore, be seen as an attempt to deprofessionalise social work, removing the need for decision-making based on professional values by substituting a bureaucratic and procedural requirement (see Chapter 6). Yet they leave social workers fearful of making mistakes.

Social work and society

Our second group of questions is concerned with the function of social work, for example:

> **What is the purpose of social work as an activity in modern society?**

> **Why do we have social work?**

Is it possible to conceive of a society without social work? Some of the newly emergent states of Eastern and Central Europe functioned under communism without a social work profession (Deacon, 1992; Constable and Metha, 1993). In recent years, these states have moved quickly to establish social work – just as they are seeking to develop non-command-style economies and introduce market mechanisms (see, for example, Munday and Lane, 1998). This drive to develop social work in such states does not of itself establish that social work is a necessary function of modern industrial societies. However, it may well be that there is a functional need for social work in modern industrial societies, for example as Lorenz writes:

> Broadly speaking, social work's origins coincide with the formation of modern Western nation states and are directly related to the internal stability that these states need. (Lorenz, 1994: 4)

Thus he argues that social work is necessary and contributes to the maintenance of social order, while Cannan et al. (1992) point to comparative and historical similarities in the emergence of social work in Northern Europe in parallel with urbanisation and industrialisation.

Perhaps the most persuasive argument that social work is functionally necessary to modern society has been propounded by Davies (1994). He argues, from a humanist perspective, that the function of social work is to help to maintain the fabric of society, a fabric that would otherwise be brittle and likely to fracture, as exemplified in the following quotation:

> In so far as there are common elements in social work they are best described by the general notion of *maintenance*: society maintaining itself in a relatively stable state by making provision for and managing people in positions of severe weakness, stress or vulnerability; and society maintaining its own members, without exception by commitment to humanist endeavour. (Davies, 1994: 40)

Interestingly, in the second edition of the book, Davies continued with a bold statement about the underlying purpose of social work:

> and its [social work's] emphasis on the idea of respect for the client, optimism for the future, and faith in the essential or at least potential unity of society. (Davies, 1985, p. 3)

We can only speculate about the reasons for the lost vision of a social work striving for a unified and harmonious society. Yet, Davies' vision of the function of social work emphasises the need to maintain the social order while seeing the operation of the state in the promotion of social work as being to further humanist ideals. The 'maintenance theory' of social work found in Davies' writings is essentially benign: he expresses a broad approval of the motives of the state and the consequent role of social work to maintain the social fabric. When a similar argument (in the sense that social work helps to maintain existing social structures) about the role of social work in society is advanced from a Marxist perspective, the timbre alters dramatically:

> Since its modern origins in the middle of the last century, social work has been one of the many strategies developed and deployed by the ruling class and the state for intervening in the lives of working people ... social work has to be considered as one of the agencies of class control and regulation. (Jones, 1983: 9, as quoted in Rojek et al., 1988: 64)

Leonard developed this argument further, suggesting that social work promotes a more compliant labour force and seeks the re-education of the 'underclass clientele who are seen as irresponsible and immature' (Leonard, 1976: 261). Here, social work is portrayed as a malignant force assisting dominant elites to maintain political and economic power over groups in society who are deemed to be a threat. In such a vision, social work is not acting in the interests of those it helps but is part of a set of social structures that oppress. However, these two different opinions – the Marxist and the maintenance theorist – do not diverge over what social workers actually do in society. It is in the significance, meaning and value of those actions, not for individuals but at the level of sociological or political explanation, that they differ. The type of position adopted by Leonard, which is critical of the position and role adopted by social work within society, leads relatively easily to the view that social work should strive for social change, in other words to refute the notion that social work is about the maintenance of society. Similar critical and radical views about the function of social work in society are located within a variety of other intellectual traditions, notably feminism (see, for example, Graham, 1992; Wise, 1995) and anti-racism (see, for example, Dominelli, 1997b; Ahmad, 1990).

New values: empowerment, consumerism, structural challenge

In the past twenty years or so, a new set of ideas, such as advocacy (for example, Simons, 1992), consumerism (for example, Allen, 1988), empowerment (for example, Adams, 1996a), participation (for example, Biehal, 1993), partnership (for example, Marsh and Fisher, 1992), user involvement (Office for Public Management, 1994) and so on, have influenced social work ideology. Braye and Preston-Shoot (1995) characterise these new and emerging social work values as 'radical' values, which are concerned with challenging oppression, as distinct from 'traditional values' which emphasise the individualised nature of the relationship between the social worker and the individual receiving help. Yet there should be no presumption that the emergence of these new values or the development of older, more traditional ones will lead to changes in professional practice. Without organisational backing or changed professional education, practice is likely to remain relatively fixed.

Let us consider as an example one of these 'radical' values in a little more detail.

Empowerment

Empowerment has been persuasively and powerfully defined by Braye and Preston-Shoot (1995: 48) in terms of:

- extending one's ability to take effective decisions;

- individuals, groups and/or communities taking control of their circumstances and achieving their own goals, thereby being able to work towards maximising the quality of their lives;

- enabling people who are disempowered to have more control over their lives, to have a greater voice in institutions, service and situations which affect them, and to exercise power over someone else rather than simply being the recipients of exercised power;

- helping people to regain their own power.

Such a definition of empowerment is centrally about people taking control of their own lives and having the power to shape their own future. For Braye and Preston-

Shoot, the concept seems to imply a general broadening and deepening of citizenship as in the large body of work of Beresford and Croft (see, for example, 1993) and is closely linked to self-advocacy (see, for example, Simons, 1992) and the assertion of users' rights (see, for example, Morris, 1997). Such notions of empowerment draw upon liberationalist ideologies and implicitly contain notions of structural change or the claiming of political and social rights for oppressed groups. For others the context of empowerment is more circumscribed and refers only to the articulation and meeting of needs (Stevenson and Parsloe, 1993). Here then empowerment becomes a social work tool for the achievement of high standards of professional practice. The growing emphasis on theoretical approaches to empowerment has been complemented by strategies for promoting empowerment in given situations, some drawing upon liberationist ideologies, others not (see, for example, Mullender, 1996; Shera and Wells, 1999; Thompson and Thompson, 2001. Hence, In essence, in its more restricted sense, 'empowerment' as an idea may not be so very different from 'self-determination' as proposed by Biestek (1961). The social context and the social construction of professional social work practice are different, but when we use words such as 'empowerment' or 'self-determination', we should ask how these professional concepts are linked or related to longstanding philosophical debates about the nature of freedom or liberty. Part of the difficulty with terms such as 'empowerment' is their very slipperiness – just like our fish! These values are defined in different ways and hence mean different things to different people. There is a considerable danger with 'radical' values such as 'empowerment' that they vanish as quickly as they came and become mere ephemera: whatever their eventual durability as professional values, they stand in need of justification for adoption by the profession. Otherwise, 'radical' values are susceptible to the same counterarguments as those advanced by Timms against the 'list approach'. They become, in essence, just another item on a list!

If we were to explore the other radical values, we might find similar problems with regard to definition, scope and potential for meaningful application to practice: for example, according to Stevenson and Parsloe, 'partnership is very vague since it suggests an equality which is rarely possible' (1993: 6). Debates about the nature of concepts such as 'partnership' or 'empowerment' are highly significant, as these debates denote the rise of user-led definitions of the nature of professionalism that stand in contention with the profession's own views.

Endnote – netting the fish

From this brief overview of professional values and ethics in social work, we may emerge in despair about the possibility of providing definitive answers to the questions posed. If this is so, however, the nature of the enterprise is misunderstood; it is not so much final answers but better refined questions that are required. This will help to establish an ethically mature professional stance for social work. Moreover, there is a great diversity and liveliness about the emerging topics for debate in this field: see, for example, the role of social workers in organ donation (Geva and Weinman, 1995), the need for social work to adopt a p ifi stance (Verschelden, 1993) or the importance of religion in social work (Ar von Hemert, 1994; Clark, 1994; Patel et al., 1998). There have recently be increasing number of published materials concerning postmodernism and social work (for further discussion of this aspect of values, see Chapter 22). There is an inevitability that 'professional values', however defined, will mediate between forms of social work practice that are essentially procedural and forms of practice that are individualised and highly creative. Forces such 'globalisation' and 'managerialism' are strongly changing the nature of social work practice. Discussion about professional values and ethics has yet to respond to these challenges – perhaps that is for the future.

Notes

1   In recent years, there has been a growth in popular interest in values and ethics and similar subjects which are part of the philosophical tradition, for example Gaarder, J. (1995) *Sophie's World* (London, Phoenix House), which was originally designed for children or de Botton, A. (2000) *The Consolations of Philosophy* (Harmondsworth, Penguin).
2   This is perhaps the most fundamental issue faced by any discipline; for a recent discussion of the key issues see Reid (2001).
3   The BASW Code of Ethics is under revision at the time of writing: a major consultation exercise is being under taken in the UK; for further details see www.basw.co.uk.
4   See the GSCC website for more information: http://www.doh.gov.uk/gscc/.

FURTHER READING

Banks, S. (2001) *Ethics and Values in Social Work,* 2nd edn (Basingstoke, Palgrave – now Palgrave Macmillan). A brief general overview of social work values designed specifically for practitioners.

Clark, C. (2000) *Social Work Ethics: Politics, Principles and Practice* (Basingstoke, Macmillan – now Palgrave Macmillan).

Hugman, R. and Smith, D. (eds) (1996) *Ethical Issues in Social Work* (London, Routledge). An edited collection containing an exploration of a range of current issues in professional ethics for social workers.

Reamer, F.G. (1993) *Ethical Dilemmas in Social Services: A Guide for Social Workers*, 3rd edn (New York, Columbia University Press). A thorough exploration of professional values for social workers from a US perspective.

Rhodes, M.L. (1986) *Ethical Dilemmas in Social Work Practice* (London, Routledge & Kegan Paul). A book which takes a series of practical examples of value problems and explores the implications.

Shardlow, S.M. (2002) *Social Work Values and Knowledge* (London, Palgrave Macmillan). A detailed overview of professional values from a UK perspective.

4

Social Work and Society

Chris Jones

Introduction

Try and find a clear definition of social work. It is no easy task, although in recent years it would appear that, for some, social work is best described as that activity undertaken by those people employed as social workers by state social service departments. This was the position taken for example by the CCETSW in its national curriculum for social work education. It is not a helpful definition in that it captures nothing of the history of social work or its essence independent of a specific context and suggests that social work can be almost anything if it is called such by a state agency. Such an unsatisfactory definition is a reflection of a real difficulty. For social work is a diverse and shifting activity, undertaken by various kinds of welfare worker, many of whom are currently employed by statutory local authority social service departments, others by voluntary and charitable agencies, still others being genuine volunteers offering social work through a wide range of community-based organisations and groups. Moreover, until the mid-1970s, the majority of people employed as social workers in Britain had no specialist training or education.

Not only is the location of social work becoming increasingly diverse in contemporary society (Parton and O'Byrne, 2000), but so too is its practice. It embraces a spectrum of activities along a wide continuum, with counselling and support at one end and statutory powers to remove liberties at the other. Furthermore, as any social work student will tell you, clients of social work, or in modern parlance service users, are in some respects equally diverse. Clients can be drawn from across the life cycle, from the oldest to the youngest, men or women, black or white, from the able-bodied to those with special needs.

This diversity of social work is one of its salient characteristics. For some clients, social work is an activity that brings solace and comfort at times of acute need; for others, it is an activity to be avoided because of the threat it poses to their liberty. Moreover, it is not a static activity. The work of social workers in contemporary social service departments has changed considerably from the pre-Seebohm days of childcare and health and welfare departments (Clarke, 1993), and there have been further profound changes since the implementation of the Children Act 1989 and community care legislation in the early 1990s (Hadley and Clough, 1996).

However, such diversity and dynamism does not mean that it is impossible to talk about social work and society in a more general sense, although one needs to be sensitive to its lack of uniformity. Social work is no different from other social activities in that it is possible to reveal much of its purpose and character by exploring its origins and development. After all, the personal social services in which social work has taken a lead role have grown to become a very significant part of Britain's welfare system. One presumes that this expansion, particularly since 1945, is based on some understanding of social work's more general role, purpose and function in society. Second, while not wishing to diminish the significance of social work's diversity and even its paradoxical nature with respect to its involvement in both social care and social control, there is a need to challenge social work's own in-house appreciation of itself, in which it has glorified its diversity in order, I would argue, to obfuscate some of its more essential and enduring features.

Social work, class and poverty

For all the attention to diversity, social work has, since its modern origins in the Victorian Charity Organisation Society (COS) through to the present day, been overwhelmingly a class-specific activity. Many social work texts might wish to avoid this conclusion by using other labels and categories for its clients, but the evidence overwhelmingly indicates that, whether the client is old or young, able-bodied or with a special need, an offender, a single parent, an abused child or partner, black or white, clients are most likely to be poor and most likely to be drawn from those sections of the population which enjoy the least status, security and power (Becker and MacPherson, 1988; Schorr, 1992). In Britain at least, it is unusual to find those with wealth and privilege making use of social workers, and one suspects that they would recoil at the prospect. This class-specificity of social work is of great importance. Its focus on and preoccupation with those at the bottom of the social hierarchy is one of the distinguishing features of social work and is a common factor through its historical development. Ironically, the modern social work enterprise, whether expressed through its courses, its professional organisation or its various organisational settings, attempts to play down this class-specificity.

The COS, during the period of its greatest influence between 1869 and 1908, was not so coy about its class-specific credentials and mission. Concerned by the threat to social order and progress posed by widespread poverty and destitution – especially in the rapidly expanding industrial and commercial centres of British capitalism – the COS developed casework as *the* method of social reform. Central to the development of casework was the idealist perspectives of the leading members of the COS, of whom Bernard Bosanquet was particularly notable. For the Bosanquets (Bernard and Helen) and Charles Loch, social work was the practical expression of idealist philosophy (Jones, 1978). Idealism gave primacy to the realm of ideas in the determination of social and economic conditions just as casework gave primacy to character and morality with respect to an individual's social and economic position and well-being. 'In social reform', Bernard Bosanquet argued, 'character is the condition of conditions' (1895: vii). In a later text, he wrote:

> Here then, seems to be the true meaning of social work. Wherever it may start its goal is the same; to bring the social mind into order, into harmony with itself. Social disorganisation is the outward and visible form of moral and intellectual disorganisation. (Bosanquet, 1901: 297)

Casework was developed as an idealist welfare practice and did much to set the tone for all subsequent social work practice and theory. The logic was impeccable once one accepted the taken-for-granted assumption that the plight of the working-class poor and destitute was not related to the fundamental nature of capitalism and its machinations. Indeed, industrial capitalism was taken as a progressive force. The dislocations incurred by its expansion and urbanisation were not problems of capitalism but rather the backwardness of people to adapt and shift, to modernise.

The problems posed by the poor and destitute were defined according to the idealism of the COS as problems of character and morality rather than of lack of resources and power. Social work in its modern origins and subsequent development, while focused on the most impoverished and disadvantaged, was neither practised nor conceived of as an activity concerned primarily with the material conditions of clients' lives. Its principal, long-term concern has been with either the moral education of clients or, where this is impossible, their supervision in order to minimise their nuisance and cost to the state. Material circumstances are considered largely as an external measure of personal and familial morality. Drawing on social Darwinism, the COS insisted that one's location in the social and economic world was in large measure a reflection of character, those at the bottom of the pile being the most deficient and disorganised. The contribution of the COS to these popular debates and understandings about social conditions and the plight of the working class in late Victorian society was the manner in which it contributed significantly to the sophistication and quality of these commonplace assumptions of the privileged towards the powerless.

The leadership of the COS was formidable. The Bosanquets in particular matched in intellectual stature and publications their counterparts the Webbs in the Fabian Society. Helen Bosanquet's work on the family had a significant impact on social policy in general and social work in particular. Her book (Bosanquet, 1906) marks one of the first systematic accounts of the importance of the family as the basic social unit. The family, Helen Bosanquet argued, was the critical institution which influenced and informed character and morality. The problems of destitution, crime, poor labour discipline, alcoholism, lack of thrift and so forth were not to be sought in social structural arrangements but in poor and inadequate parenting, especially mothering. This, rather than lack of money or influence, was the problem, and social work was created and developed as a 'mental' activity and welfare practice with overwhelming attention being given to family life and parenting. In essence, casework involved social workers taking on the role of 'good' parents with the clients as 'children'.

Social work as conservative welfare

The COS's creation of casework within an idealist paradigm and a central focus on the family established social work as a conservative welfare practice. Despite many changes in the language and knowledge base of social work since the end of the nineteenth century, social work has remained an activity that is not only class specific, but has also continued to practise as if the primary causes of clients' problems are located in their behaviour, morality and deficient family relationships. Mainstream social work, despite its immersion in poverty and among the least powerful sections of the population, has rarely ventured to seek explanations for these difficulties beyond family and interpersonal relationships and dynamics. Questioning the legitimacy of social, economic and political systems and the manner in which patterns of inequality and oppression systematically disadvantage women, minority ethnic groups, people with disabilities, children and young people, especially when located within the working-class poor, has not been part of social work's agenda.

For all its trappings of liberalism and concern, there has been no sustained or substantial tradition of radicalism within British social work. It is also probable that had social work acquired such a perspective, it would have not enjoyed state sponsorship since 1945. That is not to deny, however, the presence of critical impulses within social work, in particular the influence of feminist and anti-racist perspectives, especially since the mid-1970s (Ahmed et al., 1986; Marchant and Wearing, 1986; Dominelli, 1988; Langan and Day, 1992). For many practitioners and students, the materials generated from these perspectives provided highly valuable insights, understandings that influenced their practice with clients. Their contribution to highlighting systems of institutional racism and the manner in which much social work practice was both gender-specific and sexist has been considerable.

Nevertheless, throughout its short history, progressive ideas which seek to move the locus of explanation and intervention from the family or individual client to wider social and political systems and processes have tended to be resisted and treated by the key state agencies managing social work as contagion and dangerous. The removal of community work from social work's repertoire during the 1970s is probably one clear example of potentially troublesome perspectives and practices being eradicated. The social work establishment itself has devoted considerable energy and attention to the management of social workers in order to avert the threat of what it perceives as radical contamination. As I have argued elsewhere, many developments in social work education since 1975 can be read in part as being concerned to ensure the reproduction of a conservative and manageable workforce (Jones, 1996a, 1996b). This in turn highlights a further characteristic of social work as a site of ongoing debate, controversy and contest, and as an activity whose trajectory is, and has been, influenced by conflicting perspectives on the nature of social problems and appropriate responses.

From the point of view of clients, the history of social work has been marked by suspicion and hostility (Jones, 1997). Social work remains one of the few welfare activities that has at no time been the subject of working-class demands for expansion and development (Wardman, 1977). On the limited occasions when the voices of clients are heard, it is notable that many complain of the moralising and interfering nature of social work investigations and the sheer unsuitability of the agencies' responses to their difficulties. The claimants unions in the 1970s reckoned that social workers were worse than the social security for their snooping and the conditions which they applied to the giving of small sums of money (Carmichael, 1974). Handler (1968), in his study of children's departments, came to the conclusion that the

> operative social work principles ... are remarkably similar to those of the Charity Organisation Society, founded about 100 years ago. The close supervision of spending money is little different from the old system of relief in kind; poor people cannot be trusted to spend money that isn't 'theirs'. (Handler, 1968: 487; see also Davis and Wainwright, 1996).

As Bryan and her co-authors (1985) note, add racism to social work's underlying class hostility and the result is that 'black women's relationships with social workers have been fraught with ... antagonisms':

> Whether we are single parents, homeless young women or the parents of children in care, we are constantly confronted with racist, classist or culturally biased judgements about our lives. The social background of most social workers and the training they receive give them no real understanding of our different family structures, cultural values and codes of behaviour. It is so much easier for them to rely on loose assumptions and loaded stereotypes of us than to try seriously to address the root cause of our problems. These assumptions become the justification for everything from secret files and surveillance to direct intervention of the most destructive kind. (Bryan et al., 1985: 112)

That people mostly become clients through third-party referral (for example by the police, schools, health services or social security) rather than through self-referral further illustrates the low regard and suspicion with which social work is held among those in need (Schorr, 1992). Social work appears to be one of those welfare services which people seek to avoid wherever possible, and where entanglement has come to be associated with failure and stigma. However, remembering the caveats about diversity and dynamism noted in the introduction, it is important to note that not all clients are treated in the same manner. Social work reflects and in significant ways reinforces the moral hierarchies prevalent at any particular time. This can impact significantly on client experiences of social work, with those who are generally perceived as more deserving – single and abandoned poor fathers, some older poor people for example – having a more positive response than those held in low regard – black young offenders, young poor black single mothers and so on. Moral judgements about worth and deservedness structure social work practice with the working-class poor just as they did a century earlier. Social work, for all its claims of being a liberal and caring occupation, tends to reflect rather than challenge prevailing social mores, which again reflects its social conservatism.

Unloved social work

Paradoxically, despite this conservative tradition, social work has not enjoyed unconditional support from elite groups either. The renaissance of state social work in Britain after World War II was marked by a long process of struggle for legitimacy and acceptance, and it was not until the Seebohm Report in 1968 that social work was granted its own discrete agency. Even then, medicine was most reluctant to give up its stewardship of social work (Leonard, 1973) and has continued to demand that social work be returned to its ambit of control.

Part of social work's problem rests with the very low status accorded to its client population. In contrast to the COS, which insisted that social work was only possible with those who had shown some semblance of morality prior to their destitution – namely the deserving poor – British social work since 1945 has been principally targeted at those whom the COS described as the residuum or the undeserving poor and whom it regarded as beyond help. Influenced by eugenics and social Darwinism, it was commonplace for the undeserving poor to be condemned as human refuse incapable of being assisted and for whom close supervision and containment was the only reasonable strategy. Whetham, a prominent eugenicist at the turn of the century, represented this perspective when he wrote of the residuum:

> In dealing with men and women of this character, where we cannot hope to accomplish individual radical cure, we must, as with the feeble minded, organise the extinction of the tribe. In the old days the law attempted this extinction by hanging, a preventative of the sternest and most effective nature ... For us ... the old methods are impossible. We must attain the same result by the longer and gentler system of perpetual segregation in detention colonies, and with all mitigations that are practicable. (Whetham, 1909: 214–15)

By 1945, although these ideas were never expunged – as their re-emergence in the 1980s and 90s with the New Right's underclass concept demonstrated – they were no longer wholly acceptable. Popular opinion following World War II was revolted by such inhumanity and demanded compassionate social welfare with the state taking greater responsibility for regulating the excesses of capitalism. In contrast to social work's current lack of vision British social work after World War II enjoyed a quality of leadership which both seized upon and reflected the growing dominance of and consensus around social democracy and the promise of the Keynesian welfare state. Buoyed up by the work of Freud and the neo-Freudians, social work leaders such as Eileen Younghusband were confident that social work had the knowledge and skills to ensure that even the lowest of the low were capable of becoming full participants – citizens – in society. All that was required was that social work be given the remit and resources to intervene.

Psychoanalysis liberated casework from the straitjacket imposed by the biological pessimism of the COS, and there was tremendous optimism within social work about the contribution that a psychoanalytically informed casework could now make to resolving a range of deep-rooted social problems (see Morris, 1964; Younghusband, 1970). It was considered that such casework could eradicate the problem of the problem family, strengthen working-class families and thereby reduce the need for residential provision for children and make major inroads into reducing juvenile delinquency. These were no cautious claims. Social work leaders believed that their occupation could, with appropriate funding and training, attend to some of the most pressing social problems of the post-war period. With these claims, social work captured much of the optimism of social policy-makers through the 1950s and 60s. It believed that the Keynesian welfare state had eradicated the principal material causes of poverty, such that those who were still locked in poverty were there because of psychological problems and thereby required social work. It was quite a different context from that of the COS period, but there was no less an insistence within social work that those problematic groups at the 'bottom' of society were there largely because of the consequences of poor parenting and mothering.

Needless to say, the expansion of social work, driven largely by concerns over the working-class family and children (and much less by concerns with those who were poor and old or disabled), did not bring about the sorts of dramatic improvement envisaged by social work commentators. Moreover, there were many groups and organisations, both within the state system itself and elsewhere, which became increasingly critical of what they saw as the softly-softly approach of social work. The police and sections of the magistracy were vociferous in their opposition to the new powers granted to social workers in the 1960s for the management and control of juvenile offenders (Jones, 1978: 304–6). Reactionary critics attracted considerable attention then, as they do now, in pointing to young offenders being given opportunities seemingly to enjoy themselves when placed under the supervision of social services departments following conviction. Social security officials likewise complained that too much of their time was taken up haggling with social workers who were attempting to secure more generous benefit settlements (when there was discretion in the social security system) for those whom they believed were no more than scroungers and layabouts. Despite advances in the social sciences, in which valuable insights have been gained into the manner by which life chances and opportunities are considerably influenced by class position, gender and ethnicity, over which the individual has no control, it seems that many people continue to hold negative views of clients and public opinion is soon excited when it is suggested that they are being treated generously.

Social work and neo-liberalism

Criticisms of this sort were music to the ears of the New Right which came to dominate social policy reform in Britain and elsewhere during the 1980s. It was little wonder that social work figured so highly in their onslaught on state welfare, as it was considered by many on the radical right to epitomise all those character-istics of social-democratic welfare which they sought to root out (Franklin, 1989). Not only could they not abide social work's attention to issues of racism and sexism which was cast aside as political correctness, but they were outraged by what they perceived as social work's overlenient and sympathetic approach to those who were dependent on state welfare.

This New Right critique, which is now better understood as marking the beginning of the neo-liberal re-engineering of the welfare system, was more than just an ideological onslaught. It was in fact a recasting of the relationship of the state to the citizenry which has been characterised in part by reining in state welfare support which in turn has fallen with most dramatic effect on the poorest and most vulnerable in society. Superficially it would seem that social work, especially in the state sector, has not been too badly affected by neo-liberalism. After all, social workers are still in demand and there has been no eradication of social service departments. However a closer examination reveals some very significant changes (Jones and Novak, 1999).

Essentially, state social work no longer has a meaningful preventive brief. Unlike the 1940s and 50s when the economy's thirst for labour to work in an expanding economy pushed the state to look with 'new eyes' at problem families as potential sources of workers and saw social work as a means of tapping that resource, there is now no such economic pressure. As Nick Davies notes, those who make up the majority of social work's client population are now considered worthless:

> They are in the deepest sense redundant. Looking at them from a strictly economic point of view, these former workers and their families are worthless. More than that they are an expensive burden – at least they will be if they are to be properly housed, clothed and fed, if they are to be given decent schools and hospitals. So why bother ? ... From an economic point they are worth nothing, they will be given the bare minimum. (Davies, 1997: 299–300)

Giving them the bare minimum has become one of the hallmarks of the British welfare system at the beginning of the twenty-first century. State social work continues; its clients are as poor as they ever were, and in many respects they are more stressed (Jones, 2001), given the extent to which poverty has deepened and inequalities have widened since the late 1970s. However, there is no longer any pretence at rehabilitation with respect to children and their families. After all there is no demand for their labour, given that, for men in particular, unskilled manual work has all but evaporated. The state social work task has changed to one which is now much clearer and less confused. Its role today is essentially one of policing the poorest and holding down the costs of their dependency. And even New Labour, for all its rhetoric about social exclusion, is not interested in the most disadvantaged and vulnerable and, like the Conservatives before them, demonises them as failures lacking in any sense of social responsibility. For this group of the population, the state has taken a sharp authoritarian and controlling turn which is reflected in every part of the welfare system, social work included (Jones and Novak, 1999). Little wonder then that so many social workers today, like their clients before them, are turning their backs on state social work. For this grim situation to change, society as a whole has to reconsider its stance on poverty and inequality and fundamentally challenge the contempt in which the poorest are held. The challenge for social work is whether or not it is prepared to commit itself to that goal.

FURTHER READING

Clarke, J. (ed.) (1993) *A Crisis in Care* (London, Sage). Useful edited collection on social work and society.

Holman, B. (1993) *A New Deal for Social Welfare* (Oxford, Lion Publishing). Polemical renunciation of the New Right's impact on state social work.

Loch, C.S. (ed.) (1904) *Methods of Social Advance* (London, Macmillan – now Palgrave Macmillan). It pays to have an appreciation of the historical roots of British social work.

Mullaly, R. (1993) *Structural Social Work* (Toronto, McClelland & Stewart). Provides a lucid and critical analysis of contemporary social work and its possibilities.

Schorr, A. (1992) *The Personal Social Services: An Outside View* (York, Joseph Rowntree Foundation). An accessible and informative account of the British social services which makes clear the class specificity of state social work and its implications for practice.

Social Policy and Social Work

Carol Walker and Alan Walker

Introduction

> To claim that economic and social policy, the prevailing political ideology and a particular location within the social structure, conceptualised in class terms have a direct bearing upon day-to-day living, would hardly be contentious today. (Bailey, 1988: 197)

So wrote Roy Bailey in 1988. While few in social work would disagree with this statement in principle, in practice it is all too easy for the context within which social workers, and other professionals, work to be overlooked in the pressures of their everyday lives. In particular, it is too easy for social workers, the majority of whose service users are poor (Becker and MacPherson, 1986), to focus on the differing abilities of individuals to manage and cope within the constraints of their personal circumstances rather than compare their circumstances with those enjoyed by the wider population.

In this chapter, we focus on the social policy context within which social workers operate and their service users live. Social policy is of particular importance because it sets both the framework and constraints within which professionals work and the type and level of service they can provide. It also has an impact on the number of people seeking or being referred to social services departments, in particular on their ability to cope independently.

The current social policy context

Over the past two decades, there have been major changes in British social policy. Under the Conservative governments between 1979–97, welfare policy aimed to roll back the frontiers of the state in order to:

● increase individual and family responsibility;

● move from public to private provision;

● decrease public spending on the welfare state.

All these objectives impacted most seriously on the most vulnerable people in Britain because it is they who require total or partial support from the state, yet they have been the main losers. It is the poor who lost most in the changes which were made in the structure and administration of public welfare services. This is illustrated in a number of different services:

● Housing policy was more concerned with changing tenure (from public to private) than with meeting housing need.

● The introduction of market principles into the NHS and social service provision through the purchaser–provider split and the establishment of fund-holding GPs led to two levels of NHS provision, in which those living in the most deprived areas gained least.

● In education, the introduction of the local management of schools (LMS) and the national curriculum, in particular the publication of league tables, exacerbated divisions between pupils in poor and affluent areas and penalised those working in areas of social deprivation.

● The focus in the probation service shifted much more towards an active involvement in punishment and control.

● Changes in local authority social services saw a dramatic shift of social services departments away from providers to being managers and regulators of care.

● In response to the growing number of people dependent on social security, social security policy focused on getting people off benefit through punitive measures and ignored the continuing poverty of those dependent on benefit, in the vast majority of cases through no fault of their own.

All these changes occurred within the context of huge cuts in social spending, which led to a diminution of confidence in public services, and increasing numbers of people opting into the private sector, for example in health, education and pensions.

The New Labour government came to power in 1997 with a number of commitments relating to welfare set out in its election manifesto (Labour Party, 1997):

● We will be the party of welfare reform

- Education will be our number one priority, and we will increase the share of national income spent on education

- 250,000 young unemployed off benefit and into work

- rebuild the NHS, reducing spending on administration and increasing spending on patient care

- We will build strong families and strong communities, and lay the foundations of a modern welfare state in pensions and community care

These positive welfare aspirations were crucially constrained in New Labour's first term of office by a commitment not to increase income tax and to stick to the previous Conservative government's stringent proposals on spending. A major change, however, was the government's commitment to reduce poverty, specifically child poverty, to be achieved by changes in benefits for children and educational initiatives geared towards poorer areas. However, there was also considerable continuity following on from the Conservative years, including greater conditionality in obtaining welfare benefits, increasing importance of means-tested benefits and, crucially, no improvement in uprating benefits which remain pegged to price inflation and not to earnings as in the 1970s. The government is also committed to an involvement of the private sector in public services.

Before considering how government policy in other areas of welfare state provision has impacted on vulnerable people, we will consider the growth and persistence of poverty in Britain and its implications for social work.

Poverty and social work

The majority of social work service users are poor, yet poverty as an issue is too often marginalised in social work training, even though it is a greater cause of social exclusion than are 'race' and gender, with which it also overlaps (Walker and Walker, 1997). In social work practice, there is a danger that poverty and deprivation can be overlooked precisely because they are so common and are somehow seen as 'normal' for social work service users. However, the fact remains that a significant proportion of the British population are living on incomes substantially below the average for the rest of the population and are, as such, at risk of malnutrition, hypothermia, homelessness, restricted educational opportunities, poorer health, earlier death and being victims of crime. For example, a child born into a poor family is four times as likely as a child from a better-off family to die before the age of 20.

Under the last Conservative governments, the UK experienced an increase in income inequality unparalleled, with the sole exception of New Zealand, in the industrialised world (Hills, 1995). For example, between 1979 and 1993–94, the real incomes (after housing costs) of those in the poorest tenth of the population fell by 13 per cent, the average rose by 40 per cent, while the richest enjoyed a huge increase of 63 per cent (Oppenheim, 1997). Despite this, Conservative governments were reluctant to acknowledge the problem, to the extent that, in the 1980s, the word 'poverty' was banned from official publications. By contrast the incoming New Labour government took the issues of poverty and social exclusion on board. It set up the Social Exclusion Unit to monitor and coordinate relevant policy across a range of government departments. A number of reports on progress have been published (DSS, 1999; ONS, 2000). Tony Blair pledged to end child poverty within twenty years and pledged his government to an anti-poverty strategy comparable to that of the Beveridge Report (Howarth et al., 1998). There has been some success in reducing levels of child poverty, however, income inequality and levels of poverty continued to rise in the first New Labour administration (Rahman et al., 2001).

In the post-war period, the political debate generally shifted away from the problem of poverty towards the 'problem' of the poor. Consequently, policy tended to concentrate on influencing the behaviour of the poor, in particular to reduce their dependence on state benefits, rather than tackling the underlying factors, such as unemployment, which cause poverty. New Labour has shifted the balance back, but only a little, and really only in relation to children. Benefits for adults have become increasingly conditional upon meeting income and other work tests. The whole 'welfare to work' policy which has underpinned its social security policy is based on the premise that many people are reluctant to work. Most disappointing is the government's decision to continue to vilify benefit claimants:

> there is a tendency to 'balance' progressive social measures with a populist rhetoric which often stigmatises benefits claimants. ... the drive against poverty in the twenty-first century needs to leave behind the divisive language of the deserving versus the undeserving poor. (Fimister, G., 2001)

Britain does not have an official measure of poverty. Different measures have been used in the post-war period. First the low income statistics, which set out numbers in or on the margins of poverty according to social assistances rates. This measure was abandoned by the Conservatives in 1985 in favour of the HBAI (households below average income) figures. The HBAI statistics allow analysis of numbers living in the different deciles of income. The 50 per cent figure is now used as a definition of poverty by commentators, as this figure is used in many international studies, particularly when making comparisons across the European Union. According to the HBAI statistics, the number of people living on incomes below half-average income rose to 14.5 million in 1998–99. Of those, about one-third were in work, one-quarter pensioners, and the remainder of working age but not working. Looking at the figures by family type: one-third were couples with children, one-fifth pensioners, one in nine lone parents and the remaining quarter single people and couples with no children (Howarth et al., 1998: 23).

Who are the poor?

Poverty is not confined to any particular group or place, but it is not a random experience. Certain groups of people are particularly vulnerable because of their economic or family status. Employment is the key to avoiding poverty: those in full-time work are at less risk than those working part time, who are in turn less at risk than a household where no-one is in paid employment. The unemployed account for more than a fifth of those in poverty (according to the half-average income definition), whereas couples with two working partners make up only 2 per cent (Oppenheim and Harker, 1996).

Although, overall, people in work are better off than those not in work, there is considerable inequality within the working population. In the 1980s and 90s the gap between the low paid and the highest paid was 'wider than at any time in the century for which we have records' (Hills, 1995: 42). Between 1979 and 1999 (before the introduction of the minimum wage) the earning of the top 10 per cent of male earners grew from 2.4 times that of the poorest 10 per cent to 3.4 and for women grew from 2.1 times to 3.1 (Exell, in Fimister, 2001: 44). According to the Low Pay Unit (1996), in 1996 over 10 million people in Britain earned less than the Council of Europe Decency Threshold (£5.88 per hour), and 2 million people earned less than £3 per hour. The introduction of the minimum wage in April 1999 raised the incomes of 1.5 million workers, two-thirds of them women. However, it remains low at £4.10 per hour for those over 22, less for those between 18 and 22, and does not apply to people below the age of 18.

Vulnerability to poverty is closely associated to family status. Having children increases the risk of poverty for both couples and single people. Lone parents are the group most likely to experience poverty. A feature of growing poverty among families has been the increase in the number of children living in poor households, which rose even more steeply than the overall figures. In 1979, 1.4 million children (10 per cent of all children) were living in poverty (according to the half-average income measure); by 1993/94, this had risen to 4.2 million (32 per cent). The government has estimated that changes made during its first term of office will lift 1.2 million children out of poverty. After lone parents, the group most vulnerable to poverty are single pensioners. Women make up the majority of both of these groups. A number of other factors increase an individual's vulnerability to poverty; these include gender, 'race', age and disability. Official measures of poverty, and much social research, underestimate women's poverty because data are based on household rather than individual income. Webb (1993) has estimated that, in 1992, two-thirds of adults in poor households were women and that the women in these households had about half as much independent income as the men. Poverty among women inevitably has a knock-on effect on their children. Like 'race', age and disability, gender increases one's propensity to poverty because individuals within these groups are disadvantaged in the labour market and are more likely to be dependent on inadequate state benefits for a larger proportion of their income and for a longer period in their lives. In 1997–98 individuals in households headed by people in the black, Indian or Pakistani/Bangladeshi groups were particularly likely to be in the poorest decile of the income distribution. More than half of those in households headed by someone of Pakistani/Bangladeshi origin were in this position, compared to over two-fifths of households headed by a black person and less than one-fifth of those headed by a white person. White households were twice as likely to be in the top fifth of the income distribution compared to black or Pakistani/Bangladeshi households. (Office for National Statistics, 2000: 42). The poverty of disabled people is exacerbated by the extra expenses which many have related to their illness or disability, which are not reflected in their incomes.

But are the poor really poor?

A report commissioned by the Joseph Rowntree Foundation (Hills, 1995) revealed increasing polarisation between 'a prosperous majority and a growing minority of people living on low incomes'. A subsequent report on numerous qualitative research studies, which looked at the lifestyles of people living on low incomes, confirmed the persistence of poverty and the deprivation of poor families (Kempson, 1996: ix). Irrespective of how they define 'poverty', no-one reading this report can be left in doubt that life on a low income in 1990s Britain and beyond is a stressful and debilitating experience. People who rely on income support (IS) and related benefits, in particular, face a struggle against encroaching debt and social isolation, where even the most resilient and resourceful are hard pressed to survive.

The level of IS varies according to the type of family, the number and ages of children and a number of other criteria, such as disability and age. The weekly income of £158.10 (after housing costs) paid to a family of four (two adults, two children under 11) in 2000/01 is considerably lower than either average weekly household expenditure or average manual earnings. The increase in benefits beyond inflation for some families with children means that a couple family is £24.79 per week better off in real terms and that the gap between IS rates and the Family Budget Unit's 'low cost but adequate' budget has fallen but it is still £11.17 per week adrift for a couple family (Bradshaw, in Fimister, 2001). The failure to uprate benefits beyond inflation means that any improvement in income is at the government's whim. The pensioners' lobby have been particularly critical of being given benefits in kind rather than an increase in the real value of their pensions. The Labour government has continued the earlier policy of increasing reliance on means tests even though low take-up persists. According to the government's own estimates, up to 4.3 million people may be missing out on benefits to which they are entitled, valued at up to £3.2 billion a year.

In a study of social workers and poverty, Becker (1988: 248) found that 'As a group [social workers] appear supportive ... But as individuals their poverty awareness has tendencies towards hostility and prejudice'. In particular, his respondents tended to regard the poor both as victims and also as contributing to their situation by an inability to cope. However, as Bailey (1988) has written, there is no spare capacity in a poor household to cope with crises.

Living on a fixed income takes skill and determination. The remarkable thing is not that some people fail to make ends meet but that many people succeed. People who fail to manage their weekly budget and get into debt are often accused of being feckless. However, Kempson (1996: 26) found no evidence to support this:

> No matter how resourceful, those living on social security benefits generally find that no amount of forward planning and bill juggling is enough. They face a difficult choice between cutting back drastically on food, fuel and other essentials or falling into debt.

Debt and poverty are now inextricably entwined. Poor people's debts are most frequently for basic household bills – rent, mortgage, gas, electricity, water and council tax. Because of the nature of their debt, poor people are at risk of serious sanctions, such as disconnection of essential services or the loss of their home (see Kempson, 1997).

Food and diet

While food is one of the most basic essentials, in practice it is often the most flexible part of family expenditure. Consequently, when money is short, the food budget suffers: cheaper food is bought, families cut down on fresh fruit and vegetables, and mothers tend to go without to ensure that their children and their partners are fed (Charles and Kerr, 1985). A National Children's Home study (NCH Action for Children, 1991) found that not one of the 354 low-income families surveyed was eating a diet which met current nutrition guidelines.

The inadequate diets of the poor have often been blamed on ignorance, famously so by the former Conservative government minister Edwina Currie. However, it has been calculated that a healthy diet which meets government nutrition guidelines actually costs over one-third more than the average cost of the food intake of a low-income household (Cole-Hamilton and Lang, 1986). As a result of poor people's inability to follow a rich, nutritional diet, people in social classes IV and V are at greater risk of undernutrition, failure to thrive, vitamin and mineral deficiencies and poor dental health (Cole-Hamilton and Lang, 1986).

Family relationships

One of the first sacrifices that poor people make is to cut out 'luxuries', even if they might not be defined as such by the general population: these include leisure and social activities. This self-imposed exile means that many people lose contact with family and friends. They cannot afford to go out and may be reluctant to visit other people's homes because they cannot afford to reciprocate. This isolation, together with the constant worries about making ends meet, can put a strain on family relationships. Kempson (1996) found that this could be a contributory factor to a couple separating or to an older child leaving home:

> Little things that never mattered before are suddenly major issues and you fight over them. I fight with him [her husband], I shout at the kids, he does as well and the kids cry.

Policies on poverty

The main instrument used by governments to tackle the issue of poverty is the social security system. Social security cannot prevent poverty; at most it can only alleviate it. Over the past twenty years, there has been a decisive shift away from insurance-based benefits to means-tested benefits. Between 1978–79 and 1995–96, expenditure on the latter increased from 17 per cent of all benefits to 30 per cent. Means-tested benefits are an inefficient way of reaching the poor because a significant minority of people do not claim them, as the Labour government found when it introduced the Minimum Pensions Guarantee –

merely IS renamed. The Labour government is moving towards a system of tax credits administered via the Inland Revenue. A working families' tax credit and disabled person's tax credit have already been introduced, and further tax credits for pensioners and children are in the pipeline.

Total social security spending has reached £100 billion per year, yet this total disguises over £20 billion of cuts which were made by the 1979–97 Conservative governments, virtually none of which were reversed by the New Labour government. The main cuts were achieved by increasing benefits only in line with prices rather than earnings, but many other small and large cuts were made to reduce the benefits bill by reducing either entitlement or eligibility to benefits (see Howard, 1997). Total benefit expenditure has been falling under the New Labour government. This is attributed to falling numbers of claimants (especially unemployed people). The government also claims £1 billion savings in social security fraud. Benefit savings have been accompanied by a much tighter administrative regime, in particular by a much sharper focus on fraud detection and prevention. While fraudulent claiming is a legitimate target for action, overzealous rhetoric can have a deleterious effect on the public perception of claimants. The New Labour government has maintained the benefit fraud telephone hotline and has had a very high-profile advertising campaign on this theme.

Under New Labour, social security policy has been an adjunct to the welfare to work policy. In its *A New Contract for Welfare*, the government pledged 'work for those who can; security for those who can't'. The change of name from the Department of Social Security to the Department for Work and Pensions confirms the shift of emphasis to the first part of the mantra and not the second. The real increase in children's benefits has been one of the very few positive social security measures introduced by the New Labour government and the one area in which its policies can be seen to be very different from its predecessors.

Social policy and social exclusion

Government social policies relating to social security and employment have an obvious impact on poverty. However, there is also a close relationship between poverty and other social policies, in particular health, housing and education.

There has been a growing body of evidence on inequalities in health since the publication of the Black Report in 1980. However, the Conservative government did not accept such a link until 1994 following the recommendations of a Health of the Nation working group set up by the Department of Health. The link between poverty and health is symbiotic: ill-health makes people vulnerable to poverty because sick and disabled people have a more tenuous relationship with the labour market and because they may have higher costs related to their condition. However, poverty itself can contribute to ill-health. Poor diet and homelessness or inadequate housing are major contributory factors to ill-health. Money worries, together with the circumstances which cause them – job loss, onset of ill-health, relationship breakdown – can affect people's mental health and can lead to anxiety and depression.

Despite nearly half a century of the NHS, committed to providing health care free at the point of access on the basis of need, a health gap between rich and poor persists. People who live in disadvantaged circumstances have more illness, greater distress, more disability and shorter lives than those who are more affluent. The greater propensity of the poor to ill-health is not reflected in their use of health services.

There is continuing evidence that health resources are still not distributed equitably between areas in proportion to needs and formal health care services do not respond appropriately to the health care needs of different social groups (Benzeval et al., 1995). As a result, poorer people receive less health care relative to their health needs than do better-off people: they are less likely to see a doctor, more likely to have shorter consultations and less likely to have their children vaccinated or receive health screening. The significant health reforms which were introduced by the Conservative governments made matters worse by creating a two-tier health service (Wilkinson, 1996). The continued use of charging, for example for prescriptions, which have increased in price over 14-fold since 1979, and optical and dental charges, also puts an extra burden on many poor people. New Labour's attempts to begin to address these gaps were hindered in the first term by its spending promises.

Housing is a key parameter of social exclusion. In Britain, renting is regarded as a poor second-best to owning one's own home, and housing tenure is therefore an important source of social division and an important indicator of deprivation. Between 1980 and 1993, the average income of household heads in council housing fell from 48 to 35 per cent of the average income of household heads in mortgaged owner-occupation (Wilcox, 1996). As a result of very actively pursued and subsidised 'right to buy' policies in the 1980s and 90s, council housing tends to be concentrated on the poorest people, which 'reinforces the image of social rented housing as a residual and stigmatised provision for poor people, who have little political clout in bidding for adequate housing management and maintenance' (Ginsburg, 1997).

Another obvious indicator of poverty and social exclusion is homelessness. After peaking at 151,720 people in 1991, the number officially accepted as homeless by local authorities fell to 125,500 in 1995. However, many homeless people are not included in this statistic because they fall outside the remit of local authority responsibility. An analysis of the 1991 census suggested that

> on census day there were approximately 110,000 concealed families (such as having to live with parents), 50,000 would-be couples living apart, 140,000 sharing households, as well as the 22,000 families accepted as homeless and living in hostels and bed and breakfast accommodation. (Ginsburg, 1997)

This does not count the people who are literally 'roofless' and forced to sleep rough. The Labour government appointed a homelessness Tsar, who was much criticised by some groups for her hardline approach.

The Conservatives introduced several important educational reforms, which impacted on finance, structure and the curriculum. The reduced educational opportunities open to children in poor families were not addressed. Partly because of the social segregation caused by the housing market, the children of poorer families tend to go to schools in poorer areas. They often have access to the worst, most deprived schools. Their parents are unable to subsidise school funds and activities to the extent that this happens in more affluent areas. Children from poor families are less likely to stay on at school beyond the minimum school-leaving age and are much less likely to go on to higher education. Evidence indicates a link between educational performance and social disadvantage, both among junior school pupils (Brooks et al., 1996) and at GCSE level (Smith et al., 1997):

> educational opportunities and results have become more unequal in social terms. It cannot be the case that 'every child, regardless of background (now has) the chance to progress as far as his or her abilities allow'. Reducing educational disadvantage has been a key goal of the New Labour governments and is a key plank in its tackling social exclusion. (DSS, 1999)

Community care

Long-term care is of critical importance to older people and their family carers. From the early 1980s Conservative governments implemented a policy designed to reduce the direct provider role of public services and increase that of the private sector. This resulted in a huge increase in residential and nursing home provision and a massive rise, from £10 million to £3 billion, in social security provision for board and lodgings, which the NHS and Community Care Act 1990 was designed to control. As a result of the changes following the Act, community care was driven to a state of crisis: too little home care and no preventive work, which means that older people in particular are having to enter residential homes, despite the policy of community care; lack of choice between providers; lack of consultation with users and carers about appropriate provision; an overreliance on family carers, often to the point of breakdown; and some 40,000 older people each year having to sell their houses to fund their long-term residential care.

The New Labour government's response to this crisis was to appoint a Royal Commission on Long-Term Care for the Elderly (1999). The resulting report, *With Respect to Old Age*, is a major contribution to social care policy but the government's response (which took two months longer to arrive than the Royal Commission had deliberated) rejected the radical proposal to fund all personal care. Instead the NHS Plan (2000d) opted for the cheaper policy of funding only 'nursing care' (defined as the time spent by a registered nurse in providing, delegating or supervising care in any setting). This is an important change and will benefit some 35,000 people but it is a long way short of what the majority of the Royal Commission wanted. The government has reinforced the boundary between health and social care when its rhetoric and some other measures (such as health and social care Trusts) have been aimed at breaking down this 'Berlin Wall'. Other important changes were contained in the NHS Plan, such as disregarding from the means-testing rules the value of a person's house for the first three months of admission to residential and nursing home care; the restoration of capital limits to their 1996 values and new guidance concerning variations in charges for home care. Also the National Service Frameworks for Mental Health (DoH, 1999b) and Older People (DoH, 2001d) are promising to raise the standards of care available to vulnerable groups.

The ideal of community care as a means of supporting care by families, preventing carer breakdown and providing a source of social integration in local communities is still far from being realised. Despite increased resources for both health and social care in 2000–01, there is not sufficient to restore years of underfunding and cope with rising needs. There are still tensions between health and social services, for example over the discharge of (normally older) patients who are deemed to need only 'social' care, with social services departments being obliged, but unable, to fund suitable care packages for all those assessed as being in need. Whether or not the massive reorganisation of the NHS into primary care Trusts and the development of integrated health and social care Trusts will overcome these barriers to seamless care, at the moment, is an open question. Certainly there is no sign of the major increase in resources necessary to create high-quality, responsive and user-empowering community care services.

CONCLUSION

Social policy provides the context within which both social work professionals and their service users live and work. The development of welfare states is particularly relevant (if not the beginning and end of social policy). If housing, employment, income or health needs are not being met by the relevant service, the individual is more likely to turn to social services departments as the source of last resort assistance. The key to social workers finding a resolution to family crises may involve addressing a material need – such as adequate housing – without which family stress cannot be relieved.

The pressures built up in the 1980s and 90s to reduce the role of the welfare state, for both ideological and financial reasons, made it much more likely that vulnerable people would find themselves in need and yet much less likely to find support or material help within the state welfare system. The New Labour government made a firm commitment to support the most vulnerable and tackle poverty and social exclusion across a number of departments and policies, compromised by stringent fiscal and spending policies. Some positive steps have been achieved, but much is still be done, not least in trying to generate a climate in which the needs of the vulnerable are championed, and poor people are not vilified and denigrated. Until that is achieved, it is particularly important for those working with the poor to look beyond individual hardship – and sometimes personal inadequacy – to the structural factors which exclude the poor from sharing in the lifestyles of the wider society.

FURTHER READING

Hill, M. (1997) *Understanding Social Policy* (Oxford, Blackwell). A useful text, very broadly covering British policy processes.

Howarth, C., Kenway, P., Palmer, G. and Street, C (1998) *Monitoring Poverty and Social Exclusion: Labour's Inheritance* (York, Joseph Rowntree Foundation). Provides a baseline of a number of indicators of social exclusion against which to map future government progress. Series of subsequent reports do this.

Kempson, E. (1996) *Life on a Low Income* (York, Joseph Rowntree Foundation). A research report vividly demonstrating the realities of poverty.

Oppenheim, C. and Harker, L. (1996) *Poverty: The Facts*, 3rd edn (London, Child Poverty Action Group). An easy-to-follow guide on debates relating to poverty. More recent studies in Howard, M. (2001) *Poverty: The Facts*, 4th edn (London, Child Poverty Action Group).

Walker, C. (1993) *Managing Poverty: The Limits of Social Assistance* (London, Routledge). A helpful general text on social security policies.

Walker, A. and Walker, C. (eds) (1997) *Britain Divided: The Growth of Social Exclusion in the 1980s and 1990s* (London, Child Poverty Action Group). A comprehensive collection of articles showing how poverty leads to social exclusion and disadvantage.

6

Social Work and the Law

Suzy Braye and Michael Preston-Shoot

Introduction

The relationship between social work and the law remains complex. One tension that remains is whether the law (Beckford Report, 1985) or an ethical duty of care (Stevenson, 1988) is social work's defining mandate, or whether practitioners and managers must determine the balance to be uniquely struck between these polarities in each situation (Braye and Preston-Shoot, 1990).

Students and practitioners can experience contact with the law and legal system as stressful. They may be anxious about being found wanting or uncertain. They may lack familiarity with legal procedures, methodology and language or, conscious of the breadth of knowledge to be acquired and retained, be unaware of developments in the legal rules. Indeed, one feature of social work law is the permanence of change in the primary legislation, regulations and policy guidance that shape both the organisational structures through which social work and social care services are delivered, and the mandates for intervention with different service user groups. This vulnerability is amplified by concerns that practitioners feel unable to retain their professional values in the face of work pressures, procedural and bureaucratic forms of decision-making, increasing control and regulation of practice, and growing managerialism (Preston-Shoot, 2000a). Judicial scrutiny of practice may further provoke feelings of vulnerability, particularly in the context of diminishing resources and infrequent post-qualifying training (Preston-Shoot, 2000b).

Another tension surrounds purposes and outcomes. Law is a product of political and moral debates or controversies. It speaks volumes about the society in which it exists. The law can be used to preserve power structures and maintain structural inequalities, for instance in childcare, family life and mental health. It can be used for social engineering, identifying norms of behaviour and creating sanctions for non-conformity. Another aspect of social control, which illustrates the relationship between moral panics and legal developments, arises from the law being employed to 'solve' social problems, such as youth crime or asylum-seeking. The law may also be used to shape attitudes and behaviours. However, in relation to counteracting discrimination, the mandate is partial, omitting for instance ageism and heterosexism, and limited in its challenge to structures and attitudes that maintain inequality.

Reflecting their nature as a social construct, the legal rules contain muddled images of competency, for example of children, and potentially oppressive images of moral worth, which present challenges to practitioners. The legal mandate also contains conflicting imperatives: needs versus rights, welfare versus justice and autonomy versus intervention (Braye and Preston-Shoot, 1997). Practitioners and managers must negotiate the resulting dilemmas at the interface of practice and law, where professional values and knowledge are sometimes in uneasy juxtaposition with legislative requirements or intentions.

Intersecting law with social work practice

A distinction may be drawn between *social work law*, which includes those powers and duties that expressly mandate social work activity, and *social welfare law*, comprising statutes with which social workers must be familiar if they are to respond appropriately to service users' needs, but which do not permit or require specific actions by them (Preston-Shoot et al., 1998a). The two 'territories' exist in close proximity, as when duties towards children-in-need (social work law) interface with legislation affecting homeless families (social welfare law).

Social work law defines the individuals towards whom social workers have responsibilities. It determines the nature and extent of preventive, protective and rehabilitative intervention. It sets out the conditions under which compulsory intervention is possible, together with the safeguards and mechanisms for redress that place boundaries around, and seek to ensure, the accountability of professional practice.

The legal rules contain absolute and discretionary duties, and powers in relation to particular service user groups. These may be delegated to voluntary organisations and independent sector providers. Examples include residential care for older people (National Assistance Act 1948) and family support services (Children Act 1989). They are accompanied and amplified by secondary legislation (regulations, directions and approvals) and by central government guidance. Sometimes this is advisory (practice guidance) but, when issued under section 7, Local Authority Social Services Act 1970, is directive (policy guidance) and must be followed. Courts are often required to interpret this mandate and sanction or monitor its use. Consequently, case law becomes an important component of understanding how the legal rules can shape social work practice.

Usually these powers and duties are delegated to social workers who must adhere to statute and, when lawful, to their employers' procedures for its implementation. Occasionally, as with Approved Social Workers performing functions under the Mental Health Act 1983, powers and duties are designated to individual practitioners. Here they are personally accountable rather than as employees of a local authority.

The legal rules are translated into operational policies and procedures by local authorities and other agencies undertaking statutory duties. Research evidence (see Preston-Shoot, 2000c, for one review) and case law indicate that health and social welfare organisations, in their interpretation and/or implementation of the mandate, sometimes act *ultra vires*. Organisations can be held accountable for the definition and administration of policy, and for social work practice derived from it, through complaints procedures, judicial review and the Commissioner for Local Administration (Ombudsman). The appeals mechanisms available to service users are limited in that, in the event of finding illegality or maladministration, they can quash or criticise decisions made but not ensure or reinstate service provision. Complaints procedures, as one component of maintaining and improving the quality of services, are weakened because service users and carers lack information about them, are sceptical or fearful about outcomes of using them, and have low expectations of services and, possibly, high tolerance thresholds (Preston-Shoot, 2001). More positive is the influence of article 6 (the right to a fair hearing/trial) of the European Convention on Human Rights and Fundamental Freedoms. This has been incorporated into United Kingdom law by the Human Rights Act 1998. Together with article 13 (the right to an effective remedy), which has not been directly incorporated but which remains influential through decisions of the European Court of Human Rights, it has persuaded the House of Lords[1] to allow local authorities to be challenged in actions for negligence in their performance of statutory duties (Braye and Preston-Shoot, 2001).

The Human Rights Act 1998 requires all public authorities to interpret legislation so as to be compatible with the European Convention on Human Rights and Fundamental Freedoms. The definition of public authority includes central and local government, courts and, to the extent that they are exercising public functions, individuals, voluntary organisations and the independent sector responsible for areas of activity previously in, and/or delegated, by the public sector. Where public authorities believe there to be incompatibility between secondary legislation, or policy and practice guidance, and the Convention, they must act in accordance with Convention rights. Where there is a potential clash between primary legislation (Acts of Parliament) and Convention rights, public authorities must follow the former. If an individual then claims breach of Convention rights, a court, where satisfied, may declare the primary legislation to be incompatible with the Convention, a clear signal to parliament of the need for amendment, repeal or fresh legislation.

However, the agency context remains problematic for social workers. The conformity that practitioners and managers are expected to demonstrate to organisational policies and procedures sometimes sits uneasily alongside the allegiance to social work knowledge and values, and commitment to the rights and welfare of service users. It may conflict with the legal rules as articulated in statute, case law and guidance, requiring practitioners and managers to weigh their relationship with their employers against their obligations to service users and professional codes of ethics (Preston-Shoot, 2000a). Practising social work law, therefore, demands not only familiarity with how the law regulates decision-making, but also skills in challenging policies and procedures that are administratively unfair or illegal and/or which run counter to social work values. The Public Interest Disclosure Act 1998 offers some support here, with protection against dismissal for workers who disclose information about criminal offences, or failures to comply with legal obligations, where there has been an attempt to conceal them. However, it does not make reporting of concerns mandatory, or prevent employers from victimising staff who raise concerns by questioning their competence (Cox, 1998).

The organisational context is also being reshaped by New Labour's commitment (DoH, 1998b) to consistent quality of service provision, founded on clear, acceptable and enforceable standards. The Care Standards Act 2000 has established a National Care Standards Commission, whose remit will include inspection of residential and nursing care, children's homes, domiciliary care, fostering services, and local authority and voluntary adoption agencies. The Commission has begun to publish national minimum standards for different types of service provision, which parallel those relating to diverse service user groups to be found in Quality Protects[2] and National Service Frameworks.[3] Together with the Protection of Children Act 1999, the 2000 Act creates registers of people unsuitable to work with children or vulnerable adults.

The Health Act 1999 gives statutory backing to partnerships between health and local authorities. It allows the transfer of money between the National Health Service and local government and permits new partnership arrangements to make it easier for health and social services to work together. Specifically, funding arrangements may be pooled, with one agency delegated to commission all services for particular service user groups, thereby integrating provision into one management, financial and administrative structure. The Health and Social Care Act 2001 permits local and health authorities to merge their powers into care Trusts, responsible for commissioning services. Both Acts may be seen as attempts to break down the barriers which have unhelpfully fragmented and often frustrated the meeting of people's needs.

Nonetheless, the relevant legal rules do not necessarily provide a clear mandate and are not always supportive of social work values. Some social work values have influenced or may be found in statute. Section 95, Criminal Justice Act 1991; section 1(3), Children Act 1989; and the Race Relations (Amendment) Act 2000 all uphold social work's concern with anti-discriminatory practice. The Community Care (Direct Payments) Act 1996, particularly now that older people have been brought within its remit, reflects social work's commitment to empowerment. Other legislation, or the guidance associated with it, promotes values, attitudes and practices that would not be professionally endorsed, such as developments in youth justice (Crime and Disorder Act 1998; Youth Justice and Criminal Evidence Act 1999) or mental health (Mental Health (Patients in the Community) Act 1995). Consequently, practising social work law anti-oppressively remains a key challenge containing tensions and dilemmas. It requires a values literacy (Preston-Shoot et al., 2001), which explores in each situation the connections between social work values and social work law. From such exploration, practitioners and managers may engage with the complexity within values and legal rules, and argue coherently for action that negotiates conflicts between different interests and identifies the extent of particular principles.

Critical themes

In any setting social workers have a professional obligation critically to appraise the nature and scope of statutory provisions and, with service users, to advocate for change, the translation of social and economic rights into legal rights, and the provision of services that meet needs. The Human Rights Act 1998 merely reinforces the importance of this obligation, since it is concerned with political and civil rights which, while important, contrast with social and economic rights with which social workers are concerned through the impact of poverty, ill-health and social exclusion on people's lives. Moreover, the Act does not create a commission with responsibility to look for abuses and take action on behalf of individuals whose rights have been abused. This is unlike the Race Relations Act 1976 (Commission for Racial Equality), the Sex Discrimination Act 1975 (Equal Opportunities Commission) and the Disability Discrimination Act 1995 (Disability Rights Commission).

Conflicting purposes

Central to social work is a commitment to a value base. Whether this is interpreted traditionally as a commitment to respect for persons, equal opportunity and meeting needs, or radically as a concern with social rights, equality and citizenship, the focus is on change. Social work law and social welfare law may facilitate this focus, as when the Court of Appeal held that asylum-seekers had the right to assistance under the National Assistance Act 1948 (*R* v. *Westminster CC and Others, ex parte M, P, A and X* [1997] 1 CCLR 85). However, social work law is largely expressed as discretionary duties, whether towards groups or individuals. Entitlement is often to unspecified services, such as assessment or a care plan, rather than to a particular service or one of specific quality. Moreover, the local authority may define the extent to which it will exercise discretion, for instance in defining need and taking resources into account (*R* v. *Gloucestershire CC and the Secretary of State for Health, ex parte Barry* [1997] 2 AllER 1). Provided local authorities act reasonably in their exercise of discretion, it is difficult for service users to challenge their decisions. The present emphasis on standards, through Quality Protects and National Service Frameworks, which seeks to improve health and social care services and ensure consistent quality through tighter regulation and monitoring, does not alter this position fundamentally.

Additionally, the law can express objectives that oppress or marginalise people rather than counteract discrimination and meet needs. Enactments on asylum, social security provision, sexuality and housing are examples. The Local Government Act 1988 proscribes any action by a local authority to promote gay and lesbian lifestyles, referring to such partnerships are 'pretend family relationships'. Courts are only slowly departing from the notion of heterosexual parenthood as the ideal standard when considering matters of residence and contact[4] (section 8, Children Act 1989). The law relating to homelessness (Housing Act 1996) has tightened the definition of intentional homelessness to include unreasonable refusal of an offer of accommodation. It permits local authorities to avoid obligations on the grounds that alternative suitable accommodation is available in other housing sectors, while the duty to provide housing no longer means permanent accommodation.

The law, then, embodies value judgements and ideologies (such as increasing punitiveness, demonisation and authoritarianism towards young offenders) that social work might wish to challenge but to which, because of their position, practitioners are expected to conform. Indeed, the purposes of law are multiple and sometimes contradictory. The law may be harnessed to preserve power structures or prescribe or proscribe certain lifestyles (for example the strong presumption in favour of contact between children and separated parents, even in situations of violence and hostility). It may be used to shape behaviours and attitudes, as in anti-discrimination legislation, or express ideology (for example the primacy of the market in the NHS and Community Care Act 1990). It remains imbued with discriminatory images of competency to make decisions, and of moral worth, and with prejudicial stereotypes of race, gender, disability and sexuality. The question for social work is how to respond.

Legalism

Social work is increasingly being regulated through national standards, volumes of guidance and constrained resources. Increasingly, too, it is being judged through inquiries based on norms and practices of the legal system. This emphasis on legalism is problematic. Essentially, this is because legalism conflates good practice with 'procedurally correct' practice, the latter emphasising apparent certainties rather than acknowledging the imprecisions and choice points inherent in social work tasks. Additionally, legalism presents inherently conflictual notions as if they were complementary and thus minimises debate on the balance to be struck between conflicting imperatives such as rights and risks, needs and resources, autonomy and protection.

The statutory mandate is neither consistent nor comprehensive; it is confused and ambiguous. A child's welfare is not always paramount (compare family proceedings under the Children Act 1989, to which the paramountcy principle does apply, with financial and accommodation questions in divorce and domestic violence proceedings (Family Law Act 1996), in which the needs of, often male, adults can predominate). Children are sometimes denied the right to seek to initiate proceedings – contrast appeals to special educational needs tribunals (Education Act 1996), which children have no right to initiate, with section 8 orders (Children Act 1989), which they may seek. Government exhortations, prompted by research (DoH, 1995a), to alter the balance between child protection and preventive services towards the latter, have not been accompanied by acknowledgement of either the complexity of practice or the social context in which practitioners operate. The latest policy guidance on assessment (DoH/DfEE/Home Office, 2000) offers signposts about how to intervene in families where children are in need but cannot guarantee the right answers. Despite recommendations for legislation (Law Commission, 1995), social workers currently have limited powers to protect vulnerable adults from abuse, a feature which the latest policy guidance (DoH, 2000a) on developing and implementing multi-agency policies and procedures reinforces.

The community care mandate boasts choice and needs-led assessments, yet resources control questions of service provision, while the differential meanings of partnership, empowerment, choice and quality obscure rather than clarify the objectives to which services should aspire. Judges (*R* v. *Gloucestershire CC, ex parte RADAR* [1995] COD 253); *R* v. *Gloucestershire CC and the Secretary of State for Health, ex parte Barry* [1997]) and inquiries (Ritchie et al., 1994) have criticised government guidance for its lack of clarity, and central government for the wretched position into which it has placed councils.

Legalism does not necessarily safeguard service users. First, reliance on the law for resolving welfare questions may be misplaced because of its adversarial nature and narrow emphasis on questions of evidence and procedure (King and Trowell, 1992). The more that law becomes the main form of admissible knowledge in social work, the more difficult it may become to address awkward questions about the purpose of provision and highlight the limitation of judicial procedures in supporting vaguely defined objectives of choice, needs-led assessments and empowerment.

Second, the legislative mandate continues to marginalise the social. The policy emphasis is on individuals rather than the wider systems that frequently contribute to the difficulties that people experience. Social work should connect the personal and political, public and private, and from individual cases identify those political and structural issues that require social change as part of problem resolution. Legalism fragments this perspective, offering officially sanctioned procedures but leaving unaltered the current alignment of power and relationships. Put more starkly, people's needs are not being met (Jordan, 1990) and practitioners inherit a legal mandate still characterised by poverty of provision and meanness of spirit (Utting, 1993).

The location of social work

Social work's predominant location in local authorities has always meant the negotiation of multiple accountabilities (Braye and Preston-Shoot, 1999) – between employers, professional values, professional self, service users and the public. The challenge has always been to hold the dynamic tension that this involves rather than succumb to bureaucracy, and to find the room for manoeuvre within agencies for anti-oppressive practice and promoting service users' rights and needs. The problem here is less the law but rather how it is interpreted in policy and practice, where evidence from users and carers indicates that relationship commitments and skills are being sidelined (Preston-Shoot, 2000c). Moreover, the pressures to conform and practise unquestioningly can result in the neutralisation of moral concerns and the undermining of moral responsibility, as practice reflects dominant organisational and political interests (Preston-Shoot, 2000a).

Evidence continues to accumulate (see Braye and Preston-Shoot, 1997; Preston-Shoot, 2000a, 2000c) that agencies are failing to follow policy guidance and meet their statutory obligations to both children and families and adults needing care or services. Social work is being drawn into practices that are morally or legally suspect – withdrawing services from vulnerable adults without the required reassessment and when their needs have not diminished (*R* v. *Gloucestershire CC, ex parte Mahfood and Others* [1997] 1 CCLR 7), or avoiding formal statements of how children in need will be defined in order to escape any obligation to act (Colton et al., 1995).

This is not to underestimate the impact of the consistent underresourcing of local authorities compared with growing social need and mounting legislative duties. Indeed, government has acknowledged underresourcing (DoH, 1998b). However, ongoing resource constraints, together with increasing regulation, mean that managers and practitioners still face the unenviable discomfort of continuing to struggle with irreconcilable demands and tighter targets or performance indicators. This can result in acquiescence to the degradation of social work as the only means of survival (Jones, 2001). That sensitive and innovative practice remains in evidence is a tribute to the strength of commitment and imagination still derived from the professional social work ethos of public service. This discussion must highlight, however, the evidence of services and practitioners under strain. It must caution that the emphasis given in social work training and practice to social work law (legislation, regulation and policy guidance), and conformity in decision-making to agency policies, can amount to acquiescing to a rationing role and bypassing political and ethical questions about the purposes of welfare and social work, and about the quality of life that services should promote.

Critical debates

How, then, should social work interface with the law and social policy, and their expression in agency procedures? An empowering context for practising social work law requires a social work that is confident in interacting with legislative and local government systems, and active in initiating and contributing to debates about the goals of practice. This requires frameworks for understanding, which together construct a theory for practice, and which can strike the balance in the relationship between the law and social work uniquely in each situation. The emergence of the discipline 'social work law' (Preston-Shoot et al., 1998a), the construction of a conceptual frame informed by values and knowledge (Braye and Preston-Shoot, 1997) within which to address dilemmas of practice, and the articulation of academic and practice curricula (Ball et al., 1995; Preston-Shoot, 2000b), which counteract uncertainty about knowledge of the law and its relationship to practice, provide these frameworks.

Appraising social work law

The different purposes to which the law can be harnessed result in contradictions which, for social workers, formalise around conflicting imperatives. Thus, some procedures in child protection have to balance welfare with justice, where the requirement to promote the child's welfare conflicts with the parent's right to the justice of a fair investigative process and trial. The conflict between needs, resources and rights appears endemic within community care and services for children with special educational needs. The tension between the rights of the individual to autonomy and the rights of the state to intervene is encapsulated within the realm of health care and social care legislation, and within the Children Act 1989 and its associated guidance.

These conflicting imperatives are encountered in practice as dilemmas, for example rights versus risks, care versus control, needs versus resources, professionalism versus partnership with users, professional versus agency agendas. Determining the balance to be struck in each situation will require an understanding of social work goals and legal goals, clarity about where social work and legal purposes overlap and where they diverge, and an approach to decision-making which weighs up the claims of each polarity. It requires consideration of proportionality (Human Rights Act 1998) – where an individual's rights are to be restricted or limited, the public authority must show how such action is prescribed by primary legislation and proportionate to the aims being pursued. It requires an understanding of the nature of the interaction between social work and the law, a continuum characterised by the extent to which either legal or social work language, methodology and values dominate (Preston-Shoot et al., 1998b).

Creative practice in the arena of social work law is thus characterised by the identification and exploitation of the spaces created by the legal rules and accompanying concepts or principles for practice. It connects different areas of the law, and a social services department's organisational structure, and utilises case law and appeals procedures – all with the purpose of pushing the law's boundaries to maximise a service user's rights and access to services.

Defining welfare

When social work and legislative goals diverge, this separation should be introduced into debates about the purpose of welfare. Social work has at least three frameworks for understanding to advance here. One is an understanding of oppression and how social work risks being coopted into the task of preserving power structures rooted in inequalities. This understanding is derived from research and service users' experiences. It informs practice based on values that emphasise rights and equality, echoes of which may be found in some government guidance (DoH, 1989), and on services which strive for an optimal satisfaction of basic needs.

The second is a critical appraisal of the concepts that underpin social policy – partnership, empowerment, choice, quality and need – with particular reference to how the concepts can be recruited to serve both a New Right and an anti-oppressive agenda. This focuses on the quality of the lives of less powerful people by reference to key values and basic needs, and addresses awkward questions about the issues involved in need satisfaction, rights and resources, autonomy, protection and empowerment. It explores how social workers' accountability to different stakeholders should be managed, what a professional ethical duty of care should be, how welfare should be interpreted and needs defined, and how the legal mandate might be used with and for users. Practising social work law will involve accessing research on need in order to argue for services. It will involve enabling people to gain access to political processes by developing partnership and advocacy skills that place service users centre stage in articulating need, expressing choice and advocating change. Recent emphasis by government on the development of advocacy services (DoH, 2000b, 2001a) supports this endeavour.

The third framework draws also from research and from listening to users. It identifies and actively promotes the core elements of good practice and delineates the contextual features that presently undermine that practice. Welfare is often presented as ineffective. Social work can reclaim its effectiveness – what is valuable and important between practitioners and service users.

Reviewing organisational behaviour and practice ethics

That agencies, far from solving problems, can maintain or exacerbate them is well known. Healthy organisations, therefore, require staff who will challenge received ideas and explore different possibilities, and who can identify the elements that can combine to render agencies dangerous or abusive (see Wardhaugh and Wilding, 1993; Waterhouse, 2000). The emphasis now given in policy guidance to whistle-blowing procedures (for example DoH, 2000a), following the Public Interest Disclosure Act 1998, endorses such staff activity. Equally, given the complicated and contradictory mandates inherent in social work law, competent organisations must engage with rather than defend against the dilemmas posed by their mandates and roles. Practice here may include forming alliances with other organisations and with service users to advocate for change, and providing clear direction about the principles that are to take precedence in practice. It should name the contradictions, for example between the Children Act 1989's emphasis on welfare and the Crime and Disorder Act 1998's emphasis on individual responsibility, reparation and rehabilitation. It should articulate the impact on people's lives of contemporary social and economic policies. It should incorporate acknowledgement of the feelings that the work engenders in practitioners and managers. The challenge is to create an organisational culture where responsibility is shared through structures of support, supervision and consultation, and where it is accepted that accountability to an employer can only be fulfilled with integrity where it is consistent with the higher-order principle of effective, ethical and legal practice.

To intervene in organisations requires a factual understanding of decision-making and policy-making structures and how to gain entry to these. It requires knowledge of law and policy guidance, which relate to the concerns to be raised in order that the challenging position being taken can be justified. It demands an understanding of how organisations respond to demands for change and, therefore, sophisticated change agent skills – agenda-building, problem-defining, policy-assessing and proposal-making (Jannson, 1994), together with constructing alliances or constituencies for change. Such practice requires skills in using legislation and policy provisions to achieve clearly expressed outcomes informed by social work values, theory and knowledge, and to advance ways of understanding and tackling issues that enable organisations to perceive room for manoeuvre and respond positively.

CONCLUSION

A common question is how social workers might practise anti-oppressively in the context of social control functions, resource and employment constraints, and the absence of a legal mandate in key areas of inequality. The answer partly centres on knowledge and skills that integrate social work and the law. Knowledge includes relevant statute, case law and guidance, together with learning from other disciplines that helps to make sense of the 'what' and 'why' of each practice situation. Skills, using this knowledge, include:

- Using law and guidance that endorse anti-discriminatory practice;

- Using provisions to achieve outcomes informed by social work values;

- Challenging how authorities approach decision-making and interpret the legislative mandate;

- Presenting a clear rationale for practice, based on connecting knowledge with social work goals and tasks.

The challenge is to address the tensions and dilemmas inherent in social work law, and in the relationship between social work, social policy and the law, through a legal, policy and organisational literacy. This engages not just at the level of practice – the 'what', 'why' and 'how' of individual situations – but also at higher levels of context about the objectives of policy and the means by which they will be realised. If social work loses its ability or willingness to question and comment, it will lose its position to promote and empower a difference at the levels of individual and collective experience, and will become identified with policies, procedures and practices that evade awkward questions, mask inequality and perpetuate disadvantage.

Notes

1 *Barrett* v. *Enfield LBC* [1999] 3 AllER 193; *W and Others* v. *Essex CC and Another* [2000] 2 AllER 237.
2 DoH (1998) *The Quality Protects Programme: Transforming Children's Services*, LAC(98)28 (London, Stationery Office).
3 DoH (1999) *National Service Framework for Mental Health. Modern Standards and Service Models for Mental Health*, LAC(99)34; DoH (2001) *National Service Framework for Older People*, LAC(2001)12 (London, Stationery Office).
4 See Braye and Preston-Shoot (1997) for a review of cases.

FURTHER READING

Braye, S. and Preston-Shoot, M. (1997) *Practising Social Work Law*, 2nd edn (London, Macmillan – now Palgrave Macmillan). This book explores the tensions and dilemmas in the complex relationship between the law and social work, and offers guidance to practitioners and managers for legally competent social work practice.

Cooper, J. (ed.) (2000) *Law, Rights and Disability* (London, Jessica Kingsley). This book explores the effect of different parts of the social work law and social welfare law mandate and professional intervention on the lives of disabled people.

Cull, L.-A. and Roche, J. (eds) (2001) *The Law and Social Work: Contemporary Issues for Practice* (Basingstoke, Palgrave – now Palgrave Macmillan). Chapters in this book examine key themes and issues in the relationship between law and social work, or provide overviews of different parts of the legal mandate, or provide service user and practice perspectives.

Hill, M. and Aldgate, J. (eds) (1996) *Child Welfare Services. Developments in Law, Policy, Practice and Research* (London, Jessica Kingsley). This book reports on research critically analysing childcare legislation, policy and practice.

Roach Anleu, S. (2000) *Law and Social Change* (London, Sage). This book explores the relationship between law and social life. It considers the social conditions under which laws emerge and change, the values incorporated by law, and the degree to which a legal mandate might lead to social change.

Social Work and Organisations

Audrey Mullender and Stella Perrott

Introduction: the organisational context of social work

Although much organisational and human resource management theory has arisen from industry and commerce, it has a clear relevance to public and voluntary sector welfare bodies. Indeed, social work values can be used to evaluate management theory as we consider what organisations do to the people who work in them and the people they were set up to serve. Furthermore, if services and working conditions are to improve over time, organisations have to change and adapt, so that they foster competence, quality and learning.

Social work in its widest sense is practised in a great variety of organisations and settings. While the majority of social workers continue to work in social services departments (social work services in Scotland and health and social services Trusts in Northern Ireland, hereafter all summarised under 'SSDs'), they also work in voluntary organisations, other statutory bodies such as the probation service and Children and Family Courts Advisory and Support Service (CAFCASS) or in health, prison, housing and education services. Some social workers might be employed by a SSD and work in another setting, for example, as a hospital social worker, while others will be employed by the agency in which they are located.

In the 1990s, the purchaser/provider split became the dominant means of organising and subdividing the workforce. Social workers and their managers were often either purchasing (commissioning) services for those who were assessed as being in priority need or were directly providing the commissioned services to meet that need. In broad terms, in social work, SSDs are the purchasers of services. Most SSDs have also retained a considerable role in providing services, such as home care and residential care, to all service user groups, but they increasingly do so in partnership or in competition with voluntary and private agencies. At various times, political discussion has focused on the extent to which the statutory sector should provide any services and the New Labour government has not led to a changing balance in the enabler/purchaser/provider role for SSDs.

Since the change of government in 1997, the new 'reform' agenda for public services has also changed as the focus has turned from the markets and quasi-markets to the experience of service users, and the organisational culture has changed to delivering 'Best Value' services. More recently, the trend towards 'person-centred' services has led to multidisciplinary teams or co-location/one-stop shops for services. For example, learning disability teams may include social workers, occupational therapists, psychologists, community psychiatric nurses (CPNs), housing and employment staff, or social workers may be located in schools or health centres to enable access to social work through less stigmatising routes and as an extension of another universal service. Thus it can be seen that organisational forms and responsibilities can only be fully understood within a political and social context.

Organisational forms and issues

Organisational definitions

> An organization is a consciously co-ordinated entity, with a relatively identifiable boundary, that functions on a relatively continuous basis to achieve a common goal or goals. (Robins, 1990: 4)

Organisations encompass or involve workforces and structures of staffing, systems of working and markets of demand for goods or services, as well as less tangible facets such as culture, ethos and patterns of power and influence (Clegg, 1990: 3). Organisations are also places where identities can be formed (when introduced to someone socially, the first question is often, 'And what do you do?'), social lives and careers established and political aspirations realised. Work can be the vehicle of achieving personal needs and ambitions, or a site of oppression and unhappiness. Clearly, then, we need multi-layered and complex ideas in order to develop an understanding of how organisations function.

Organisational forms: from hierarchical bureaucracy to feminist collective

We owe to the sociologist Weber the development of organisation theory as a discipline of thought in the modern world. Observing the economically driven society around him, he conceptualised the model of the bureaucratic organisational form and praised it for its efficiency in carrying out large-scale administrative tasks (Weber, 1947).

So dominant did the bureaucracy become that its development explains most forms of working life in the Western world. In manufacturing, bureaucracy led to the differentiation of tasks and the production methods which came to be known as 'Fordism' (in reference to the separated, repetitive jobs on the automobile production line), while, in the professions, it led to specialisation, the development of standardised services, hierarchical lines of management control and the application of rules and procedures, even though professionals retained more autonomy than did factory-floor workers, owing to their specialised knowledge and the influence of their external professional associations and training bodies (Mintzberg, 1989: 347). In this regard, social work in the statutory sector is something of a hybrid. It lacks the autonomy of professions such as medicine and is governed by a considerable amount of legislation, regulation and guidance while, in the voluntary sector, and in some statutory roles such as when acting as children and family reporters and family court advisers, social workers have considerable scope to practise as 'autonomous professionals'. The development of the General Social Care Council, which came into force in October 2001, and equivalent bodies in other parts of the UK will change the dynamics between central regulation and guidance, training and independent review. The Council will establish minimum qualifications, minimum levels of continuous professional development and make demands on employers to provide the environment in which these expectations can be met. This, combined with an increase in the length of training for social workers, National Occupational Standards and increased levels of specialisation, should lead to a more highly skilled, confident workforce but with inevitable tensions between individual professional autonomy, employer control and professional regulation.

Additionally, social workers will continue to experience competing identifications, not only with professional bodies, but also with trades unions, special interest groups and personal reference groupings such as women's and/or black workers' groups.

Of course, there have always been real alternatives to (as opposed to modifications of) bureaucratic, hierarchical structures, and the voluntary sector of welfare provision in the UK is one of the richest sites of these. Those with the longest history include all-women organisations (Hawxhurst and Morrow, 1984; Dominelli, 1990) such as women's aid and rape crisis, sometimes run solely by black women, as in specialist black refuge services, or by lesbian women as in lesbian helplines. In these, the distinctive organisational form has been that of the feminist collective (Iannello, 1992). Its wider legacy includes rotating the chairing of meetings, delegating tasks, sharing information and equalising access to resources (Freeman, undated). Some of the current interest in tribal/extended family group decision-making (Family Rights Group, 1994), according to Maori, native American and other traditional cultural patterns, relates to a similar search for alternative means of working in partnership, often within a more holistic ethos than Western society retains. Gay and lesbian groups, too, have developed wholly new thinking on organisational principles, such as approaches to recruitment and recording where confidentiality is paramount.

Non-traditional organisations come under tremendous pressure from the more traditional, however, to behave in ways the latter can recognise and understand. If difference is noticed at all, it is registered as some kind of inferiority – as disorganisation, inefficiency or unprofessionalism. Also, at the points where the two organisations need to interact, for example through access to funding, power may be used to force the smaller to become more like the larger. Increasingly, for instance, local authority contributions to the funding of posts in women's organisations are accompanied by pressure to move away from equality of pay and status, with 'project directors' appearing in former collectives. On a wider scale, voluntary agencies fear that competing for contracts to sustain their funding base will distance them from their pioneering roots and reduce their capacity for advocacy. As only the widest diversity of projects can reflect the more complex understanding of human need we have now acquired, the challenge to the large public agencies is to support and emulate where appropriate, rather than impose uniformity.

In more recent management thinking, there has been a widespread interest in moving beyond simple bureaucracy to alternative organisational forms which are better able to deal with complexity. As information processing, diversification of operations and interdisciplinary liaison have exerted greater demands, control has spread sideways to section heads in various technological and specialist fields. Other factors influencing change have been a developing awareness of the value of the human 'resource' (as opposed to narrowly defined technical efficiency) and, in industry and commerce, the desire to emulate ways of working thought to underlie the post-war growth of the Japanese and the younger 'tiger' economies led to organisational changes in the 1990s before the Far East economic bubble burst.

Clegg (1990) identifies the more complex 'postmodern' organisation as one that offers a differentiated service or product but has a dedifferentiated, that is, multiskilled workforce. 'Teamworking' has replaced the production line in many manufacturing organisations, the responsibility for the quality of the output being shared between all members of a multiskilled and non-hierarchical team. Alongside this, 'quality circles' have been introduced. The 'dot.com' revolution has more recently focused management attention on speed of delivery and technological solutions and, in the public sector, this can be seen in the development of 'smart' housing for people with disabilities, thereby providing independence and a reduction in the needs for intrusive care; 'info-webs' where service users or their carers have access to a whole range of information about services via the internet; and internet 'chat rooms' where virtual communities such as those who are housebound can communicate with each other. These developments are not yet widespread but are already changing the social work role and involving other experts in the service provision task.

Increasingly, too, social workers are using new technology to enhance their day-to-day practice, for example the use of the Social Care Institute for Excellence (SCIE) CareData database to gain access to up-to-date research findings; interactive computer programmes for use with looked after children; computerised assessment tools; integrated care recording and information management packages and so on. The developments in statutory social work, however, are particularly slow, with only a few authorities taking a lead in reducing the bureaucratic demands on their staff.

Along with technological advances has come increased labour market 'flexibility', with heavy reliance on part-time and short-term staff, 'the flexible fringe' (Handy, 1990: 77), where women have traditionally dominated. In the 1980s and 90s, during periods of recession, social workers' employment was insecure and some sectors, most notably the probation service, made a number of staff redundant. As the economy has improved and, along with it, the desire to improve public services, there are insufficient staff to meet demand, particularly in the southeast of England and employers are searching abroad to fill vacancies. Increasingly, too, as the voluntary sector has expanded under the Sure Start scheme and as the Quality Protects programme has led to a number of new, and apparently more attractive, social work posts, so core childcare teams have been depleted. The current major challenge for social work is the recruitment and retention of sufficiently high-calibre staff and support for those now working with heavy workloads under considerable pressure.

'Flexibility' in the labour market, it is true, has tended to lead to the creation of more temporary and part-time jobs, both in industry and social work, the latter also relying heavily on employment agencies to fill vacancies. Part-time employment in social services increased by 50.4 per cent between 1988 and 1992 (Local Government Management Board and Association of Directors of Social Services [LGMB and ADSS], 1993: 27), with women predominating. Part-time middle management (team leader) posts in social services more than quadrupled between 1988 and 1992 (LGMB and ADSS, 1993: 28), and over 90 per cent of these are held by women (p. 29). However, part-time working tends not to be offered (or tends to be disadvantageous for career prospects) at the most senior managerial levels, where men still heavily predominate.

Organisational culture and leadership

As old-style rationality and bureaucracy have proved inadequate to guarantee efficient performance in complex contemporary organisations, greater interest has begun to be shown in 'softer' concepts such as culture, emotions and even sexuality (Hearn and Parkin, 1995). The human messiness that the Weberian legacy viewed as 'inimical to rational, efficient capitalism' has, ironically, become an essential part of theorising about organisations (Clegg, 1990: 150). Organisations are not, after all, peopled by automata – staff bring their personalities, feelings and social roles to work and are affected, in turn, by the way in which they find themselves treated there.

In social work, issues such as a culture of blame, the risk of violence, inadequacies of staff care policies, racism from users and colleagues, and, simply, the degree of stress in the job (NISW, 1995a) all require an awareness of the impact of organisations on the people who work within them. Tribunal cases and out-of-court settlements involving social workers who received no help when their health was suffering under pressure of work (Thompson, 1996b), as well as a national survey indicating that 'half the profession had considered leaving social work in the preceding three years because of stress and frustration' (*Professional Social Work*, 1996: 1), illustrate recent grounds for concern. There is a need to foster social work agencies as 'competent workplaces' (Pottage and Evans, 1994) rather than environments which can actively contribute to stress (Thompson et al., 1996).

The work of Peters and Waterman (1982) began the exhortation to organ-isations of all kinds to create and harness a more positive climate. They emphasised people over roles, and the need for value-driven rather than efficiency-obsessed activity. The line of interest in culture and 'quality' has, in general terms, been unbroken from then with the 'Investors in People' (IIP) award scheme currently emphasising the reliance of every successful organisation on each member of its workforce. This is certainly true in social work, where the lowest tiers of workers are all in direct contact with the public.

Widespread efforts to develop 'quality assurance' (DoH, 1992; Kelly and Warr, 1992) – a bottom-up involvement of all members of an organisation in setting and meeting agreed quality standards – have provided many teams with positive opportunities to work towards the improvement of service design and delivery. At its most creative, work on quality has merged with thinking on equality (National Association of Race Equality Advisers, 1993: 9). This has allowed some groupings of black and female staff to incorporate their demands into mainstream rethinking about the accessibility and appropriateness of all services.

More recently, and particularly in the private sector, attention has moved from developing quality systems and approaches to developing leadership and entrepre-neurial 'behaviours' throughout the organisation. The argument for this approach is that the world is changing so fast (as are consumers' views) that it is impossible to control organisations, and traditional organisational/control structures reduce capability, leaving organisations trailing as new modern networked organisational forms are able to respond quickly to environmental and consumer changes. E-commerce companies are often cited as exemplars and, while many early companies are now bankrupt, the skills and the learning acquired by the staff working in them are widely sought. Ceding control while maintaining influence through leadership is now a desired management and staff 'model, leadership not being confined to any role within an organisation (Senge et al., 1994; Bragg, 1996; Kotter, 1996). The network of relationships that achieve results through individual behaviour that is outcome focused but sensitive to environmental and political changes (with a small 'p') will be familiar to social workers working across agency boundaries with a variety of service users, families and professionals. What will be less familiar both to social workers and their managers will be the reduction in the use of control mechanisms, as these have grown considerably in social work over the last three decades, and the requirement for individual initiative and entrepreneurship at practitioner level. The development of new methods of work such as family group conferencing provides an example where these key behaviours might be demonstrated. Conference outcomes are highly dependent on the skills of the facilitator and the work undertaken in preparation for, during and after the conference. The facilitator has influence rather than power, but through careful relationship-building and sustaining can assist families to achieve workable solutions, many of which are innovative.

Equal opportunities

Direct and indirect discrimination against an individual who is a current or potential employee are now unlawful to the extent of the definitions in the Sex

Discrimination Acts 1975 and 1986, the Race Relations Act 1976 and the Disability Discrimination Act 1995 (the latter covering physical disability, learning difficulties and mental illness). There is no equivalent legislation covering unfair treatment at work for gay men, lesbians or older workers. Although Britain now has a minimum wage, some of the lowest-paid workers in the country (disproportionately women, black people and those deprived of training; Phillipson, 1988) are still responsible for the quality of life of many thousands of people in group and domiciliary care settings.

The existing equal opportunities Acts cannot be said to operate particularly effectively, even on their own terms, if we work from a baseline which regards racial and other oppressions as endemic (Macpherson, 1999). Furthermore, the legislation depends on individuals taking cases and, by definition, fails to tackle entrenched, structural oppression.

Equality in social work organisations appears to be most effectively pursued – through codes of practice, equality standards and the like – by designated staff in high-level equality units (Thobani, 1995). Formal and informal measures can combine practical support, such as dependency leave and childcare provision, with personal encouragement through mentoring and coaching, mutual support networks, fostering skill and career development, women-only and black-only management training, appraisal schemes, consultancy, secondments and job swaps, and opportunities to 'act up' to a higher level.

There is a growing literature on the organisational impact on women's careers, and similar work is needed in relation to other oppressed groups. For women, there are studies which identify the problem (DoH/SSI, 1991b), clarify what aids or hinders progression (Coleman, 1991; Allan et al., 1992) and warn that a male backlash is inevitable (Cockburn, 1991). This thinking has begun to work its way through into self-help guides (Clarke, 1992), including those for women's career development in social work (Foster, 1996), and into the social work literature more broadly (Grimwood and Popplestone, 1993). Male-managed environments are recognised as obstructive and often hostile contexts for women, particularly when much of the work itself involves the need to challenge violent and abusive men (Perrott, 1994). Within the above movement for change is some awareness that black women (Martin, 1994), lesbian women and disabled women face compounded forms of discrimination, that they may be more visible, more isolated and less trusted once in management posts, that they may lack appropriate role models, and that there is less scope to make mistakes when many others depend on you to forge a path to the top for them while everyone else expects you to fail. There are also moves to target other groups underrepresented in managerial grades, for example through a survey of male and female black managers in public services (Andrew, 1996).

The feminisation of management

Meanwhile, human resource management theory is beginning to explore the hitherto undervalued, especially the 'feminine', qualities such as interpersonal and intuitive skills that can contribute to organisational success. Whereas classical management theory concerned itself with men managing men in masculine ways –

controlling, rational – so that women's contributions were invisible (Hearn and Parkin, 1995; cf. Spender, 1980), gendered management thinking reveals that women's ways of interacting – teamwork, running democratic meetings, drawing out each other's strengths rather than competing – can make organisations more effective, particularly in handling more diverse demands and more complex lines of communication. Up to now, men's style of talk (Tannen, 1996) – 'bantering', putting others down, self-promotion – has made them seem natural leaders, with women avoiding what they regard as boasting, while playing down their own authority and helping others to contribute. Now, organisations are beginning to question whether they need leaders or facilitators (cf. Mullender and Ward, 1991), whether they require so many managers or more project teams devoted to innovative and responsive thinking, and whether relationship skills might not be just as important as business acumen. There is even a new business interest in 'values-aware' and 'responsible' management within an environmental context (Baty, 1997).

The recognition of stereotypical expectations helps to explain why workplaces can be intensely uncomfortable for gay and lesbian staff members. Not only is there crude homophobia and heterosexism in daily conversation (Hearn and Parkin, 1995), but also rigid gender hierarchies devalue women's contributions and reward only those men who act out the 'macho' role. Black people, too, may find themselves valued only in as far as they conform to white norms. The latest formalised manifestation of this has appeared in psychometric testing standardised around white test results, which is associated with lower rates of appointing black staff to posts (Skellington with Morris, 1992: 135–6).

Thus, it is not just (or even predominantly) the traditionally excluded groups who need to change, but those who stereotypically and disproportionately hold the power in organisations. Here, there are emergent theories about the ways in which managements and masculinities reinforce one another and how both might be transformed (Collinson and Hearn, 1996). Male practitioners are urged to think how they operate in organisations, whether they should absent themselves from whole areas of work such as those directly involving survivors of sexual abuse (Pringle, 1992/93), and whether they have a special responsibility in all settings where men could usefully reconsider prevailing models of masculinity (for example Bensted et al., 1994, writing about work with offenders). Additionally, accountability to women is viewed as crucial in the direction of projects aimed at changing men (Mullender, 1996a). Again, this thinking could usefully be extended to other anti-oppressive agendas.

Achieving organisational change

Since it is not always possible, or even desirable, to set up wholly new organisations, the wider challenge to professionals is to seek planned change within their own agencies (NISW, 1995b), wherever they observe that services or employment practices are outdated or oppressive.

A parallel stimulus from managers towards organisational change is being triggered by the need to balance increased demand and higher expectations with a shortfall in resources (George, 1996). Restructuring within existing agencies has become the hallmark of the age, so that organisations are needing sophisticated ways to manage, and to help their staff to weather, processes of change. While stable and static organisations concentrate on efficiency and tend to be centralised and bureaucratic as a result (Mintzberg, 1989), those which face greater complexity tend to decentralise and become more organic, developing and adapting as needed.

A number of change techniques are nowadays considered more appropriate than the mere assertion of managerial authority. Styles of change management include (Kotter and Schlesinger, 1979):

- education and communication;

- participation and involvement;

- facilitation and support;

- negotiation and agreement;

- manipulation and cooption;

- explicit and implicit coercion.

Their deployment depends on the circumstances. Legislative change, for example, is usually interpreted as a need for new information and is managed through education and communication, while an imminent budgetary crisis elicits stronger measures in varying degrees of manipulation, cooption or coercion to impose cost-cutting measures, for example redundancies. It is likely that imposed change techniques will lead to later problems within the organisation, however, as anger and resentment engender resistance and lowered morale. Nor is effective change only a matter of altering what other people do (Pugh, 1993). A rigid or unreflexive approach, that is, one where we are unable to see our own part in what is happening, creates fresh resistances in others and new obstacles in operating systems.

While some organisations are actively empowering, most show some resistance to change (cf. Pernell, 1986: 112). Many, for example, are skilled at reinterpreting new ideas in accord with their own norms, demanding compromises and spinning out decisions until momentum is lost. 'Covert resistance' (Whitaker, 1975: 426) – verbal assurances without active support – can be far harder to deal with than out-and-out opposition. Also, the change process itself virtually always takes longer and creates more unforeseen problems in existing performance levels (Carnall, 1990) than has been allowed for.

To smooth the way, Pugh (1993: 110–12) has devised a number of 'rules' for the successful implementation of change in organisations which encompass full participation, long-term planning, and the avoidance of change for change's sake. Social work also has its own model of 'managing change through innovation', developed at the NISW (Smale, 1993). Its message involves breaking down both the planning and the actual change process into clearly defined components, and placing considerable emphasis on the 'people' aspects such as enabling, convincing, reassuring, forming alliances and partnerships on the one hand, and avoiding and bypassing where necessary on the other. Change is possible, then, but it requires vision, persistence and strong alliances, preferably between staff and service users pursuing shared objectives.

CONCLUSION

Constant agency reorganisations, expectations on workers to develop transferable competences and demanding performance criteria have made 'managing change' an essential skill in professional social work. Within this pursuit of change can be perceived opposing trends in management thinking. There is, day by day, increasing regulation and guidance – the traditional bureaucratic response to problem-solving – while there is a need for more responsive, relational, networked leadership relying on influence rather than bureaucratic systems of control.

The quality agenda remains important but requires stable staffing, systems and procedures to maintain consistency of experience for service users and this may be antithetical to (much needed) entrepreneurial activity at all levels of the organisation. In such an environment, different organisational forms, management styles and sets of working relationships may be needed and congruence with task may be more important than organisational consistency across the whole organisation or sector.

FURTHER READING

Clegg, S. R., Handy, C. and Nord, W. (eds) (1996) *Handbook of Organization Studies* (London, Sage). A useful organisation 'textbook' which covers theories of organisation, current issues and research.

Itzin, C. and Newman, J. (eds) (1995) *Gender, Culture and Organisational Change: Putting Theory into Practice* (London, Routledge). This book focuses on gender in organisations and on feminising the workplace and service delivery. It provides useful case histories of successful change in and across organisations.

Kelly, D. and Warr, B. (1992) *Quality Counts: Achieving Quality in Social Care Services* (London, Whiting & Birch). An edited collection which provides the most accessible general introduction to quality assurance in social work and social care.

Mabey, C. and Mayon-White, B. (1993) *Managing Change* (London, Paul Chapman in association with the Open University). A widely read and practical introductory text on managing change in organisations.

Morgan, G. (1986) *Images of Organization* (Thousand Oaks, CA, Sage). An exploration of organisations through metaphor and symbols – for example the organisation as a brain or a psychic prison – which provides insights into how organisations work and what they mean to their members.

Social Work through the Life Course

Lena Robinson

Introduction

During the late 1980s, social work education 'became increasingly aware of the impact of oppression and discrimination on clients and communities' (Thompson, 1993: 1). For example, CCETSW requirements for the DipSW award attached a high priority to an anti-discriminatory approach in college and placement teaching and assessment (see CCETSW Paper 30, 1991). The CCETSW document which outlined the guidance notes for the teaching of childcare in the DipSW course stressed that:

> all social work students should have a sound knowledge of human growth and development, [and] the significance of race, culture and language in development must be understood. (CCETSW, 1991: 14)

The Children Act 1989 states that the race, culture, language and religion of children and young people must be addressed in the provision of services. In order to meet the needs of and help the development of any child, black or white, it is essential that social workers operate with adequate knowledge, understanding and sensitivity.

Life course study may draw on different theoretical perspectives – sociological, economic, political, biological, anthropological and psychological. Social work has turned to the social sciences, particularly psychology, for accounts of human behaviour which can be applied in practice. This chapter will focus mainly on the psychological perspective. It argues that traditional psychological theories have not had sufficient explanatory power to account for the behaviour of black people. The term 'black' in this chapter has been used to describe people from Asian and African-Caribbean backgrounds.

As British society has become more heterogeneous, cross-cultural effectiveness has emerged as an essential skill for all social workers who work with children and young people. Over the last two decades, social scientists (mainly in the USA) have become increasingly aware of the contributions that cross-cultural research findings can make to our understanding of human development (for example Segall et al., 1998). Little of the current social work literature in the UK has addressed the issue of cross-cultural development.

The issues discussed in this chapter are offered as the initial steps towards an understanding of some concepts covered in the literature on the life course from a cross-cultural and black perspective: attachment theory, black identity development, the family and older people. These perspectives have been widely researched and developed in the USA (Cross, 1971, 1980; Greenfield and Cocking, 1994).

Inadequacies of Western psychology

The conventionally accepted paradigms and discoveries of Western psychology do not provide an understanding of black children, adolescents and older people. Even a casual observation of the history of psychology will demonstrate that psychological literature from the past 100 years has been based on observations primarily on Europeans, predominantly male and overwhelmingly middle class. A model of white middle-class personality has been 'utilized as a measuring stick against which all other psychological development is assessed' (Sinha, 1983: 7), 'the standard against which others must measure up' (Segall et al., 1990: 93).

The formulations of such notable thinkers who have shaped the thought of Eurocentric psychology, such as Sigmund Freud ([1913]1950) and Carl Jung (1950), have all directly or indirectly asserted the superiority of European races over non-European races. Despite the diversity of the various schools of Western psychology, they seem to merge unequivocally in their assumption of the Eurocentric point of view and the superiority of people of European descent. It is not surprising, therefore, that the conclusions reached from the application of their concepts and methods are invariably of the inferiority of non-European peoples (Robinson, 1995).

A main feature of Eurocentric psychology is the assumption among psychologists that people are alike in all important respects. In order to explain 'universal human phenomena', white psychologists established a normative standard against which all other cultural groups were to be measured. What appeared as normal or abnormal was always in comparison to how closely a specific thought or behaviour corresponded to that of white people. Hence, normality is established on a model of the middle-class, Caucasian male of European descent. The more one approximates this model in appearance, values and behaviour, the more 'normal' one is considered to be. The obvious advantage for Europeans (whites) is that such norms confirm *their* reality as *the* reality and flaunt statements of their supremacy as scientifically based 'fact'. The major problem with such normative assumptions for non-European people is the inevitable conclusion of deviance on the part of anyone unlike this model. In fact, the more distinct you are from this model, the more pathological you are considered to be (Robinson, 1995).

Social workers in Britain and the USA have been influenced greatly by the psychoanalytic approach in psychology. This approach is based on Sigmund Freud's work but has been developed by neo-Freudians (for example Erikson, Melanie Klein and Jung). In contrast to the critiques of Freud for sexism (Mitchell, 1974; Frosh, 1987), the racism of the psychoanalytic approach is relatively unknown. Mama criticises Freudian psychoanalysis for:

> its universalism and ethnocentrism ... A theory which takes sexual repression and taboo as the bedrock of 'civilisation' is also highly culture-bound. (1995: 127)

Fernando (1991) notes that Freud (1930) envisaged the development of civilisation being dependent on suppressing instinctual behaviour under the guidance of the super-ego, elaborated into a 'cultural super-ego'; it was natural for him that the 'leadership of the human species' should be taken up by 'white nations' (Freud, 1915, 1930) and that 'primitives' have a lower form of culture' (Fernando, 1991: 41). In his book *Totem and Taboo*, Freud ([1913]1950) refers to the practices and behaviours of African peoples as 'savage' or 'primitive'. However, 'although Freud adhered to racist thinking, it was Jung who integrated racist ideas more fully into psychological theories' (Fernando, 1991: 42).

Carl Jung (at one time Freud's star pupil) has been referred to as the father of 'transpersonal psychology'. He believed that certain psychological disorders found among Americans were due to the presence of black people in America. He noted that:

> The causes for the American energetic sexual repression can be found in the specific American complex, namely to living together with 'lower races, especially with Negroes'. (Jung, 1950: 29)

Jung identified the modern African as 'primitive' in every sense of the word. Dalal (1988) maintains that Jung considered black people to be inferior rather than just different.

Erikson's (1968) psychoanalytical theory focuses on one distinctive feature of adolescence: the development of a sense of identity. He proposed a process whereby adolescents begin with an unclear sense of their identity, experience a 'crisis' and achieve a clear sense of their identity. He felt that 'identity crisis' was normative to adolescence and young adulthood. Erikson (1964) spoke of ethnic self-doubt and a pathological denial of one's roots as being seminal to Negro identity. He could not conceive that, for some individuals, their colour might actually be a source of pride. In an article 'Memorandum on identity and Negro youth', he states:

> A lack of familiarity with the problem of Negro youth and with the actions by which Negro youth hopes to solve these [identity] problems is a marked deficiency in my life and work which cannot be accounted for by theoretical speculation. (Erikson, 1964: 41)

Towards a black perspective in psychology

There is a consensus among most black psychologists and professionals that explanations of black behaviour which are alternative to white European perspectives must be developed. A black perspective in psychology is concerned with combating (negative) racist and stereotypic, weakness-dominated and inferiority-oriented conclusions about black people. This perspective is interested in the psychological well-being of black people and is critical of research paradigms and theoretical formulations that have a potentially oppressive effect on black people. Black psychologists (mainly in the USA) have presented alternative perspectives on black child development. However, the research of black scholars, who have unique insights into the problems of minority children and adolescents, has largely been neglected by mainstream developmental psychology (Spencer, 1988).

Cross-cultural considerations

How can a cross-cultural perspective contribute to our understanding of human development? Gardiner (1994) has pointed to a number of important benefits. First, looking at behaviour from this perspective compels researchers to reflect seriously on the variety of ways in which their cultural beliefs and values affect the development of their theories and research designs. Second, increased awareness of cross-cultural findings provides an opportunity to extend or restrict the implications of research conducted in a single cultural group, most notably the USA and similar Western societies. Third, this perspective reduces ethnocentrism – by looking at behaviours as they occur in another culture. Although it is essential for social workers to have a basic understanding of black people's cultural values, there is the ever-present danger of overgeneralising and stereotyping. Information about Asian and African-Caribbean cultural values should act as guidelines rather than absolutes. Members of every group are shaped by culture, but also by acculturation, gender, roles, age, income, education and so on. Recognising intra-group differences is critical and helps avoid stereotyping. Race, gender and class inequalities all play a part in shaping dominant and minority groups' cultures, defining opportunities and moulding traditions (Mirza, 1992).

Attachment

An example of a developmental theory criticised for its assumptions of universality is attachment theory, as described by Bowlby (1969). In this section, I will briefly examine the concept of attachment. This concept refers to the special bond that develops between the infant and the care-giver. Attachment provides the child with emotional security. Once attachment is established, babies are distressed by separation from their mothers (called separation distress or anxiety). Ainsworth et al. (1978) have delineated three different styles of attachment: secure, avoidant (children who shun their mothers) and ambivalent (children who are uncertain in their response to their mothers). One of the assumptions about the nature of attachment in the USA and Britain is that secure attachment is the ideal. Cultures differ, however, on their notion of 'ideal' attachment. For example, German mothers value and promote early independence and regard avoidant attachment as the ideal, seeing the 'securely' attached child as 'spoiled' (Grossman et al., 1985).

Some cross-cultural studies (for example, Tronick et al., 1992) also challenge the notion that closeness to the mother is necessary for secure and healthy attachment. Indeed, this notion is prevalent in traditional theories of attachment based on research in the USA. Tronick et al. (1992) found the children in their study to be emotionally healthy despite having multiple care-givers.

Theories of attachment appear to be central to social work practice with children and families. However, most of the social work literature on attachment is Eurocentric and does not address issues of working with black children and families. A recent text for social workers, Howe's (1995) *Attachment Theory for Social Work Practice*, refers briefly to 'cultural variations in the distribution of the different types of attachment patterns' (Howe, 1995: 78) but takes no account of Britain's black population. Recently, Howe et al. (1999: 33) note that:

> cross-cultural and intercountry comparisons of attachment patterns confirm that the modal type is that of the secure attachment, typically around 55–60 per cent infant–mother dyads showing the pattern.

Gambe et al. (1992: 30) argue that:

> the processes of colonization, migration, refuge-seeking and the effect of immigration controls have led to black families developing the capacity to maintain relationships and attachments over vast distances and time.

Attachment theory fails to take into account such issues and fails to appreciate the strengths of black families. Thus, the Eurocentric bias of attachment theory 'can contribute to inappropriate and racist assessments, [and] inappropriate interventions' (Gambe et al., 1992: 30).

There is still much to be done to understand the attachment patterns in other cultures. The studies that do exist, however, are clear in suggesting that we cannot assume that what is seen most in Euro-American culture is best or most descriptive for all. Notions concerning the quality of attachment and the processes by which it occurs are qualitative judgements made from the perspective of each culture. Each culture has values different from but not necessarily better than those of others.

Black identity development

This section argues that the model of psychological nigrescence (a Latin word that means the 'process of becoming black') is more relevant to the psychological life experiences of black adolescents in Britain than are the more traditional psychological theories. It will enable us to gain a better understanding of the difficulties experienced by black adolescents in Britain.

Black identity has been discussed extensively in the social science literature using various terms and measures. According to Looney (1988: 41), 'Black identity deals specifically with an individual's awareness, values, attitudes, and beliefs about being Black'. It can also be viewed as 'an active developmental process which is exposed to various influences within and without, and [which] can be selective and/or adaptive' (Maxime, 1986: 101). These definitions will be used as the 'operating definition' in the discussion of black identity development.

A perspective that has largely been ignored by traditional Eurocentric psychology is the research on the psychology of nigrescence. Nigrescence models tend to have four or five stages, the common point of departure being not the change process per se but an analysis of the identity to be changed. These models are useful as they enable us to understand the problems of black identity confusion and to examine, at a detailed level, what happens to a person during identity change. Perhaps the best known and most widely researched model of black identity development is Cross's (1971, 1980, 1991) model of the conversion from 'Negro' to 'black'.

Cross suggests that the development of a black person's racial identity is often characterised by his or her movement through a five-stage process, the transformation from pre-encounter to internalisation–commitment. Briefly, the five stages are:

1. *Pre-encounter.* In this stage, the individual's racial identity attitudes are primarily pro-white and anti-black. That is, the individual devalues his or her ascribed racial group in favour of Euro-American culture.

2. *Encounter.* Encounter attitudes describe the awakening process experienced by black people. This awakening is often the result of a critical incident in one's life that leads the individual to reconceptualise issues of race in society and reorganise racial feelings in one's personal feelings. For example, a white individual with racist attitudes and practices may act as a catalyst to racial identity attitude change.

3. *Immersion–Emersion.* This stage involves learning and experiencing the meaning and value of one's racial group and unique culture. Immersion attitudes are pro-black.

4. *Internalisation.* This is the stage of racial identity in which the individual achieves pride in his or her racial group and identity.

5. *Internalisation–Commitment.* In this stage, the person finds activities and commitments to express his or her new identity.

The internalisation and internalisation–commitment stages are characterised by positive self-esteem, ideological flexibility and openness about one's blackness.

There is an extensive empirical literature that confirms Cross's model of black identity development (see Cross, 1971, 1991). Although Cross' identity development model has been developed with African-American samples in the USA, it is argued by various authors (for example, Maxime, 1986; Sue and Sue, 1990) that other minority groups share similar processes of development. In Britain, Maxime (1986) has used Cross's model in the understanding of identity confusion in black adolescents.

Parham has expanded Cross's nigrescence model. Parham considers that:

> The process of psychological Nigrescence ... is a lifelong process, which begins with the late-adolescence/early-adulthood period in an individual's life'. (1989: 194–5)

More recent developments in nigrescence theory and research have both added to the expansion of specific stages (see Cross et al., 1998 for a detailed description) as well as opened the model up to renewed criticisms (Constantine et al., 1998). Emphasis on stage theories for capturing racial/ethnic identity formation has fallen under heavy criticism by some researchers as being too linear and not recognising the multidimensional nature of ethnic identity (Phinney, 1990; Yeh and Huang, 1996). Work continues on advancing the nigrescence construct (Cross et al., 1998).

An understanding of Cross's model should sensitise social workers to the role that oppression plays in a black individual's development. Maxime (1993) has used Cross's model in the understanding of identity confusion in black children and adolescents in residential, transracially fostered and adoptive care settings. It was clearly apparent from Robinson's study of racial identity development and self-esteem among African-Caribbean adolescents in residential care in a city in the West Midlands that residential care staff found Cross's model extremely useful in therapeutic work with African-Caribbean youngsters (Robinson, 2000).

Cross's model serves as a useful assessment tool for social workers to gain a greater understanding of black youth. Pre-encounter attitudes have been linked to high levels of anxiety, psychological dysfunction and depression (Parham and Helms, 1985; Carter, 1991), and low self-regard and self-esteem (Parham and Helms, 1985). Young people's perceptions of the social worker are likely to be influenced by their racial identity development. Thus, young people at the pre-encounter stage are more likely to show a preference for a white social worker over a black worker.

Finally, social workers need to be aware that raising children in a white-dominated society places special pressures on the black parent. Although the basic mechanisms for socialisation are the same for black and white children – reinforcement, modelling, identification and so forth – the transmittal sources and content may exhibit some subtle and some obvious differences for black children. The need for adaptive responses to social, economic and political barriers helps to shape the socialisation of black children (Harrison et al., 1990). Peters (1985) indicated that many black parents focused on racial barrier messages and emphasised learning to cope with and survive prejudice in a white-dominated society. Hill (1999) noted that racial socialisation was nearly universal among black parents, 'who can scarcely escape talking about racism and racial pride and who engage in myriad subtle strategies to challenge the denigration of blackness' (Hill, 1999: 102).

Social work with black families

This section will focus on the dominance of pathology models of black family functioning – with reference to models of African-Caribbean and Asian family structures in social science and social work literature and practice.

Many social work texts paint crude cultural stereotypes of black families. The 'norm' against which black families are, implicitly or explicitly, judged is white. The norm presents a myth of the normal family as nuclear, middle class and heterosexual. Black families are seen as strange, different and inferior. The pathological approach to black family life is evident in the British research on black people. It is also evident in social workers' perception of black families. Barn notes that social workers' 'negative perceptions of black families led them to develop a "rescue mentality" which came into force very quickly when dealing with these families' (Barn, 1993: 120). Various studies (for example, Barn, 1993) have indicated the high presence of black children in the care system. Social workers tend to rely on Eurocentric theory and practice that devalues the strength of black families (Ahmad, 1990). For example, Stubbs observed:

> the ease with which negative models of Afro-Caribbean culture and family functioning, already prevalent within the social work literature ... fit into the frameworks of knowledge held by social workers to be relevant to their task. (1988: 103)

Asian families have also been described in terms of cultural stereotypes. Parmar (1981: 21) notes that:

> the traditional Asian household organised through the extended family kinship systems is held out to be responsible for a number of problems that Asians face in the context of British society.

It is argued that the 'rebellion' that

> Asian parents face from sons and daughters is ... to be expected and deserved particularly if they [Asian parents] insist on practising such 'uncivilised' and 'backward' customs as arranged marriages. (Parmar, 1981: 21)

Young people, particularly young women, are said to be torn between two cultures (Anwar, 1976), unable to tolerate strict rules, particularly arranged marriages, and ill-equipped to integrate into British society. Complex family situations tend to be reduced to simplistic, catch-all explanations such as 'endemic culture conflict', which offer no real understanding and fail to give any positive regard to the client's cultural roots (Ahmed, 1986). Implicit in the idea of 'culture conflict' is the assumption that the values of the British family are modern and superior while the Asian culture is in some way backward and inferior.

White social workers are more likely to tolerate intergenerational conflict between parents and adolescents in white homes than in black homes. However, the little research that exists suggests that young Asians, for example, are no more alienated from their parents than are any other group of young people (Westwood and Bhachu, 1988).

Dwivedi (1996) argues that if social work perceptions and practice are largely Eurocentric, the Children Act 1989 can easily work against the best interest and protection of the black child. Thus:

The instrument of 'race, culture, religion and language' can be easily abused to perpetuate the dominance of professional control as a manifestation of their perception of ethnic minority families as culturally deficient, dysfunctional or pathological from whom the children need to be rescued on the one hand, to a justification of non-intervention even when a child desperately needs intervention and protection, so that the professional could appear to be culturally sensitive in case abuse is culturally acceptable! (Dwivedi, 1996: 9)

According to O'Hagan (2001) social work has 'no roots in cultural sensitivity or cultural competence' (p. 116). He argues that 'even today its literature adopts a distinctly anti-cultural stance, compatible with its monocultural theories and practices' (p. 116).

Social work with older black people

Older people, both black and white, face discrimination on the grounds of age or 'ageism'. Fennell et al. define ageism as follows: 'ageism means unwarranted application of negative stereotypes to older people' (1988: 97). Unlike other older people, black elders face additional problems arising from racial, cultural and economic differences and disadvantages.

The comparative literature on black and white elders is dominated by the theme of 'double jeopardy'. This concept, first popularised in the USA (National Urban League, 1964), asserts that the adverse living conditions of black elderly in America is compounded by the social fact of their overall treatment as minority group members (Jackson et al., 1982). In Britain, the term has been applied to 'emphasise the double disadvantage of being poor (in income, housing, health, status and role) and a member of a minority group which suffers racial discrimination' (Patel, 1990: 5). In addition to 'race' and age, gender and social class are also important dimensions to inequality (Patel, 1990). Thus, older blacks could face triple jeopardy, which is defined as the combined impact of race, age and social class on the lives of people in disadvantaged minorities (see Jackson et al., 1982).

British research has suggested that the service needs of elderly people from black groups may be considerable as a result of low incomes, poor housing, isolation and comparatively poor health (Askham et al., 1993). However, older black people 'have been virtually neglected by statutory bodies and have seldom found provisions addressing their specific needs (Farrah, 1986; Holland, 1986)' (Dominelli, 1988: 117). In a recent study of the housing and care needs of black elders in Tower Hamlets, London, Bowes (1998: 41) concludes that 'existing provision ... is not appropriate and is not meeting their needs'. Despite earlier research studies, the housing and care needs of black elders remain unmet (Bowes, 1998).

Dominelli notes that myths about the support of the extended family in caring for its older members have been used by white social workers and their institutions to deny the need for making appropriate provisions available. (Dominelli, 1988: 117)

This approach ignores the fact that 'immigration controls since 1962 have made it virtually impossible for black family units to exist in their totality in Britain'

(Dominelli, 1988: 96). Therefore, not all older Asians live with family members and, even when they do, they may still have problems of isolation and lack of daytime support. The strains on the extended Asian families, partly as a consequence of cramped accommodation, have been mentioned in many of the reports presenting the need for Asian day centres (for example, Rochdale County Council, 1986). Older black people, especially older Asians, are ill-informed about their welfare rights and the social services. Positive action is, therefore, required by social services departments and other organisations to increase awareness (Askham et al., 1993). However, social work practice in this area is largely ethnocentric, if not colour blind.

The dominant psychological theories on ageing do not provide an adequate understanding of older black people. For example, disengagement theory (see Cumming and Henry, 1961) claims to be universal, but the theory is based on a model of middle-class, white, older people living in the US Mid-west (Hochschild, 1975). Blakemore and Boneham (1994: 138) suggest that:

> ethnicity and race do make a difference to the experience of ageing, whether this is in connection with ... roles in the family ... culture-specific needs for care by voluntary and statutory services, or problems of racism and stereotyping.

Thus, the main theories on ageing 'need to be reconsidered with ethnic and racial diversity in mind' (Blakemore and Boneham, 1994: 137).

CONCLUSION

The issues discussed in this chapter indicate that black and white people have different experiences at different stages of the life course. Social work training and practice must question whether theories which have originated in Euro-American settings have relevance in working with black clients in Britain. A Eurocentric perspective in psychology has meant certain theoretical deficits when social workers attempt to apply it in practice. Traditional psychology perpetuates a notion of deviance with respect to black people. Social workers need an understanding of the black perspective in psychology and social work theory in order to be able to deliver effective services to black clients and communities.

Research which focuses on attachment theory, identity development, the black family and black elders from a black perspective will enable social workers to gain a better understanding of the difficulties experienced by black children, teenagers and adults in Britain.

FURTHER READING

Blakemore, K. and Boneham, M. (1994) *Age, Race and Ethnicity* (Buckingham, Open University Press). This is an important reference book for social workers who want to gain an understanding of ageing among black people in Britain.

Cross, W.E. (1992) *Black Identity: Theory and Research* (Philadelphia, Temple University Press). This book provides a detailed discussion of racial identity development models.

Cross, W., Parham, T. and Helms, J. (1998) 'Nigrescence revisited: theory and research', in Jones, R.L. (ed.) *African American Identity Development* (Hampton, VA, Cobb & Henry). This chapter provides a detailed discussion of nigrescence models and directions of future theorising and research.

Dwivedi, K.N. and Varma, V.P. (eds) (1996) *Meeting the Needs of Ethnic Minority Children: A Handbook for Professionals* (London, Jessica Kingsley). This book provides social workers with theoretical and practical information on the health, education and social care of black children.

Phinney, J.S. and Rotheram, M.J. (eds) (1987) *Children's Ethnic Socialization: Pluralism and Development* (London, Sage). This comprehensive book discusses black children's development.

Robinson, L. (1995) *Psychology for Social Workers: Black Perspectives* (London, Routledge). An essential introductory text for all social workers in training and practice.

Robinson, L. (1998) *'Race', Communication and the Caring Professions* (Buckingham, Open University Press). This book aims to provide social workers with a precise framework in which to view and define the diverse factors at work during inter-ethnic communication.

Personal and Professional Development

Joyce Lishman

Introduction

> Social Work involves entering into the lives of people who are in distress, conflict
> or trouble. To do this requires not only technical competence but also qualities of
> integrity, genuineness and self-awareness. (Lishman, 1994)

Discussion of personal and professional development must be set in the
uncertain, demanding, complex and changing context of social work. The
current emphasis on vocational training and the achievement of discrete technical
competences in a culture which promotes market forces, consumerism and
managerialism (Holman, 1993; Banks, 1995; Clark, 1995; Dominelli, 1996) is at
the expense of fundamental aspects of social work including:

- a concern about individual people and the enhancement of their lives and
  relationships;

- a commitment to social justice and the eradication of poverty and discrimination;

- a commitment to social work as a moral and ethical activity;

- a holistic approach to practice, where relationships and process as well as
  outcomes are addressed;

- a commitment to partnership and involvement with users in developing
  services to meet their needs;

- a commitment to evaluating practice as a means of developing it;
- a recognition that the worker's use of self is integral to social work activity.

Examination of personal and professional development in this chapter is based on a definition of social work which includes these fundamental aspects. We cannot, however, ignore the tensions between this holistic approach and the current culture and context in which professional definition and identity have been challenged both by the political ideology of the New Right (interestingly and paradoxically sustained and continued by New Labour), with its adherence to managerialism and efficiency savings, and by a competency-driven approach to training and professional development (Banks, 1995; Sheppard, 1995; Vanstone, 1995).

This chapter examines both the context of personal and professional development in social work, and essential elements of personal and professional development. In particular, our motivation for social work, and our capacity to manage complexity, change and uncertainty, involve both personal and professional development, and each is discussed in turn. Three critical aspects of professional development are then examined: the use of supervision, the articulation and promotion of good practice along with the development and evaluation of models of practice and service provision, and the need for commitment to the next generation of entrants to social work.

The context and nature of personal and professional development in social work

The ideological, political, economic and financial context has already been alluded to and is hostile to the concept of reflective professional practice on which this discussion of personal and professional development is based. The complex and uncertain nature of social work, with its ethical base, legal accountability, responsibility for complex decision-making and risk assessment, public profile and constantly changing legislation, requirements, structures and organisation requires social workers to engage in ongoing development, personal and professional, if they are to survive, respond effectively to users and clients, and manage the uncertainty which is endemic to the profession.

The ethical issues in social work summarised by Banks (1995) involve tensions between individual rights, public welfare, inequality and structural oppression; they lead to moral dilemmas and a balancing of rights, duties and responsibilities for which there may be no 'right answer'. An ethical response may conflict with financial accountability and resource availability; it may inform or conflict with legal accountability.

Social workers engage in complex decision-making, often about relative risks, safety, harm and protection. They do so in the context of a breakdown of consensus about social and collective responsibility and a rise in the value accorded to individual choice and responsibility. Paradoxically, 'society' has simultaneously experienced widespread economic insecurity and increasing marginalisation and vulnerability, in particular in relation to people who are unemployed, in poverty or homeless, or have mental health problems (Parton, 1996). Social work is closely interlinked with these changes, and social workers' dilemmas and actions reflect and symbolise wider preoccupations with insecurity, safety, marginalisation, risk and control. The Labour government's emphasis on social inclusion recognises and seeks to address societal diversion, marginalisation and exclusion. However, it is not clear that social work is seen as a major driver of this agenda (Jordan, 2000), despite its inherent involvement with people who are vulnerable and marginalised.

Such inherent complexity in the social work task is compounded by the pace of change which social work has experienced. Change is not unique to social work, although we may feel we have been bombarded by it! Since the late 1980s, policy and legislative change has included: the National Health Services and Community Care Act 1990; local government reorganisation, 1996; the Children Act 1989; the Children (Scotland) Act 1995; and the overall reorganisation of social work into childcare, community care and criminal justice (with the loss in England and Wales of probation as part of social work training) (Criminal Justice Act 1991; Children Act 1989; Children (Scotland) Act 1995). In social work education and training, new initiatives for qualifying training were introduced in 1990 and revised in 1995 (CCETSW, 1995). More recent reviews of CCETSW and social work education and training (J.M. Consulting, 1999) have led to further proposed changes, welcome in that qualifying education and training will be set at honours degree level. However, the implication for each of the devolved countries remain to be decided in detail.

This history suggests that the external environment of social work will constantly change. Internally led change and development in practice and service delivery which is responsive to user/client views and based on the evaluation of practice and service delivery is also essential. However, such rapid policy, legal and organisational change adds to the uncertainty and complexity we experience in our practice.

The context of social work practice has not been favourable to personal or professional development. As Pietroni (1995: 38) argues:

> a short social work basic training, no nationally recognised career path or consistent professional development structures, an inhibition or an antipathy towards individual authority and excellence and a context is produced which is intrinsically antagonistic to thoughtful practice.

Other barriers to professional development and learning include:

- a tension between a local authority's requirement for a technically competent worker, and a professional requirement for critical reflective practice, which may include criticism of the agency practice;

- a lack of agency recognition in terms of pay and status for the achievement of professional development, the practice teaching award being one example;

- a lack of time allowed for professional development;

- a lack of access to professional development; for example, Dominelli (1997a) raises issues about access to higher education for women which are also relevent to professional development in social work and social care, where women with family commitments may have difficulty in terms of finance and time in pursuing relevant professional developments.

The new proposals for qualifying education and training should address the problem of the 'short social work basic training'. The establishment of regulatory bodies for the legislation of social workers and over time all social care workers and the development of codes of conduct and practice are strategic attempts to change the organisational and cultural problems identified in relation to continuing professional development and learning in social work (see, for example, the Scottish Executive, *The Way Forward for Care*, 2000b).

We may ask why social workers should undertake any professional development when it may not be organisationally valued and is unlikely to be financially rewarded. In future, it will be a requirement for professional registration, but there are clear reasons why all professional bodies require social workers to update their knowledge on a regular basis. Professional development is essential to develop, use and promote more effective models of practice and service delivery in a context of rapid change of policy and legislation. Personal development is essential to underpin professional development, since our use of self is part of the service we offer to users and clients. The need for continuing professional development is not the prerogative of social work. Qualifying training, in any profession and whatever the length, is inevitably limited in input, both breadth and depth, and opportunities for application to practice. Professionals also need to update their expertise as knowledge and methods change and develop:

> One central purpose of continuing professional education is to bring practising professionals into contact with new knowledge and ideas. Sometimes this is conceived in terms of general updating, sometimes as a stimulus to critical thinking and self evaluation, sometimes as the dissemination of a particular innovation, sometimes as part of the process of implementing a new mandatory policy. (Eraut, 1994: 25)

Put briefly, but too simply, two contrasting models appear to influence continuing professional development: the competency-based approach underpinning the National Vocational system, adopted to some extent by CCETSW for both qualifying and post-qualifying awards and used by TOPSS; and an approach which values reflective practice and the learning process, and stresses the role of the professional as a reflective practitioner (Schön, 1987).

The 'competency' model is based on functional analysis which:

> breaks the job down into functional units and the units into elements each of which has to be separately assessed to cover a range of situations according to a list of performance criteria. (Eraut, 1994: 118)

This model is inappropriate for education, training and professional development in social work because it results in fragmentation of the complexity of social work and lacks a holistic approach to the necessary integration of knowledge, values and skills and the processes whereby these are integrated and applied.

This chapter bases professional development on the second approach, the reflective practitioner model. Schön (1987) acknowledges the need for academic rigour but also its limitations in the messy reality of practice (see also Chapters 11 and 23). By reflection and analysis, we can adapt and develop the theories we use to new, complex and out-of-the-ordinary situations.

Our motivation for social work

Why do we become social workers, and why should this be relevant to our personal and professional development?

Motivation for social work, like social work itself, is varied and complex. Cree (1996) found that reasons for entering social work training were family background, significant life experience of loss, illness or disability, and adult choice including social work as a vocation to care for individuals, as a means of 'changing the system' and promoting social justice or as a career. Rochford (1991) drew attention to the experience of loss, both normal and exceptional, as a major factor in motivation for social work. Cree (1996) also highlights gender differences in motivation for social work. Men are entering a profession in which their promotion prospects are high but the qualities and abilities required of them are not stereotypically male. For women, the opposite is true.

Why does motivation matter, and why should it be an issue for personal development? Think about your own motivation. Was it political, was it your experience of racial or gender discrimination, or did it arise from your personal experience, as a child or as an adult? How do you think it influences your practice?

We need a personal element in motivation for social work whether it arises from our experience of structural oppression or personal difficulty. It can give us compassion, empathy and insight into the lives of people with whom we work and a commitment to challenging injustice and discrimination. However, we must not be driven in our practice by our personal experience, attempt to impose the experiences which motivate us on our clients or users, or work out our agendas (personal or political) through their lives.

How may we harness the positive and empowering aspects of our motivation and avoid the potential danger of using our clients or users to meet our own needs rather than responding to theirs? Developing and maintaining self-awareness is one way, supervision, potentially, another.

Self-awareness and reflection

We need to develop our self-awareness and capacity for critical reflection in order to ensure that our motivation and past experience are used to enhance our practice. Self-awareness is also necessary if we are to recognise our impact on others. Do we convey authority and expertise where required? Do we convey a non-judgemental attitude to aspects of clients' lives which are potentially shocking, for example violence, abuse or deprivation? What sense of empowerment do we convey to our users? How do we remain aware of our impact on others?

Self-awareness and critical self-reflection are also necessary to ensure confidence that our responses arise from the client's or user's situation rather than our past or needs. This requires self-awareness and:

> awareness of situations and topics which generate most personal anxiety to the worker since intense anxiety is likely to lead to inattention, poor listening, and inappropriate responses and action. (Lishman, 1994: 60)

Finally, we need to use self-awareness and reflection to meet the complex demands of social work. Carter et al. (1995) suggest that in social work we experience a tension between the uniqueness of each situation and the need to develop generalised responses to 'familiar social work problems':

> We have to think things through, for every case is unique. When we forget this, problems arise. If we simply label people as a 'housing problem' or whatever, and then go through our 'housing routine' we are liable to miss all sorts of things ... Of course, we rely on routines: it would be intolerable if we had to work things out from first principles for each and every situation. However, these routines have to be open to feedback from the situation. (p. 8)

They argue that this requires both 'reflecting-in-action' and 'reflection-on-action'.

We need to develop a discipline of reflecting on what we have done and how we have behaved, 'reflection-on-action' (Schön, 1987), in order to learn, confirm good practice, analyse mistakes and develop alternative actions and responses. Questions contributing to reflection-on-action include:

- How did I engage with that person or in that situation?
- What previous experiences influenced me?
- What did I do?
- Why did I do it?
- On reflection, how might I have responded differently, if at all?

By practising such discipline, we may increasingly be able to 'reflect in practice', where questions have a more immediate focus and may include the following:

- What am I feeling?
- How am I presenting?
- Do I need to change my approach or focus?
- Why do I feel uncomfortable?

Managing complexity

We have noted the complex demands of social work, but its very essence is complex and ambiguous, involving tensions between a focus on the alleviation of individual distress and misery and on challenging structural oppression and inequality, and between meeting individual need, promoting empowerment, ensuring the protection of vulnerable children and adults, and carrying out functions of social work control. Practice is equally complex. For example, faced with families in poverty, in isolation, with difficulties in childcare and control (Walker, 1995), what, out of the range of relevant knowledge and theory, do we draw on? What focus do we select? What methods do we employ? Equally, how do we manage the complexity of our feelings, of being overwhelmed, of feeling inadequate and helpless, of empathy, of frustration?

Such complexity and need 'stirs up powerful and primitive feeling in all professionals' (Trowell, 1995: 195). One danger is that we become paralysed by attempting to manage all the complexity and by our inability to do so effectively. Walker (1995) warns of the dangers of the wish to be omnipotent: 'the belief that I could or should be brilliantly effective' (p. 56). An alternative danger is that we attempt to limit and simplify the complexity, for example, by:

- providing 'concrete responses' such as providing a service or aid but ignoring the feelings and relationships which surround the problem; for example, providing a Zimmer frame may be necessary for the user's functioning but not sufficient for their well-being, because issues about dependency and anxiety about 'failing' may need to be addressed.

- 'splitting' and 'projection':

  Splitting arises from the existence of utterly contradictory feelings that seem impossible to countenance simultaneously and which are therefore kept in separate compartments ... Projection occurs when a feeling or characteristic which in reality belongs to the self is first externalised and then ascribed to another person. (Brearley, 1991: 52)

  Splitting and projection are defence mechanisms which began in infancy in order to cope with the powerful good and bad primitive feelings and can be helpful essential mechanisms in coping as adults. As workers, however, if we use splitting and projection in relation to our clients/users and work, we are in danger of distorting a complex reality.

We have to be able to contain, for example: worry and concern for a mother on her own, depressed, in debt and without the very basic material props of parenting, for example a washing machine; our anxiety about her child's emotional and physical needs; our anger with the political and social security system which allows if not promotes this; and resonances with our past and our childhood experience of need and dependency. If we split, for example by focusing entirely on the child's needs and vulnerability, or project, for example by rage at the system, we cannot manage and balance the complex task of addressing ways of improving resources and parental care, and improving the ways in which the parent's and child's needs can be met.

How can we develop this personal capacity to contain and manage such complexity? In part, we need to recognise this as a continuing area of personal and professional development; in part, it requires a commitment to the maintenance and development of self-awareness; in part, it requires a capacity for reflection in and on action; and, in part, we need to be able to analyse practice and therefore learn from and build on previous experience. Practice supervision may offer the opportunity to examine our responses to complex cases with real needs, vulnerability and risks and engage in the same processes for personal development and learning. We also need to be allowed to make mistakes and get things 'wrong', provided that we learn from the experience and are not dangerous to our clients.

Managing uncertainty

Uncertainty faces us in a number of ways. We face uncertainty about our value base as we are challenged to examine, for example, how racism, sexism, heterosexism, ageism and other forms of oppression may influence us, without our necessarily recognising this. In working with users and clients, we face uncertainty about how to respond appropriately, how to choose the 'right' response to the myriad of feelings, impressions, theories and experiences which form our working practice. Uncertainty is not unique to social work but is a component of 'professional' activity. More specifically, uncertainty in social work arises because individuals and their problems are unique; there is no set causal link between a problem, a response and an outcome; risk assessment is problematic (Kemshall and Pritchard, 1996); the organisational context has been constantly changing and the political context is hostile and unpredictable.

Dealing with uncertainty means realising that often there is no right response, although there may be a wrong one. The danger here is that, again, we try to simplify, which may involve:

- demanding certainty and answers where none are available;

- giving answers and information which are definite but may be wrong;

- dealing with the discrete parts of a problem which may have an immediate solution and ignoring the more messy and uncertain areas.

Such strategies for denying uncertainty can be dangerous as they may lead us to impose 'certain' but wrong action on our clients or users.

How may we better deal with uncertainty? Perhaps we first have to recognise it as an essential part of life, not just social work! We need to consider how we deal with uncertainty in our lives, what helps and what hinders. 'We need to avoid jumping to closed conclusions and keep open the possibility of change as a result of reflecting in action and dialogue with others' (Carter et al., 1995: 9). We need to use the experience of training, supervision and our colleagues to help us examine our own ways of dealing with uncertainty and, where we find they are inappropriate, to explore and practise other ways.

Managing change

We have seen that the recent context of social work has been of rapid, constant and externally imposed change. Change is not unique to social work. In our personal lives, we have to adapt to changes of biological maturation and ageing, and life cycle social and emotional changes.

More generally, we need to be aware (Marris, 1974) that any major change, be it voluntary or imposed, will involve loss for the participants – an initial loss of their previous 'taken-for-granted' view of the world, sense of security and established sense of meaning and purposes. Such loss is met with ambivalence, analogous to grief, involving conflict between contradictory impulses: to remain the same and keep what is valuable from the past, and to move on. Marris argues that the management of change necessitates the expression of ambivalence and conflicting impulses before the participants can move on to accept the change (whether it involves new perspectives, skills or organisational structures) and integrate it into a continuity of experience and meaning. Such an analysis helps us to understand why change, even where we can see that it brings rewards, is met with apparently irrational resistance. While such resistance to change is not intrinsically bad – for example, it may delay ill-thought out or ill-advised changes (Coulshed, 1991) – change is essential if an organisation is to be responsive to its environment and develop and thereby survive, and in order to develop better services and practice.

In our personal and professional development, it is important to pay attention to how we manage change. At the extremes, do we totally resist it or embrace it without thought for the past? We need to examine our personal responses because they will influence how we respond to clients or users who are facing change, for example in relationships, dependency or physical location, how we respond to changes in the organisation and delivery of social work, and how open we are to new ideas, without discarding hard-earned knowledge and skills from the past.

Managing complexity, uncertainty and change is demanding and stressful, and it is impossible to prescribe methods and techniques to do so 'successfully'. What can help? At a personal level, we have seen the need to develop and maintain an awareness of our own strengths and weaknesses, a capacity to tolerate and contain our irrational feelings and responses, and a discipline of self-critical reflection.

To support and help us in this, we can use specific training courses, discussion with colleagues, mulling over particular cases and incidents, recording, reflection and evaluation, and, perhaps potentially most important, supervision.

Supervision

> Supervision is an effective tool for professional staff development which managers would be foolish not to consider. However, many managers subvert the supervision process into a means of controlling or instructing staff, instead of as a means of developing staff. (Turner, 1995: 127)

The above quotation indicates the potential dilemma and danger of supervision. It can become a management tool of accountability and efficiency. Equally, it can be used to enhance professional development and thereby practice and service provision.

What should you expect of supervision? Ideally, it should be provided on a regular and reliable basis. It should involve mutual trust and an awareness of issues of authority and responsibility. It should provide support and an opportunity to express feelings and go 'below the surface' in the analysis of problems and situations. It should address particular issues which workers identify as problematic, including facing pain, anxiety, confusion, violence and stress. Its content and process should be anti-oppressive and anti-discriminatory, with a professional development focus of empowerment. It should focus on learning.

There is a gap between what should happen and what actually does happen! Areas of discrepancy which will hinder professional development include:

- the unavailability of supervision;

- the abuse of power, for example where the dissemination of information is controlled or supervision is used to exercise the supervisor's power or control as negative power, for instance by blocking and restricting, or by punishment (Grimwood and Popplestone, 1993);

- a lack of emotional or feeling support:

    Supervisors often cut off from the pain in clients' lives. The worker, unable to share and thereby receive support from her line manager, is left on her own with the loss and grief of her clients. (Hanmer and Statham, 1988, in Grimwood and Popplestone, 1993: 47)

- a lack of acknowledgement and support in issues connected with violence: often as workers, we are left to deal with fears of and responses to violence as our personal responsibility rather than being offered support and the oppor-tunity for reflection, process and analysis in supervision.

It is important to seek good supervision. In particular, it can help us to manage anxiety and confusion. Turner (1995: 126) argues that:

Many workers feel they must appear to be coping well with their work at all times. What they see as their less acceptable thoughts, feelings and actions are suppressed, denied and avoided, for fear of being seen as not a good enough worker. It is important for supervisors to demonstrate in supervision their own capacity to contain anxiety and remain thoughtful about whatever the worker brings, rather than avoiding the painful issues, rushing for solutions, or giving 'neat' packages of instructions.

Such a capacity for containment, empathy, reflection and their encouragement of analysis in depth can help us to cope with the pain, violence and anxiety we may encounter. It can also help us to become more able to take responsibility for our own work, to make our own judgements and then improve them. As Brown and Bourne (1996) argue, supervision is time for exploration, reflection, learning and problem-solving.

We also need to remember our accountability to the organisation employing us. As Coulshed and Mullender (2000) argue, supervision should meet individual support needs, educational and developmental needs and managerial and administrative needs. These managerial needs include workload and caseload management, ensuring that staff work with the policies and developments of the agency and giving feedback about performance.

There is an inevitable tension between the different potential users of super-vision, but in terms of professional development it is essential to recognise the requirements of the agency, the need to perform appropriately and the need for supervision as a time to reflect and seek support.

Promoting and developing good practice and service provision

The development of good social work practice and service delivery is a collective responsibility of all qualified social workers. We need constantly to examine critically and review practice and service delivery. We need to identify what are the ingredients of 'good practice' and how can they be applied elsewhere. We need to identify areas for improvement and gaps in service delivery and responses to user need, in order to begin to change services and provide new ones. This is, of course, within a context of lack of resources. *Community Care* (1996) found that most social workers had to refuse services that clients needed because of a lack of resources. However, *Community Care* also regularly provides examples of innovative developments in practice and service delivery to meet gaps in service provision or unmet need.

We need to develop and maintain ways of learning from others: we should not be reinventing wheels in each unitary authority or voluntary organisation. How can we keep abreast of new developments which we may usefully be able to apply? One problem is the overload of information we receive and the need to select from it. Conferences and training courses are specific and therefore targeted clearly for us in terms of application to our particular practice and service develop-ment needs, but they are expensive. However, they can put us in touch with other workers' relevant experience in relatively informal but productive ways.

We can learn by reading. *Community Care* provides relevant articles about good practice and service development. It also reviews relevant literature from which we can select what may best apply to and develop our current expertise. More general texts may be useful at post-qualifying level (see Further Reading). The Social Care Institute for Excellence has been set up to promote the dissemi-nation of both qualitative and quantitative research-based evidence to underpin social work practice and policy development. It will recognise the complexity of social work practice and not rely entirely on evidence from the 'gold standard' experimental research of the randomly controlled trial (RCT) (see Lishman, 2000 for a critique of this approach).

We can engage in the formal post-qualifying training continuum. CCETSW has set out a framework for post-qualifying training which involves two levels: post-qualifying and advanced. The requirements are difficult to summarise and the details are set out in the CCETSW Paper 31, revised in 1995 (CCETSW, 1995). The main features of the post-qualifying level are 'the development of competence, confidence and professional credibility beyond the qualifying level' and either the development of specialist expertise in one area of practice or the responsibility for the management of an aspect of social work. At the advanced level, candidates may be assessed in practice, education and training, management or research, but all candidates have to demonstrate a range of competence including the analysis of practice and service delivery, the development and improvement of services, the critical evaluation of values, theories, models, methods and policies, and the management of innovative change. Future developments in relation to registration may change the precise requirements but should retain the principles.

We need to articulate our practice, on lines indicated by the post-qualifying framework. We need to do this, for example, in supervision in order to learn from what we do and change and develop our practice. We need to articulate our practice to colleagues from other disciplines. We need to articulate our practice so that other social workers can learn from what we do. We may be working on behalf of our users and clients in excellent innovative ways which benefit them, but if we do not articulate this practice, others cannot learn from it and have to reinvent the wheel. We need to articulate practice for the political survival of the profession and our users, in order to demonstrate to the government, press and public what we do well (even though they may not necessarily listen).

We need not simply identify good practice, but also evaluate it. As Ian Shaw (1996) argues, evaluating practice has historically been a problematic aspect of social work. However, there are good reasons why we should engage in the evaluation of practice and service delivery. Evaluation examines our effectiveness and can help us to improve it, can increase our accountability to users and clients, develops our knowledge and identifies gaps in knowledge, and helps us to develop new models of practice and service delivery (Shaw and Lishman, 1999).

If we develop a new method, project or service, we need to examine how well it works for its users. More problematically, the continued funding of innovative projects is often linked with the evaluation of effectiveness, where definitions of effectiveness may not necessarily be shared by the funder and the project and its users. Evaluation, we need to recognise, can be part of a political and resource context. Nevertheless, we need to engage with it: as Ian Shaw (1996) argues, 'it holds the promise of keeping social work honest'.

How to evaluate our practice can appear threatening, with connotations of the scientific experimental method, although, as Everitt et al. (1992) suggest and Everitt argues in Chapter 10 of this volume, the social work process of finding and collating evidence, hypothesis-forming and assessment, intervention and hypothesis-testing, review, further assessment, revision of intervention and further review is not dissimilar to qualitative research methodology. Shaw and Lishman (1999) demonstrate the range of methodologies appropriate to social work evaluation and Smith (2000b) argues that 'evidence' is drawn from users' and practitioners' views and that evidence from RCTs needs a contextualised 'realistic' application.

Educating and training the next generation

There are inevitably many valid reasons for not becoming a practice teacher or providing input to social work eduction, including a lack of financial or career recognition, a lack of resources including staff, space and time, and a lack of organisational support where management is preoccupied with service delivery and cuts in resources.

In such circumstances, educating and training the next generation can be seen as a luxury. Why should you become involved in practice teaching or any other teaching input to social work courses? Good reasons include the need to ensure the continuation of professional service delivery to clients and users, the professional and value component of generativity (Erikson, 1965), that we should put back into the profession as we have received, and the enhancement of our learning and expertise. Students question and challenge us in ways that ensure we explore, examine, reflect on and evaluate our practice.

Teaching others often provides the best opportunity to articulate our own practice, to question and examine what we do and why, and, if we are open to challenge, to identify gaps and failures in practice and provision. Students then provide a challenging external scrutiny of what we do. By educating and training them, we provide the future development of our profession, and workers who can learn from and develop our experience.

CONCLUSION

Personal and professional development, in this context, is a very broad agenda: it lasts a lifetime and depends on definitions of social work and its functions. It can be undermined by ideology (for example, the emphasis on technical competence or managerialism), a lack of access (by gender, class or ethnicity), a lack of organisational support and reward, and a lack of resources including time.

This chapter focuses on themes of self-awareness, reflection and critical self-evaluation which underpin both personal and professional development, and not on models of development involving discrete technical competences because social work is a complex, uncertain and value-based activity in which we work with people from different backgrounds who are likely to have experienced structural oppression, discrimination, personal difficulty, loss or tragedy. Despite the barriers identified, we owe it to our users and clients to maintain our personal and professional development and thereby contribute to the development and improvement of the social work practice and services they receive.

FURTHER READING

Brown, A. and Bourne, I. (1996) *The Social Work Supervisor: Supervision in Community, Day Care and Residential Settings* (Buckingham, Open University Press). This book, although focusing on supervision, is invaluable in drawing attention to issues of professional development and support for social workers and potential blocks to them.

Carter, P., Jeffs, T. and Smith, M.K. (1995) *Social Working* (Basingstoke, Macmillan – now Palgrave Macmillan). This edited collection of chapters by practising social workers identifies major issues in professional development by analysing social work practice from the perspective of experienced social workers, including the main processes: a 'hands-on' approach to examining and articulating practice and learning from it.

Eraut, M. (1994) *Developing Professional Knowledge and Competence* (London, Falmer). This book contains a valuable multidisciplinary analysis of issues in professional development and pressures which deal with complexity.

Shaw, I. and Lishman, J. (eds) (1999) *Evaluation and Social Work Practice* (London, Sage). This book presents critically a range of ways of evaluating social work practice, arguing that evaluation should not be just *applied* to practice but should be a direct *dimension* of practice.

Yelloly, M. and Henkel, M. (1995) *Learning and Teaching in Social Work: Towards Reflective Practice* (London, Jessica Kingsley). This edited collection addresses issues in the post-professional education of social workers and related professionals, examining the concepts of professionalism, competence, knowledge and anti-racism, with an emphasis on how professionals learn and maintain a self-critical and reflective approach to practice.

10

Research and Development in Social Work

Angela Everitt

Introduction

Social work has long had a somewhat ambivalent relationship with research. Concerns have been expressed that practitioners do not read research, do not inform their practice with findings from research, do not influence decisions on what is researched, do not commission research and do not undertake research themselves. There is not space in this one chapter to consider all these issues. Instead, taking account of recent policy initiatives, the chapter suggests some approaches to research and development that might be particularly relevant for social work. In this, social work is understood as a professional activity wherein practitioners engage in their craft to contribute to policy and practice with a view to reducing inequalities in society and ameliorating the local and personal effects of these.

Enhancing research in practice

A range of initiatives have been introduced in recent years to enhance the relevance of research to policy and practice development. Some, such as the practitioner-research programmes at York University (Whitaker and Archer, 1989) and the Social Work Research Centre at Stirling University (Fuller and Petch, 1995), focus upon providing opportunities for social workers to undertake small-scale research relevant to their practice. Others, such as the Joseph Rowntree Foundation, in its publication of *Findings*, and *Research Matters*, published twice a year by the magazine *Community Care*, concentrate on making the findings of research accessible to practitioners. Still others take the form of action-research projects, such as the Department of Health's pilot scheme, set up in 1995 with social services departments in the southwest of England, designed to promote the use of research findings in practice and involve practitioners in identifying needs for research.

The state of research in health and the personal social services was the focus of two working groups established by the Department of Health: the Smith review of personal social services' research reported in June 1994 (Smith, 1994) and the Culyer review of NHS research the following October (Culyer, 1994). Both were prompted partly by concerns about how research and development would fare in the market economy of health and social care. With purchaser–provider changes in the organisation of services, and short-termism in funding and projects, questions were being asked on where and by whom research and development would be undertaken. It was thought that research and development might well diminish, with purchasers attracted by the cheapest and providers driven to reducing costs. Furthermore, a decline in local government research was anticipated as unitary authorities disappeared and others struggled with depleted budgets. Both reviews, acknowledging the gap between research, policy and practice, emphasised the importance of the usefulness, relevance and ownership of research by those expected to be influenced by findings. Both recommended that practitioners should feel ownership of research, be involved in deciding what should be researched and take part in dissemination and implementation exercises. They should be trained to be research literate, and researchers should have a clear responsibility to make research findings accessible. Links between health and personal social services, and other services such as education, should be fostered and partnerships introduced for commissioning and conducting research across professional and organisational boundaries. The Culyer Report recommended that more attention be paid to health research in primary and community health. Both reviews recommended that research and development strategies be developed nationally, regionally and across the personal social services and the health service.

Considerable attention has been paid to developing research-based and informed practice with children in care. Indeed, there is some evidence that the Children Act 1989 was itself informed by research (Harwin, 1990). Attention has been paid to making childcare research findings accessible to practitioners (Kahan, 1989; DoH, 1995a, 1996, 2001c). The development of research-informed practice (Parker et al., 1991; Ward, 1995) is key to the Department of Health-funded research and development project *Looking After Children: Good Parenting, Good Outcomes* (DoH, 1995b). This is concerned with assessing outcomes in childcare work and developing practical instruments, action and assessment records. These records, for social workers to complete with children in care, are intended to ensure that childcare research findings inform practice, work with children in care is pursued systematically, data are generated for departmental review and monitoring purposes as well as comparatively across social services departments, and the child growing up in care is able to capture her or his own history. Similar to structured questionnaires, they comprise questions derived from research findings on good parenting which social workers are expected to build into their ongoing conversations with children and young people in their care.

At first sight, to the researcher, the *Looking after Children* project is impressive. It is systematic and meticulous, and care has been taken to include every detail important to the child in care. It has attracted a wealth of expertise from research units and university social work departments, and is being adopted widely by social services departments and social welfare organisations in other countries. It is interesting and innovatory in its approach to bridging the gap between research and practice. However, it is through this very gap that the project could fall into technical and unthinking ways of working. Whereas some practitioners may, and undoubtedly do, adopt the action and assessment records as valuable instruments for research and professional practice, others may merely engage in it, or alternatively resist it, as yet more of the procedural form-filling that has replaced so much professional practice.

New managerialism in health and welfare has been accompanied, even strengthened, by an array of what might be seen as research and development activities: monitoring, evaluation, inspection, performance review, output and outcome measurement, and evidence-based practice. While the central assumption of this chapter is that social work practice, and the policy context in which it operates, should be systematically subjected to the scrutiny of research and developed to take account of evidence of effectiveness, there is little doubt that these recent initiatives are experienced as a part of increasing managerial control. Rather than approaches designed to enquire into, and ensure the effectiveness of, policies, procedures and practices, they can be more like technical intrusions into what should be professional practice:

> The extravagance of professional expertise was to be replaced by a range of review techniques including quality assurance, clinical audit, performance indicators in various forms and guises. Much of this scrutiny was external to the professions concerned and seen as a direct attack on clinical autonomy. (Rafferty and Traynor, 1997: 17)

This technical recording of practice has been exacerbated in social services through departmental defensiveness in the wake of child abuse inquiries and the evidence of abuse experienced by children and adults in their care. It can serve to prevent or obscure the interrogation of professional practice, particularly through the public pretence that services and practices are informed by research. Professional practice must be subject to rigorous scrutiny and public debate, and should itself be concerned with opening up social services and policies to such processes. What is important in professional practice, and in closing the gap between research and practice, is that social work practitioners are research-minded (Everitt et al., 1992). This is a necessary condition not only for doing research and implementing research findings in practice, but also for ensuring that practice makes a difference for people in trouble. As Utting reminds us:

> To get the best out of research you need an inquiring mind, the desire to improve performance and a critical and sceptical intelligence ... Research is a means, not an end in itself – a tool with which to improve and perfect one's business, whether this be making policy, managing services or working face to face with people: it is not a machine which dispenses neat answers on cardboard squares. (Utting, 1989)

The process of researching is one of questioning, generating and being open to evidence. It is about teasing out values and theoretical assumptions with a preparedness to engage in debate with those who may interpret the evidence differently. It contrasts with polemic, rhetoric and common sense. It disrupts routine and procedure. There is now quite a research literature available for social workers on undertaking research and reading published research critically (for example, Whitaker and Archer, 1989; Everitt et al., 1992; Broad and Fletcher, 1993; Shakespeare et al., 1993; Hart and Bond, 1995). Indeed, the literature on research methods for practitioners generally, teachers (for example, Altrichter et al., 1993; Burgess, 1993), nurses (for example, Sapsford and Abbott, 1992) and leisure (for example, Veal, 1992) is quite considerable, indicating that the problem is with the relationship between research and practice generally rather than with social work in particular.

In nursing, a large part of the problem is attributed to the power of members of the medical profession (Rafferty and Traynor, 1997). It is not only that they decide on research priorities and claim the major slice of the research resource, but also that they set the prevailing ideas of what constitutes respectable and credible research. This has led to a predominance of randomised control trials with little acknowledgment of the value of smaller-scale studies yielding qualitative data. At the same time, claims that qualitative studies are more likely to contribute to social change must be treated with caution. We only have to compare the detailed large-scale studies of poverty and health that have been undertaken over long periods of time (for example, Townsend et al., 1988) with the one hundred and one case studies of people successfully making their journeys back from long-term unemployment (Booth and Mallon, 1994) or with the current prevalence of focus groups falsely occupying the space of research and consultation (Preston, 1996) to be rightly sceptical of seemingly genuine stories of people's lives and concerns. The underlying issue here is power. Processes that are dressed up as research, and come to be accepted as such, are powerful in that they produce knowledge that is thought to be credible, to be 'true'. It is important to be critical, not only of professional practice, but also of research and knowledge, and to be mindful of the ways in which some explanations and understandings come to be thought of as 'true'. Such truths may serve to maintain the status quo and continue and strengthen oppressive practices.

Theory and practice in research

The *Wider Strategy for Research and Development relating to Personal Social Services* (Smith, 1994) adopts the official definition of research as used by government in its research policy and funding strategies. It separates 'basic research' (that is, 'experimental or theoretical work ... to acquire new knowledge') from 'strategic research' (that is, research that is applied but where no specific applications have been identified) and 'applied research' (that is, 'to acquire new knowledge' but 'directed primarily towards practical aims and objectives').

For social work, the distinction which separates theory from practice is unhelpful. It feeds into practices that do not enhance social science's potential contribution to the amelioration of social problems and the reduction in social inequalities. One effect, for example, of the 'basic' and 'applied' split is the hierarchy that can develop between those who, in elitist and prestigious ways, regard themselves as social science theorists looking down upon those in more applied academic areas and probably not noticing practitioners at all. On the one hand, this serves to let such social scientists off the hook: in the position they adopt they have no need to ensure that their research makes a difference to 'private troubles and public issues' and accept no responsibility for this. On the other hand, it promotes in social workers anti-theoretical and anti-academic feelings, voiced as 'they're out of touch', 'not engaged in the real world', 'irrelevant'. This finds expression in social services departments and social welfare projects where there is no time to research, even to read, in order to reflect upon what is happening in practice and to keep up to date with developing knowledges.

In the 1970s, these tendencies separating theory from practice were noted by social theorists and those engaged with radical social work. Alas, Gouldner's opening lines are as relevant today as they were then:

> Social theorists today work within a crumbling social matrix of paralyzed urban centres and battered campuses. Some may put cotton in their ears, but their bodies still feel the shock waves. It is no exaggeration to say that we theorise today within the sound of guns. (Gouldner, 1970: vii)

Cohen, reflecting on his encounters with social workers, wrote thus:

> the most familiar reaction we encounter is encapsulated in the phrase (often quite explicitly used): 'it's all right for you to talk.' The implication is that, however interesting, amusing, correct and even morally uplifting our message might be, it is ultimately a self-indulgent intellectual exercise, a luxury which cannot be afforded by anyone tied down by the day-to-day demands of a social-work job. (Cohen, 1975: 76)

Gouldner and Cohen had in mind the radical activist, the practitioner with an urgency to change and a commitment to 'the tangible outcomes of pragmatic politics' rather than 'the intangible outputs of theory' (Gouldner, 1970: vii). Today, practitioners are often more likely to be concerned with the measurable outcomes of depoliticised practices as they follow departmental and govern-mental rules, guidance and procedural manuals. Their haste is more likely to be to be generated by a concern to get home, away from their alienating, under-resourced, overburdened and ill-regarded places of work.

In contrast, the field of disability politics provides a positive illustration of the coming together of academics and activists. Here, disabled academics have been significant in changing understandings of disability, through theorising, research and personal experiences. Shakespeare (1996) has pointed out that, in the disability movement, academic interventions are closely related to the ongoing struggles of disabled people, social theories of disability arising from the wider political movement of disabled people in the 1990s. Retheorising disability was necessary to social change. People such as Oliver (1990) and Morris (1991) alerted us to ways in which research had shaped how we thought of disabled people within medical labels and categories. Disability was individualised, disabled people pathologised, subjected to treatment, sympathy and charity. Particular professional groups became experts in knowing better about their needs than disabled people themselves, telling them how they should behave, what they should expect from life, how they should feel and how they might improve. Social theorists such as Oliver (1990) conceptualised disability as social, to do with restrictive environments and disabling barriers, rather than to do with individual failure and personal tragedy. This social model of disability disrupted the medical model to become adopted by disabled people's organisations such as the Union of the Physically Impaired Against Segregation. It allowed the experiences of disabled people to be articulated and heard. There is not the space here for all the empirical data, or the massive social changes, that have arisen through disabled people bringing together theory, research and practice. It serves, however, as an exemplar for research and development throughout social work. It is not a rational, technical model wherein research findings are fed into policy and practice, where, unless the status quo is socially and/or economically ready for a change, they will hit stony ground (Pahl, 1992). It is a political model of praxis.

It is important that research and development in social work is understood as a process of praxis involving the theorising of practice and the development of theory through practice. The term 'praxis' is used, as in Stanley, to adopt:

> a political position in which 'knowledge' is not simply defined as 'knowledge *what*' but also as 'knowledge *for*'. Succinctly the point is to change the world, not only to study it ... [and to engage in] a social science endeavour which rejects the 'theory/research' divide, seeing these as united manual and intellectual activities. (Stanley, 1990: 15)

Praxis involves a commitment to understanding in order to take action, a recognition that understanding comes through engagement and debate with others, and a preparedness, through deliberation, to make judgements about 'the good'.

Critical social research

In taking seriously research and development for 'good' practice, practitioners must consider carefully the kinds of research likely to be useful to them and users of their services that will accord with anti-discriminatory practice. This requires an understanding of theories of knowledge and theories of methods, of epistemology and methodology:

> Epistemology is the study of theories of knowledge. What is knowledge? What can we know about the social world? Who can become knowledgeable? What do we choose to know? These are important epistemological and methodological questions. (Everitt et al., 1992: 6)

The prevailing view of both research and policy development assumes processes imbued with objectivity, neutrality and rationality. Bulmer presents this view wherein:

The task of social research is to provide as precise, reliable and generalisable factual information as possible ... This information, when fed into the policy-making process, will enable policy-makers ... to reach the best decisions on the basis of the information available. (Bulmer, 1982: 31)

The Seebohm Committee, which recommended the establishment of research sections in the new social services departments, talked in similar terms: suggesting that 'better decisions depend on better information' (Seebohm Committee, 1968).

This 'objective' approach is informed by a particular understanding of research (how we come to know about the social world) and development (how we intervene to bring about change). Here, 'research' and 'development' are seen as separate functions, research informing development. It is an understanding which assumes objectivity in both the research process and the policy process. Research is understood as an activity undertaken under conditions controlled to ensure objectivity as far as possible. It demands and produces expertise and requires considerable time and resources. The 'scientific method' of such research separates it from policy and practice processes and researchers work from the 'outside', usually located in universities and central government research institutes and centres, but increasingly in private consultancy agencies. This is a top-down model: policy is expected to be informed by research, practice to be informed by policy.

This supposed objectivity in social research is used to justify particular approaches to policy research that bear little resemblance to research as an enquiring activity involving the critical scrutiny of assumptions, values, policies and practices. As already noted in this chapter, research undertaken technically in the form of feasibility studies, monitoring and evaluative studies now accompanies policy initiatives almost as a matter of routine. These are often expedient activities in the name of research to put on a public show that something is being done, and indeed the funding mechanisms of the marketplace, where outputs are purchased from public, voluntary and private providers, have spawned a considerable 'research' industry in monitoring and evaluation. This may be valuable in providing work for academics, freelancers and private consultants, and in justifying the continuing existence of projects and programmes, but will have done little to bring about much-needed research-informed developments designed to tackle inequalities (Everitt, 1995).

The 'objective' approach to research and development purports that researched knowledge, together with research processes for generating and according credibility to knowledge, is value-free. However, that this very supposition is so generally accepted is itself highly political. Research and policy processes are depoliticised, making both seem rational and disguising the presence and exercise of power. The work of critical social scientists, feminists and members of other new social movements provides social work with credible alternatives that recognise research *and* development as political activities. To suppose that they are not, to fail to reveal the political nature of research, is to leave the prevailing bias of our society untouched and closed to questioning and debate, a bias that is sexist, homophobic, racist, classist, ageist and disablist. The values, assumptions and cultural beliefs of those who shape the research and development agenda, who raise the research questions and who, through observation and interaction, seek data to answer these questions are influential in research and development processes. Unless particularly addressed, the world will continue only to be known through the lenses of those with power and resources. As Harding argues, the perspectives and beliefs of researchers and those who determine the research agenda should be treated, like data, as evidence:

> open to critical scrutiny ... Introducing this 'subjective' element into the analysis in fact increases the objectivity of research and decreases the 'objectivism' which hides this kind of evidence from the public. (Harding, 1987: 9)

Thus, feminists and other critical researchers attempt to be clear, with themselves and others, about the standpoint from which they understand the world. Furthermore, attention is paid to researcher/researched relations and to the researched becoming researchers so that those usually objectified through research have the opportunity to articulate, become conscious of and develop understandings of their own experiences. Value is placed on revealing and acknowledging the experiences of researchers and the researched, while, at the same time, experience is not treated as unproblematic. It needs to be theorised to understand ways in which it is shaped through structures and processes (Maynard, 1994).

Analysing research as a powerful process, and understanding its power to produce knowledge regarded as credible, raises a number of questions. How do phenomena and people come to be known, identified and categorised in particular ways? Who falls into which categories and with what effect? What views are respected and whose are not? Who decides what should be researched, what questions should be answered, how and by whom? As we have noted from the reviews of research in the personal social services and the NHS (Culyer, 1994; Smith, 1994), government has in recent years turned its attention to such questions and introduced a number of policy initiatives designed to shape research and development. These are now explored a little more to bring them to the attention of practitioners who might be able to shift the research and development agenda towards addressing social problems and inequalities.

Users and beneficiaries of social work research

The White Paper *Realising our Potential* (Cabinet Office/Office of Public Service and Science/Office of Science and Technology, 1993) emphasised the need for government-funded research to produce useful knowledge. Focusing upon science, engineering and technology, the White Paper probably escaped the notice of social work. Yet it has had considerable influence upon the ways in which research priorities are set in all fields, including the social sciences and health and social care. It recommended that decisions about what to research should be made through partnerships of academics, professionals, industrialists and government, and that research designs should take account of those intended to benefit or take account of research findings.

Following the White Paper, all research councils which fund research were required to change their charters, policies and procedures. The Economic and

Social Research Council is now committed to funding social science research that is likely to enhance economic competitiveness and public welfare. Each year, it prioritises themes for research. It does this through consultation exercises with learned societies, universities and 'users of research in government, business, public life and the media' (Economic and Social Research Council, 1996) and in response to the government's Technology Foresight Sector Panels. These panels of partners forecast research priorities for sectors of society including, for example, health and life sciences, and leisure and education (Office of Science and Technology, 1994).

There are two key themes within these research and development policy developments: useful research and users of research. The policy changes clearly indicate that research should only be funded from public money if it is seen (by whom?) as potentially useful. Furthermore, those who are expected to make use of research should be involved in deciding on research priorities. It is these same themes that were confirmed and strengthened for social work and social care by the research and development reviews (Culyer, 1994; Smith, 1994). The final section of this chapter will briefly explore these themes for their meaning for research and development in social work.

An awareness of the relationship between knowledge and power, and a recognition of the success of the New Right in shaping our thoughts, language and curricula for learning, should make us sceptical of the emphasis upon partnership in determining research agendas. It fits more with Conservative political mechanisms that have served to control the autonomy, creativity and critical thinking of academics and professionals than it does with notions of democracy in science and knowledge. Writers in the field of adult education distinguish 'useful knowledge' from 'really useful knowledge' (Hughes, 1995). They have reminded us of the Society for the Diffusion of Useful Knowledge set up in the early years of industrialisation to provide workers with knowledge useful to the emerging economy (Kelly, 1962). This 'useful' knowledge was contrasted with 'really useful knowledge', which:

> meant knowledge that sought to make sense of the causes of hardship and oppression in working-class people's lives ... must help to make sense of intolerable circumstances with a view to their challenge. (Hughes, 1995: 99)

Evidence-based social work is one response to the requirement that practice should be informed by research evaluating effectiveness. Yet, evidence-based approaches may be based on a relatively restricted view of the kinds of experimental research which is authoritative. For example, they may take note of traditional experimental research based on random controlled trials and ignore qualitative research. Evidence-based approaches have a contribution to make to better practice, but should themselves be regarded critically, as Webb convincingly argues (Webb, 2001). On a broader front, qualitative research, informed by critical feminist perspectives, makes an invaluable contribution to progressing social work theory and practice in key areas such as domestic violence (Taylor-Browne, 2000) and gender issues in community care (Orme, 2001). Social workers should be active in influencing research agendas to ensure that all that they learn of the intolerable conditions of poverty and racism through their daily practice is exposed and understood. Practitioners have important roles as 'social investigators' (Sinfield, 1969) to reveal the harmful effects of structures and policies such that some people live in fear in their own homes and neighbour-hoods without the means to participate as full members of our society and without hope for the future.

Scrutiny of policy and practice does not, however, exclude the practice of social workers themselves. Power is exercised through all our practices, including research, and to be research-minded is to be constantly alert to the ways in which our talk, our assessments, our inspections and our behaviours affect others. For example, research on user and carer participation in needs assessment reveals a lack of dialogue with users and carers (Ellis, 1993) and, as Utting points out in his foreword to the research report:

> Occupations which trade on non-judgementalism are shown to be as moralistic in their approach as any lay person. The ways in which some workers discouraged 'dependency' should impress the most fervent advocate of Victorian values, and shows that the Poor Law is alive and kicking nearly 50 years after its official internment. (Utting, 1993: 3)

The research demonstrates examples of good practice but also reveals 'stereo-typed responses ... [and a] lack of creativity' (Ellis, 1993: 7). If social work is concerned with challenging the discriminatory contexts of the lives of users and of their own practice, then to be enquiring and critical is essential in the repertoire of practice skills. As Utting forcefully points out, the assumptions that social workers can and do make about policies, resources and values would often not stand up to rigorous questioning and scrutiny, and serve to discriminate against users of social services. Furthermore, while social workers engage in anti-oppressive talk, speaking the correct words, any critical analysis of their practice might well reveal a totally different reality.

Empowerment and participation are ideas associated with important contrib-utions of principle and practice in the fields of social research and social develop-ment (Nelson and Wright, 1995). The word 'participation' can be regarded as rhetorical or as expressing a real commitment to involving people. Traditionally, programmes, projects and research into their effectiveness originated in goals and standards imposed by outsiders with little attempt to match them to people's local wishes and needs. A paradigm shift took place where workers began to prioritise people designing and running their own projects and carrying out the evaluation research themselves. New paradigm or collaborative research develops the idea that the people researched are coopted as collaborating researchers who join the research before the goals are set and the methods and methodologies are discussed (Reason and Rowan, 1981). Participatory research and development is associated with the aim of achieving sustainable development in social development projects in many countries (Chambers, 1995).

In reflecting on the users of research in social work, it is perhaps helpful to distinguish between users and beneficiaries. In participating in research and development, through setting research agendas, commissioning and undertaking research, social workers themselves should be users of research for the benefit of those who use, or are likely to use, their services. They should also, however, develop ways of providing opportunities for users of social services to become users of research in their own right. Feminists, disability researchers and action-research approaches have demonstrated the potential value, to both knowledge and action, in people becoming knowledgeable about their own lives. Hopefully, having read this chapter, you will know that this makes sense theoretically, politically and professionally.

FURTHER READING

Broad, B. and Fletcher, C. (eds) (1993) *Practitioner Social Work Research in Action* (London, Whiting & Birch). A useful collection of articles giving examples of research by practitioners having a real effect on practice and policy.

Everitt, A., Hardiker, P., Littlewood, J. and Mullender, A. (1992) *Applied Research for Better Practice* (Basingstoke, Macmillan – now Palgrave Macmillan). A helpful introduction to research for improving practice, with an anti-oppressive focus.

Fuller R. and Petch A. (1995) *Practitioner-research: The Reflexive Social Worker* (Buckingham, Open University Press). A thoughtful guide to practice research.

Hart, E. and Bond, M. (1995) *Action Research for Health and Social Care: A Guide to Practice* (Buckingham, Open University Press). A useful guide to implementing research techniques as part of practice.

Sapsford, R. and Abbott, P. (1992) *Research Methods for Nurses and the Caring Professions* (Buckingham, Open University Press). Helpfully views research from a multidisciplinary focus.

Theories for Practice in Social Work

11

Social Work Theories and Reflective Practice

Malcolm Payne

Introduction: reflecting on reflecting

The first part of this book has presented ideas about the nature of social work and the social and political world in which social workers operate. As Part I has shown, we need to approach such ideas critically because many of them are in debate. Understanding the purposes and context of our work does not, therefore, give us any easy answers, and we must find ways of connecting our knowledge and understanding of society, policy and people with the actions we will take as social workers. Part II examines some examples of important and well-known 'practice theories' which seek to explain in organised ways how social workers may usefully act, using their knowledge about the social world in which they operate. Practice theories are no less debated than the material considered in Part I, so we have to come to a view, as practitioners, not only about the most helpful knowledge of the social world to use, but also what ideas we can use to apply that knowledge to the particular social and interpersonal situations we are dealing with. If we are to practise from this knowledge and theory, we must have ways of thinking which turn thinking into practice action. Reflection is a way of doing this.

Reflective practice has become increasingly important in the 1990s and now has a central place in the relationship of theory to practice. This is partly because the critique of social work practice theories from the 'evidence-based' position has sought to promote only a limited range of practice that can be empirically tested. However, the social work task is too complex and the demands made of social workers too variable to be restricted in this way. With its connections to critical practice (see the companion book to this one, *Critical Practice in Social Work*,

Adams et al., 2002), reflective practice offers an apparently rigorous way of working, without the stringencies of evidence-based practice. Connections to ideas of reflexivity, important in research and feminist thinking, make links to current ideological concerns and offer interesting insights into implementing reflectiveness (Taylor and White, 2000; Healy, 2000). Reflection seems the answer to handling the range of practice theories available: research by Marsh and Trisel-iotis (1996) has shown that social workers are critical of and confused by the profusion. Another attraction of reflective practice is the hope that it seems to hold out for personal professional development and the transfer of learning from one setting to another (Cree and Macaulay, 2001). Martyn (2001) argues that reflection can help people to make sense of the circumstances presented to social workers in complex situations, relating them to agency requirements. For similar reasons, reflective practice has become influential in health care professions (Bulman and Burns, 2000; Taylor, 2000).

Many hopes rest on reflective practice; therefore, we must ask if it can bear the strain. There are several different meanings of 'reflection' in social work and two concepts related to the idea of 'reflective practice'.

Meanings of reflection

Thinking issues through in all their complexity and acting towards clients and others in a considered, thoughtful manner is the common-sense meaning of reflection. It sometimes encourages a particular style of practice – slow, considered, thoughtful, thinking out all the angles, checking out all the details before taking the plunge. This has relationships with other important ideas in social work theory and practice, and with widely accepted views about the role of social workers. Reflection in this sense connects with study and diagnosis. Modern social work practice replaces the medical associations of these terms with ideas such as 'assessment', but the implication remains of trying to put together a full picture of what difficulties a client faces from a multitude of different pieces of evidence, some of which might not be immediately obvious. Very often, this is a formal responsibility of social workers, for example when they write pre-sentence reports for courts or carry out community care assessments for clients needing packages of services. It means not only reflecting on what is apparent or what is said in the early stages, but also looking for clues to important issues from many different and possibly insubstantial sources.

Boud and Knights (1996), drawing on their previous work, describe a three-phase process of reflection: returning to an experience, attending to feelings connected with the experience and re-evaluating the experience through recognising its implications and outcomes. They include the ideas of reflection-in-action, that is, while events are going on, and reflection afterwards. Inevitably, in their view, reflection must be grounded in our personal experiences, which have shaped us as a thinker, and our objectives. They give importance to attention, that is, noticing and applying our minds to particular events. Experience helps us to identify when particular aspects of a situation are important.

Being a 'reflective practitioner', according to the ideas of Donald Schön, is a more complex way of understanding reflection, based in the ideas of pragmatic philosophies, which see education as concerned with practical problem-solving (Ixer, 1999). These ideas similarly influenced Perlman's (1957) social work theories. Schön argued that some professions deal with work (such as building bridges) which use 'technical rationality'; that is, you can calculate through mathematics and scientific thinking exactly what the consequences of your decisions and actions will be (and so be sure that the bridge will not fall down when you have completed it). Schön thought that some kinds of work deal with such complex and variable situations that complete technical rationalism is impossible. Theories in this kind of work offer guidelines for action in the average daily situation, rather than complete rules about what to do. When we come across something new, complex or out-of-the-ordinary, this causes us to stop, think over our guidelines and amend them. Thus, our guidelines (theories) grow every time we deal with a yet more complicated bit of human life, but they will never cover everything.

The implication of Schön's ideas are that people doing jobs such as this (for example teaching and social work) should be educated to expect that their theories and guidelines will only help them so far. We should learn how to identify when existing theories are not helpful enough and should be trained in techniques of reflecting on situations and theory together so as to develop theories further. His particular concern is education for such techniques, and several of his examples use a supervisor, as in social work, for an exploring and questioning discussion. He describes reflection (Schön, 1983: 76–104) as having 'a reflective conversation with the situation'. Issues in our work are reframed into different kinds of problem, so that an alternative way of dealing with them can be worked out. Gould (1996) describes this as 'imaginisation', that is, creating images in our mind of the problems that we are dealing with. In Schön's view, we argue out the implications of our new approach, leaving it open to rethink our rethinking if our new premise does not seem to work. We bring past experience to bear on new unique situations and try out a rigorous 'on-the-spot experiment' to see whether our ideas work.

Schön emphasised that reflection takes place in a 'virtual world' (1983: 157–62) of our own constructions about the problem and possible answers to it; it is not reality and action itself. He takes it for granted, however, that professionals would agree about the most appropriate way of reflecting and the most appropriate outcome and that we are dealing with rational processes which can be understood and explained. In social work, and probably in most other professions, there are different points of view which could be taken about similar situations, and legitimate debate about appropriate professional responses. These points of view and debates are represented by different practice theories, explored in Part II, which suggest different ways in which social workers may interpret and react to the situations they face.

The third, still more complex, idea about reflection comes from Mattinson's (1975) work. She shows, in a study of social work supervision, that social workers very often *reflect their relationships* with their clients in their behaviour towards their supervisor. So if a client is frightened of getting things wrong, and becomes dependent on their social worker, always coming for advice and guidance before doing the simplest thing, the social worker will start doing this, in an out-of-character way, with their supervisor, too. This is also common sense if you think about (reflect – in the first sense – on) it. You, the social worker, are being presented with everything in a complicated life and have to advise someone who is worried about what to do. As a result, you take on all the pressure of being worried. Therefore, you lose some of your own self-confidence, passing on to your supervisor some of the pressure and also, probably unwittingly, some feeling of what the relationship you are dealing with is like. In working with clients, you can use this idea that your relationship with them reflects their relationship with others. If a mother, for example, is making you feel anxious because she is very dependent on you and demanding, this might be a clue to how she experiences her daughter's dependence on her. So, again, being reflective about how you feel about your client as part of what is going on can cause you to think and do something about how she is feeling about her daughter. This view of reflection comes from the psychoanalytic idea of transference which suggests that the nature of relationships with important people in our past influences current important relationships.

These three meanings of being reflective emphasise the point that it is not enough as a social worker to travel along guidelines and conventions. Schön (1983) suggests that much of the time this will be satisfactory. However, any situation may need us to develop and change our guidelines, responding to new aspects of the work and social circumstances that we meet. We must look underneath the surface relationship and events which are presented to us. At any time we may need to think again and think differently. Because this kind of flexibility is the essence of dealing with any human being and being effective in working on complex human problems, critical awareness and reflection is an important practical implementation of the social work value of respecting human individuality and rights.

However, it is not divorced from the real world in which we practise. Jones and Joss (1995) incorporate the idea of reflective observation into Kolb's model (1984) of experiential learning. We have a concrete experience, which we observe and reflect on, construct new ideas about and then experiment, leading us to have a further concrete experience about which we can reflect. This model emphasises the importance of using observation (Briggs, 1995), that is, testing our reflection against what we see and experience, not allowing it to become divorced from, and indeed enabling it to build upon, the real world which we experience. Reid (1994) expands Kolb's model using Gibbs's 'reflective cycle', where we start from description (what happened?), and move to feelings (what were you thinking and feeling?), evaluation (what was good and bad about the experience?), analysis (how can you make sense of what happened?), conclusions (what alternatives did you have?) and an action plan (what would you do if it happened again?).

In summary, then, we can see reflection as taking place in our minds both as we act (reflection-in-action) and afterwards as we think about and try to understand the events we have experienced (reflection-on-action). Reflection implies attending to particular situations, and using observation, imagining alternative ways of understanding those situations (imaginising and reframing). Reflection, then, leads us to experiment with alternative approaches which eventually become incorporated into our ways of thinking and acting in social work. Practice theories, such as those reviewed in Part II, help us to express and identify those alternative approaches in models of practice which we might use when we act as social workers.

Two related concepts

Reflexivity is easily confused with reflectiveness. It means the circular process by which our thoughts affect our actions, which affect the situation we are dealing with and therefore offer feedback through the reactions of others involved, which can affect how we understand and think about the situation. This sets off another cycle in which our thoughts affect our actions. Circularity is important because social work is active. We do not just think and assess but act on the situations we deal with. Reflexivity means that we constantly get evidence about how effective or worthwhile our actions are, and we can change what we are doing according to the evidence of its value. To do so, of course, requires being reflective, because we have to be constantly alert to the possibility that what we are doing needs to change and we have to keep our minds open to changing according to the evidence we see about the effect we are having. Thus, reflexivity gives reflection a chance to work.

There are, however, broader implications to reflexivity. In research, the idea is used to draw attention to the way in which the researcher's presence and involvement affects the situations being investigated. A researcher is never a neutral inquirer. Neither, of course, are social workers, because the whole point of social work is that their involvement helps to achieve change, individual or social or both. Taylor and White (2000) argue that by a detailed understanding of the evidence about how interactions with people have effects, we may build up a more flexible and broadly applicable base for understanding and action than specific evidence-based practice theories can offer. These ideas also help to emphasise how the experience of social work will change the worker, and how interpersonal practice experiences can help to build the knowledge to apply in broader social and political action, to make the personal become political.

Praxis is a Marxist term which takes this idea a little further. It emphasises that our thoughts and the circular reflexive process are affected by our ideology, that is, what we believe the social world is like and how we think it should be. Our ideology causes us to think and therefore act with particular objectives. This interacts with the world, and praxis proposes that we should allow the evidence of how the world is to reform and affect our beliefs. Marxist ideas emphasise the importance of using praxis to experience the inequality and oppression in the world that we deal with, so as to strengthen our ideology of opposition and desire to work effectively within the world to change it.

The ideas of reflexivity and praxis emphasise how our thoughts interact with practice to affect clients and service users, and how their reactions and experience come to affect our own view of the world and our thoughts. Reflection, then, is one of the processes through which clients participate in social work. We are forced by our experience of their world and problems to *think* carefully about their experiences and respond to them. Social work does not impose a set of prescriptions on clients. Instead, it reacts to clients and the world in which they live, and it does so through reflection. All three meanings of reflection are involved: thinking things through, questioning our guidelines and developing our theories to respond to new situations, and understanding how our relationships with clients reflect their own experiences and relationships and give us access to how they are experiencing the world.

However, there are some aspects of using theory and knowledge in an organised way which the idea of reflection does not help us with. In the first place, reflection in 'reflective practice' takes place almost in a social vacuum. It is often assumed that the issues that we consider will easily arise out of the problems that we face, that our assessment of clients and their situation will inevitably raise the issues that we must reflect on. Many people find, to the contrary, that it is difficult to identify and criticise our own actions and raise broader issues for social change or our own professional development from them. In this way, focusing on reflection may be oppressive, because it leads to a lack of clarity both for workers and clients, which may allow prejudiced attitudes to intrude. We can be interested in the ideas raised in Part I, but find it hard to identify them when they arise in everyday situations. Second, it is unclear what the process of reflection actually is and how it connects with the practice theories that we want to use. Practice theories are supposed to convert our understanding of the social world and our assessment of the client into ideas for usable action, but we have to integrate our general understanding and our assessment into a view of the situation to which the practice theory can be applied. It is this process that the various chapters in Part II examine. Third, this action must take place in a set of services geared to a range of social needs and organisations; these services are explored in Part III. The remaining commentary in this chapter is therefore concerned to provide a model of the use of reflection in the context of social work practice, first through understanding the aims of social work that we are taking up in our practice, then through understanding how we can reflect on practice theories as we work and finally through integrating knowledge about the social world from Part I in our thinking. We can take this capacity for reflection forward into practice within particular social work services which are considered in Part III.

Reflecting on the social work role

The starting point of using practice theory lies not in the theories themselves but in how we understand social work and its role in society. This is the same distinction that Shardlow (Chapter 3) makes between the narrow scope of social work ethics and mid-range or broad descriptions of the very nature of the thing we are doing. Practice theories are about *effective* behaviour with clients, just as values are about *ethical* behaviour with clients A theory cannot tell us how to be effective unless we can say what our aim is and therefore what direction we want to be effective in.

There are three basic views of the nature and role of social work (Payne, 1996a), the distinctions between them having some support in Harrison's (1991) research on how social workers decide what to do in particular cases. He found that social workers either had one typical approach to all their work based on one of these views, or used two or more in succession if their usual approach was not relevant.

Individualist-reformist views

These views see social work as providing services effectively to help individuals' personal problems and adjust well to the society around them. Dominelli, in Chapter 1, called these 'maintenance' and traditional views. Such practice is prevalent in most official agencies, whose job is to provide efficient social services to meet the needs of members of the public, sorting out their practical and emotional problems, getting other services to respond better to their needs and perhaps raising problems which affect a lot of people to improve the administration or provision of services. Workers would take their functions from the defined responsibilities and role of their agencies, using their interpersonal social work skills to implement a set of well-established conventions and approaches derived from agency policy or conventions of social work practice.

Care management to organise a package of community care services, or effective planning of a network of support to prevent parents from physically abusing their child, is a typical kind of service. Clients are dealt with mainly as individuals but perhaps in groups and in their community, particularly if, through community organisation, local people can get together to improve services through self-help or improving the general environment. This approach to social work recognises that, in complicated modern societies, many people may need help in hard times or if they are affected by longstanding problems. Individualist-reformist theories, such as task-centred or cognitive-behavioural work, set clear targets and involve the planning and delivery of services and personal help in an organised and focused way.

Reflexive-therapeutic views

These views see social work as helping individuals (and perhaps groups and communities) to achieve personal growth, self-actualisation and personal power over their environment, that is, to identify and fulfil satisfactorily their human wishes and needs. Dominelli, in Chapter 1, called these 'therapeutic' views. Personal growth and fulfilment not only increases the humanity of services and values the humanity of people in need, but also enables people to deal more effectively with the issues that face them. So, these views argue that individualist-reformist work, sorting out practical situations and teaching people skills (as in task-centred work) or providing services and checking up on behaviour, does not deal adequately with the fundamental problems of people who are struggling with disability or parenthood. Workers use models of practice such as psychosocial work and counselling to explore clients' views and understanding of their problems, to try to understand and help clients to gain insight into the complex social and psychological origins of the problems that they face and help them to plan new ways of responding to the challenges in their lives. They would develop a warm relationship with their client, using their personal skills to help the client feel valued and supported. Workers in these approaches would be non-directive, and they assume that the job is about releasing clients' own skills and capacities to achieve what they want.

For example, a colleague works with people dying of brain tumours. There are practical things to do in an individual-reformist way, such as sorting out disability benefits and helping the struggle against increasing illness at home. But there is more besides. She helps very frightened people die in dignity, helps their families prepare for and say goodbye at their death, and tries to set the still living on a path for satisfying relationships in the future.

In one case, she helped a West Indian mother dying at 29 with practical and social security matters and developed a relationship with several members of the family. After the death, the nine-year-old son refused to go to the funeral, and the family were very distressed about this. The day before the funeral, she took him to the church where the funeral would be, suggested that she could come with him, showed him where they might sit at the back out of everyone's view and suggested that, as an alternative, they might sit in the park opposite, so as to be there, if not actually in the church. They sat there, and he revealed that he did not want to go because he was embarrassed by the possibility of his aunts giving extravert displays of grief. She thought that he feared breaking down in tears himself. They agreed to sit in the park, and she accompanied him there on the day of the funeral. He decided to go into the church with her. She herself became tearful. This allowed the boy to cry with her. The family appreciated her commitment and help, and the genuineness of her emotion; also, no doubt, the boy was helped to grieve appropriately for his mother and this probably prevented or reduced emotional distress in the future.

Socialist-collectivist views

These views are transformational; in Chapter 1, Dominelli called them 'emancipatory'. That is, they propose that, rather than helping people to adjust to society to deal with their problems, we should change fundamental structures in society which are the origins of most people's problems. Society is organised so that some people are in groups, such as ethnic minorities, or people with disabilities, which are oppressed by inequalities with other groups and the resultant injustices. Often mere difference, as in gender inequalities, create oppression.

Using feminist, radical and anti-oppressive practice, workers engage in a dialogue of equals with clients to help them raise their consciousness of the ways in which their problems arise from inequality and oppression. The aim is to create cooperative alliances between people with shared problems and other organisations with concerns for injustice and inequality. Thus, people can gain experience of the effectiveness of working together to resolve their own problems, rather than being blamed for their own inadequacies and seen as 'a problem' or becoming alienated from others who share similar difficulties through developing their own personality and skills. Such experiences of cooperation can be empowering and help to overcome feelings of helplessness. Very often, such cooperative work can be successfully developed in particular localities and among groups with shared interests and is an integral part of community work.

For example, a young woman, Sandra, came to a women's refuge having been frequently beaten by her husband. Thinking she was alone and blaming herself for her husband's behaviour, she was surprised to find that many other women shared the same problem. Her husband found out where she was and other women kept him out of the house, much to Sandra' relief. She welcomed this mutual support and realised that, together, relatively powerless people could defend themselves. Eventually, Sandra was able to help others in similar crises before being rehoused in a different part of town. Some years later, Sandra was confident enough to be part of a group of women who described their own experiences to an audience of mainly men at a trade union conference, which sought to gain support for the refuge and the group that ran it, as well as making an influential group of men more aware of weaknesses in their 'macho' view of themselves. In this way, the women's group sought to make a contribution to changing the social expectations which led to violent patterns of behaviour among men.

Some people criticise socialist-collectivist views because it seems impractical for individual social workers, or even groups, to achieve sweeping social changes. However, such changes are often achieved through many small steps of progress, and socialist-collectivist ideologies help us to keep a long-term perspective in the daily pressure of small-scale events. Moreover, they avoid the tendency of individualist and therapeutic approaches to focus problems on individuals' failings, thus 'blaming the victim' of structural problems, rather than focusing on changing the root causes of difficulties.

Reflecting on the three views

These three views are opposed to each other, but also have something in common. Individualist and therapeutic approaches both focus on individuals and are thus often regarded as 'traditional' social work as opposed to 'radical' socialist views. Therapeutic views often criticise the inhumanity of individualist approaches and the tendency of socialists to focus on social change rather than meeting the human needs in front of them. Individualists criticise the socialist idea that social workers employed in an official agency might transform society. Reflexive-therapeutic work is also criticised by individualists for its unrealistic ambitions for personal changes through therapeutic means. Both socialist and therapeutic views criticise individualism for a lack of ambition and imagination about what might be possible and the prosaic, rather oppressive, methods of practice proposed.

In some cases, one view joins another to criticise a third, then joins with the third to criticise the former ally. Each of these views is part of a continuing discourse abut the priorities, objectives and value of social work which has been going on ever since it started (Payne, 1996a). None of them represents a complete view of social work. None of the oppositions among them is full-scale conflict. Aspects of otherwise bitterly critical views are shared: both therapeutic and socialist social work, for example, focus on insight and consciousness-raising.

Social work contains elements of all three views, and their influence and role is constantly varying and debated. Reflective practice requires us to interpret our role in the world and focus on the particular combination of elements that social work takes up in the situation before us. More widely, politicians, the public and the press constantly debate the role and value of particular occupational groups. Professional groups such as social work negotiate their role with others around them, such as nursing, teaching and medicine, in a constantly changing network of services, legislation, knowledge and value bases, educational and professional structures and clients' views and expectations. Since the role and pattern of social work is uncertain and debated, we inevitably have to reflect constantly on our actions. Practice theories provide organised statements about the world which help us to have our debates and carry forward our reflections with an agreed terminology and some aspects of shared understanding.

Using theory reflectively

Theories are sometimes presented, as in the chapters in Part II, as more or less complete perspectives on how we should try to understand the world or as models of how to respond to particular situations. Theories are said to explain and justify why particular perspectives or models are valuable to social workers. How do we identify which theory or theories to use, and how do we use them? In this section, we explore how we can reflect on theories as we apply them in three different ways: selectivity, eclecticism and critical engagement. Each of these ways of reflecting on theory tries to answer the question of whether it is realistically possible to understand and implement a wide range of theoretical ideas.

Selectivity

This approach to using theory proposes that we should select just one, or one group of related theories, and apply that to all the situations that we deal with. The advantage of this approach is that we can go into the ideas of the theory in depth, become comfortable and assured in applying them and act consistently throughout our work. There are, however, problems with this approach, both practical and theoretical.

Among the practical problems are that most social workers operate in (sometimes multidisciplinary) teams with others who may not share the particular theory they use, and the theory may not make sense to clients either. Many workers who operate selectively are supported in doing so because they work in agencies (for example psychiatric units or specialist centres such as women's refuges) where workers share a theoretical position, often in a fairly small group of people who work together consistently, as in a day or residential care setting.

The theoretical problems with selectivity lie in the difficulty of one theory extending into a wide range of different situations. Many theories, such as psychoanalytic or cognitive-behavioural theories, claim this possibility and some, including these examples, are extensively developed. However, it is often enthusiasts who claim this, and observers often consider that such theories are overstretched, overcomplex and hard to follow, or ignore large areas of work which their theory does not fit. For example, both of these examples are primarily therapeutic in character and do not deal well with the practical problems of people in poverty or suffering from racist abuse in an inner-city housing estate.

Eclecticism

The eclectic approach suggests *either* that workers should select aspects of different theories and use them together, perhaps all at once or perhaps successively, in a case *or* that workers should use different theories in different cases, depending on which is appropriate. Eclecticism enables different ideas to be brought to bear, helps to amalgamate social work theories when they make similar proposals for action, deals better with complex circumstances and allows workers to compensate for inadequacies in particular theories.

As with selectivity, however, there are theoretical and practical disadvantages. Workers may be unable to decide which set of ideas to select and how they should put them together. Also, it is difficult to know many complex theories well enough to take parts of them and use them appropriately. Social work theories may produce similar action proposals, but this often implies different ways of understanding issues. So, in contrast with the selective approach, eclecticism may confuse clients and workers by bringing together ideas in inconsistent patterns. Epstein (1992), therefore, proposes that eclecticism should be built up by continuing reflection, agreement and debate, and recommends doing this cooperatively in a team rather than encouraging individual flexibility from moment to moment in our practice. Approaches to reflective practice suggest using a mentor or supervision as a structure within which you can reflect carefully and critically (Taylor, 2000).

An important focus of eclecticism is systems theory (Pincus and Minahan, 1973). This biologically based perspective on practice emphasises working at different levels in society: the individual, the 'system' surrounding individuals and the more extensive systems which form a context for lower-level systems. This allows practice with agencies and other people and groups on behalf of clients to be theorised, and Roberts (1990) argues that systems theory was part of a trend in the 1970s to integrate many different aspects of social work into a generic form of practice. Systems theory's integration is at least partly eclectic, since it suggests that different theories might be used at different levels (for example therapeutic theories with individuals, radical theories with social systems) and with different systems (for example family therapy with a family, task-centred work with peer groups). Since it provides a model for analysing the different systems and levels with which workers might operate, it provides a basis for deciding which aspects of a case might have different theories applied to them. However, it does not help to decide which level or system to work on or which theory to choose and how it may be integrated with the other theories chosen.

Critical engagement

An alternative way of using theories to help in reflection is by using them critically against one another. We have seen already that there are different views of the nature and aims of social work and that many social work theories offer criticisms of other theories. Differences between theories can help reflection in practice by enabling alternative and opposing theories to criticise practice which used a particular theory.

Mrs Jones, for example, is a single parent who is very depressed and is unable to care adequately for her three preschool children. The social worker focused on her depression and found that this comes from isolation and loneliness. Her general practitioner supplied anti-depressants and the worker thought through with her the life she has led so far and plans for the future. Reflecting on this, radical theory would criticise the individualised approach. It does not look at how single parents may be stigmatised, put in the worst housing and blamed for not bringing up a conventional family. Feminist theory would draw attention to the oppression of women by forcing them into caring roles and not validating their aspirations for the future. Cognitive-behavioural theory tells us that she might benefit from learning different ways of thinking which would enable her to cope better with the world, instead of our approach of being concerned with her feelings and responses to her present situation. By reflecting on these alternative views of the situation, the worker can criticise and develop her approach, even if she does not use them to guide her practice according to their own model of action.

This 'critical contrastive approach' is one of a number of approaches to engaging in critical reflection using theory (Payne, 1996b). A dualities approach looks for conceptual opposites to inform our understanding. For example, if we say that someone's behaviour is childlike, what do we mean by adult-like behaviour, and how does it differ? A special case of this is the 'thinking-feelings' approach. If we are concerned about clients' thinking, we should ask ourselves how their emotions are coming out in this situation, and vice versa. In the case of the bereaved boy described above, we saw how the focus of work was on his feelings in a very distressing situation. A useful counterbalance might well be to progress to rational planning for the future. In every case, using the dualities and thinking-feeling approaches, we should look for what we are *not* doing and for what is *not* coming out.

Another approach to critical engagement is the three views of social work outlined above. If we are focusing on providing a service to an individual, we can ask ourselves how alternative views of social work would criticise this. Are we forgetting about building the client's personal capacity and emotional strength? Are we forgetting to look at the consequences of oppression and the inadequacies of social provision in this case? Our answer may give us clues to alternative social work theories which would pay dividends, or confirm us in the approach that we are currently using.

Reflecting on integration and dissent

So far, we have examined the complexities of the idea of reflection and some related concepts and, following that, some of the difficulties which arise in reflecting on practice theories. The argument has been that the idea of reflective practice is often discussed in a social vacuum and that we need to reflect in a context of awareness about debates around the nature of social work and the value of the practice theories we are considering. We have to incorporate in our reflective practice an understanding of the interaction between the ideas we are using to guide our practice, and we have to have models for thinking the interaction of ideas out.

Our reflection must also include the material considered in Part I about the social. Reflective practice must integrate this into our thinking about action, because our action needs to use this knowledge. Complete integration is neither possible nor desirable, however, because, as Part I demonstrates throughout, there is no agreement about how we should interpret and act on much of this material. So, again, our reflection must incorporate the possibility of dissent and disagreement.

Practice theories and the social world

Theories of the social world allow us to use knowledge from a variety of sources to guide our understanding of how clients might react and why events have turned one way rather than another. In particular settings, we might need to use other theories. For example, in hospital and health-related social work, medical knowledge might be useful, in education welfare work, educational theories and so on.

Some theories of the client world relate closely to social work practice theories described in Part II. Learning theory relates closely to behavioural work, and social learning theories have developed into aspects of modelling and cognitive practice. Attachment theory about child and adult behaviour derives from the interest and work of psychoanalytic practitioners, which also influenced psychosocial theory. Radical, feminist and anti-oppressive practice is strongly influenced by Marxist sociology and political theory, and by feminist and black social and artistic perspectives.

However, much theory and knowledge is not represented directly in social work practice theories. Much of it can be used with any practice theory. For example, research in aspects of the life cycle from different perspectives may be incorporated into most approaches to social work practice. Sociological knowledge about families, groups and communities can influence any form of social work. One important area of debate in social work, however, has been whether the characteristics of particular theoretical positions can incorporate particular areas of knowledge or values. For example, psychosocial theory has sometimes been criticised for its historical tendency to stereotype women as carers and as subordinate to men, and cognitive-behavioural theory has been criticised for its inability to incorporate black and minority ethnic communities' perspectives on behaviour within a structure of thought which assumes a consistent and, some would say, Eurocentric approach to learning and thinking. Some of the inadequacies and strengths of particular theories in taking into account various aspects of psychological and social knowledge form part of the arguments around why one theory is thought better than another. So, weaknesses in its being able to incorporate important knowledge may cause us to be cautious about what a particular theory has to offer. Social workers need to understand in detail what theoretical positions can offer as part of their evaluation of the use of particular theories in practice.

Theory, the law and the agency

One of the difficult aspects of applying theory is understanding its role in relation to the legal basis of social work practice and agency requirements. Part I of this book shows that these two factors influence and constrain how social workers practise. Magistrates and judges reading presentence reports and managers looking at our practice are not likely to concern themselves with which theory was used.

Colleagues in a multidisciplinary team are interested in the results we produce, not explanations of how it all came about. Lay people are naturally entitled to have reports and explanations of practice presented in clear, non-technical language, and colleagues are entitled to expect our practice to be competent and successful. This does not, however, make theory irrelevant to our practice.

Everything we do implies a theory about the circumstances that we deal with. Obviously, as we undertake social work activities, we use theory, even if it is not one of the formally stated ones. Knowing about and using the formal statements of theory help to clarify and organise ideas about what we do. It helps report-writing and justifying ourselves to managers and magistrates if we can be clear about why we took this or that action. Occasionally, a particular case goes wrong and there is a formal inquiry. Happy the social worker who can refer to the organised statement of well-established practice contained in a recognised theory as the basis for what they did. Even if this does not happen very often, our practice and everyday activity will display greater self-confidence and consistency if we have an organised view of what we are doing and why. Colleagues and clients will also have their own theories about the world, both formally organised and informal. Our own understanding of theory enables us to see where their theory is situated in the constellation of possible views of the world. We can also identify more easily inconsistencies and difficulties in decisions that they have chosen to make. Where colleagues' theories agree with our own, we can cooperate and work together on a more common basis and cement multidisciplinary work more effectively.

Theory, then, can be used for accountability to agencies and external institutions such as the law, because it clarifies our ideas about what we do. Moreover, applying, and being able to refer to, an established form of practice enables us to justify our practice to outsiders.

Theory in practice

Perhaps the most important group to whom we can justify our practice by using theory is our clients. They are entitled to know that we have an organised view of what we are doing and why and gain understanding and explanation of what we are doing, so that they can agree or disagree with it. This is one of the claimed advantages of approaches such as cognitive-behavioural practice and task-centred work, since a clear and often written agreement is made between worker and client. It is one of the essential features of radical, feminist and anti-oppressive theory, which requires a dialogue between equals rather than an expert therapist helping a disempowered client.

Obviously, clients do not need to be involved in every technicality. However, Secker's (1993) study of social work students suggests that students who succeeded in applying theory with confidence had certain important characteristics. Their skills in using theory were not about intellectual ability, but about skill in working openly with clients. Their use of theory started from the clients themselves. They listened well and responded to what clients told them. They did not put clients in theoretical categories. Instead, they used theoretical ideas all the time in discussing matters with clients. As a client said something, they might say, 'That reminds me of an idea ...'. They picked up ideas and talked them over with clients; they did not keep them to themselves. They worked together with clients to test out their ideas, first in discussion and then in what Schön (1983) calls 'on-the-spot' experimentation.

Using theory, then, does not require great intellect, it requires the application of exactly those social and interpersonal skills in working openly with people that social workers most like to claim. It involves reflecting theoretically *with* clients and also with colleagues, making reflection-in-action and reflection after the event an everyday part of what social workers do. Also, it means having the self-confidence to be open about your ideas and willing to experiment, alongside your clients, in putting your ideas into action.

Using Part II reflectively

The chapters which follow, in Part II, offer a beginning in using social work's theoretical ideas. The first three chapters explore three basic forms of social work: counselling, groupwork and community work. None of these belongs to social work alone, and there is debate in these chapters about the extent to which these forms of practice interact with other professionals' practice. These debates draw attention to the way in which social work is increasingly part of multidisciplinary intervention from a network of allied professions or occupational groups. Nevertheless, social work uses these forms of practice and applies, as Cosis Brown in particular shows, a variety of other theoretical models of practice within them.

The next two groups of accounts of theory describe broadly individualist and therapeutic models of practice (psychosocial, cognitive-behavioural and task-centred) and then socialist-collectivist models (radical, feminist, empowerment and advocacy, and anti-oppressive). These are not the full range of possible models, and for a more extended review you could refer to Payne (1997). However, these accounts from proponents of and enthusiasts for each model will allow you to begin the process of critical engagement with different models. How far, in the first group, is practice required to be individualist-reformist or reflexive-therapeutic? How far are the ideas of psychosocial theory in conflict with cognitive-behavioural theory? What ideas do they share? You could also examine your own reactions. Would you feel comfortable with the structure and clarity of task-centred work, for example, or do you think that psychosocial theory offers a more rounded view of human beings and their needs? Are all these approaches inadequate? Do they leave you turning towards socialist-collectivist models for a change of focus? Are there links as well as oppositions between the first group and the second? Looking at the second group, what are the crucial differences between radical and later socialist-collectivist models? Do these ideas give you clear concepts of how to practise, or are they just theories which give you a different view of the world? Whatever you think about their clarity as practice models or world-views, which do you find most useful and why?

The final chapter, on postmodernist ideas, proclaims that it is different. It tries to offer a way of thinking about people and the social situations in which they live. These are some of the very latest ideas influencing social work at present. They seek to help us to understand and explore the complexity, uncertainty and ambiguity of the world that we inhabit, whereas many of the other theories discussed here try to clarify and organise our thinking about the world according to their own point of view. Among other things, postmodernist theory argues that such clarifications and certainties are only limited representations of the world's complexity which we may agree as useful social conventions, but which reflect social and power relationships whose complexities we should try to understand.

CONCLUSION

This approach to theory suggests that we should be cautious and critical of all simplifi-cations of the world. Indeed, it argues that we should be critical and reflective in all our dealings with other human beings. We should never use theory to pigeon-hole and restrict the infinite variety of humanity. Instead, theory should be a guide to be used together with clients to explore, understand and transform the social world in which we live together.

FURTHER READING

Burns, S. and Bulman, C. (eds) (2000) *Reflective Practice in Nursing: The Growth of the Professional Practitioner*, 2nd edn (Oxford, Blackwell Science). Recommending a book about nursing demonstrates the interlocking nature of ideas within the network of related professions, and this book offers a range of practical articles about reflective practice which can be applied to social work.

Payne, M. (1996) *What is Professional Social Work?* (Birmingham, Venture). This book contains a more extended account of many of the ideas about views of the nature of social work discussed in this chapter.

Payne, M. (1997) *Modern Social Work Theory*, 2nd edn (London, Macmillan – now Palgrave Macmillan). A more extended critical review of social work theories than is possible here.

Schön, D. (1983) *The Reflective Practitioner: How Professionals Think in Action* (New York, Basic Books). The classic, creative and easy-to-read book about how some professions benefit from learning how to use 'reflection-in-action' to inform their practice.

Taylor, C. and White, S. (2000) *Practising Reflexivity in Health and Welfare: Making Knowledge* (Buckingham, Open University Press). This is a thoughtful book directly based on research into practice and full of ideas and stimulating insights into social work practice.

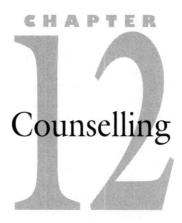

CHAPTER 12

Counselling

Helen Cosis Brown

Introduction

This chapter explores the relationship between social work and counselling, and the use of counselling theories, values and skills within social work practice. It covers the changing context of counselling within social work, the different theoretical underpinnings to counselling ideas and skills relevant to social work, counselling theory and skills within social work practice today and some current issues emerging from counselling and social work. The current context of this exploration is radically different from that which gave rise to the Barclay Report of the early 1980s. The report argued that it was:

> essential that social workers continue to be able to provide counselling and we use the word to cover a range of activities in which an attempt is made to understand the meaning of some event or state of being to an individual, family or group and to plan, with the person or people concerned, how to manage the emotional and practical realities that face them. (Barclay Committee, 1982: 41)

Barclay, on the same page, argues that social workers have themselves seen counselling 'as the hallmark of their calling'. Brearley (1995) documents the social, political, legislative and policy changes that have impacted on social work since the mid-1970s that have altered social workers' relationship to counselling. Today it would be more likely that social workers would see their hallmark as brokerage or care management rather than counselling. Social work students are often resistant to undertaking direct in-depth work with service users, seeing 'counselling' as something they feel they are neither prepared for nor trained to undertake.

Social work practice is (with a few exceptions) located within a legislative context. Where counselling is employed by its practitioners, it will be alongside other interventions and within a legislative, procedural and organisational context, compromising it as a form of 'pure' counselling, it being instead one of several possible social work methods of intervention. Social work practitioners, in all their various manifestations, have traditionally had a complex relationship with counselling. Bringing together the separate enterprises of counselling and social work has posed theoretical, organisational, ethical, practical and practice dilemmas. They are two separate areas of helping interventions, governed by different professional bodies, underpinned by separate bodies of knowledge and offering different outcomes, while at the same time sharing many of the same values, intentions, processes, ideas and methods. They are both interested and engaged in the processes of change, and they are both predominately preoccupied with the psychosocial. It might well be difficult to distinguish some social work interviews from a counselling session. Social work training has traditionally drawn heavily on counselling methods when teaching social work interviewing skills. However, it is often argued that, despite the very close relationship between social work interviewing and counselling, they are separate activities, one being the practice of counselling and the other the utilisation of counselling skills. Feltham points to the different views of professional bodies in relation to this distinction; the British Association for Counselling (BAC) arguing that social workers are employing counselling skills rather than practising counselling, whereas the Group for the Advancement of Psychodynamics and Psychotherapy in Social Work have occasionally argued that casework can be not just counselling, but also indeed psychotherapy (Feltham, 1995: 72). Historically, social casework, as practiced by psychodynamically oriented social workers, would hardly have been discernible from counselling. Today, within some social work settings, it is difficult to make a distinction; for example, in-depth work being undertaken by a social worker within a child psychiatric department in a hospital setting with an anorexic young woman may be difficult to distinguish from a counselling session undertaken by a counsellor with a similar young person.

Social work students and practitioners now occupy a New Labour era and are engaged in discourses different from those of the Barclay Report. One change has been the gradual de-emphasis on the 'collective' and the re-emphasis on the 'individual' and the individual's responsibility to facilitate change, whether that be social, economic or personal. The past twenty years have seen the corresponding mushrooming of personal therapies, the increased professionalisation of counselling, the growth in numbers of private counsellors and psychotherapists, and the explosion of related trainings. The same period has seen counselling being relocated within the social work context, into the 'provider sector', and a growing reluctance on the behalf of social workers to undertake counselling with service users, seeing it as outside their remit, theoretical and skills base and outside the realm of the possible, because of time and resource constraints. A cynical observer might comment that one major development in the differentiation between counselling and social work has been that the former is now rarely other than for the benefit of the bourgeoisie and the latter for the working class.

Social work practice today, in its many different forms and contexts, still needs to employ counselling as a possible method of intervention in specific and appropriate contexts, at the same time drawing on counselling theory and skills to inform its knowledge and skills repertoire more generally. Social workers still have to 'do the work' with service users, whether it be in-depth, long-term work or as part of an assessment in order to devise a care plan. Without counselling theory and counselling skills, social work practice is likely to be ineffectual and inefficient.

Theoretical groupings within counselling

Before looking at some of the broad theoretical groupings of ideas underpinning different 'schools' of counselling, it may be important to say something about what counselling is. The word 'counselling' is often used interchangeably with the word 'advice' For example, it might be more accurate to refer to careers 'advice' given in schools rather than careers 'counselling'. Dryden et al., emphasising the distinction between the spontaneous giving of help and professional intervention, write:

> counselling is a more deliberate activity and in its definition of the term the British Association for Counselling spells out the distinction between a planned and a spontaneous event. 'People become engaged in counselling when a person, occupying regularly or temporarily the role of counsellor, offers or agrees explicitly to offer time, attention and respect to another person or persons temporarily in the role of client'. (Dryden et al., 1989: 4, quoting from BAC, 1985: 1)

One of the most comprehensive definitions of counselling is offered by Feltham and Dryden (1993: 40), who describe it thus:

> a principled relationship characterised by the application of one or more psychological theories and a recognised set of communication skills, modified by experience, intuition and other interpersonal factors, to clients' intimate concerns, problems or aspirations. Its predominant ethos is one of facilitation rather than of advice-giving or coercion. It may be of very brief or long duration, take place in an organisational or private practice setting and may or may not overlap with practical, medical and other matters of personal welfare.

This definition illustrates why there may be some confusion over what it is, precisely, that makes counselling and social work perceived as being so different, as well as offering some insight into why BAC might need six separate divisions within it adequately to reflect all its constituent parts.

What are the 'psychological theories' that are referred to within this definition? As it pertains to social work practice, counselling has two areas related to it that have been of significance to its practice and knowledge base: the theoretical underpinning of different 'schools' of counselling and their related skills application. There are very many different counselling approaches built on a number of diverse theoretical perspectives. Only some of these have been influential upon social work and they may be grouped under four general headings: psycho-dynamic, cognitive-behavioural, humanistic person-centred and eclectic and integrative. These headings represent whole sets of ideas separate from counselling, which can be traced in relation to their influence on social work practice, and the ideas related to each heading can be shown to have been influential upon both social work and counselling at similar historical moments. For example, the interrelationships between psychodynamic ideas and social work and psychodynamic ideas and counselling, seen earlier this century, are similar for both social work and counselling (Yelloly, 1980; Jacobs, 1988; Pearson et al., 1988; Payne, 1992; McLeod, 1993: 23; Brown, H.C., 1996; Fleet, 2000). Theoretical developments are part of an economic, social, geographical, histor-ical, racial and gendered context; both social work and counselling have been subject to similar influences in their different processes of professionalisation since the beginning of the nineteenth century. Both professions developed in an often defensive relationship to their more orthodox and (often perceived as) intellectually superior relatives psychoanalysis and psychotherapy. Both social work and counselling have suffered from developing in their shadows, despite their undoubted enrichment as a result of their close liaisons. There is no clear, singular, linear relationship between psychoanalysis, psychotherapy, counselling and social work, neither in their historical development nor in their theoretical underpinning. However, the myth and to some extent the reality of their inter-dependency has had a powerful influence.

Psychodynamic ideas

Jacobs (1988) offers what is still a very useful account of the interrelationship between psychodynamic ideas and counselling. This is one of the most complex theoretical areas drawn on in counselling, utilising a whole range of evolving ideas developed by many different individuals (Freud, Jung, Klien, Bion, Fairbairn, Winnicott and Bowlby to name just a few of the originators) over a considerable period of time. Key psychodynamic concepts relevant to counselling would include the unconscious, the structures of the mind (the id, the ego and the super-ego), the past being relevant and impacting on the present, psychosexual development (oral, anal, phallic (Oedipal), latency, adult sexuality), defence mechanisms, envy, depression, transference and countertransference, projective identification, ambiva-lence, attachment, separation, loss and crisis. It is beyond the scope of this chapter to detail the meaning and different interpretations of these concepts. McLeod offers a useful précis of their development and application to counselling. Psycho-dynamic and psychoanalytical ideas have had a profound impact on the way in which we view human development and have been integrated into our cultural heritages in ways that subtly influence our understandings about ourselves and others. These influences have also impacted on counsellors:

> All counsellors and therapists, even those who espouse different theoretical models, have been influenced by psychodynamic thinking and have had to make up their minds whether to accept or reject the Freudian image of the person. (McLeod, 1993: 43)

Psychodynamic counselling has attracted much criticism, including its normative and potentially pathologising tendencies and the question of its efficacy. Questioning the outcomes of psychodynamic interventions has been raised alongside the problem of resourcing what was often long-term intervention that had no measurable outcome. The development of 'brief-therapy', associated with people such as Mann, Sifneos, Malan and Davanloo, has been significant in relation to this (McLeod, 1993: 38). The development of brief-therapy has been highly significant to counselling, as by its nature it is about facilitating the mobilisation of the client's inner and outer resources to manage a particular life event or set of circumstances, circumstances where limited interventions are often appropriate, as opposed to, in the case of psychotherapy, often long-term intervention focused on personality change. This development has not just affected psychodynamic counselling, but has also had a general impact on counselling (Dryden and Feltham, 1992).

Both humanistic person-centred and cognitive-behavioural counselling developed partly, but not exclusively, in response to some of the perceived difficulties and limitations of the psychodynamic approach.

Humanistic person-centred ideas

The development of humanistic person-centred counselling has its roots located within the broad developments of both phenomenological and existential influences within philosophy and psychology during the post-war period. Its inception is often associated with a talk given by Carl Rogers in 1940 (Rogers, 1942), in which he emphasised clients' potential to find their own solutions:

> The emphasis on the client as expert and the counsellor as source of reflection and encouragement was captured in the designation of the approach as 'non-directive' counselling. (McLeod, 1993: 63)

Coulshed (1991: 52) writes that the

> theory base and important concepts devolve from a philosophical background of the existential tradition which respects an individual's subjective experience and places emphasis on the vocabulary of freedom, choice, autonomy and meaning.

Although this approach can be associated with broad theoretical and philosophical developments outside psychology, it was also part of the so-called 'third force' (the first and second being associated with the work of Freud and Skinner) within psychology, person-centred counselling being one development within that 'force'.

As a set of theories and methods, the person-centred approach is associated with an optimistic view of human nature but tells us little about human development. Although Dryden et al. (1989) are right in seeing the necessity of contextualising these theories, with their emphasis on 'self-actualisation', within the Californian culture of the 1960s, they are still important in having established the central significance of empathy, warmth and genuineness as key to the effectiveness of counselling interventions. The emphasis here is on counselling intervention rather than explanation of human behaviour. This approach and its theoretical underpinnings have been highly influential in social work, particularly on ideas relating to social work interviewing skills. Egan (1994) is seen as a bridge between counselling and social work interviewing, and is still highly influential in social work training courses. He is also seen as a bridge between the humanistic person-centred and behavioural approaches (Dryden et al., 1989).

Cognitive-behavioural ideas

Cognitive-behavioural ideas and their influence on counselling have been associated with developments within mainstream psychology, with its emphasis on scientific methods, and the growth of behavioural and cognitive psychology in the post-war period. These ideas built on work undertaken drawing on animal experiments earlier in the century, associated with people such as Pavlov, Watson and Thorndike. From the 1950s onwards, they were built on by Eysenck, Rachman, Skinner, Wolpe and others, who were chiefly interested in behaviour and learning, and with understanding how behaviours are learnt and what interventions will enable behaviour to change. They were not interested in understanding the inner meanings of acts or causation other than how those acts were learnt.

Feltham (1995: 83) notes that 'behaviour therapy is based on what can be observed, studied, measured and reliably changed'. These are a different set of criteria from psychodynamic or humanistic person-centred preoccupations. Within this tradition, there are numerous types of behavioural and cognitive counselling interventions, drawing on specific theories including respondent conditioning, operant conditioning, observational learning and cognitive learning to name but a few. These interventions are interested not exclusively in behaviour, but also in thought and feelings, and how these then impact upon and affect behaviour.

There have been moments in the history of social work when it has been fashionable to be derisive about behavioural interventions, but their relevance to social work is important. They have been shown to be effective with specific conditions, for example enuresis, agoraphobia and anxiety. One strength is their capacity to be adopted and practised by ordinary practitioners, be they social workers or community psychiatric nurses, who have not had to receive such extensive training as would be expected of, for example, a psychodynamic counsellor in order to facilitate an effective outcome. Behavioural interventions are often seen as successful in the short term and focus on management, focused change, measurement and monitoring. In the current climate of social work, these methods might be seen as fairly closely matching the needs of the professional roles.

Social work has traditionally drawn on a wide range of counselling theories and methods, a combination of psychodynamic, person-centred and cognitive-behavioural approaches, often in a haphazard way rather than in a theoretically and therapeutically logical manner that considers efficacy and professional integrity.

Eclectic and integrative approaches

The eclectic approach, which is sometimes referred to as integrative, is where the theory and the corresponding method of intervention are chosen as the most relevant and appropriate to meet the needs presented by the client or service user's specific circumstances. It can be seen as a way of maximising the beneficial aspects of the three different schools. This leads to the potentiality of the practitioner having an underlying psychodynamic understanding, taking a person-centred approach to the counselling relationship, one that is characterised by warmth, respect and empathy, while having the capacity to, where relevant, employ behavioural techniques. This, to many, smacks of heresy, but there is a growing literature looking at the validity of integration. McLeod notes the difference between an eclectic approach, which is a more accurate description of the above, and one that is integrative:

> An eclectic approach to counselling is one in which the counsellor chooses the best or most appropriate ideas and techniques from a range of theories or models, in order to meet the needs of the client. Integration on the other hand, refers to a somewhat more ambitious enterprise in which the counsellor brings together elements from different theories and models into a new theory or model. (1993: 99)

For social workers, their approach is likely, more often than not, to fall within the eclectic category, one they are already overfamiliar with and one that is often used against them, reinforcing the perception that social work has a flimsy, incoherent theoretical base in practice, whereas, in fact, eclecticism can be a potential strength.

Counselling and social work

Social work, within the statutory sector, at the beginning of the twenty-first century, comprises a set of activities and interventions that are primarily focused on assessment, administration, care management, risk analysis and monitoring. It can be argued that the focus social work did have, or was perceived as having, on the facilitation of change, whether it was at the level of the individual, household, group or community, has slowly been transferred out of the statutory sector and into the provider sector, one that is increasingly private and voluntary. Within the provider sector, social workers both practise counselling and employ counselling skills. Within the areas of drugs and alcohol, palliative care, mental health and family work, there are social workers employed who will be negotiating a counselling component to their overall work with a service user. This counselling work will rarely be 'pure' counselling, as by definition it will, as with social work practice more broadly, be located in the context of a wider intervention context.

It can be argued, and the author is among those who do, that counselling has to remain as an integral part of social work wherever its location or context. This is 'counselling' in its broadest sense, focusing primarily on the application of counselling skills and the deployment of specific or integrative theories of counselling. If we examine the processes of assessment, be they in relation to family support and child protection, assessment and care management in community care or the assessment undertaken by the key-worker under the Care Programme Approach in mental health (DoH, 1996), these processes necessitate the social worker having the competence to deploy counselling skills to undertake a full and comprehensive assessment. This link is made explicitly by Smale et al. (1993) when they consider the skills needed to enable competent work to be done when assessment work is undertaken. Pearson (1990), from a counselling perspective, also explores what it has to offer to social support and care management. It is interesting to note that two publications that look explicitly at social work competence make very little direct reference to counselling (Thompson, 1996a; Vass, 1996).

Egan (1994), over a number of decades, has provided social work educators with a relevant and applicable model for the application of counselling skills to social work interviewing. Utilising both person-centred theory and behavioural ideas, he developed his model. Coulshed lists seven qualities that counsellors (here she is referring to the context of social work) should have, qualities that are often associated with person-centred counselling and ones that are central to Egan, these are empathy or understanding, respect, concreteness or being specific, self-knowledge and self-acceptance, genuineness, congruence and immediacy (Coulshed, 1991: 45). Egan's model can be summarised as having four components: exploration, understanding, action and evaluation. It is easy to see why Smale et al. have built on and adapted this model for application with assessment and care management in community care. It has real strengths, including its commitment to working with, and not for, the client. It is a model that fits well with ideas of, and emphasises the importance of, engagement, clarity, focusing, planning, prioritising, negotiating realisable and relevant goals, action and review, and evaluation, all aspects of competent social work practice whatever its context, congruent with a culture of increasing openness and practitioner accountability. While the Egan model has received much criticism for its focus, foundations and crises-free assumptions, it is a model that can be adapted and built on to enhance effective social work intervention, as demonstrated by Smale et al. (1993).

It has been argued that in the current social work context social workers are more likely to offer counselling only within the provider sector, which is increasingly made up of private and voluntary organisations. However, to be effective, social workers within all contexts, need to apply counselling skills and be informed by counselling ideas to be effective. This remains particularly pertinent within the statutory sector, where the majority of assessment work is still concentrated, the application of counselling skills being fundamental to the processes of assessment and care management.

Issues

Egan's model is one that draws on behavioural and person-centred ideas and methods. It largely ignores psychodynamic ideas, and that can mean that it has limited application. To focus on 'a problem', without an understanding of causation, may mean that the intervention has limited effectiveness. Also, to ignore the contribution of systemic ideas to social work could mean that 'the problem' is seen outside its context, again limiting the effectiveness of the intervention. For the model to be effective, it needs to be located within a familiarity with and understanding of both psychodynamic and systemic ideas.

COUNSELLING **147**

There has been much written recently about the reflective practitioner (see Chapter 11; Schön, 1987; Yelloly and Henkel, 1995; Thompson, 1996a). Thompson writes that the reflective practitioner is:

> a worker who is able to use experience, knowledge and theoretical perspectives to guide and inform practice. Reflective practice involves cutting the cloth to suit the specific circumstances, rather than looking for ready-made solutions. (Thompson, 1996a: 222)

Reflective practice also needs the practitioner to have what was earlier referred to as self-knowledge. It requires the practitioner to be able, and be committed, to reflect upon their own perceptions, responses and feelings in any given situation, requiring an understanding of countertransference. Countertransference is a complex and fraught area of both psychoanalytic and psychodynamic theories. 'Social work accessible' explanations of these ideas are available (Salzberger-Wittenberg, 1970; Jacobs, 1988; Pearson et al., 1988; d'Ardenne and Mahtani, 1999). Without this theoretical base underpinning the application of counselling skills, we will not achieve reflective practice.

As ideas in counselling and social work have developed, so there has been a growing acceptance by both professions of their limitations in offering an appropriate service to a cross-section of all our communities. Not only have these two professional groups been unable to reach all communities, but they might also have been both overtly and covertly, deliberately and by default, discriminatory and oppressive to both individuals and specific communities. Anti-oppressive practice has become an accepted part of the discourse of social work. Within counselling, as well, there is a substantial literature developing, demonstrating a general acceptance that both ideas and models may need to be adapted to integrate anti-oppressive practice (Noonan, 1983; d'Ardenne and Mahtani, 1989; Scrutton, 1989; Crompton, 1992; Atkinson and Hackett, 1995; Davies and Neal, 1996). When social work deploys counselling skills and ideas, it needs to take cognisance of the developing literature of counselling and anti-oppressive practice.

CONCLUSION

A key issue for counselling and social work is social work's gradual defensive rejection of and timidity towards its use of counselling and counselling skills. It has been argued that both are still and will remain central to the roles and tasks of social work. Counselling skills are integral to the processes of assessment and care management, and there will remain a need for counselling within the social work context, certainly within the provider sector. If we are going to achieve the goal of a profession that is made up of competent and reflective practitioners, we will need to draw on counselling skills and models that enhance effectiveness and make use of counselling theories that inform practice. This could enable professional reflection to take place when working with the needs of specific, unique individuals within their own context and lead to the deployment of sensitive, relevant and effective interventions that facilitate negotiated change.

FURTHER READING

Atkinson, D.R. and Hackett, G. (1995) *Counseling Diverse Populations* (Madison, Brown & Benchmark). Offers a general coverage of anti-discriminatory practice issues in counselling.

Brearley, J. (1995) *Counselling and Social Work* (Buckingham, Open University Press). This book covers areas directly pertinent to the content of this chapter.

Dryden, W., Charles-Edwards, D. and Woolfe, R. (eds) (1989) *Handbook of Counselling in Great Britain* (London, Sage). An excellent general introduction to counselling.

Feltham, C. (1995) *What is Counselling?* (London, Sage). An accessible introduction to counselling.

Fleet, F. (2000) 'Counselling and contemporary social work', in Stepney, P. and Ford, D. (eds) *Social Work Models, Methods and Theories: A Framework for Practice* (Lyme Regis, Russell House Publishing. A useful chapter looking at social work and counselling.

McLeod, E. (1993) *An Introduction to Counselling* (Buckingham, Open University Press). A helpful introduction to counselling theory and practice.

Seden, J. (1999) *Counselling Skills in Social Work Practice* (Buckingham, Open University Press). This book looks in detail at the application of counselling skills to social work practice.

13

Groupwork

Dave Ward

Where has all the groupwork gone?

How things have changed! My immediate reaction on being invited to contribute this chapter on groupwork was a mild panic. Although I see groups and groupwork as central to much that we do, in both our private and professional lives, 'groupwork' seems, almost without being noticed, to have faded from view. This invitation brought it back to my attention with a start: where has groupwork gone?; why?; what might be its future?

The 1970s were a golden age for groupwork. Students on social work courses would actively seek, and talk proudly about having done, 'groupwork' on placement. Groupwork had a secure place on the curricula of social work training courses within which the four 'methods' – casework, family work, *groupwork* and community work – dominated. These provided a framework for organising a potentially overwhelming mass of material and hinted at an exclusive knowledge and skill base which was seen then as necessary for an aspiring profession.

The late 1970s and 80s saw an outpouring of British texts focusing on the generic basics of groupwork (for example, Davies, 1975; Douglas, 1978, 1983; Brown, 1979, 1986; Houston, 1984; Heap, 1985; Whitaker, 1985; Preston-Shoot, 1987) and in 1988 *Groupwork*, the first British journal devoted to the method, was launched. However, this output was failing to keep up with deeper changes that were taking place in society at large.

Little of this vibrancy and expansiveness is visible today. One or two of the established authorities have continued to pursue the method (Brown, 1992; Douglas, 1993), joined by a few others (Adams and O'Sullivan, 1994; Vernelle,

1994, Doel and Sawdon, 1999), but I see little evidence of its take-up in field practice. *Groupwork* continues as a thrice-yearly publication. However, a scan of its contents since 1990 reveals that, of the papers published, more than one-third were by foreign authors. Few addressed groupwork practised in the statutory social services. Indeed, Doel and Sawdon (1999: 21) observe that groupwork is increasingly being practised by people who are not social workers, perhaps based on a view that groupwork is not appropriate for statutory social work. While there are rich veins of practice experience and conceptual analysis, little of this is grounded in the mainstream of social work. In parallel, the basic texts tend not to address directly the issues faced in the settings in which most social workers work. Much of this literature must seem remote to social work students with prior experience in statutory agencies. As an external assessor to social work qualifying programmes, I have frequently commented on how the few students who do undertake groupwork in their practice placements rarely refer to the basic texts in their practice studies, but rather apply concepts and methods from non-groupwork sources to their work with groups. Doel and Sawdon (1999: 21) suggest that the real question 'may, therefore, be less of "where has all the groupwork gone?" and more of "why have all the social workers gone?"'.

The 1990s saw tremendous changes in the vision and practice of social work as a result of pressures from several directions. In some respects, these forces are in conflict, but, in sum, they have had the effect of putting the notion of a social work organised around the four core methods into terminal decline. They include the drive towards specialisation, the emergence of the law as a central concern, new approaches to the education and training of social workers, the impact of 'new managerialism' and, finally, the searching and scathing critiques of theory and practice from radical, feminist and anti-racist perspectives. This list is neither complete nor exclusive, but will enable me to sketch the context within which I believe an identifiably different groupwork has come into position.

The demethoding of social work

The child abuse scandals in the 1970s and 80s had a profound impact. They cast doubt on whether social workers managed, organised and trained generically had the specialist skills to deal with complex childcare cases (for example, Blom Cooper, 1985). Outcomes traceable to this are a trend towards specialisation and a concern for safety-first practice (DoH, 1995a). The law, as the framework within which social work is practised and which provides legitimacy, is given great prominence in training and, manifestly, stands to the fore in the minds of social workers (Sanfacon, 2001).

In the probation service, another set of changes were taking place. A national survey (Caddick, 1991) revealed that groupwork was being practised widely in the service, much of it 'providing developmental or enabling experiences for the members' (p. 211). However, in 1992, the punishment-oriented Criminal Justice Act was introduced, establishing a new direction which, by the turn of the millenium, had fundamentally changed the culture of the service:

an offence specific practice developed ... decreasing appreciation by practitioners of the dynamics of the groupwork process and concentration on the task in hand rather than the process. (Senior, 1993: 35)

Alongside these developments, and reflected in them, have been wider changes in the culture of Britain, developing momentum throughout the 1980s following the Conservative election victory in 1979, but only institutionalised in social work practice in the 1990s. One element is 'new managerialism', with its focus on concrete and measurable outcomes, in a drive towards greater economy, efficiency and effectiveness (McLaughlin and Muncie, 1994). As Youll (1996: 39) argues:

what is not directly observable and therefore easily measured and described gets left out: mindfulness, the process and nature of relationships, managing the affective component of the work, the 'artistry of social work'.

Inexorably, the attention moved away from the 'how' of the job. This is illustrated vividly in a probation text (Raynor et al., 1994) in which a chapter on 'a programme to reduce offending', which is predominantly group based, covers rationale, aims, content and evaluation but nothing on groupwork skills and methods.

Echoes of these developments can be seen in profound changes in social work education. Responding to accusations of inadequate training, most stridently made in relation to childcare practice, qualifying training has been reorganised around greater specialisation and a competence framework (CCETSW, 1996). While there is much debate about the efficacy of a competency approach, the fact is that such an approach, consistent with the imperatives of new managerialism, concentrates attention upon precisely framed identifiable and measurable behaviour (Cannan, 1994/95). What is lost is the synergy of bringing skills together to form, collectively, a method.

The final factor I wish to note as influencing the 'demethoding' of social work has been the so-called 'progressive' critique of traditional social work. This has interrogated not only the reactionary policies and practices flowing from the New Right, but also how good intentions can be damaging. It began with the radical social work movement in the late 1970s and early 1980s, moving on into the trenchant critiques from feminist, disability, gay and lesbian, and anti-racist perspectives from the mid-1980s. I do not question the rectitude of the critiques – indeed, I have been an unashamed participant – but merely highlight their impact, alongside other factors, in changing the face of social work.

The four methods were a product of a time that has now passed. They made sense as part of the knowledge base of an aspiring profession which confidently saw itself progressing to heightened status and security. Battered from all sides, those conditions no longer apply. Social workers' confidence in themselves has been profoundly shaken. It is not surprising that they have come to feel safer operating within instrumental but more clear and defensible frameworks, reflected in buzz words such as 'competences', 'risk assessment' and 'case management'.

Groupwork and work-in-groups

In contemporary social work, there is a good deal of evidence of a continuing interest in groups. Indeed, there is a considerable amount of work taking place *in* groups. However, it is not recognisable as groupwork. It does not pay substantial attention either to the knowledge base of group dynamics or to the practice base in groupwork methods and skills. Nor does it incorporate the democratic and collective values that are, as we will see, at the core of real groupwork. It is to be found in cognitive-behavioural work, particularly with offenders; in residential and daycare; in 'self-help'; in research and service evaluation; and, organisation- ally, in teamwork. In some cases, for example in so-called 'What Works' practice with offenders (McGuire, 1995; Chapman and Hough, 1998; Underdown, 1998), the guiding texts simply pass over groupwork knowledge and skills. In other areas, for example residential and daycare or management, the evidence is that groupwork is not taken seriously, although some theoretical work has highlighted its importance (for example, Brown and Clough, 1989).

Work-in-groups involves moving away from a notion of the group as an '*instrument*' (Douglas, 1993) or 'medium' (Whitaker, 1985) for help and change, where group members work together to explore and exploit group resources (Douglas, 1993: 31), to a greater emphasis on the group as '*context*':

> in which a powerful and knowledgeable resource, usually one leader, operates ... in which all group members have a primary relationship to the group leader who works with each individual in turn in the context of the group. (Douglas, 1993: 33)

an orientation quite consistent with the changes in social work outlined.

Douglas (1993) sees a close connection between groups as 'instrument' or 'medium' and 'concepts of equality and democracy' (p. 31), and for A. Brown (1996: 83) 'groupwork is anti-oppressive in its context, purpose, method, group relationships and behaviour'. Indeed, what has historically distinguished groupwork from forms of practice focused on the individual has been:

> an emphasis on the commonalities of problems and situations and the concomi- tant commonality of feelings to which they give rise. In groupwork each issue that is raised, even when that issue at first glance seems to have no relevance to others in the group, does have applicability for all. The worker who practises real groupwork draws out that applicability and elicits the commonalities and asks members to examine the issues of others. (Kurland and Salmon, 1993: 10)

At its best, groupwork can offer (Coulshed, 1991: 161, summarising Yalom, 1970):

- a source of power for members;
- mutual support;
- an exchange of information;
- motivation and hope;

- opportunities to learn and test interpersonal and other social skills;

- a sense of belonging;

- role models;

- feedback on behaviour and coping attempts;

- a chance to help as well as be helped.

Furthermore, if affiliated to a purpose, which explicitly rejects the splintering of public issues from private troubles, and also to a set of practice principles which stress the potency of self-directed action and non-elitist leadership, groupwork can be the preferred method for anti-oppressive practice. Bringing together people with common needs and problems to work together on their own behalf represents the essence of empowerment (Mullender and Ward, 1991: 12).

Instead, in the mainstream, we find groups that are predominantly 'one-to-one treatment with the rest of the members acting as bystanders'. Such groups are boring, suppressing and run by people who must maintain control. Process is used to enhance conformity; dissenters may be humiliated; revealing is required, with punishment if refused (Konopka, 1990, cited by Kurland and Salmon, 1993: 8).

Although Kurland and Salmon are writing about the American scene, British writers have similar observations. Brown (1994: 45) notes a trend towards groups that are increasingly task-oriented, with decreasing emphasis being paid to process:

> reducing groupwork ... to a rather sterile exercise in which group members receive packaged group programmes of limited usefulness, making no real impact on them as unique individuals often caught up in oppressive social conditions of poverty.

Senior (1993) acknowledged that the individualised task focus had produced some high-quality training materials, for example, the catalogue of 'accredited programmes' for use by probation and prisons (Home Office, 2000b), but was concerned that:

> unless groupworkers were skilled enough to use the group process appropriately, opportunities for personal development of clients were left undone. (Senior, 1993: 35)

As an example, Cowburn and Modi (1995) critically evaluate approaches, predominantly based in groups, to working with male sex abusers. They see in the prevalent cognitive-behavioural programmes and, in particular, in the practice of individual confrontation, oppressive Eurocentric and heterosexist assumptions, grounded in conformity and obedience, which are potentially dangerous in reinforcing abusers' minimalist views of their own responsibility and the harm their actions have caused. Effective practice, they argue:

> needs to help to develop a person's positive sense of identity as a firm base from which knowledge, skills and understanding about offending behaviour can be

brought together to avoid re-offending ... it needs to be experienced within a context that is not oppressive (Cowburn and Modi, 1995: 204–5).

Real groupwork may have become unfashionable precisely because it acknowledges that groups develop a life of their own over which the worker cannot ever have complete control. In a group, the agenda is likely to be holistic. Group members will raise what is important and significant to them, no matter what 'ground rules' and boundaries have been set. Such free-flowing characteristics are out of kilter with the current climate, emphasising, as it does, discipline, individual responsibility and, at an organisation level, preset objectives and audited outcomes. The outcome is many projects and workers for whom the ideas of real groupwork are unfamiliar and regarded with suspicion (Drakeford, 1994: 237).

However, there is a danger of throwing the baby out with the bath water. The drive for efficiency seeks, wherever possible, economies of scale, and this means gathering people together. Whenever this happens, group process and the need for groupwork skills will come to the fore.

A continuing need for groupwork

Sustaining Caddick's (1991) findings, work-in-groups has continued to develop as a vital activity across the probation service, but along the dimension of 'the modification of offending or offence related behaviour' rather than 'towards providing developmental or enabling experiences for members' (Caddick, 1991: 210–11). Cognitive-behavioural approaches developed in North America have provided the received model (Ross et al., 1989). Cowburn and Modi (1995) have highlighted the risk of deconstructing fragile identities in such group-based work with sex abusers. Instead, they urge a groupwork approach which 'allows offenders to feel power and consequently a strong sense of self ... [which] ... will allow them to develop non-offending ways of finding self-affirmation (Cowburn and Modi, 1995: 205). As noted, recent texts on 'What Works' cognitive-behavioural practice pay minimal attention to group dynamics, group process and groupwork methods and skills.

Likewise, in residential and daycare, sometimes called group care, there is a dearth of literature with a groupwork base and practice examples. Exceptions have been Douglas (1986) and, particularly, Brown and Clough's (1989) *Groups and Groupings: Life and Work in Day and Residential Centres*. Brown and Clough built on the premise that better practice lies in understanding the complexities of the 'mosaic' of more or less formal groups which straddle the experiences of users and staff in day and residential settings. A particular contribution of this work was to extend attention beyond inter- and intra-group processes (Douglas, 1986) to the 'rediscovery' of the open and large group as contexts which require special consideration and skills (see also Ward, 1993).

In the organisation and management of social services, the problem is not the lack of literature on groups, organisations and management per se. Rather, it is the failure to apply the knowledge and understanding of group process, and to use groupwork skills, in the management of social work agencies as 'mosaics' and front-line teams as groups. The culture of 'new managerialism' has led to a top-down style preoccupied with obedience, performance indicators and output measures, features which are an antithesis of groupwork. According to one former senior civil servant, this leads to a narrowing of vision, driving out initiative and distorting priorities, a flattening of the levels of performance leading to conformism, a reluctance to question received ideas and 'ultimately to secrecy and defensiveness' (Faulkner, 1995: 69). The capacity of groupwork, applying techniques of problem analysis, objective-setting, prioritisation and evaluation to enhance creativity and generate team spirit and enthusiasm for the tasks in hand, goes unconsidered in such a culture.

In the rapidly expanding field of 'self-help', much initiative takes place in group settings. There are two sides to the self-help movement. Negatively, it can be seen as substituting for properly resourced, high-quality welfare services, providing an ideological smokescreen for cuts, contracting out and, at worst, the unpaid and unsupported care of the poorest by the poorest. On the other hand, self-help groups, besides providing the quality of empathy and support that only those in the same predicament can extend to their peers, have raised the profile of hitherto unmet need and brought about significant changes in policy and provision. Adams (1990, 1996a) shows the importance of an understanding of group process if workers are to mobilise and empower, rather than stifle, the creativity and commitment of those involved. Crucially, Adams (1996a) goes beyond a checklist approach (see, for example, Wilson, 1986, 1988, 1995), to assert and explain how, to achieve these purposes, groupwork skills must be set within a paradigm of practice principles which is explicitly anti-oppressive (pp. 117–18).

Finally, I have come increasingly to note the use of groups in research and evaluation (Ward, 1996). This has come into public view with the prominence given to the use of 'focus groups' by political parties in devising their appeals to the electorate. While there is a technical literature on focus groups (for example, Morgan, 1988; Krueger, 1994), there is little acknowledgement of group and groupwork matters in the research methods literature, even where participative, ethnographic, feminist and other anti-oppressive approaches are advocated. It is self-evident that the knowledge of group process and a measure of groupwork practice skill should be components in such methodologies. Indeed, the potential impact of research on groups studied, and indeed its capacity to empower or oppress, should be central ethical considerations for all researchers (Fleming and Ward, 1996; Taylor, G., 1996).

Re-establishing groupwork

A. Brown (1996: 90) identifies three key considerations for the future of groupwork: values, practice-based model-building and sustaining groupwork and groupworkers into an uncertain future. Up to this point, I have identified forces which have undermined the presence of groupwork in mainstream social and probation work and how this may be counterproductive from both ethical and practice perspectives. What I would like to propose now is a practical reassertion of groupwork which can encompass the three considerations set out by Brown. A briefing by the National Institute for Social Work (1996) highlights that a major cornerstone for social policy, and challenge for social work, in an enlarging Europe is the fight against social exclusion. The briefing argues:

> The challenges of reducing social exclusion through working with those individuals and groups currently denied access to employment or services demands new approaches ... The absence of such an aim in the United Kingdom has profound implications for the practice of social work.

In this context, I am prompted to recall Douglas's (1993) observation, cited earlier, of the historical connection between groupwork and equality and democracy. I discern in other countries of the European Union, where unemployment, demographic changes and the apparent inability of governments to sustain their welfare provision have created various forms of social exclusion, conscious efforts being made to reframe welfare services in ways which enhance an inclusive group-oriented approach. In contrast, in the UK, we have barely begun to address

> the role of social workers as agents in the fight against social exclusion and the development of a model of practice that can incorporate a broader community focus as well as an individual or family approach. (NISW, 1996)

The challenge of social exclusion demands that we take account of what we have come to know about the systematic oppression of excluded groups, anti-discriminatory practice and empowerment (Mullender and Ward, 1991; Rees, 1991; Thompson, 1993; Adams, 1996a), and, in this context, groupwork reasserts its significance. This is because the group can be, according to Butler and Wintram (1991: 77):

● a source of immediate support, of friendship, where the knowledge that a meeting will take place regularly provides a safety net in itself;

● a place to recognise shared experiences and their value;

● a way of breaking down isolation and loneliness;

● the source of a different perspective on personal problems;

● a place to experience power over personal situations with the capacity to change and have an effect on these.

Also, beyond these foundations, 'in groups there is a better chance of addressing the inseparability of private troubles and public issues' (Breton, 1994: 31). Even though matters may surface as private troubles, in groups these private troubles soon become shared troubles, providing the ground for the *analysis* of their structural sources, and *action* together to bring about change (Mullender and Ward, 1991).

Butler and Wintram (1991), Lee (1994) and Mullender and Ward (1991) have articulated specific models for practising anti-oppressive groupwork. What is distinctive is their insistence on taking account of an interconnectedness of values, methods and skills right through practice. Helpful guidance can be found in Brown (1992), who provides an invaluable inventory of areas for attention, but one which – distinctive and essential to anti-oppressive groupwork – must be set within a searching exploration of underpinning values (Mullender and Ward, 1991). Brown (1992: 152–80) draws attention to: group composition; supervision and consultation; style format and group culture; ground rules; putting race and gender on the agenda; confronting racism, sexism and other forms of discrimination when they occur within the group; co-working; worker self-preparation; and work within the group and its external environment.

To illustrate what is possible, I will conclude with practice examples from arguably the least promising areas of social work practice.

Butler (1994) writes about a group for women whose children were adjudged by social services as at risk of significant harm from their parents. She explores how the 'facilitation' style of groupwork engendered an atmosphere of equality, enabling the women 'to explore the humour, sadness and strains of family life and no longer remain silent about these' (Butler, 1994: 178). Central to the group agenda emerged structural dilemmas facing members: women's sexuality and relationships with male partners, which were entangled with the processes of racism and the difficulties of bringing up mixed-parentage children. Faced with relentless hardships, the women easily identified the politics of poverty. Unpacking structural and individual issues was critical to these women's empowerment and the creation of their own solutions to the threats and dilemmas they faced (Butler, 1994: 163).

In the completely different setting of a young offenders penal institution, Badham (1989) and colleagues worked with the inmates to develop a through-care service which the young men would see as useful and relevant by enabling them to raise issues and complaints within the institution and prepare themselves for release. The workers sought to draw out of the young men, and provide opportunities for them to learn skills and knowledge which would help them to survive both 'inside' and after release. Confronting racist and sexist attitudes was part of this, and the worker team included women and black workers. The young men controlled the group's programme producing, amidst wide-ranging discussions, advice booklets and arranging speakers on welfare rights, housing, parole and temporary release. For invited speakers, including the governor, the group prepared their briefs, organised invitations and devised questions so that they acquired the information they wanted. The governor acknowledged the value of the forum and saw in this different context hitherto unrecognised capacities in these inmates. One young man said on leaving the group, 'It made you feel as though you *can* do something with your life while you are inside' (Badham, 1989: 35).

This, then, is the shape of an anti-oppressive groupwork practice to tackle the processes of exclusion. Like so many other catch words that have gone before – participation, citizenship and, sadly, empowerment – there is, of course, the ever-present danger of the 'fight against exclusion' being coopted and watered down to become meaningless, ideological deodorant. Some insurance against this can lie in interlinking with an anti-oppressive approach grounded in the practice of 'real' groupwork. It is an opportunity to begin to bring British social work with groups back in from the cold.

FURTHER READING

Brown, A. (1992) *Groupwork*, 3rd edn (Aldershot, Ashgate); Doel, M. and Sawdon, C. (1999) *The Essential Groupworker* (London, Jessica Kingsley). These books are excellent best basic texts on practising groupwork. The former has an excellent, if slightly dated, bibliography for follow-up reading.

Adams, R. (1996a) *Social Work and Empowerment* (London, Macmillan – now Palgrave Macmillan); Breton, M. (1994) 'On the meaning of empowerment and empower-ment oriented social work practice', *Social Work with Groups*, 17(3): 23–38; Mullender, A. and Ward, D. (1991) *Self-Directed Groupwork: Users Take Action for Empowerment* (London, Whiting & Birch). These three texts are most helpful in unravelling the notion of empowerment and providing practical guidelines for practising groupwork in that direction in mainstream social work settings.

14

Community Work

Marjorie Mayo

Introduction

'Community work has a long history as an aspect of social work' (Payne, 1995: 165). Essentially, community work brings a focus upon helping

> people with shared interests to come together, work out what their needs are among themselves and then jointly take action together to meet those needs, by developing projects which would enable the people concerned to gain support to meet them or by campaigning to ensure that they are met by those responsible. (Payne, 1995: 165)

Community work has generally been associated with holistic, collective, preventative and anti-discriminatory approaches to meeting social needs, based on value commitments to participation and empowerment.

'As stated,' Payne continues, 'this looks innocuous.' Public policy statements, both in Britain and internationally, abound with commitments to the values of participation and empowerment. In practice, however, as Payne goes on to point out, 'community work has proved controversial and problematic', having the capacity to draw 'attention to inequalities in service provision and in power which lie behind severe deprivation' and so to become part of struggles 'between people in powerless positions against the powerful' (Payne, 1995: 165–6) This has been offered as an explanation for the British government's decision to conclude its own experiments in community development (the Community Development Projects – CDPs) in the 1970s, for example (Loney, 1983).

Why then, given its potentially controversial and problematic characteristics, has community work not merely survived from the 1970s, but taken on an apparently new lease of life from the 1990s onwards into the twenty-first century? This chapter starts by exploring some aspects of this question. Having summarised key features of the current context, this chapter will move on to provide some 'mapping', including a brief discussion of different definitions of key terms, together with a rapid summary of the recent history of debates around community work as an approach to social work.

The discussion will then focus on issues and debates in community work today. What are the main theoretical perspectives, and what are their varying implications for community work practice? At what levels, and in which types of practice setting, is community work most relevant and appropriate? What are the key areas of knowledge and skills which are required? This chapter will also consider a number of the more negative features and some of the key dilemmas of the contemporary context, in terms of both policy and practice. This will then provide the basis for concluding with an overall appraisal of community work's contribution, both actual and potential. What has community work to offer as an approach to reflective social work practice? And what changes in social policy might be required if community work's contribution were to be enhanced?

The context

The economic and social policy context within which social work and community work operate has changed significantly since the 1970s. These changes have been characterised in terms of 'globalisation', an expression which has become increasingly fashionable since the 1980s, 'when it began to replace words like "internationalization" to denote "the ever intensifying networks of social and economic relationships"' (Dominelli and Hoogvelt, 1996: 46). These changes have also been described in terms of a number of 'posts' – post-industrialism, post-Fordism, post-structuralism and postmodernism (Taylor-Gooby, 1994; Dominelli and Hoogvelt, 1996; Penna and O'Brien, 1996). There are key differences between these terms, as Penna and O'Brien point out, the first two referring predominantly to debates within political economy, the latter two having been more concerned with debates within cultural studies. These differences are beyond the scope of this chapter.

What these different terms share in common, however, is a common sense that the old order of 'modern' industrial society is in a state of flux and transition, on a global scale, whether this is in terms of economic change, or in terms of social, political and cultural change. These changes have fundamental implications for welfare states in general, and more specifically for the social policy context for social work and community work.

In summary, despite national and local differences, there are powerful global trends, it has been agued, including trends towards increasing marketisation, increasing privatisation, increasing fragmentation of services and the technocratisation of social work itself, in the contract culture (Dominelli and Hoogvelt, 1996). These changes pose significant threats. They also pose new contradictions. For community work in particular, the current focus upon the role of the community sector, within the mixed economy of welfare, could be seen to represent new opportunities as well as new challenges. Only, this increased emphasis upon the role of the community sector is taking place within the wider context of reduced public resources, including reduced public resources for the support and development of the community sector itself. Similarly, the current focus upon the promotion of self-help, diversity and choice offers new opportunities for some, against a background of reduced opportunities and choice for others. This makes it more important than ever that those engaged in community work are actively aware of these divergent tensions and critically reflective in their practice.

'Mapping' community work: definitions and recent history

This need for clarity starts with the concept of 'community' itself, a term which has over time been the subject of confusion and contestation (Crow and Allen, 1994; Mayo, 1994a; Payne, 1995). The uses of the term 'community' which have greatest relevance for community work can be broadly summarised as follows:

- 'community' as shared locality – a common geographical area, for example a neighbourhood, a housing estate in an urban or suburban context, or a village in a rural area;

- 'community' as shared interests – these might be interests based upon cultures and identities, as in the case of ethnic minority communities, or upon common identifications of particular needs (as in the case of the parents of children with special needs, or ex-users of mental health services, for example).

The term 'community' is frequently applied to services to differentiate them from institutional forms of provision (for example community care services for the elderly in their own homes and/or in day centres in their localities, rather than in residential homes or geriatric hospitals). The term 'community' is often contrasted with 'state', as in the case of the 'community sector', which has been associated with small, relatively informal and 'bottom-up' forms of service provision, in contrast to the larger, more bureaucratic forms of service provision typically associated with the public sector. Community-based services have been associated with the promotion of unpaid caring and self-help (often in response to widening gaps between shrinking services and increasingly unmet social needs). Also, community-based services have been associated with more participatory and more empowering approaches to social welfare provision, based upon enhanced respect for the diversity of users' and carers' own perspectives.

As has already been pointed out, community work has a long history as an aspect of social work, predating the current focus within the mixed economy of welfare. Broadly speaking, community work has been defined as being concerned 'with enabling people to improve the quality of their lives and gain greater influences over the processes that affect them' (AMA, 1993: 10). Twelvetrees has suggested that, at its simplest, community work is 'the process of assisting ordinary people to improve their own communities by undertaking collective action' (Twelvetrees, 1991: 1). Community work has been particularly concerned with the needs of those who have been disadvantaged or oppressed, whether through poverty or through discrimination on the basis of class, race, gender, sexuality, age or disability.

Community work developed from the late nineteenth-century settlement houses, starting with Oxford House (founded in 1883) and Toynbee Hall (founded in 1885), linked to social work as well as to community education. Through the work of the community association movement in the interwar period, and community work in the new towns, after World War II, community work developed as a professional activity, alongside the unpaid work of volunteers and activists in community organisations and social movements. At the end of the 1960s, the government launched its own Community Development Project as part of its efforts to combat poverty and deprivation through more holistic and more preventative approaches to social welfare (Loney, 1983), approaches which were emphasised in the Seebohm Committee's conception for the future of the social services:

> directed to the well-being of the whole community and not only of social casualties, seeing the community as the basis of its authority, resources and effectiveness. (Seebohm Committee, 1968: 147)

Similar arguments were put forward by the Barclay Committee's Report in the early 1980s (Barclay Committee, 1982).

This emphasis upon the role of the community, and the need for partnerships between social service departments and the local communities they served, re-emerged, at the end of the 1980s, in the changing context for social work in the mixed economy of welfare (Bamford, 1990). In particular, the Griffiths Report (1998) on care in the community took up the theme of closer partnerships between statutory services and local communities as part of the new welfare pluralism. The NHS and Community Care Act 1990 enshrined both increasing marketisation and a potentially increasing emphasis upon community work, at least in theory if not necessarily in practice. Whatever the varying outcomes in reality, following these and related changes in social policy and local government, it is hard to imagine social work reverting to previous models within all-encompassing local authority social service departments, as the Seebohm Committee had envisaged. This all goes to demonstrate the significance of the challenges for community work.

Community work and social work

Community work has a long history as an approach to social work. In the context of the NHS and Community Care Act 1990, there has been particular interest in community work in relation to community care, promoting care in the community, as well as enabling service users and carers to participate in planning, monitoring and evaluating community care services. Community social work has not, however, been confined to community care. Community-based social work has been and continues to be relevant across a wide range of social work practice, including preventive work with children and their families, for example, as studies by Cannan and others have demonstrated (Cannan, 1992; Smith, T., 1995).

While community work has a continuing role, as an approach to social work, however, community work has not been confined to social work. Community work has featured as an approach to youth work, and it has featured and continues to feature within other professional settings, including housing and planning, and more recently in relation to area regeneration. In addition, community work has also been carried out, and continues to be carried out, by volunteers and unpaid activists within communities.

There have been long-running debates on whether or not community work should be defined as a professional activity at all, professionalisation having been posed as potentially undermining to community activism and autonomous community movements (Banks, 1996). In summary, then, community work has its place as an approach to social work, but community work is not confined to the social work profession.

Alternative perspectives and implications for practice

By this time, it should have become apparent that community work can be and has been based upon competing perspectives, associated with both right and left positions on the political spectrum. Community work has been promoted to encourage self-help and informal caring, compensate for reductions in public service provision within the context of the increasing marketisation of welfare, support strategies to combat poverty and oppression, and facilitate community participation and empowerment.

Texts such as Twelvetrees have distinguished between alternative community work perspectives, contrasting the 'professional' approach, which seeks to promote self-help and improve service delivery within the wider framework of existing social relations, with the 'radical' approach. This latter 'radical' approach seeks to go further, contributing to shifting the balance of existing social relations through empowering the relatively powerless to question the causes of their deprivation and challenge the sources of their oppression, 'drawing upon insights from neo-Marxist structural analyses, together with insights from feminism and from anti-racist analyses' (Twelvetrees, 1991). This is the type of approach which supports minority ethnic communities, for example, in drawing attention to inequalities in service provision and 'in power which lie behind severe deprivation' (Payne, 1995: 166).

While these distinctions have relevance, the terms 'professional' and 'radical' have inherent problems, in the current context, as Twelvetrees himself has also recognised. In particular, in recent years, the term 'radical' has become even more confusing, since its adoption by the 'radical' right. The use of the term 'professional' to describe one perspective could also be taken to imply that the alternative perspective was in some way 'non-professional' or even 'unprofessional' (although this was not actually suggested by Twelvetrees himself). Given that professional values, knowledge and skills are essential to community work, whatever the perspective in question, it has been suggested that it would be less confusing to categorise community work perspectives in terms of a 'technicist' approach on the one hand, and a 'transformational' perspective, emphasising community empowerment and social transformation, on the other hand' (Mayo, 1994b).

These two broad types of community work perspective have also been broken down into further subdivisions and related to the different types and levels of community work practice. Dominelli, for example, has characterised the traditional, 'neutral' views of community work in ways which are comparable to the 'technicist' approach. She defines these views in terms of their assumptions that 'the system' is basically sound, although individual and community pathologies need to be ironed out through the community work process; she quotes Biddle and Biddle's comment that 'the poor and the alienated must overcome their inner handicap practically through the cultivation of their own initiatives' as a classic text to illustrate this approach (Dominelli, 1990: 8).

Dominelli then goes on to characterise three models of community work – community care, community organisation and community development – in terms which can be related to this broad type of 'traditional', 'neutral' or 'technicist' approach. Community care schemes based on the use of unpaid and typically white, middle-class women volunteers to cover gaps in statutory provision would fit into this 'neutral' approach, for example, although the effects may be far from neutral, in terms of reinforcing inequalities of race, gender and class, in service provision. Similarly, Dominelli places community organisation[1] – or community work which focuses on improving the coordination between various welfare agencies – as typically forming a tool of corporate management rather than a tool for more fundamentally challenging the inequalities in resource allocation (including the specific inequalities experienced by women and black people). Third, Dominelli considers the community development model, which focuses on the promotion of self-help skills, and fits this, too, into this broad type of approach; this is especially the case, it is suggested, when leadership in community development programmes is provided by outside professional experts brought into so-called problem areas to tackle social problems as defined by the state. However, Dominelli also points out that, where community development

Table 14.1 Two perspectives on community work

Perspective	Goals/assumptions
'Professional'	To promote community initiatives, including self-help
'Traditional'	To improve service delivery (within the framework of existing social relations)
'Neutral'	
'Technicist'	
'Radical'	To promote community initiatives, to improve service delivery and to do
'Transformational'	so in ways which empower communities to challenge the root causes of deprivation and discrimination, and to develop strategies and build alliances for social change (as part of wider strategies to transform oppressive, discriminatory, exploitative social relations)

involves collective struggles to achieve groups' demands, this community development model may turn into 'community action'.

In contrast, Dominelli considers three models which would be more consistent with the 'transformational' approach, as outlined above – class-based community action, feminist community action and community action from a black perspective. These models are all, in their different ways, about more fundamental social change (including a change in the consciousness of those affected), whether focusing upon addressing inequalities of class, gender and/or race. Dominelli describes class-based community action in terms of bringing people lacking power together 'to reduce their powerlessness and increase their effectiveness' (Dominelli, 1990: 11), typically using conflict, direct action and confrontation as well as negotiation to achieve their ends. Feminist community action has

> transcended the boundaries of traditional community work by challenging fundamentally the nature of capitalist patriarchal social relations between men and women, women and the state and adults and children. (Dominelli, 1990: 11)

Community action from a black perspective has made the struggle for racial equality central to their work – while anti-racist feminist community work has been committed to eliminating both racial and gender inequality.

As Dominelli and others have also recognised, however, there is, in practice, a degree of overlap between these different models, 'particularly in the areas of techniques and skills adopted' (Dominelli, 1990: 7), and there have been continuing debates, including debates about differences within both feminist and anti-racist approaches, which are beyond the scope of this particular chapter. (For a guide to these debates, see, for example, Williams, 1989.)

As has already been suggested, in the context of the particular pressures and tensions of the mixed economy of welfare, this makes it all the more important that community workers are critically aware of the potential implications of different models and reflective in their practice. More specifically, this context requires increasing knowledge and skills, as community workers have to operate within the more complex and more fragmented environment of the mixed economy of social welfare provision. Whatever the history of community organisation, in terms of whether or not this model has necessarily implied a more traditional, less structurally challenging/transformational perspective in the

Table 14.2 A continuum of community work models?

Model/level of work	Perspective typically associated with model
Community care Community organisation Community development	'Professional' 'Traditional' 'Neutral' 'Technicist'
Community action Feminist community action Community action from a black perspective	'Radical' 'Transformational'

past, in the current context community workers neglect community organisa-tion work at their peril (not to mention the potential peril of the communities they work with professionally). The local authority, although a key player with overall responsibility, can no longer be expected to be the key provider of relevant services. Communities may need to negotiate with a wider range of agencies, public sector agencies, quangos, private sector agencies, voluntary, not-for-profit and other community sector organisations. In the current policy context, considerable emphasis is being placed upon 'partnership working', including the development of partnerships between private, statutory, voluntary and community sector agencies. Partnership working is far from unproblematic however, and partnership structures can be experienced by the less powerful groups and communities as being effectively excluding and disempowering (Balloch and Taylor, 2001). Community workers have a potentially more vital role than ever, here, in empowering communities to address these situations effectively. Community workers need to be effective, then, at the levels of inter-agency work and at the levels of local and regional planning, as well as at the level of grass-roots neighbourhood work.

Similarly, I would argue that, in the current context of the mixed economy of welfare, a considerable proportion of community workers will be needing to address community care issues, whatever their own perspectives. Models of community work practice, which place community care at one end of the spectrum, through to community action and feminist, black and anti-racist community work at the other end of the spectrum, need to be reconsidered in the light of these changing conditions (Popple, 1995).

Community care can be approached, in any case, from different perspec-tives – from traditional perspectives which focus upon the promotion of self-help and volunteering in ways which substitute for rather than enrich public service provision, or from more transformational perspectives which address issues of immediate needs within the context of wider strategies for community empowerment, supported by anti-discriminatory, anti-oppressive community work practice. Such an approach has been set out, for example, in the chapter by Shaw which addresses the possibilities as well as the problems for community

Table 14.3 Beyond a continuum? Alternative perspectives on community care, community organisation and community development

Models	Alternative perspectives and practice	
	Traditional/technicist *for example:*	Radical/transformational *for example:*
Community care	Promote volunteering	Empower users and carers
Community organisation	Promote interagency coordination	Negotiate/campaign for organisational change to improve services/support for the community sector
Community development	Promote self-help to tackle concentrations of deprivation	Empower communities to develop strategies to tackle deprivation and disadvantage

care, drawing upon the Scottish experience (Shaw, M., 1996). The point to emphasise here is that, whether community workers are focusing upon community care issues and/or tackling interagency community organisation issues, they need to reflect upon their practice critically. Is their practice informed by relatively traditional, 'technicist' perspectives on community work, which focus upon managing social problems and containing social needs? Or, alternatively, how far is their practice informed by more transformational perspectives, geared not only towards meeting social needs, but also towards addressing the causes of oppression and discrimination and promoting community empowerment?

Whatever their underlying perspective, however, community workers need an increasingly sophisticated core of background knowledge, techniques and professional skills (see Beresford and Trevillion, 1995). Broadly speaking, as a starting point, community workers need to be confident of their skills in the following areas:

- engagement (with a range of individuals, groups and organisations);
- assessment (including needs assessment, via area profiles);
- research (including participatory action research with communities);
- groupwork;
- negotiating (including working constructively in situations of conflict);
- communication (across a wide range of contexts);
- counselling;
- the management of resources (including time management of self);
- resourcing (including grant applications);
- recording and report-writing (for a wide range of purposes);
- monitoring and evaluation.

These are, of course, typically skills which are widely transferable. In addition, community workers need a sound background knowledge of social policy and welfare rights, together with a specific knowledge of the fields in which they are predominantly operating, such as health and welfare policies and practice in relation to community care, child protection legislation for those concerned with children and families in the community, and housing and planning legislation for community workers involved in housing, planning and urban or rural regeneration programmes, for example. In addition, as it has been argued elsewhere:

> community workers need to have knowledge and understanding of the socio-economic and political backgrounds of the areas in which they are to work, including knowledge and understanding of political structures, and of relevant organisations and resources in the statutory, voluntary and community sectors.

And they need to have knowledge and understanding of equal opportunities policies and practice, so that they can apply these effectively in every aspect of their work. (Mayo, 1994b: 74)

Some current issues and dilemmas

In recent years, community work has had to respond to the criticism that it is an area of practice that is 'both imprecise and unclear' (Popple, 1995: 1). In a period of increasing pressure to target scarce resources more precisely, with clearer performance indicators, there has been decreasing scope for generalist, preventive community work, the type of work with children and families in deprived areas that Holman (1983), for example, has carried out and analysed so effectively and with such inspiration. Crisis management in child protection, for example, has tended to divert resources from community-based approaches to the support of children and families in need (for example through community-based family centres and particular initiatives such as childcare projects and credit unions).

More specifically, community work has tended to be promoted within particular, short-term initiatives, such as projects to promote community participation in government-initiated urban regeneration schemes such as 'Single Regeneration Bid' programmes. By their very structure, as short-term schemes, these have had a focus upon short-term outcomes and very specific performance indicators (such as the numbers of trainees attending training courses). The point to emphasise here is absolutely not that there is a case for exempting community work from the fullest public accountability. However, the contemporary emphasis upon short-term interventions, evaluated by overly narrow performance indicators, has risked being ultimately self-defeating, marginalising the more holistic, preventive, longer-term approaches to community work – the type of community work which has been pioneered by Holman, for example, and developed, for instance, in the more community-based family centres (Holman, 1983; Cannan, 1992; Smith, T., 1995; Durrant, 1997). While there are some encouraging signs of increasing recognition of the need for longer-term strategies to promote regeneration and neighbourhood renewal, there is still some way to go in terms of more holistic approaches to evaluation.

Area-specific programmes can be potentially divisive in communities, too, where community groups find themselves competing against each other for limited resources. The point to emphasise here is that, even if particular groups and individuals take a more positive view of programme outcomes, communities overall could be left even more fragmented and alienated following community regeneration interventions. Community workers need to be critically aware of this potential for negative as well as for positive outcomes. This is a key point and one which relates to a long history of debates over how far community work, like other approaches to social work, can be controlling rather than caring and enabling. There are parallels here with debates around contemporary notions of communitarianism, including debates about how far this actually focuses upon responsibilities rather than rights, upon communities policing themselves and/or competing with neighbouring communities for limited resources, eked out via self-help, rather than working together to challenge the policies in question.

CONCLUSION

In the contemporary context of the mixed economy of welfare, community work has a potentially more vital contribution than ever to make. Community workers can support communities in coming together to work out their needs, and then take action together to meet those needs. Also community workers can work in ways which empower communities to develop strategies to challenge inequalities in service provision and indeed to begin to challenge the underlying causes of discrimination and deprivation.

Conversely, however, this contemporary context is also more problematic than ever, with the risk of further fragmentation and increasing inter- and intracommunity conflicts. This means that community workers need greater professional expertise than ever. Most particularly, their practice needs to be informed by critical theory if they are to address these challenges as reflective practitioners.

Without significant changes in the wider context, including significant changes in the social policy context, however, community work risks remaining severely constrained as an approach to social work. It will continue to be hampered by the short termism which has reduced rather than increased support for the community sector and focused upon crisis management, to the detriment of longer-term and more holistic strategies of meeting social needs in preventive and anti-discriminatory ways, ways which are both participatory and empowering.

Notes

1   The term 'community organising' has been used somewhat differently in North America, generally being associated with 'community mobilisation/community.

FURTHER READING

Balloch, S, and Taylor, M. (2001) *Partnership Working: Policy and Practice* (Bristol, Policy Press). Explores aspects of partnership working.

Beresford, P. and Croft, S. (1993) *Citizen Involvement: A Practical Guide for Change* (London, Macmillan – now Palgrave Macmillan). A discussion of user involvement.

Bulmer, M. (1987) *The Social Basis of Community Care* (London, George Allen & Unwin). The background to sociological and social policy debates.

Cannan, C. and Warren, C. (eds) (1997) *Social Action with Children and Families* (London, Routledge). Readings in community social work with children and families.

Dominelli, L. (1990) *Women and Community Action* (Birmingham, Venture Press). Issues of gender, race and class in community work.

Popple, K. (1995) *Analysing Community Work* (Buckingham, Open University Press). A textbook on community work.

Psychosocial Work

David Howe

Introduction

It would be possible to argue that, in essence, social work *is* psychosocial work if by psychosocial we mean that area of human experience which is created by the interplay between the individual's psychological condition and the social environment. Psychosocial matters define most that is of interest to social work, particularly people who are having problems with others (parents, partners, children, peers and professionals) or other people who are having a problem with them. There is a simultaneous interest in both the individual and the qualities of their social environment.

For example, a woman neglected as a child may have low self-esteem, feel anxious and agitated in close relationships, becoming depressed when she feels unable to control what is happening to her. She needs to be loved and valued but can never take other people for granted or trust them. Her partner comes from a similarly adverse 'socio-emotional' background. Their relationship is characterised by mutual anxiety as each fears that the other may abandon them, and mutual anger as each believes that the other is capable of causing them hurt. The result is that their relationship is full of conflict and turbulence, anxiety and depression. The emotional needs of both people are so great that any children of their union are, in their turn, likely to experience an emotionally disturbed upbringing. The woman's past social experiences affect her emotional make-up. These influence the way she approaches and handles *current* social experiences. The way her partner and children react to her behaviour then creates yet another round of family life to which she has to respond. And so on.

The basic dynamic between psychology and setting can be used to explore all aspects of people's psychosocial functioning. The developmental frameworks that help to analyse social behaviour and the quality of people's past and present relationships provide social workers with a powerful theory to guide all aspects of practice, including observation, assessment, evaluation of risk, decision-making, the choice of methods of help and treatment, worker reflectivity and models of practitioner supervision.

Although the research and knowledge base which underpin this perspective continue to develop apace, the main features of the approach were recognised and described as early as the 1920s and 30s. Perhaps the most articulate and coherent rendition of the psychosocial approach was, however, made by Florence Hollis, best captured in the second edition of her book *Casework: A Psychosocial Therapy*, published in 1972. In this work, she defines the essential elements of a psychosocial approach, in which she argues that clients and the contexts in which they find themselves have to be thought about and handled simultaneously. Using the knowledge bases of her time, Hollis was inclined to use Freudian psychology to inform the 'psycho' element of the approach, and social systems theory to develop the 'social' component of the practice.

Attacks during the 1980s by Marxists, early feminists and behaviourists on much of social work's traditional knowledge bases, including psychoanalytic theory, dealt a severe blow to the use of psychosocial outlooks in welfare work. A few core concepts and practices remained, including those of loss, grief and mourning, but the basic approach went into steep decline, at least in social work. However, in psychology, particularly developmental and clinical psychology, the concept of the 'psychosocial' continued to develop and grow, playing a major part in providing the discipline with a powerful perspective on understanding people's psychological development and behaviour in various social and cultural contexts (see, for example, Rutter and Smith, 1995). It is ironic that social work, which had such early claims on the 'psychosocial', now finds itself turning to other social sciences to rediscover the rigour, relevance and usefulness of adopting socio-emotional outlooks on human relationships.

The socialness of self

Although the idea that we are 'social selves', whose being and personality form within social relationships, is not new, there has been a resurgence of interest in the 'socialness of self' in the social sciences (see, for example, Bakhurst and Sypnowich, 1995; the phrase 'the socialness of self' is used by Mulhall and Swift, 1995). The self and personality form as the developing mind relates with and tries to make sense of the world in which it finds itself. As it does this, it takes on many of the properties of the environment which it seeks to understand and negotiate. How we understand, think, feel, see and conceptualise, although heavily influenced by inherited temperamental and biological dispositions, is also shaped by our social, cultural and linguistic experiences. Individuality is socially based, and personality forms as social understanding develops (Burkitt, 1991: 2).

The developmental implications of this perspective are that the *quality* of relationships with other people during childhood has a direct bearing on the development of personality and the emotional make-up of the individual. The poorer the quality of people's relationship history and social environment, the less robust will be their psychological make-up and ability to deal with other people, social situations and emotional demands:

> it seems that the postulate that a lack of continuity in the loving committed parent–child relationships is central has received substantial support ... What has stood the test of time most of all has been the proposition that the qualities of parent–child relationships constitute a central aspect of parenting, that the development of social relationships occupies a crucial role in personality growth, and that abnormalities in relationships are important in many types of psycho-pathology. (Rutter, 1991: 341, 361)

Therefore, the way in which different personalities handle and develop their *current* social environment is in large measure a product of *past* relationship experiences. Current social performance hints at people's earlier social experiences. Past relationship histories help us to understand current levels of social competence.

Inner working models

Different types of personality indicate the different ways in which people attempt to make sense of and adjust to their relationship environment. Adverse environments which lack love, mutuality and empathy are less conducive to the formation of secure and confident personalities. Children who lack responsive, consistent and predictable relationships find it more difficult to handle the emotional stresses that life inevitably throws up. The coherence of people's psychological organisation reveals the type of psychological adjustments which they have had to make in order to cope with their social environment. The models used to represent relationships gradually become internalised, forming the basis of personality (Bowlby, 1988). The individual's personality is judged by the characteristic ways in which he or she makes sense of and handles social relationships and experiences. In our development, what is on the social outside therefore establishes itself on the psychological inside. In this sense, external relationships become mentally internalised (Howe, 1995: 24).

As they seek to understand what is happening around them, babies create mental representations to interpret the confusion of experience. Once established, these models act as templates within which subsequent experiences of that type are interpreted. Of central concern is the infant's need to understand the relationship she has with her prime care-givers. Attachment figures (in the first instance, usually, but not necessarily or only, the mother) provide the child with security and her first opportunity to be in a relationship. To be a competent player in the relationship, the child needs to make sense of the selected attachment figure emotionally and socially. In order to do this, however, she has to understand her own self, other people and their shared relationship. For this to be possible, the young mind has to build up an internal working model of the mother so that her actions, feelings, beliefs and intentions can be read (Bowlby,

1988). Here are the beginnings of social understanding. The more open, full and accurate the communication between mother and child, the more the child learns to understand the mother, her own self and their shared relationship. Such mutuality encourages reciprocity, empathy, responsiveness, cooperation, regard and respect. Experience helps to generate the models, and the mental models then aid in the interpretation of future experience. In this way, *past* experiences influence how *present* experiences are approached and understood (Bowlby, 1988; see also Howe, 1995).

Everyday life is a matter of understanding and negotiating the world of other people. The more children are able to make sense of their social world and understand their own place within it, the more adept, skilled and relaxed they can be in social relationships. In turn, this improves their chances of developing mutually rewarding friendships, entering reciprocally based intimate relationships, becoming caring parents and emerging as socially competent beings.

Frith (1989: 169) reminds us that, 'The ability to make sense of other people is also the ability to make sense of one's self'. Children learn about their own psychological states within relationships. The more sensitive, empathic and reciprocal the communication within relationships, the more fully will children learn to understand the nature and effect of their own mental states on themselves and those around them. The more they can understand the basis of their own thoughts and feelings, the more skilled will they become at understanding and interacting with other people. Imbalances, insensitivities and inconsistencies in the care-giver/child relationship mean that the infant's attempts to model interpersonal experience are more difficult to achieve. Not being able to make sense of experience is confusing, stressful and anxiety-provoking. When other people are unpredictable and not susceptible to influence or control, children are less able to learn how to conduct themselves socially. The argument is that, if human beings are social beings, the ways in which we develop social understanding and become socially competent are of great relevance to those who work with parents and their children.

Attachment and relationship-based theories are examples of a psychosocial perspective. Attachment theory is a good example of how a psychosocial perspective can help us to understand and assess the quality of people's social relationships. The success with which people relate with others is a measure of their 'social competence'. Attachment theory provides us with a coherent, well-researched and elegantly argued set of ideas about the feelings, behaviours and psychological strategies we all use in our dealings with others, particularly if those others are our partners, parents or children (see Bowlby, 1979, 1988). Parents are the people most likely to provide children with their early, close relationship experiences. Attachment theory explores how the qualities of children's relationships with their carers affect their socio-emotional development, which then influences the way in which they relate to and deal with other people. Therefore, if we are to understand the quality of children's social environment, we also have to understand the parents, their personalities and the kinds of relationship they generate with each other and their children. If the social outside influences the child's psychological inside, we need to pay careful attention to the quality of the relationship between the two.

Attachment behaviour

Attachment behaviour is a biologically adaptive response designed to ensure that babies get into close, protective relationships. They need to get into such relationships at times of danger and when they feel anxious. They also need to be in close relationships with their prime care-givers in order to develop social understanding, interpersonal competence and language. By the time they are one year old, most children have established strong *selective attachments* to one or more adults or older children.

Attachment behaviours are triggered when children experience stress or anxiety. At such times, children seek out their attachment figure. This person is experienced as a 'secure base' – a place of safety and comfort. When children are not anxious or in need of comfort, they are free to explore and learn about their environment. It follows that children who experience a lot of anxiety have less time and emotional energy to explore and learn how to become socially adept.

Four types of relationship experience and their impact on psychosocial development and competence

Researchers and clinicians who have studied interactions between parents and their children have observed that the type of relationships they form depend on the parent's physical and emotional availability, sensitivity, reliability, predictability, responsiveness, level of interest and level of concern. Children who experience their attachment figures as usually available and responsive feel *secure*. Those who do not experience their attachment figures as reliably available and responsive feel varying degrees of *insecurity*. Ainsworth et al. (1978) worked with many of Bowlby's ideas and were the first to formulate an attachment classification system. Others have added to and refined the original classification, but the basic framework remains in good shape and of great relevance to social workers.

Although there are now many refinements, we might recognise four basic types of attachment experience. Each type represents a certain kind of emotional relationship within which a child has to make particular kinds of psychological adjustment if he or she is to cope and survive in the social world. We have already said that aspects of the child's personality and ability to develop social understanding form within these important relationships. Natural temperaments, degrees of resilience and cultural contexts certainly have a strong part to play, but the classification remains extremely useful in helping childcare workers to understand children's emotional experiences and psychosocial functioning. The theory insists that many features of our personality and emotional life form within the history of our relationships with others. Therefore, the different patterns of attachment lead to particular personality and relationship styles during childhood and beyond into adulthood. We might consider four types of attachment:

1. secure attachments;

2. insecure, ambivalent attachments;

3. insecure, avoidant attachments;

4. disorganised attachments.

A basic understanding of these four relationship environments helps practitioners to make sense of the way in which children and adults react to and deal with the social and emotional demands of others.

Secure attachments

In secure parent/child relationships, care is loving, responsive, predictable and consistent. There is a sensitivity to children's needs, thoughts and feelings. Communication between care-givers and children is busy and two-way. There is mutual interest and concern in the thoughts and feelings of the other. Within such relationships, children begin to understand and handle both themselves and social relationships. They feel valued, socially competent and interpersonally effective. Other people are seen as trustworthy and available. These children are usually sociable and well liked by peers. They cope reasonably well with the conflicts, upsets and frustrations of everyday life. As they mature into adulthood, they continue to feel good about themselves. In Main et al.'s terms (1985), these are 'autonomous' and 'secure' people who have a broadly realistic, accurate and workable view of themselves, other people and the relationships between them. Such people are only likely to come the social worker's way at times of great environmental stress (hospitalisation, a disaster, the physical demands of a disability or old age) or in the guise of a resource (foster carer, adopter or volunteer).

Insecure, ambivalent attachments

When parental care is inconsistent and unpredictable, children begin to experience increasing levels of anxiety. The problem is one of neglect and insensitivity rather than hostility. Parents often fail to empathise with their children's moods, needs and feelings. Misunderstandings and inaccurate communications abound. The child is never quite sure where he or she is within the parent/child relationship. The child becomes increasingly confused and frustrated. Distress and anxiety lead to a clingy dependence. To this extent, children feel that the world of other people is hard to fathom and impervious to their influence and control. Love comes and goes in what seems an entirely arbitrary way. This generates a fretful, constant anxiety. Children become demanding and attention-seeking, angry and needful. They create drama and trouble in an attempt to keep other people involved and interested. Feelings are acted out.

Insensitive and inconsistent care is interpreted by children and adults to mean that they are ineffective in securing love and sustaining comforting relationships. Their conclusion might be that they are not only unworthy of love, but also might be unlovable. This is deeply painful. It undermines self-esteem as well as self-confidence. Thus, there is a need for closeness but a constant anxiety that the relationship might not last: 'I need you, but I am not sure I can trust you. You may leave me and cause me pain, so I feel anger as well as fear.' Such feelings provoke jealousy, conflict and possessiveness in relationships. Children, indeed adults, who have grown up in such relationships are racked by insecurity. There is a reluctance to let go of others, yet a resentment and fear that they may be lost at any time. The result is that people cling to relationships, yet conduct them with a high level of tension and conflict.

No matter how fraught, for those who feel anxious and insecure, it often feels better to be in an 'active', noisy relationship with the world. Silence and isolation trigger feelings of emptiness and despair. Lives, therefore, are full of drama and crisis, many of which will appear on the social worker's doorstep.

Insecure, avoidant attachments

Children who develop avoidant patterns of attachment have parents who are either indifferent, hostile, rigid or rejecting. Although these parents may respond reasonably well when their child appears content, they withdraw when faced with distress and the need for comfort and attention. The clinging, complaining behaviour of children in ambivalent attachment relationships serve no purpose in these cooler styles of parenting. Attempts at intimacy only seem to bring rebuff and hurt. Carers encourage independence and de-emphasise dependency. When separated from their parents, these children show few signs of distress. Upon reunion, the children either ignore or avoid their attachment figure. Adults cannot be trusted or relied upon. It seems better to become emotionally self-reliant. Feelings are suppressed. To experience such rejection must mean that the self is unlovable or even bad. Self-esteem is very poor.

Lack of emotional involvement and mutuality mean that both children and adults find it hard to understand and deal with feelings. Empathy is poor. Anxiety and frustration easily lead to anger and aggression. These may not be popular people. They can be unfeeling, even cruel. They may find it difficult to form intimate, emotionally reciprocal relationships. Getting too close brings the fear of rejection and pain. As children, they may bully and try to get their way through physical force rather than social skill.

Disorganised attachments

Many children who suffer physical abuse and maltreatment seem to show a confused mixture of resistant and avoidant patterns of attachment (Main and Solomon, 1986). The parent may not be wholly hostile or rejecting, but there are times when they are either dangerous or very frightening to the child. Relationships of this kind produce *disorganised* and *disturbed* attachment patterns in which the parent's violent or scary behaviour causes the child to feel extremely anxious. Anxiety normally triggers attachment behaviour in which the child approaches the parent for comfort. But in these cases, the attachment figure is the cause of the anxiety, so to approach him or her actually raises the level of anxiety. The child is therefore faced with a dilemma. There is an urge both to *approach* and *avoid* the attachment figure. The result is that the child is deeply confused and either physically or emotionally 'freezes'. This confusion extends to dealings with other people. Distress and undirected, agitated behaviour is often the result when children find themselves in close relationships. They do not know how to seek comfort nor do they seem to know how to respond to other people's warmth and concern. There is a general air of helplessness and disorientation.

Assessments

Using a psychosocial approach places a great deal of emphasis on making thorough, carefully observed, theoretically informed assessments of people, their relationships and their sociocultural environment. We need to know how people act and relate with each other, how they behave with their children, neighbours and officials, how children respond to parents, peers and teachers, and how they play and react to demands and difficulties. How people react to 'outer world' events tells us about their 'inner world'. Indeed, among the 'people professions', social work remains peculiarly well placed to appreciate how people bring feelings to situations and how situations provoke feelings in people (Winnicott, 1964; Schofield, 1996). There is a need to identify the stresses in people's lives. Do they have unsupportive partners, live in poverty or experience isolation? What children and adults say and do, then, needs to be interpreted within the logic of a psychosocial framework. The character and quality of people's current behaviours and relationships tell us about their internal working models, defensive inclinations, emotional states and personality. Although working within a psychosocial perspective does not require social workers actively to enquire about people's past experiences, large amounts of information will in practice be acquired about their childhoods, relationships with others, including sexual partners, encounters with authority, emotional states, material problems and interpersonal ups and downs. This information can be fed into the assessment to help the social worker to understand the way people are relating to their social and material environment.

Practice

A detailed psychosocial assessment allows social workers to begin to make sense of what people say and do. It sees links between past and present relationship experiences. Connections can be made between the emotional and behavioural impact of people on each other. The ability of people to feel in control of their own mental, social and economic state is recognised as fundamental to their general well-being. When control is absent, anxiety rises. And when anxiety mounts, a variety of feelings and behaviours may be triggered, including anger, despair, worthlessness, aggression, denial and avoidance, which brings them to the attention of social agents. Using a psychosocial approach allows social workers to understand and 'stay with' the apparent confusion and complexity that seems to characterise the lives of so many clients. The ability to make sense of what is going on allows practitioners to respond calmly and clearly. In this way, they are able to contain difficult emotional situations and continue to be available to people who feel frightened and confused, angry and impotent. Such client/worker relationships provide the opportunity for reflection, emotional growth, rational planning and decision-making.

Working within a psychosocial perspective defines two major areas of interest for the practitioner. The first concerns the notion of *risk factors* – what elements of the individual's psychosocial environment place their development, emotional well-being and social competence at risk. Social workers and clients need to identify such risks so that they may be avoided, decreased, changed or removed. Risks range from the obvious (for example, physical and sexual abuse) to the more subtle (for example marital discord, the absence of emotional support, neglect, social isolation and financial worries). The second requires the social worker to identify the *protective factors* in an individual's psychosocial environment – what elements are promoting their well-being, sound socio-emotional development and social competence. Social workers and clients seek to increase, introduce and improve factors which strengthen and protect psychosocial functioning. *Emotional, social and economic support* are among the most effective protective measures we can receive (see, for example, Brown and Harris, 1978). Such support may be introduced in a variety of ways. Conflict may be reduced between parents. Depressed mothers may be encouraged to meet other women at a family centre. Social workers may provide frequent, low-intensity visits (Jones, 1985). Attempts may be made to increase social security benefits. In extreme cases, in order to reduce risks to psychosocial functioning, clients may need to be removed to new social environments, as happens in the case of the adoption of older children or the transfer of an old person into a residential home.

CONCLUSION

At a deep level, a psychosocial approach taps into important contemporary debates about the development of behaviour and personality, and the social nature of being human. Increasingly, social scientists are recognising that our natures and development are the exclusive result of neither genes nor experience. Rather, there is a complex interaction between the two, in which the way our inheritance expresses itself and develops depends on the physical and social environment in which we find ourselves, and the way in which our environment is shaped and reacts depends on our individual characteristics (see, for example, Plomin, 1994). These insights provide the basic intellectual outlook of a psychosocial approach. Not surprisingly, psychosocial theory has been seen to have greatest relevance in childcare and family work. However, the perspective is being increasingly used in work with other client groups. The quality of the social environment appears to be an important factor in understanding the onset and experience of those at biological risk from either schizophrenia or depression. Social developmental models might help us to understand the various kinds of relationship that develop between elderly parents being cared for by their adult children, bearing in mind that the children themselves are the product of the care and attachment environments generated by their parents.

Always at the heart of practice, psychosocial theories are being revitalised in social work as other disciplines, particularly in the psychological sciences, exploring how people develop (or fail to develop) social understanding and interpersonal competence. If social work is about people's emotional well-being, personal develop-ment and social behaviour, a psychosocial approach provides theories which help to both explain personal experience in a social context and to guide practice.

FURTHER READING

Dunn, J. (1993) *Young Children's Close Relationships: Beyond Attachment* (Newbury Park, CA, Sage). A stimulating read, written by a leading developmentalist, that takes a well-rounded look at young children's development in the ever-changing context of family, peer and cultural relationships.

Durkin, K. (1995) *Developmental Social Psychology: From Infancy to Old Age* (Oxford, Blackwell). A solid, comprehensive introduction that provides a good understanding of personal growth and the role of developmental processes in building social relationships throughout the lifespan.

Howe, D. (1995) *Attachment Theory for Social Work Practice* (London, Macmillan – now Palgrave Macmillan). A broad outline of the main features of attachment theory, backed by a comprehensive review of the research literature, and aimed at social workers both in training and in practice.

Howe, D., Brandon, M., Hinings, D. and Schofield, G. (1999) *Attachment Theory, Maltreatment and Family Support: A Practice and Assessment Model* (London, Macmillan – now Palgrave Macmillan). The application of developmental attach-ment theory to child abuse and neglect.

Mattinson, J. and Sinclair, I. (1979) *Mate and Stalemate* (London, Institute of Marital Studies). A first-hand account, backed by analytic and attachment-oriented theories, of working with marital problems in a social services department, packed with case examples.

Rutter, M. and Rutter, M. (1993) *Developing Minds: Challenge and Continuity across the Life Span* (Harmondsworth, Penguin). An examination and review of the research literature that looks at human development over the course of life, paying particular attention to the continuities and discontinuities in the psychological growth process.

Cognitive-behavioural Practice

Katy Cigno

Introduction

The rapid expansion in recent years of theoretical and empirical research in applications of learning theory has not been matched to the same extent by growing awareness and interest of social work practitioners. Fischer's (1974) 'quiet revolution' has gained some ground in the British context but, at nearly three decades hence, not as much as expected. Later in this chapter, we shall consider some of the reasons for this.

During this same period, terminology changed, reflecting shifts in emphasis. For example, Payne, writing in 1991 about theories in social work, divided the cognitive from the behavioural and discussed their theoretical bases in separate chapters. The journal *Behavioural Psychotherapy* changed its name to *Behavioural and Cognitive Psychotherapy* in 1993 with volume 21, number 2, in line with the title of the association which publishes it. Sheldon revised his 1982 text *Behaviour Modification* and published it in 1995 as *Cognitive-behavioural Therapy*, including sections on the role of cognition in the development of problems and in helping to determine which behaviours will be performed. Note that the hyphen denotes a linking of cognition and behaviour: a deliberate indication of how the one informs the other and how both elements are important for therapeutic practice. Sutton (2000a) gives an excellent account of the development of cognitive-behavioural theory.

A careful examination of the role cognition plays in deciding whether a behaviour will be repeated or not, or how it helps, on the one hand, in the learning of behaviours, and on the other, in eliminating unwanted behaviours, is a particular contribution which social workers (although, of course, not uniquely; see, for example, the earlier work of Herbert, 1987a, 1987b; Falloon, 1988; Falloon et al., 1993; Webster-Stratton and Herbert, 1994) have made and should make to the literature as well as to the enhancement of practice skills. Social workers' broad remit, attention to both the immediate and wider environment and their tradition of intervention in the client's own home setting put them in an ideal position for developing applications of cognitive-behavioural theory to the real and often untidy, oppressive world of clients of social welfare in local authority and other non-clinical settings. This chapter will concern itself with such applications.

The policy context of social work

Superficially, the recent and actual political and social policy climate would seem favourable to the advancement of the principles of cognitive-behavioural practice. Pragmatic concentration on presenting situations and problems, planned, focused work, contracts, the attention to goals, outcomes and evidence for 'What Works': does this not fit in with value for money, managerialism and performance indicators of Best Value and effectiveness? Furthermore, current legislation and procedures, while rarely acknowledging the influence of learning theory and competency-based approaches, have nevertheless absorbed several of their essential principles. Some examples are:

- the Children Act 1989 and its 'working together' guidance, especially the new version (DoH/Home Office/DfEE, 1999), with the emphasis on working in partnership with professionals, parents and children, clear assessments, written, negotiated plans and systematic reviewing;

- the frameworks for quality services for children (DoH, 1998c) and for assessing children in need and their families (DoH/DfEE/Home Office, 2000);

- the National Health Service and Community Care Act 1990, with its user involvement and needs-led assessments within a context of what is realistic and possible;

- CCETSW's Paper 30 (CCETSW, 1991) and the revised version (CCETSW, 1995): their evidence-based approach to assessment incorporates the direct observation of student social worker skills, identifies knowledge and values necessary to the social work task and lists progress indicators for judging the success or otherwise of a student's intervention.

Some of these trends in the world of social work have 'good guy' and some 'bad guy' connotations since the legacy of the reverses of the welfare state during the years of Thatcherism (Hutton, 1996) but are largely helpful. At the same time, a backlash against such approaches within the broader agenda of 'What Works' and evidence-based practice has already begun (see, for example, Gorman, 2001, writing in *Probation Journal*). We need to consider why this should be so.

First, many misconceptions prevail about learning theory approaches: they are mechanistic; they are about punishment; they are concerned with institutions and token economies. This view ignores the many research-based British texts published over the past two decades (for example, Hudson and Macdonald, 1986; Falloon et al., 1993; Sutton, 1994, 1999, 2000b; Iwaniec, 1995; Scott et al., 1995; Sheldon, 1995) as well as the smaller but significant number of case studies written by social workers from the position of mainstream social work and social services (Iwaniec et al., 1985a, 1985b; Bunyan, 1987; Bourn, 1993; Cigno, 1993; and see Cigno and Bourn's 1998 book of case studies and practice examples). Thus the convincing body of research and its availability increases at a pace not commensurate with practitioner readiness to base work on sound theory and effective approaches (Sheldon and Chilvers, 2000).

This leads to the second point: keeping up with the research on effectiveness of different social work approaches is hard work, although there are some reviews available to make the task easier (for example, Macdonald et al., 1992; Macdonald, 1994; Sheldon, 1994; the University of Exeter's Centre for Evidence-based Social Services' *Newsletter*). It requires considerable commitment to seek after truth and carry out our ethical duty of using only those approaches where there is evidence that they work in that situation, with this family or person, with those problems (Cigno and Wilson, 1994), rather than following our own predilections. Apart from a love affair between social workers and 'family therapy', Payne (1991) noted that social workers still use psychoanalytic theory and do not find cognitive-behavioural theory attractive: this is still largely true today. Decisions to use one approach rather than another do not appear to be based on research evidence of 'what works' (Newman et al., 1996).

The third reason is that some North American research is based on clinical studies of what hard-pressed local authority social workers would rightly regard as esoteric problems unlikely to come their way in their work with the disadvantaged, poor, oppressed, multiproblem section of the population in crowded inner cities or isolated, amenity-deprived rural areas. This, of course, ignores the important and ground-breaking studies by social work academics such as Thomas (1974), Fischer (1978) and Gambrill (1983, 1997).

To sum up, many practitioners may be reluctant to use cognitive-behavioural therapy because they object 'on vague philosophical grounds ... they just don't like the look and sound of anything "behavioural"' (Sheldon, 1995: 31), although Hollin et al. (1995) point out that client resistance is much less than that of practitioners.

We now go on to consider more precisely what we mean by cognitive-behavioural practice, its underpinning theories and how an understanding of it can help us to identify people's problem behaviours as well as work out programmes with them to improve significant aspects of their lives.

Cognitive-behavioural practice

Before describing procedures and giving examples of their relevance to social work settings, I shall attempt, in the space available, to define and discuss what is meant by learning theory (or, more properly, theories) on which cognitive-behavioural intervention is based.

Behaviour is, largely, a result of prior learning, and what we learn is acquired in different ways. Sometimes we learn, so to speak, inadvertently or without deliberate intention. This kind of learning by association is known as classical conditioning: Pavlov's dogs produced saliva at the sound of a bell or approaching footsteps which they had learned to associate with the bringing of food; a child's fear of the dentist who has drilled into a tooth after an unpleasant injection may spread to fear of other people in white coats in clinical-like settings.

We also learn through others' reactions to our behaviour or through environmental consequences: our behaviour is established and maintained by reinforcement, which we sometimes like to think of as a 'reward', although it may not necessarily look 'rewarding'. A volunteer may work in an Oxfam shop because she finds it a pleasant environment in which to meet people and also because it makes her feel good to be doing something worthwhile, but many of us would not work unless we got paid. This kind of learning is known as operant conditioning. Here we can already see how our thoughts, or cognitions, have a role to play in deciding whether a behaviour will be repeated or not, as well as whether it is reinforced.

Many behaviours, such as the way we talk (regional accent?), walk (swagger or glide?), cook or drive a car, are acquired by watching or listening to someone we like or respect doing it. This is called modelling or vicarious learning. We may think about others' performances and talk it over with ourselves (what effect will we have?, will we be able to imitate the behaviour successfully?) before we repeat the action. Sutton (1994) uses the term 'social learning theory' which encompasses a good deal of what we have briefly outlined above. She describes it in a clear and useful statement:

> Social learning theory comprises a large body of concepts which, happily, are recognised by researchers in the disciplines of both psychology and sociology. It concerns how children and adults learn patterns of behaviour, as a result of social interactions, or simply through coping with the environment ... it suggests how to focus upon the practical rather than the pathological, upon people's strengths and potentials rather than upon their weaknesses or shortcomings, and upon how to empower those with whom we work. (Sutton, 1994: 5–6)

Clearly, the effects of what we do are going to determine which behaviours will be repeated and in which circumstances. It is this knowledge of how and why we learn that enables the cognitive-behavioural practitioner to make a thorough assessment of a 'problem' behaviour which, according to its possessor or to one or more significant others, needs changing. It may be that more of the behaviour is desired, as for example in cases of non-school attendance, or less, as in cases of adults who have difficulty in controlling their anger. Scott (1989) has written about social work with parents where the focus is on controlling anger which leads to the potential or actual abuse of children, and where techniques include relaxation, role-rehearsal and self-talk. Getting a child back to school often entails changing the parent's or the teacher's behaviour, which may be the reason for the child's absence from the classroom in the first place. Fear of maths or sports, worsened by a teacher's sarcasm or shouting, may be the antecedent to sickness or truanting.

Fundamental to cognitive-behavioural therapy is the observation that being aware of our thinking does not necessarily alter behaviour. Understanding, achieving 'insight' into why we do what we do, by no means inevitably leads to behaviour change. We may think 'This is bad for my teeth' as we reach for another chocolate, or 'These harm my health' and 'I must see about giving this up' as we light a cigarette, or 'This never really works and I shouldn't do it' as we raise a hand to smack a child. We listen to the sound of our voice as we quarrel with our loved ones and think 'This is awful; I'm making things worse.'

Scott et al. (1995) give examples of how cognitions – anxious thoughts, maladaptive interpretations of self, unrealistic expectations of others and disturbing ruminations – affect behaviour in many, often serious, ways. An awareness of these processes is a start, but a consideration of our own, our friends' and our clients' experiences tells us that this alone does not usually lead to the desired behaviour change. Crucially, strategies are also required. Cognitive restructuring – challenging, for example, negative thoughts about ourself ('I'm no good') and teaching others to do so – has been described and applied by social workers, such as Scott and colleagues (1995); much cognitive-based work derives from the studies of Beck (1976) and Beck and Emery (1985). There is still much work being done in this area, but most practitioners would agree that a mainly cognitive approach needs to be evaluated by indicators of behavioural and environmental change. One has only to think of the implications of a client with a serious addiction or a parent whose child has been identified as being at risk of overchastisement telling the worker, 'I think things are better now', and of the practitioner going away satisfied that the intervention has been a success on this evidence alone. In social work, therefore, a careful combination of cognitive and behavioural techniques can be useful and appropriate, provided that clearly defined behavioural goals are identified to ensure that an evaluation of practice as 'a success' is soundly based.

Areas of practice and links with effectiveness

There are, then, many areas where research and experience indicate that help with behaviour problems is required. Herbert (1987b), in his preface to a book on helping children and their parents with problem behaviours, describes his conversion to a behavioural approach. When he was practising as a child psychologist, a despairing mother told him that she wanted to know what to *do* when her child screamed and cried. As we have said, understanding is not enough; people want strategies to help them cope.

One area where families of children with learning difficulties do not get sufficient help is behaviour problems (Burke and Cigno, 1996). Sinclair et al. (1995) report that 30 per cent of children in the care system are referred because of problematic behaviour. Research shows that helping parents to learn different responses to their child's behaviour and teaching them parenting skills can help to prevent abuse or stop it escalating (see Cigno, 1995, for a review of the literature, and Chapillon, 1996, for a student social worker's account of a parenting skills group).

Social skills training (SST) has been used effectively with different client groups, including people with various degrees of learning difficulty (for example, McBrian and Felce, 1992; Cullen et al., 1995), with adults in different situations and with diverse problems (Hollin and Trower, 1986), with people with mental health problems (Hudson, 1982; Oliver et al., 1989; Oliver and Hudson, 1998), with young people leaving care (Biehal et al., 1992) and with young offenders and alcohol-related crime (McMurran and Hollin, 1993). Some undesirable results of a certain kind of punitive 'training' were discovered by Gendreau and Ross (1987) in their research on 'boot camp' rehabilitation. After such treatment, there is evidence that the young offenders become leaner, fitter criminals. The authors conclude that cognitive-behavioural intervention, rather than short, sharp shocks, works (see also Gendreau and Andrews, 1990).

Old people are not often thought of as having goals or indeed as being suitable for the attention of social work intervention. Gambrill (1986), however, reports a successful, step-by-step approach to helping older people in the community express what they would like to achieve. They can be assisted to improve the quality of their lives by, for example, making telephone calls to friends and organisations to increase social contacts. The behaviour can be rehearsed then reinforced by encouraging comments; as calls achieve success, they become self-reinforcing. Cigno (1993, 1998) describes a behavioural programme carried out in residential care with a 70-year-old woman to decrease unwanted aggressive behaviour and increase helpful acts and contacts in the wider community (see below).

Motivational interviewing (see Rollnick and Miller, 1995) developed from learning theory principles such as the use of positive modelling, cognitions and selective reinforcement of self-statements to change the behaviour of adults, including young offenders, with addictions (Tober, 1991, 1998; McMurran and Hollin, 1993). Indeed, motivational interviewing, because of its promising results, is now used in other fields, too.

In the area of child welfare, what is familiarly known as the Dartington research has drawn attention to key criteria for assessing outcomes with young people (Bullock et al., 1993, 1999; DoH, 1995a). In order to evaluate outcome, it is not only important to take into account factors such as maturation and other variables which operate externally to the intervention (Hill and Aldgate, 1996b), but also to draw up a baseline on features of well-being such as health, educational achievement, level of social skills and troubled behaviour of the person concerned prior to intervention and service provision. It is possible, for example, to assess outcomes for children and young people according to how far they conform to accepted social norms of behaviour.

Consumer research, from the early British study of Mayer and Timms (1970) to the many studies now available, confirms that clients of all ages value attributes such as reliability, openess, honesty and clarity in their social worker, quite apart from any particular approach adopted (Stein and Carey, 1986; Howe, 1989). Happily, these qualities are the basis for the client/worker relationship within which cognitive-behavioural social work is practised. Freeman et al. (1996) report the feelings of young people on being let down by social workers over such matters as cancelled visits and postponed meetings. Some missed visits may be inevitable, but many are due to poor planning and lack of consideration of the meaning of such disappointments for vulnerable and relatively powerless clients. Similar findings of appreciated practitioner attributes are found in a study by Cigno (1988) of the views of mothers attending a family centre.

The evocative accounts of users of being on the receiving end are important feedback as long as other, more objective, outcome criteria are employed alongside (Cheetham et al., 1992). All the technical skills in the world are to no avail if the practitioner lets the client down by oppressive practice such as missed appointments and lack of openness over further action. It is crucial that students learn this during their practice placements, for one of the ways we learn is by modelling ourselves on others' behaviour. 'Show me' is a reasonable position for a student to take vis-à-vis experienced, qualified practitioners. It is very common often not to connect one's own behaviour with those to whom we are close and over whom we have influence. As a parent once said apologetically of her child, 'I don't know why he **** swears like that. I'm always telling the little **** not to **** well do it.'

Assessment and intervention

The key to good practice is thorough assessment. In the case of cognitive-behavioural approaches, this needs to be detailed. Apart from adhering to basic social work values such as those mentioned above, social workers need to practise from within a relationship of warmth, genuineness and empathy. Assessments may vary, but a good starting point for many situations where the aim is behaviour change is an ABC (Antecedents, Behaviour, Consequences) analysis. It has the advantage of being easy to remember and is an excellent guide to the questions to be asked. In brief, these are as follows:

- *Antecedents*. What are the circumstances in which the behaviour takes place? What happens just before the behaviour in question? (It is often useful to obtain information about more distant antecedents, too.)

- *Behaviour*. How can the actual behaviour be described? What does the person do?

- *Consequences*. What happens immediately after the behaviour?

The worker and the client together discuss the relationship between the three. Many of our clients, living in poor housing, jobless, ill-educated and often suffering from health problems, exhibit what Seligman (1975) has called 'learned helplessness'. They do not think or feel that they can make any impact on their situation; it is their destiny to suffer the 'slings and arrows of outrageous fortune'. In some areas of their life, and in the immediate term, this may be true; however, if they can learn to take action in one small part of their life, the results can be greatly reinforcing, can increase self-esteem and encourage the client to take small steps to improve other aspects of living.

Ms A's three children were on the child protection register because of her ex-partner's abuse and her own lack of parenting skills. The children, aged three, five and seven, were, according to their mother, 'out of control' and 'did what they liked'. She attended a parenting skills course where she constantly said 'Things are no better'. Gentle exploration of this statement by the worker revealed that she was now managing to get the children to school and that she was thinking of taking a course at the local college, 'but I'm thick'. She was surprised when the worker praised her for her efforts and discussed how she might go about getting information about courses. A home visit indicated that Ms A was now talking to the children and had some control over them. She subsequently went to the library to obtain leaflets about part-time courses. Pointing out to her and giving her credit for the changes she was making to her own behaviour and how she was able to influence her children's behaviour to their benefit made her smile. She was further encouraged by the other parents in the group 'evaluating' her progress by telling her 'You should have seen how you were a month ago'.

Pointing out that Ms A's negative self-statements were not true was a start. Tracing her attempts to improve her management of the children, praising her for getting them to school and talking to them at home, and observing how they responded to this encouraged her to continue with these new behaviours. She began to see that, with encouragement, she could take steps to change some elements in her environment and was not forever destined to be a 'bad mother' and 'thick' (for a discussion of these issues from a user self-help perspective, see Adams, 1994).

The above is an example of challenging learned helplessness of a mother where there was risk of neglect and abuse to children, and of shaping coping behaviour mainly through cognitive restructuring and positive reinforcement. The next example is of a case where careful observation of a person's environment, behaviour and its consequences led to an ABC assessment, hypotheses, intervention plan, review and evaluation. It is based on Sutton and Herbert's ASPIRE assessment framework (Sutton, 1994), where AS stands for Assessment, P – Planning, I – Intervention, R – Review and E – Evaluation (see Burke and Cigno, 2000, for an example of the use of ASPIRE in work with a child with learning disabilities).

The problem concerned a young man, C, attending a centre for adults with learning disabilities. Various activities took place, and, as well as participating in these, service users were encouraged to take responsibility for other tasks. C was often asked to take messages from one member of staff to another. He was willing and pleased to do this but usually returned after a long while with the message undelivered. Staff could not understand why this was so and renewed their attempts to impress upon him where he had to go. One worker volunteered to study the problem, observing C over the space of two weeks. Her analysis was as follows:

- *Antecedents*: An activity room, often the education room (because one of C's goals is to improve his literacy skills). C is asked to take a message to someone in another part of the building.

- *Behaviour*: C sets off. Talks to the manager on the way. Walks round the building, sometimes stopping at different rooms. Returns to where he started, message undelivered.

- *Consequences*: Staff express disappointment. C misses much of the teaching/activity session. C cannot tell why he has not delivered the message. C's learning goals are not achieved.

One hypothesis is that C enjoys wandering about rather than participating in an activity. If so, it is good that he is having a pleasant time but less good that he is not achieving his own learning objectives. The second is that he fails to understand the instructions given or understands but forgets. Further observation showed that both hypotheses are partly right. C likes being entrusted with a message but also enjoys chatting to the manager and walking about. Nevertheless, he is not happy when he realises that he has failed to carry out the task, nor when he misses an activity.

The volunteer observer discovered that the instructions given to C did not follow the same pattern. This is related to the second hypothesis. Here are some of the instructions he was given over the observation period:

Take this to Mr Jones
Take this to Mr Jones' room
Tell Mr Jones the forms are here
Take this to the craft room
(and so on, with the substitution of another name or room)

So he is sometimes directed to a person and sometimes to a room or activity in a fairly random way. After a while, and particularly after a chat with the manager, C would either have forgotten where he was going or would not remember the name of the person to whom to give the message. Writing the name down for others to read would reduce C's responsibility. This longstanding problem was solved by giving C, along with the message, something to remind him of his destination: a piece of wood, a cotton reel, a tube of paint, a book and so on. The manager was also asked to prompt him by asking to see the object he was carrying. This programme worked: messages were delivered, C's pride in his achievement and competence increased and he spent more time on improving his literacy and other skills.

Putting this plan into operation required working together as a staff team in order to achieve a coherent response. Otherwise, C's wandering behaviour and failure to complete a given task would have been intermittently reinforced, perpetuating his confusion over what was expected of him.

The next situation also demonstrates how important it is to try to make sure that anyone involved in a behavioural programme is aware of how essential it is not to respond in different ways to a behaviour targeted for elimination or increasing. (Parents will be well aware that the child refused sweets, staying up late, going out to play and so on by one parent may achieve success by making the same request to another parent or a grandparent!)

Gambrill (1983, 1986) writes about how professionals often do not consider that old people have goals. Neither are they often the subject of 'casework' but rather of the allocation of resources, important though the latter may be. Similar points, albeit from different perspectives, have been made by Wilkes (1981) and Erikson et al. (1986). Yet, in both field and residential settings, the quality of life of older people and their family or co-residents can be improved.

A detailed account of the case of Miss B, a resident in a home for elderly people, is given by Cigno (1993, 1998). Miss B's problems were that she shouted, upsetting and frightening other residents as well as exasperating staff.

Sometimes she would throw things on the floor during mealtimes. This got her attention from staff, while at other times, when she was calm or helpful, she tended to be ignored. The places where these behaviours took place could be almost anywhere and could be triggered by a look perceived as hostile (antecedents). Miss B would then shout, swear, insult someone or argue (behaviour), resulting in complaints from residents and scolding from staff, sometimes ending in a shouting match (consequences). Further consequences were exclusion from a social event because of fears that she would make a scene.

Miss B was helped, by the use of a chart, to record periods free from outbursts and, by rewards which she selected, to reduce her aggressive behaviour and increase her social skills. Gradually, the charts were withdrawn as the changes in Miss B's behaviour began to alter the way in which residents and staff reacted to her. In other words, enough reinforcements were present in the natural environment to render the use of a chart redundant.

Devices such as charts and other symbolic rewards and monitoring systems are useful for clarifying and establishing desired behaviours with some clients – a diary is often a good way of recording and reviewing progress – but these should be withdrawn once the behaviour has been firmly established or eliminated. Tangible rewards, such as special outings, comfort food and so on, should always be accompanied by social rewards such as smiles and praise.

CONCLUSION

Therapeutic approaches have a place in mainstream social work. There is a case for thoughtful, systematic intervention – what used to be called 'casework' – as part of a 'package of care' to be carried out by the practitioner and not referred to other professionals (Sinclair et al., 1995). Once the therapeutic component of social work is lost through privatisation or loss of competence, it is doubtful whether it will ever be regained. As our American colleagues have advocated, 'Say you're a social worker!' (not a therapist or a case manager).

Although social work and social services (now often referred to as social care) will continue to go through many stress-provoking changes, social workers should make sure that their work is as competent as it can be in the light of current knowledge of what works. Learning about cognitive-behavioural intervention is part of this preparation. To do this, we need the best prepared people to practise social work: to paraphrase Pearson (1983), if this is elitist, so should we all aspire to be.

FURTHER READING

Cigno, K. (2002) 'Helping to prevent abuse: a cognitive-behavioural approach with families', in Wilson, K. and James, A. (eds) *The Child Protection Handbook*, 2nd edn (London, Baillière Tindall).

Cigno, K. and Bourn, D. (eds) (1998) *Cognitive-behavioural Social Work in Practice* (Aldershot, Ashgate). This book, containing case studies and practice examples by distinguished contributors to cognitive-behavioural therapy and evidence-based practice, draws on a wide range of research as well as practice experience. It covers a broad area of intervention with different client groups in a variety of settings, including childcare, probation and youth offending, mental health, addictions, disability and older people.

Cognitive Behavioural Social Work Review. Published twice a year for its members by the Cognitive Behavioural Social Work Group, it is also available in many university libraries. It contains practitioner accounts of intervention as well as more academic articles, information and book reviews. Contact Rosemary Strange (Secretary), Copper Beeches, 96 Heath Lane, Earl Shilton, Leicester LE9 7PD.

Iwaniec, D. (1995) *The Emotionally Abused and Neglected Child: Identification, Assessment and Intervention* (Chichester, John Wiley). A major and timely contribution to the literature as more attention is focused nationally and internationally on the lasting damage caused by the prolonged emotional abuse and neglect of children.

Sutton, C. (1994) *Social Work, Community Work and Psychology* (Leicester, British Psychological Society). The author, whose practice and research have roots in social work and psychology, provides an account of human development across the life-span and evidence-based practice, covering different settings in the context of a multicultural society. Carole Sutton has continued to publish in the field of working with children, familites and adolescents, and on parent training, throughout the 1990s and into the twenty-first century.

17

Task-centred Work

Mark Doel

Introduction

One of the biggest challenges facing the social work profession is how to square professional practice with the 'circle' of organisational constraints. The break-up of social work into its constituent tasks and the increasingly proceduralised nature of the work of agency practitioners are two factors which lead back to Brewer and Lait's question of 1980, *Can Social Work Survive?* (Brewer and Lait, 1980).

This chapter will present task-centred social work not as *the* answer to the question of survival, but as one of the best available. It will also seek to clarify what task-centred social work is, in the light of misconceptions deriving from its name.

Task-centred social work has its roots in North American casework practice. It is widely known that Reid and Shyne's (1969) research project, *Brief and Extended Casework*, looked at the effectiveness of short-term casework, but perhaps fewer understand that what they experimented with was a curtailed form of long-term work, cut short after a number of sessions. They found that the interventions which were allowed to run their full course were no more and no less effective than those which were foreshortened. It was Reid and Epstein (1972) who made a virtue of the short interventions by developing a short-term therapy, making positive use of a time limit to achieve a 'goal gradient effect'; in other words, the closer we approach a deadline, the more motivated we are to take action.

From these beginnings in the mainstream of social casework, the model has grown and adapted to a wide variety of contexts. It has been tried and tested in work with children, families and elders; in large public welfare agencies, small voluntary agencies, probation, school and hospital settings; in fieldwork, day, domiciliary and residential work; by students, experienced practitioners and managers; with individuals, groups and communities; with a wide range of difficulties and problems; and with people from diverse cultures and backgrounds (see Doel and Marsh, 1992: 118–22 for a comprehensive guide to the task-centred literature). In short, task-centred social work is a generic practice method whose effectiveness has been subject to more evaluation and scrutiny than any other social work practice method.

In the process, task-centred casework has become task-centred practice, an indication of its development from individualised, therapeutic beginnings to a broader stage; a move away from relatively conservative practices into more radical territory, embracing notions of partnership, empowerment and anti-oppressive practice, and signalling practical ways of realising these ideas.

Task-centred work and other social work ideas

The influences on task-centred social work have been broad and various. From its inception in the psychosocial tradition, it soon became embroiled in the heat of the inquisition over behaviourism – just how behaviourist was task-centred work? In a debate which now seems as unfashionable as loons and flared trousers, task-centred work was seen as merely 'soft' – as opposed to the 'hard' behaviourism of those whom traditionalists considered beyond the professional pale. What these questions served to show was the growing influence of learning theory as a way of understanding why people behave as they do. This in turn led to consideration of alternative patterns of behaviour and an increasing focus on outcomes and the ways in which these can be defined and measured (Jehu, 1967). All of this was consistent with the developing technology of task-centred practice, with its aim for a more precise statement of problems and goals, and a philosophy of 'small successes rather than large failures'.

As the behaviourist controversy faded, systems theory became the latest fashion statement, its essential design being detailed by Pincus and Minahan (1973). The systems approach in general, and the task-centred one in particular, contributed much to providing a unified approach to social work practice. More recently, in an example of 'retro' style, Tolson et al. (1994) make a strong case for task-centred as a generalist practice, using concepts from systems theory to demonstrate how task-centred practitioners can move within and between systems at different levels. This approach places the problem centre stage, so that it is the problem rather than the person which is 'the client'.

Task-centred practice is a member of the family of problem-solving models. In addition to developing its own techniques, such as the task planning and implementation sequence (Tolson et al., 1994: 73), it borrows from many others (such as 'positive reframing' from family therapy). The vogue for social skills training in the late 1970s and early 1980s made its mark on the task-centred methodology, for example in the use of techniques such as 5W+H (what? when? who? where? why? and how?) when investigating the specific nature of the problem, and coaching and rehearsal methods to help people to achieve success with tasks (Priestley et al., 1978).

In the 1980s, task-centred practice was well placed to give voice to the clients' rights/consumer choice movement (BASW, 1979). With its emphasis on working with people around issues which they considered prime, it provides a strong counter to paternalistic professional practice. Its links with open and shared recording (Doel and Lawson, 1986) and the requirement for explicitness about the purposes of the work, gave task-centred practice an ambiguous attraction to both radical and managerial elements in social work. This tension continued into the 1990s and beyond; task-centred practice provides a visible means of shaping the good intentions of partnership and the concrete expression of anti-oppressive principles, while also attracting interest from agency managers keen to have measurable outcomes and explicit systems of accountability.

Task-centred practice is primarily about learning. Indeed, the task-centred encounter between social workers and service users can be likened more to a teaching session than, say, a medical consultation, an administrative interview, a salesperson's pitch or a therapy session. The task-centred encounter should have the feel of a highly participative workshop.

The essence of task-centred work

A brief description of the components of the task-centred model will help to place in context the themes and issues which are raised in this chapter. For a detailed exposition of the British variant of the task-centred model, see Doel and Marsh (1992). In addition, briefer summaries are available in Doel (1994) and Marsh (1991).

Task-centred casework was first described as a method to help people with 'problems of living' (Reid and Epstein, 1972). It is a systematic model of social work with a coherent and explicit value base. It has a 'practice technology' which has developed out of a body of research to examine what works well and what works less well. There is, therefore, a 'how to' aspect of the model, in addition to a clearly expressed 'why'. Its value base is anti-oppressive in that it addresses issues of power and oppression, both in the immediate encounter between worker and service user and in the broader social context.

There are three phases in task-centred social work, plus entry and exit.

Entry

The point of entry for a social worker is often muddy. The purposes of any contact may be unclear for the worker, the service user or both. Conversely, the participants may have clear but contrary purposes. Unlike most other services, the social work service might be unwelcome.

It is essential that practitioners use a method of work which accommodates these complex factors. It should not enforce consensus where none exists, but should ease the process of reaching agreement where one is possible. Above all, it should be sensitive to the service user's 'world' – the context in which the work occurs and the relative power of the participants.

There is, rightly, a debate about the extent to which partnership is really possible. Dominelli (1996: 157) writes that 'the real extent to which "clients" gain control through task-centred approaches remains a matter of controversy'. She sees financial constraints, policy imperatives and the practitioner's value base as setting boundaries which pre-empt the possibility of real power-sharing. Of course, these are factors common to all social work interventions, whichever method is used. However, the task-centred model ensures that discussion of power is part of the work itself.

Phase 1: Exploring problems

There is no neat 'cut-off' between the entry period and the first phase of exploring problems. In many instances, the early parts of the investigation of problems will confirm or challenge the mandate for further work. The worker may have spent much time helping the person to 'engage with the problem'; de Shazer (1988) uses the term 'visitors' for those people who think that the problem is someone else's.

The encounter between the task-centred worker and the service user is a systematic approach which links areas of concern to desired changes, which are achievable through a relatively brief and intensive plan of action. As well as an outcome, there is an explicit attempt to learn from this particular experience of problem-solving, in order to generalise to other circumstances. The learning is mutual; the service user learns to generalise to problem-solving with other life difficulties, and the practitioner evaluates this example in the light of other task-centred encounters in order to learn what tends to works and what tends not to work.

This first phase is composed of a number of smaller stages:

- Problem-scanning, which involves a wide review of problematic areas (the 'headlines') and a deliberate avoidance of explanations and solutions.

- Additional problems, consisting of problem areas evident to the practitioner but not mentioned by the service users.

- Detailing each of the identified problems, with an investigation which focuses on the problem as a way of gaining a better understanding of it, rather than to provide causal explanations or fodder for a social diagnosis. Questions such as 'What will be the first sign that you are overcoming the problem?' and 'What are you doing that stops things from being worse?' help the person to colour in the details (George et al., 1990: 10).

- Selecting a problem (or, to use the jargon, 'targeting'), in which the service user makes a choice about the problem area they want to work on, based on their informed judgement and having considered factors such as the feasibility of working on the various problems. There may also be 'mandated' problems, which the worker is sanctioned to work on, even though they are not recognised as a problem or a priority by the client.

Phase 2: Agreeing a goal – the written agreement

Having focused on difficulties, problems and concerns, the work now turns to what it is the person wants. Goals may already have been mentioned, and they can often been confused with problems ('I need to get out of this house' sounds like a problem but it is in fact a goal, and it may not be the best way to address the problems it is intended to resolve). All involved in the work need to be aware of how the the agreed goal(s) will resolve or alleviate the selected problem(s). The goal must be one which is within clients' control to achieve, one which they are well motivated to work towards and which workers consider ethically desirable (in other words, they can lend their support to it).

A significant factor in the success of the goal is to decide a time limit by which the goal will be achieved, an agreed pattern for contact between worker and client, and concrete indicators of how success will be recognised. The time limit sets the work in a framework, and the indicators for success allow all involved to pace their progress and gauge the distance to achievement.

Together, the selected problem(s), the agreed goal(s), the time limit and frequency of contact make up the agreement. This should be recorded (usually written, with copies for all involved), but other formats should be considered in work with people with a visual impairment or difficulties with literacy.

Phase 3: Planning and implementing tasks

Once the written agreement is in place, the rest of the task-centred work follows a recognisable pattern from one session to another, in which past tasks are reviewed and evaluated, and future tasks are developed and implemented.

The 'task' is a central construct of task-centred social work, yet there is much confusion over this notion. The everyday English use of the word carries misleading implications, for example that tasks are always 'physical doings' when, in task-centred practice, they can be cognitive reflections, mental lists, a log of feelings and so on. Everyday tasks are usually free-standing ('My task today is to get the ironing done'), which is why many practitioners consider that they are working in a task-centred way when all they are doing is performing tasks. In task-centred work, tasks are carefully negotiated steps along the path from the present problem to the future goal. They build in a coherent fashion, sometimes completed in the session itself, sometimes completed between sessions, some for the user and some for the worker, some repeated, others unique (see Doel and Marsh, 1992: 60–79, for a full account of the significance of task development and review).

The importance of task development to the service users' success in achieving their goal has led to a five-stage task planning and implementation sequence (Tolson et al., 1994). This is based on research into what promotes task achievement. Reid (2000) provides a comprehensive guide to possible task 'menus' in a wide range of circumstances.

Exit

The end of task-centred work has been planned from the beginning; indeed, the built-in time limit is a powerful motivator for success, whether the intervention is a short, intensive burst over a few days or a number of sessions spread over several months. The length of work is a judgement based on how long it is likely to take to achieve the goal. Any change should be negotiated explicitly rather than allowing a sense of drift.

In situations where there is long-term contact between the service user and the agency (for example in residential care), task-centred agreements can be negotiated periodically.

Issues

A systematic practice method

It is evident from the preceding description that task-centred work is a systematic method of practice. One way of illustrating what is meant by 'systematic' is to consider one task-centred practitioner acting as 'a fly on the wall' watching the work of another. Although the observer has not been involved in the work and knows none of the background or context, he or she will recognise the practice as task-centred, identify the particular phase of the work and any specific technique being used, and predict the shape of the next sequence of work. For example, the observer might state:

> This is the middle phase of the work. They have been reviewing the work on the tasks agreed at their previous session, using the scoring method to help the clients make a judgement about their success. They are now developing new tasks. The practitioner is helping them to generate these by using the Headlines technique, usually associated with the earlier problem exploration stage. The practitioner might provide some coaching later, depending on the nature of the tasks, and the tasks will certainly be recorded so that they all have a copy. They will agree a time by which the tasks should be completed and the practitioner will probably refer back to the original agreement, so they are all clear about why these tasks are relevant and when the work will end.

The observer will even be able to make some comments and judgements about how well the work was progressing and how skilled the observed practitioner was:

> I've never seen the Headlines technique used at this stage – that was very imaginative and I'm going to try it myself. I liked the way the practitioner asked '*What* changes have happened since I last saw you?' rather than '*Have* any changes happened since I last saw you?' I think the worker should have been clearer about the reasoning behind the scoring – even when a task has not been completed, there are things to be learned from that failure and the practitioner came over as half-hearted at that stage ... and so on.

Although each task-centred encounter is recognisable as such, it is not a question of 'painting by numbers'. The mood and feelings of the clients, their particular circumstances and the context of the work all guide the practitioner, so that each encounter is unique. It has been likened elsewhere to a tidal progress, often slow and with one pace back for each two forward, but overall there is movement (Doel, 1994: 23).

Who is task-centred work for?

In an earlier section, we explored how task-centred practice has been influenced by psychosocial, behavioural, systems and problem-solving theories, in addition to broad movements such as clients' rights and anti-oppressive practice. Is the task-centred model, therefore, a coat of many colours?

There is certainly anecdotal evidence that many practitioners subscribe to task-centred practice. Payne (1995: 119) suggests that it is 'a popular model of social work, widely used in the UK'. In a survey of 25 student placement reports, 17 mentioned that task-centred practice had been used. (Second was counselling, mentioned in 7 reports.) However, there is a suspicion that if social workers wish to convey a sense that their work is purposeful and active, they label it 'a task-centred approach'.

Task-centred practice is fast becoming the new eclecticism, popular but undifferentiated. In the audit of practice undertaken in the *Social Work in Partnership* action research, which employed a task-centred model of practice, Marsh and Fisher (1992: 41) found that the initial response from participants was 'We do all that already.' It is an irony that its apparent simplicity makes task-centred practice a victim of its own success, yet the explicitness and clarity of the process of task-centred work should not be mistaken for easiness.

If social work is appropriate and possible, task-centred work is appropriate and possible. Social workers find themselves in situations where they are not practising 'social work' (for example when they are policing or administering), and task-centred work will not be appropriate in these circumstances. Similarly, if the service users' capacity for rational thought is severely limited, the use of the method will be similarly limited, as will other methods of social work practice.

Task-centred work and empowerment

In using a problem-solving approach, task-centred practice links us all, users of social work or not. The task-centred philosophy does not pathologise service users but sees them as fellow citizens who are encountering difficulties. These difficulties are often more severe and more enduring than those which non-service users experience (and clients have fewer resources at their disposal to overcome them), but the problem-solving techniques used in task-centred practice are universal, even if the specific application in task-centred work is unusually systematic. In effect, the service user undergoes a training course in problem-solving techniques, and – with appropriate coaching from the worker – can use this method independently when the agency leaves.

Although the focus of task-centred work is primarily with individuals, families or groups, the method recognises the significance of context on individuals' problems (Tolson et al., 1994: 395). In other words, there is often a dissonance between the level at which analysis takes place (structural) and the level at which effective action can be taken (local). The reasons a person is without a job might be analysed at a macro-economic level, but the possibility of doing something about it remains micro. Task-centred work helps expose the subtle relationships between these different systems.

CONCLUSION

Professional practice in an organisational context

Task-centred social work helps the practitioner and the service user by providing a framework to consider whether there is just cause for the work to begin. Whatever methods practitioners use for the ensuing encounter with the client, the idea of developing a mandate for the work is one of the most valuable contributions which the task-centred model has made to social work practice. Social workers practise in diverse fields, with a broad range of systems and in uncertain circumstances, and task-centred practice offers a unifying model of practice for social work in all these circumstances.

Practitioners must behave professionally. This means an ability to handle uncertainty, use discretionary power and responsibilities, and subscribe to a code of ethics drawn from outside any particular employer. Practitioners are under equal pressure to behave bureaucratically, by following procedures established in large organisations, driven increasingly by administrative and financial considerations. In these circumstances, it is necessary to establish ways of working which allow professional practice to engage with agency realities. Task-centred work can provide the cog which gears profession to organisation.

Task-centred work lends itself to professional practice because of the skills needed to negotiate with the service user in ways which are truly empowering and anti-discriminatory. The explicit focus on power and discrimination, and the emphasis on qualitative outcomes, means that it is significantly more than a systematic procedure.

There are also aspects of task-centred work which could fall foul of professional practice, if not properly exercised. For example, it could be seen as routinised practice, in which the instruments of the model are used to exercise 'pure' social control; tasks (or failure to complete tasks) become sticks with which to beat the service user or provide evidence of their incompetence or lack of motivation.

There are aspects of task-centred work which fit well with agency imperatives, such as the accountability of an explicit approach, the potential to quantify outcomes and the potential economy of time-limited interventions. However, the emphasis on negotiation could be problematic if it implied a willingness to work on issues which might not, at first sight, be defined as the kinds of problem with which the agency dealt. Moreover, the need for relatively 'short, fat' interventions, rather than 'long, thin' ones, might not fit well with agency culture.

The task-centred model has proved itself to be an effective method which is popular with practitioners and service users. It has the potential to maintain professional practice while satisfying agency requirements. However, this degree of accommodation can appear ambiguous and perhaps explains why the task-centred method is described, on the one hand, as 'supporting managerialist objectives' (Dominelli, 1996: 156) and on the other as 'offering much potential for empowering clients' (Ahmad, 1990: 51).

A systematic strategy of training in the task-centred method, from prequalifying to post-qualifying levels, is the best way to retain a clear understanding of what it means to undertake work which can be called 'task-centred'. Only when there is confidence that task-centred work *is* task-centred work can agencies, practitioners and service users benefit from experiences which are commonly understood.

FURTHER READING

Doel, M. (1994) 'Task-centred work', in Hanvey, C. and Philpot, T. (eds) *Practising Social Work* (London, Routledge). Offers a brief overview of the task-centred method.

Doel, M. and Marsh, P. (1992) *Task-centred Social Work* (Aldershot, Ashgate). Offers a detailed account of the task-centred model in contemporary British practice.

Reid, W.J. (2000) *The Task Planner* (New York, Columbia University Press); Tolson, E.R., Reid, W. and Garvin, C.D. (1994) *Generalist Practice: A Task Centered Approach* (New York, Columbia University Press). These two books provide interesting accounts of recent developments in the task-centred model, especially with regard to its position as a generalist practice method, and task-centred techniques.

Reid, W.J. and Epstein, L. (1972) *Task-centred Casework* (New York, Columbia University Press). Allows you to understand the origins of the model by returning to the first text.

18

Empowerment and Advocacy

Michael Leadbetter

Being on the receiving end of services

It is said that stories speak louder than words. I have a fairly serious eye condition that necessitated a referral to a low vision clinic. My appointment was for 9 am; at 9.20 am I overheard the following conversation.

'Has he been here before?' 'Don't know, can't find his file, I don't think he has, but we should have a file, there must be a referral letter.' 'Let's go and look.'

The conversation continued between a nurse and an administrator in the corridor where I was waiting. I was seated while they were standing.

'I don't think he's been here before.' 'No, I know, but we should still have a file. Let's wait until Mr X (the low vision consultant) comes.'

At that point I could stand it no longer and intervened. It was clear that no harm was meant but where such attitudes exist in organisations they are damaging, dehumanising and crucially ineffective. I should have been included in the conversation as an equal as opposed to it taking place over my head as if I was invisible. It is hugely disempowering, discourteous and offensive.

One is left asking questions about the involvement of service users and the need for advocacy for frail and vulnerable people, many of who would have felt uncomfortable or unable to intervene.

The failure to have a meaningful dialogue with service users is also highly ineffective and future historical analysis of the current situation will look in astonishment at the demonstrable arrogance of public and private services. Many people's recent experiences of delays on the road network, in airports and on the rail network can testify to the lack of attention to customer care. The casual way in which passengers are treated, cramped waiting conditions and a lack of information almost go without comment, yet are the lived experience of so many people.

This absence of involvement affects both the public and private sector and raises the question, how on earth can any services be delivered which meet service users' needs without the crucial elements of ongoing and robust dialogue? The debate is a fundamental one and must therefore touch on the psychology and psychopathology of organisations and individuals.

Concepts of empowerment and advocacy

Empowerment and advocacy are both concerned with a shift of power or emphasis towards meeting the needs and rights of people who otherwise would be marginalised or oppressed. Beyond this generalisation, the concepts of empowerment and advocacy are not simple and as such are almost impossible to define. Where the term 'empowerment' is used it often covers a whole range of activities from consulting with service users to involvement in service planning. Empowerment has been described as

> a process in which individuals, groups or communities become able to take control of their circumstances and achieve their own goals, thereby being able to work towards maximising the quality of their lives. (Adams, 1990: 43)

In this definition the emphasis is on power being taken and its use determined by the goals of its possessor.

Rees envisages empowerment as a political activity comprising five essential concepts (Rees, 1991: 10): using people's biographies; developing the use of power; developing political understanding; deploying skills in evaluation, administration, negotiation and advocacy; and recognising the interdependence of policy and practice. Lee regards empowerment as 'the keystone of social work' and as having three interlocking dimensions: developing a 'more positive and potent sense of self'; constructing knowledge and the 'capacity for a more critical comprehension of the web of social and political realities of one's environment'; and cultivating 'resources and strategies, or more functional competence, for attainment of personal and collective goals' (Lee, 2000: 34).

Advocacy can take a number of differing forms, such as self- or group advocacy and can be considered as a further form of empowerment. It has been described as a process by which 'people are given a say that they have previously been denied and can turn paper entitlements into real rights' (Beresford and Croft, 1993: 85).

Brandon argues that there are only three kinds of advocacy: self-advocacy by the person affected; paid or professional advocacy by someone such as a lawyer, accountant or trade union official; and unpaid or amateur advocacy (Brandon, 1995: 1).

Empowerment and advocacy are challenging concepts

Empowerment and advocacy are multifaceted concepts informing many aspects of theory and practice in social work. They are also approaches in their own right. Empowerment and advocacy are part of the professional literature but, in contrast with traditional approaches and methods such as task-centred, crisis and systems-based social work, they represent ideas and practices in the public domain which any consumer of services can draw on and apply. They represent a challenge to traditional social work, because people receiving services and their carers can use these ideas independently of professionals to achieve what they want by gaining power. Professionals and social work clients practising empowerment and advocacy are likely to encounter dilemmas because of contradictions inherent in these concepts and approaches. These become visible in those circumstances where professional intervention involves exercising legal powers, for example in child protection or mental health. Such actions will be likely to de-skill and/or disempower the service user and emphasise dependence on professionals. But practice dilemmas arise more fundamentally because they are inherent both in the diverse interests of professionals and clients, and in the diversity of interests of members of families and other groups of people.

Which term to use for the 'client' of social services?

So far in this chapter, several words have been used for the person who receives services: client, consumer or service user. This diversity is healthy in one way but, as we reread the paragraph above, we recognise it is also a sign of uncertainty and confusion in the professional literature. Several of these terms are questioned by people – 'consumer' conjures up the image of a purchaser of a predesigned service in contrast with the notion of care planning in consultation with people; 'user' has connotations with drug or alcohol abuse; 'client' is reminiscent of traditional power relationships between professional therapists and people. No single term exists to describe the person receiving services which satisfies all requirements, from the perspectives of agencies, professionals and the public.

Where did empowerment and advocacy originate?

While empowerment and advocacy are concepts and approaches which have only matured in British social work since the late 1980s, the ideas have a longer history.

Empowerment, in the sense of self-help, has roots in the mutual aid and friendly society movements which in Britain date at least from the eighteenth century. But much more significant from the perspective of contemporary social work are the links between empowerment and protest. Empowerment has antecedents in the social and political activism of oppressed groups in the USA from the late 1960s. In Britain, various traditions of radical and socialist political and social protest since the 1960s were enriched greatly by feminist theory and practice. From the 1990s, large-scale protests using networks through mobile phones and the internet, particularly against schemes to develop new trunk roads in countryside of outstanding beauty or special scientific interest, and groups such as Reclaim the Streets, have demonstrated that people can exercise power collectively to influence policies.

Advocacy by professionals has its origins in the legal advocacy which solicitors and barristers provide for their clients (Payne, 1997: 267), while amateur advocacy can be traced back to the origins of Christianity (Brandon, 1995: 1).

Legal, policy and organisational contexts

Current legislation requires social services and social workers to work with service users in partnership and in empowering ways. The goal of social services departments is to protect and improve wherever possible the lives of vulnerable people, many of who are significantly disadvantaged and excluded. There is a need to support the necessity to change and continually adapt to meet the changing needs and aspirations of the people who use the service. However, senior managers and government policy-makers are often a long way from the day-to-day lived experience of staff and this 'distance' creates problems. Some policy changes represent a move away from professional autonomy and relative freedom of action towards a system which is more accountable, responsive and consistent across the country. On the other hand, there is a trend away from traditional 'command and control' styles of management towards a management culture based on influencing rather than directing people, respect for people, shared goals with people, common values and partnership with people.

The Health Act 1999 provides legislation which allows for the NHS and local authorities to work together in new ways by enabling them to pool resources, delegate functions and move resources from one agency to another and enable a single provider to provide both health and social care services. This will lead to the opportunity to develop localised care Trusts merging health and social care services under joint management arrangements. Local service provision and other planning activity will need to meet the government's expectations of the full involvement of service users, carers and local communities. To be effective, robust arrangements, which enable empowerment and access to advocacy services, will need to be available and accessible.

Practice issues

There is a need for local practice to conform to required standards and accountabilities. Within these, there should be freedom for local authorities – politicians, managers and practitioners – to work in partnership with people and empower them. Power should be devolved to the local level to enable people to come up with local solutions. Sometimes this will entail services being provided. At other times, people may be encouraged and enabled to reach their own solutions to their problems. At the same time, staff need empowering. Professionals should be rewarded for how well they do the work and paid accordingly.

Underpinning all this is the issue of choice – the right for service users to have choice of providers and the ability to change. Is there anything here with which we would strongly disagree? We accept consumer choice for holidays, shopping and many other essential items, surely it should also be a prerequisite for public service – within proper limits and with proper safeguards and accountability but choice nevertheless.

Service user involvement

Involvement of service users is already highly developed in a significant number of social services departments. This needs to increase and crucially we need to share our expertise with health service colleagues. In Essex, for example, we are in partnership with health service colleagues planning a workshop led by our participation and advisory group sharing best practice for services user involvement across the county. Health colleagues enthusiastically embrace this agenda and have also recognised that there is much they can learn from social services. Service user involvement is one of our strengths but we must never be complacent; there is still a long way to go in making sure that the voice of the service user is pivotal in our planning, commissioning and monitoring of services – not to mention involvement in interviews.

Promoting independence

All our services, be they provided or commissioned, must be aimed wherever humanly possible to promote and support independence – deally with people living in their own homes and sleeping in their own beds. In order to achieve this, we need to be more creative and strengthen our partnerships with housing partners to change and adapt housing to match people's needs. Where independent living is not a viable option, we must ensure that residential and nursing care meets the requirements and standards laid down by the National Care Standards Commission so that service users are appropriately supported and cared for.

Family group conferencing

Family group conferencing is a process of supported mediation that allows the wider family to find solutions for themselves as opposed to solutions being found for them by statutory agencies.

The success of family group conferencing in re-engaging with members of the family is well documented. These family members without fail come up with ideas and a willingness to go the extra mile to support children staying within the family network. Family group conferences are symbolic of the move away from professionals having a disproportionate share of power towards a more proportionate allocation of power and responsibility. This is not easy for some staff but, easy or not, it is essential.

Direct payments

Direct payments offer an opportunity for people receiving care and/or supportive services to receive the cost of the services in the form of a payment, which allows them to purchase/manage their own care arrangements.

As with family group conferencing direct payments present a challenge to professionals and the status quo – one we must grasp. There is a quid pro quo in this question of equalising power relationships and I will say more about this in my concluding comments on leadership and social exclusion.

Service users as citizens

As well as being a consumer of services, the service user is much more than that; similarly, as citizens we are consumers but we are more than just people who consume. We have responsibilities. As professionals move, as they must, to greater sharing of power, increased participation in decision-making, full and appropriate sharing of information and so on, the consumer as a citizen also has his or her own responsibilities. This raises difficulties because the majority of people who use our services are to a greater or lesser extent less well placed financially, emotionally and materially than the people providing the service. Yet, even if people are relatively disadvantaged, they still have responsibilities.

As we move from what has been historically a paternalistic service (you will have what's given to you and be grateful) to services based on need and shared responsibility, this has implications for the people who use our services.

This climate of opinion and certainty is inimical to a requisite debate between professionals, citizens and service users as citizens exploring the complexity of the relationship or the allocation of resources.

As a very young social worker, I visited people with learning disabilities in what were then called 'sub-normality hospitals'; also, people with chronic mental health problems living in appalling conditions in the back wards of hospitals and, still in the 1970s, people who had epilepsy who were consigned to an 'epileptic colony'. What were the factors behind these policy decisions which today appear so bizarre? They were:

- A desire for safety for the people in the institutions.
- A desire to exclude people who were different from one's challenged perceptions of normality.

In many ways social services departments represent in the public mind groups of people who within living memory were not regarded as citizens and were not valued members of society. Social services work daily with disadvantaged and socially excluded people. Is it surprising therefore that, within parts of the media and some parts of the public consciousness, social services are associated with aspects of society that, whether we like it or not, some people would, at best, wish to ignore, marginalise or pretend did not exist or, worse, wish them excluded and returned to isolated locations.

Since their inception, social services departments have represented, supported and advocated for these groups of people. Things have now moved on and, increasingly, the social services' role, quite rightly, has to change as well. Self-advocacy, direct payments, family group conferencing and user empowerment all take this debate forward and this is right and proper.

There will always be difficulties, defeats, disasters. Mistakes will occur. But it is crucial to remember that it is our task, knowing what we know and given our limitations and strengths, to use all our endeavours to change the world for the better.

Impediments to empowerment and advocacy

Empowerment and advocacy have attracted increasingly prominent attention, not only in social work but generally in the public services since the 1990s. But from a critical perspective it can be argued that the reality of benefits to people does not match up to the rhetoric. The many reasons for this include the following factors which operate within social work.

Impediments to empowerment

First, the concept of empowerment may be diluted to mean simply enablement. The language of facilitation is very different, and implies less of a leadership role for the agency and the professional.

Second, policy-makers and managers may colonise the concepts and practices associated with empowerment in ways which do not empower staff but are disguised means of control. Managers may empower subordinates by delegating responsibility and devolving budgets. Key gatekeepers of resources, such as local managers of residential or daycare, may be given independence from agency management but required to keep spending within non-negotiable limits.

Third, professionals may use empowerment to curb demands from clients by developing policies and practices associated with self-help, disguising the withdrawal of state funding and statutory responsibility for service provision under the rhetoric of giving people the power to shape their own services and meet their own needs.

Fourth, in circumstances where social workers must exercise statutory powers to intervene in people's lives, the imperative of public and personal protection from risk or harm may contradict the goal of empowerment.

Impediments to advocacy

First, advocacy remains associated largely with meeting the needs of people who are in any case marginalised in the health and social services, such as people with disabilities and people with mental health problems.

Second, the fact that the disability movement and survivors groups in mental health have taken a lead in advocating their own interests has been accompanied by a lack of prominence of advocacy in the professional domain, as is evidenced by the relative lack of publications – research and critical commentary – in contrast with areas such as child protection.

Third, related to the previous point, whereas areas such as child protection are often prioritised as involving a high risk of harm to children, advocacy in areas such as disability tends not to be given a similarly high priority.

Debates and controversies

The multifaceted nature of empowerment and advocacy reflects and feeds into controversies about their nature and applications.

Empowerment is regarded as a legitimate goal for citizens, and complaints, campaigns for causes and collective protests are regarded as legitimate, but, in the aftermath of violent protests and terrorist incidents, the question tends to be raised about what constitutes legitimate social activism. Since the mid-1970s community action has lost prominence in community work and the roles of statutory community workers as social activists have been called into question.

The extent to which a professional or organisation can or should give a client power may be questioned, since paradoxically this makes professional and organisational power more visible and therefore real.

It is debatable how far welfare rights advocacy is part of social work (Payne, 1997: 270). Citizen and peer advocacy are regarded often as activities in which volunteers, clients and carers and members of the general public should become involved, rather than professionals.

CONCLUSION

Empowerment reminds professionals of the essential contribution to be made to the quality of services by the people receiving them. Advocacy signals the necessity to validate the experience of clients and patients and ensure that their rights, wishes and needs are met.

There is a risk that empowerment will be taken over by policy-makers, managers and professionals and diluted to the point where it hardly benefits the users of services. Also, advocacy could be dismissed by social workers as not part of their job. Empowerment and advocacy could be associated largely or wholly with radical activity in social work. This would have the serious disadvantage of marginalising their use for people receiving services. It is preferable for empowerment and advocacy to be treated as part of mainstream social work. We should work to ensure that they are reflected in policy and practice and are owned by managers and professionals. Ironically, though, we need to be constantly on our guard against dilutions in the strength of these approaches, or their cooption by managers and professionals, in terms of promoting the interests of clients, service users and carers.

The need for organisations to listen to those people for whom they provide services goes far beyond legislative requirements. The collective sum of the lived experiences of service users should form the basis upon which evolutionary organisational change takes place. Without such change, those providing services have nothing to strive for or any comprehension as to whether the work they do actually makes any difference to the lives of the people who use the services they provide. If services are to grow and change, then the actual and symbiotic nature of the relationship between service provider and service user needs to be understood and nurtured. Through this the expectations and aspirations of all concerned can be realised.

FURTHER READING

Brandon, D. (1995) *Advocacy: Power to People with Disabilities* (Birmingham, Venture Press). A good source of stimulating ideas about advocacy in practice.

Bereford, P. and Croft, S. (1993) *Citizen Involvement – A Practical Guide for Change* (Basingstoke, Macmillan – now Palgrave Macmillan). This book is intended to support people trying to increase their own and other people's say and involvement. Within this, it provides a comparator for people's own experiences and an opportunity for reflection and action.

Braye, S. and Preston-Shoot, M. (2000) *Empowering Practice in Social Welfare* (Buckingham, Open University Press). This book looks at the changes ushered in by the NHS and Community Care Act 1990 and the changes this has brought to the relationship between health and social care professionals and service users and carers.

Hoyes, L., Jeffers, S., Lart, R., Means, R. and Taylor, M. (1993) *User Empowerment and the Reform of Community Care Studies in Decentralisation and Quasi-markets* (Bristol, School for Advanced Urtban Studies Publications). This paper compares the approach of four contrasting local authorities, looking at the differing implementation strategies for service user and carer empowerment against the background of the NHS and Community Care Act 1990.

Jack, R. (ed.) (1995) *Empowerment in Community Care* (London, Chapman & Hall). This book looks at how people work to gain control over their own lives, trying to empower themselves, and the way in which health and welfare professionals working in the community can either help or hinder them.

Joseph Rowntree Foundation (2001) *Consulting with Disabled Children and Young People* (York, Joseph Rowntree Foundation). This paper looks at the 'Ask Us' Project that engaged young people in influencing policy development related to Quality Protects.

Lee, J.A.B. (2000) *The Empowerment Approach to Social Work Practice: Building the Beloved Community*, (New York, Columbia University Press). A comprehensive, critical discussion of concepts, approaches and examples of practice which, while based in the USA, has many parallels in the UK.

19

The Legacy of
Radical Social Work

Mary Langan

Introduction

Although the moment of radical social work has now passed, many of its defining values – community and commitment, equality and empowerment, feminism and anti-racism – have entered the mainstream of social work practice. Indeed these values were endorsed by the child protection and community care legislation of the 1990s and became a feature of the new framework for social work training and practice introduced by the New Labour government after 1997. Although supporters of the principles of radical social work have many reservations about recent developments in the field of social services, they have broadly welcomed the adoption of these principles by the authorities as an indication of the potential for shifting practice in a progressive direction.

Is this a postmodern paradox: that radical social work has triumphed despite the demise of the movement that launched it? Or is it a more familiar irony: that the rhetoric of radical social work has survived the containment of the movement's radical impulse? To grasp the ambiguous legacy of radical social work, it is necessary to trace its evolution over the past three decades.

In the course of the 1990s, the discourse of radical social work, a movement loosely mobilised around *Case Con*, published between 1970 and 1977 and self-styled as 'a revolutionary magazine for social workers', seemed to permeate the highest levels of the system (Bailey and Brake, 1975; Langan and Lee, 1989). Olive Stevenson recalled how 'many, including myself, were astonished to see the idea of empowerment articulated in government guidance in community care' (Stevenson, 1994: 175). She quoted guidelines published by the Department of Health Social

Services Inspectorate, which defined the policy objective as 'the empowerment of users and carers' (DoH/SSI, 1991a). This was 'revolutionary stuff', commented Stevenson, greeting it as a 'very influential' statement which gave 'authority and impetus' to radical initiatives within social services departments.

The trend towards the official endorsement of what were formerly regarded as radical causes had been gathering momentum for some time. Frost and Stein welcomed as one of the 'progressive aspects' of the 1989 Children Act the imposition on local authorities of a duty to consider a child's 'religious, racial, cultural and linguistic' heritage (Frost and Stein, 1990). The 1991 Criminal Justice Act and the 1990 NHS and Community Care Act contained similar formulations reflecting official acknowledgement of issues of oppression and discrimination.

The ascendancy of feminist and anti-racist principles in the world of social policy reflected their wider rise in public approval in the early 1990s. Unions and employers drew up codes of conduct on issues of sexual and racial harassment, and local authorities promoted high-profile campaigns proclaiming 'zero tolerance' of violence against women. The police and the courts adopted a more sympathetic approach towards victims of rape and domestic violence, and the judiciary arranged courses in 'race awareness' for its members. The Football Association, together with individual clubs, took a firm stand against racist chants on the terraces.

It was in this climate that the controversy in 1992–93 around CCETSW's statement on anti-racism took place (CCETSW, 1991: 46). A number of journalists and academics condemned the formulation in Paper 30 that 'racism is endemic in the values, attitudes and structures of British society', accusing CCETSW of 'political correctness' (see Jones, 1993, 1996b, 1996c; Dominelli, 1996). In response, some Conservative politicians exploited the populist potential of the issue, accusing CCETSW of being excessively preoccupied with 'ologies and isms' (Tim Yeo, then Social Services Minister) and of pushing equal opportunities 'to extremes' (Virginia Bottomley, then Minister for Health). This barrage prompted the newly installed CCETSW chief executive to organise a prompt review of the statement.

An editorial in *Community Care* (9 September 1993) expressed bemusement at the furore over a statement which had been adopted in 1988 and considered uncontroversial: 'Paper 30 has been almost unanimously supported by senior social work professionals. It was revised in 1991 without any objection.' Indeed, the first official reply to complaints about Paper 30 was that 'the Department of Health fully shares CCETSW's commitment to equal opportunities for all' (*Sunday Times*, 11 October 1992). Thus, although some found social work's radical anti-racist policy a convenient target for sniping, the substance of the policy was approved not only by the professional social work authorities, but also by the government itself.

The radical response to the right-wing attack on CCETSW's anti-racist stand was uneven, fragmented and mostly defensive. Many agreed that there had been some excesses in 'race awareness training' and grudgingly accepted a more anodyne redraft of the anti-racist statement, notably omitting the word 'endemic'. On the other hand, the broad approach of anti-discriminatory practice continued to enjoy official approval. In fact, far from signalling a major conflict within the world of social work, the Paper 30 controversy revealed the extent of the convergence between the radical critics of the 1970s and the social services authorities of the 1990s. To understand this convergence, we need to consider the roots of radical social work.

The roots of radical social work

According to David Marsland, CCETSW's anti-racist policy was 'the final folly of the sixties' (*Daily Mail*, 21 June 1993). In the sense that many of the values associated with radical social work originated in the upsurge of youthful radicalism in the 1960s, there is some truth in this. In the late 1960s, the movement that emerged out of the struggle for civil rights in the American South and gathered momentum in the campaign against the Vietnam War reached a crisis. Writing in 1966, two activists summed up the prevailing sense of frustration and the quest for a political alternative:

> As it becomes more difficult to carry The Movement with freedom songs and slogans, and as the complexities of social change in the overdeveloped society become apparent, the early idealistic non-political thrust has been blunted. To function 'out there' demands the use of politics. (Jacobs and Landau, 1967: 78)

For some, the way forward lay in the 'community organising movement', which, according to one authority, 'established far more clearly than any other actions or tendency a coherent set of ideas for the New Left as a movement' (Young, 1977: 56). Young summed up the 'central components' of the movement in terms that sound familiar:

> The stress on community; local focus and decentralised organisation; the notion of participatory democracy and direct control of decisions; the emphasis on do-it-yourself direct-action politics; the extra-parliamentary character of the projects; the anti-paternalism and suspicion of 'do-gooding' (implying substantial self- and soul-searching); the belief in organising all the poor (inter-racially); and finally the concept of building counter-institutions. (Young, 1977: 56)

In response to their recognition of the difficulty of making major changes in the way in which American society was ordered, the young radicals scaled down their objectives. The focus shifted from the state to the 'grass roots', from the level of society to the level of individual lifestyle and the local community.

American community activism had a strongly individualistic outlook. As Jacobs and Landau (1967: 81) recognised:

> there is radical activity on many issues, but as yet no coherent intellectual force has replaced the moral obligation to put one's body and mind on the line in order to oppose large-scale and deep-rooted injustice and humanity.

The elevated subjectivity of the radical movement was expressed in its activists' courage and commitment – and also in their lack of ideological and organisational cohesion.

Given the middle-class origins of the radical activists and the gulf that separated them from a working class deeply divided along racial lines and long quiescent, they tended towards a condescending attitude towards the American masses. The recurrent themes in the writings of the New Left were of the need for education to overcome ignorance, the moral corruption wrought by mass consumption and the cultural impoverishment resulting from the influence of the mass media. The implicit (and sometimes explicit) assumptions were of a society made up of people who were at best apathetic and at worst bigoted, people who had been bought off by the consumer durables of the 'overdeveloped society' and duped by television. Concepts such as 'consciousness-raising' and 'empowerment', which emerged out this movement, presupposed a mass of people who lacked consciousness and power. Another result of the lack of social weight of the radical movement was that, despite its anti-statist rhetoric, it tended to rely on the authority of the state to implement its policy agenda. Thus the central focus of civil rights agitation was on legislative reform and the feminist focus on the Equal Rights Amendment reflects a parallel juridical preoccupation. The subsequent emphasis on 'affirmative action', 'positive discrimination' and 'equal opportunities' policies reflects the continuing affinity of radical campaigners for the state enforcement of anti-discriminatory policies.

The radical social work diaspora

Although the ideals of the US radicals found a ready resonance in Britain, the context was significantly different. The most striking contrast was the existence in Britain of a labour movement, indeed one which was itself undergoing a remarkable rejuvenation in the rising tide of industrial militancy which reached a peak in the great strikes of the early 1970s. Despite the narrow focus of working-class activity, the high level of solidarity of the trade union movement made it a powerful force in British political life. Much of the activity of the early feminist and anti-racist campaigns in Britain was conducted under the umbrella of the labour movement.

The New Left in the USA emerged in a country in which the 'old left' had been crushed in the McCarthy era and the unions were generally conservative and corrupt bureaucracies. In Britain, however, the left had retained considerable vitality and it grew rapidly in the radical upsurge. Whereas in the USA radical community activists influenced the outlook of the left, in Britain the influence operated in the opposite direction.

Case Con was launched by a rank-and-file group in the local government workers' union. The leading activists were members of 'International Socialism' (IS), one of several radical left organisations which had expanded rapidly in the late 1960s. Mike Simpkin, a *Case Con* veteran, later explained the appeal of IS:

> It attracted support from many of the 1968 generation who had joined the public sector and wished to pursue activist politics outside the Labour Party. The essence of IS was an emphasis on rank and file activism which appealed to those social workers who were concerned with encouraging democracy and participation in their union, their department and their work with clients. (Simpkin, 1989: 165)

We see here some of the familiar themes of American community activism given a characteristically British labour movement inflection. Given the strength of collectivism, the more individualistic features of American community activism appeared in Britain in a much weaker form – at least in the early years. Radical social workers placed the highest priority on the collective mobilisation of groups such as benefit claimants, council tenants, squatters and others, and explicitly disparaged the 'pseudoscience' of traditional 'casework':

> We are supposed to 'help' our 'clients' by making them 'accept responsibility' – in other words, come to terms as individuals with basically unacceptable situations. We must counterpose to this the possibility of changing their situation by collective action. We can only do this by acting collectively ourselves. (Bailey and Brake, 1975: 145)

A commitment to the 'self-activity' of the working class, almost an article of faith in the IS tradition, far outweighed any notion of radical activists 'empowering' working-class clients.

At a time when trade unionists were openly defying state legislation and even bringing down a government, the notion of youthful radicals conferring power on the working class did not have much appeal. For much of the ensuing decade, when American radicals were falling back on state power to push through their agenda, activists in Britain could still look to the labour movement as the agency of progressive reform.

By the late 1970s, however, the moment of radical social work had passed. The onset of recession in 1973 inaugurated a new era of mass unemployment and austerity. The election of a Labour government in 1974, which embraced fiscal orthodoxy and moved rapidly from restraining wages to curtailing welfare spending, proved disorienting for the left. Disillusionment with Labour paved the way for return in 1979 of a Conservative government, committed under the leadership of Margaret Thatcher to an abrasive free-market agenda. If, after 1974, radicals in social work and elsewhere were on the defensive, after 1979 they were in retreat. In the course of the 1980s, radical social work underwent a transformation, characterised by an increase in the influence of American radical ideas whose impact had previously been lessened by the peculiar strength of the labour movement in Britain.

The defeat of the labour movement resulted in a shift of radical social work away from the working class. Writing in 1981, Bolger et al. criticised the Labour Party's approach towards social work on the grounds that it expressed a 'social democratic fear of the working class':

> In fact this probably reflects a more fundamental fear that the working class is racist, sexist, individualist and does not actually want the state services that are being imposed on it. (Bolger et al., 1981: 12)

Labour's defeat in 1979, following the defection of many traditional Labour voters to the Conservatives, led some radicals to blame the working class for Thatcher's success. The tendency to disparage working-class people as racist, sexist and, worst of all, lacking in gratitude for state munificence, which Bolger et al. recognised in the Labour Party, became increasingly influential in the world of social work.

Radical disillusionment with the working class led to a greater reliance on state agencies. Radical social workers tended to thin out at the grass roots as they rose up the social services hierarchy or went into teaching or the social work establishment. Like the American movement a decade earlier, British radicals now concentrated on working for improvements in the local community. The higher profile of, first, feminism and, later, anti-racism expanded the world of radical social work but also reflected a shift away from the labour movement towards an involvement with what became known as 'new social movements'. The collectivist outlook of the earlier radical movement was undermined by a new emphasis on difference and rights. While many welcomed this shift, it also reflected the atomising trends of modern society and an increased reliance on juridical processes.

A more pedagogical approach now replaced the propagandist methods of *Case Con*. The emergence of 'race awareness training' illustrates the way in which this trend developed through the introduction of an approach developed in the USA in the 1970s into social work education – and into local government more widely in Britain in the 1980s. Based on Judy Katz's thesis that 'racism equals prejudice plus power', race awareness training insisted that the first step towards anti-racism is to recognise and eradicate our own racism (Katz, 1978; Dominelli, 1988). Because this technique sometimes unleashed angry confrontations, and because of its emphasis on inculcating 'correct' attitudes, it attracted media condemnation as a manifestation of 'political correctness'. In its cruder forms, race awareness training has long been abandoned by most authorities and it is now regarded with some embarrassment by radicals who once championed it. Yet the basic approach survived: according to a book published by BASW in 1993, awareness training had 'a major part to play' in promoting anti-discriminatory practice and acted as 'a foundation for other forms and levels of training' (Thompson, 1993: 152). The most significant feature of the concept of race awareness training was how it revealed the shift in the attitude of radical social work. A movement which a decade earlier had regarded working-class people as the agency of the revolutionary transformation of society now assumed that the same people required professional training to eradicate their prejudices.

Radical social work in the 1980s was increasingly promoted from above. While college lecturers conducted awareness training for social work students, radical policies on equal opportunities, harassment, anti-discriminatory practice and other issues were introduced by social work employers in local government and other agencies. Simpkin commented on the dramatic reversal experienced by a movement which had placed such emphasis on mobilising at the grass roots:

> Indeed much of the radical rhetoric which remains is at present experienced as being imposed from above, whether by progressive Labour councils or by senior managers. (Simpkin, 1989: 160)

The end?

The paradox of the 1990s was the apparent ubiquity of the rhetoric of radicalism at a time when the radical spirit seemed to have long evaporated. To explain this paradox, we have to examine the convergence of different political trends in the peculiar ideological climate of the times. The wider political context was set by the collapse of the Soviet Union and the Eastern bloc, and the ending of the Cold War. The resulting combination of social stasis and political exhaustion, with the attenuation of class allegiances and conflicts and the dissolution of traditional collectivities (affecting the right as well as the left), had a highly disorienting effect at all levels of society.

One thing that unites people today is the conviction that society is falling apart. At every level, there is a perception of social disintegration, a growth in crime and a decline in civility, a collapse of discipline in schools and an apparently unstoppable trend towards the breakdown of the family. The widespread sense of living in a society out of control leads inexorably to the quest for new ways of regulating society and containing disintegrative trends. It has rapidly become apparent that traditional methods no longer work and no amount of sermonising about Victorian values or Blair-style homilies about family values is going to restore their influence.

One of the most significant trends of the past decade has been the deployment of formerly radical themes in a new framework of regulation. The use of the term 'empowerment' and the promotion of 'anti-discriminatory' practice in social work illustrate this trend.

Writing in 1991, Ward and Mullender commented that 'empowerment' had become such a 'bandwagon' term that it risked becoming meaningless. Emerging, as we have seen, in the US radical movement of the 1960s, the concept of empowerment enjoyed a new lease of life in the 1970s as an expression of right-wing commitment to liberate the individual through unleashing market forces. In the 1990s these trends merged in a common hostility to the state as a barrier to individuality, creativity and enterprise.

What, then, does empowerment now mean? It implies an individualistic conception of power, which, by reducing social relationships to the interpersonal level, obscures the real power relations in society. Thus the playground bully appears as a major public menace, while the state, the real seat of power in society, appears powerless. Confusing the problem, empowerment offers illusory solutions. Measures of support or counselling make coping and surviving the ultimate objective. This is the crux of empowerment: once the perspective of social change is eliminated, just getting by becomes the zenith of aspirations (for an illustration of a parallel process in the sphere of health, see Wainwright, 1996).

Empowerment also means inviting people to participate in decisions over which they have no control. Thus, for example, parents are said to be empowered by being invited to attend child protection case conferences; they thus become complicit in measures of state intervention in their family life decided on by professionals and the police. Applicants for community care are empowered by the fact that their designated social worker is also the manager of a devolved budget which is limited by criteria quite independent of the applicant's particular needs. Too often, empowerment means reconciling people to being powerless. For radical social work, this is the ultimate irony: in essence, it means returning to the traditional model of social work. According to Chris Jones, for all its 'rhetoric about user involvement and participation', social work 'has never been so antagonistic towards or dismissive of its clients' (Jones, 1996a). In this climate, the elitist and paternalistic elements inherent in the concept of empowerment in its American origins came to the fore.

When, in November 1988, CCETSW adopted its anti-racist statement, it may not have examined the form of words chosen very carefully. This position had, however, in substance, already been adopted by the BASW, the profession's leading body, and the statement reflected the prevailing consensus (Bamford, 1990: 60).

In one of the few critical commentaries on CCETSW's anti-discriminatory policy to be written before the 1992–93 furore, David Webb (1990–91a: 151) noted 'an ironic resonance with the strident tendency in the Conservative party' in the council's 'claim to occupy the moral high ground'. He characterised the new morality as a form of puritanism, with 'an unswerving faith in the worth of certain actions':

> Judgement, censure, righteousness and watchfulness – all of which must perforce attend anti-sexism and anti-racism if they are to succeed – are also the defining attributes of the ideal-typical puritan. To the puritan falls the heavy obligation of practising extreme strictness in matters of morals and a developed sensitivity to breeches in the correct code of behaviour or thought. (Webb, 1990–91a: 151–2)

The radical commitment to liberation appeared to have been transformed into a mechanism for regulation.

Given the subsequent furore over Paper 30 and its anti-racist appendix, a casual observer might be forgiven for losing sight of the main objective of the document: to promote a model of social work training with 'much greater employer involvement in training and assessment' (Cannan, 1994/95: 11). It marked the latest stage in CCETSW's drive to subordinate social work education to the concerns of management, marginalise academic social science and elevate vocational training ('competences model') over the pursuit of intellectual excellence. Cannan (1994/95: 12) commented on how 'equal opportunities language and principles' were used 'in a new way' to promote 'populist and anti-academic prejudices' and 'encourage individualistic rather than egalitarian solutions'.

CONCLUSION

Writing in 1996, Webb drew attention to the way in which 'exhortations to repudiate discrimination sit alongside what is in effect an endorsement of neo-liberalism' (Webb, 1996: 186). He endorsed Brewster's view that CCETSW had become 'an almost perfectly designed vehicle' for the conservative modernisation of social work (Brewster, 1992). It is difficult to avoid the conclusion that, in addition to providing a mechanism for regulation, CCETSW's anti-discriminatory policy also offered a radical image for a highly conformist agency.

As for radical social work, Simpkin's judgement has proved prescient:

> while radical practice has in some ways become more integrated, radicalism itself has become diluted and fragmented. (Simpkin, 1989: 171–2)

========= **FURTHER READING** =========

Bailey, R. and Brake, M. (eds) (1975) *Radical Social Work* (London, Edward Arnold). The foundation text of the radical social work movement, edited by two key activists.

Cannan, C. (1994/95) 'Enterprise culture, professional socialisation and social work education in Britain', *Critical Social Policy*, 42, Winter, pp. 5–19. A comprehensive critique of current trends in social work education by a veteran of the radical social work movement.

Dominelli, L. (1997) *Anti-racist Social Work: A Challenge for White Practitioners and Educators*, 2nd edn (London, Macmillan – now Palgrave Macmillan). The case for anti-racist social work in the 1980s by one of its leading advocates.

Jones, C. (1996) 'Anti-intellectualism and the peculiarities of social work education', in Parton, N. (ed.) *Social Theory, Social Change and Social Work* (London, Routledge). A spirited attack on the philistinism of CCETSW by one of the most consistent defenders of the radical tradition against the imperatives of managerialism.

Langan, M. and Lee, P. (1989) *Radical Social Work Today* (London, Routledge). A review of radical social work from the perspective of the late 1980s, by two survivors of the early movement.

20

Feminist Social Work

Joan Orme

Introduction and context

Feminist social work is not a separate way of intervening in the lives of those who are users of welfare services. Rather it is a way of understanding, explaining and undertaking social work practice, informed by feminist theories. Social work is informed by feminism in a number of ways. Feminist theories inform practice (including management). Increasingly the research base for practice draws on feminist analysis and utilises feminist methodologies. In attending to knowledge, theory and practice, feminist social work also contributes to continuing discussions about the value base of social work. The influence of feminism in social work has developed gradually over the last two decades. During the same period feminist theories have been refined, reviewed and revised in a dynamic dialogue with practice, drawing on the experiences of women and men. This chapter will plot how social work has been informed by feminist theories and explore future challenges for both social work and feminism.

Most social work is undertaken by women and with women, either as clients in their own right or as part of an infrastructure on which agencies depend to support services. Older women, women with disabilities or mental health problems and women in the criminal justice system receive services directly. More often, women are users of social services in their role as mothers or carers of older people, those who are sick, disabled or experience mental health problems. In the criminal justice system, women are sometimes the focus of intervention simply because they are partners of delinquent males.

Attention to both the condition of being a woman and the conditions that women experience has been a feature of feminist analyses of social work since the 1970s. Initially associated with the radical critique (Statham, 1978; Wilson, 1980), a shared concern of both feminist thought and women in social work was the family and women's role. However, feminism as a movement was critical of women social workers, questioning whether they worked in women-centred ways. It was argued that opportunities for advice-giving led them, at best, to reinforce roles as carers based on gendered stereotypes. At worst, women who were in touch with social work agencies were pathologised, held responsible for their own problems and the problems of those for whom they had responsibility (Dale and Foster, 1986). This led to ambivalence about whether there needed to be a synthesis of feminist theory for social work. Early commentators such as Brook and Davis (1985) eschewed the need, suggesting that this would both institutionalise and marginalise feminist theory, thus negating its dynamism and creativity. This chapter argues that an articulation of feminist social work has occurred which draws on substantive feminist theory to provide both a critique of mainstream social work and opportunities for further theory and practice development. Feminist theories in and for social work have enhanced understanding of the experiences of women and contributed a reflexivity, a way of responding to the conditions of women. The notion of feminist social work praxis has emerged which demands attention from both women and men workers, and sees as its project understanding the situations of both women and men.

Feminist social work, or women-centred practice, is now included in standard texts on social policy, welfare and health care and is given separate chapters in texts such as this (see also Davies, forthcoming). In the more traditional discourses of social work theory, feminist social work is described alternatively as a movement to raise consciousness and give women control of their lives (Howe, 1987), or as an analysis of oppression and modes of empowerment – for women (Payne, 1991). These early texts identified limitations of feminist social work theory for women who are providers and users of social work services.

The most consistent criticism has been that adopting a separatist approach detracts from the need to permeate all practice. Feminist social work has also been described as a form of crude reductionist sociology, with contradictory theories which create a hierarchy of oppression imposed by a form of ideological imperialism (Sibeon, 1991). In concentrating on the oppression of women, feminist social work was accused of avoiding or negating class, race and the imperative to work with men. It has also been suggested that insights into causes of oppression do not necessarily clarify how to intervene, that feminist theory has not informed social work practice (Payne, 1991). However, a growing canon of literature, which is specifically feminist (Hanmer and Statham, 1999; Coulshed and Mullender, 2000; Orme, 2001; Dominelli, 2002) and which is neither institutionalised nor marginalised, addresses the complexities of women's lives and offers guidance on the principles and practices of intervention. These texts and others (Cavanagh and Cree, 1996) also address the need to work with men.

Drawing on this and other literature, this chapter will identify the contribution that feminist theories have made to social work practice. In doing so, it will address the critiques of feminist social work, arguing that it has both provided a commentary on mainstream social work and contributed to practice developments which have enhanced the profession of social work.

Feminist social work practice

A crucial factor in debates about feminist social work is the recognition that there are a number of feminist theories, or, more accurately, feminist theorising can lead to different understandings and different recommendations for practice. Feminist thought has influenced writing about social work practice in a number of ways. In the analyses of the 1980s (Dale and Foster, 1986; Wearing, 1986) there was agreement about the source of women's oppression, described alternatively as men or patriarchy. Over time, explanations of the source and process of oppression have drawn alternatively on liberal, reformist, Marxist, socialist and separatist approaches. Any form of theorising is of limited value to social work, if the understandings gained do not inform ways of intervening in the lives of service users to bring about some form of positive change. For feminist social work the challenge is to contribute to the transformation of social and structural relations and thus empower women through social work practice and interventions. As we shall see, the wider challenge is to understand how feminist analysis can also inform work with men. Hence an exploration of how feminism has influenced social work involves four themes:

- The conditions of women;

- Women-centred practice;

- Women's different voice;

- Working with diversity.

The conditions of women

Social work has consistently dealt with the conditions of women by ascribing female roles and defining female behaviour. In this way social work is predicated on the expectations of women. Paradoxically, traditional theories and explanations of service users were gender neutral, they took for granted a status quo that involved women's contribution to the household and invoked stereotypical views of women and men. At times there was a reinforcement of these roles, for example in childcare practice informed by theories of maternal deprivation.

Early feminist analyses of social work therefore argued for greater attention to the conditions which women experience. For example, over time the economic position of women has meant that they are traditionally among the poorest in society. Although the participation of women in the labour force is increasing, their earnings are consistently lower than those of men (Central Statistical Office, 1995). Also, because of childcare and other responsibilities, when women are not in paid work their entitlement to benefit or their dependence on male earners means that they constitute the poorest in society. Such socio-economic conditions often mean that women become dependent upon social services, they are caught up in the web of service provision and regulatory practices. However, social workers rarely see the focus of their work with women as the alleviation of their poverty, but focus on the attitudes, behaviour and coping strategies of individual women. Drawing on Marxist analysis, Wilson (1980) argued that the welfare state sought to keep women in the role of housewife, mother and carer, and, as employees of that welfare state, social workers themselves were purveyors of the repression of the state (Wilson, 1980).

Other research highlighted how women were expected to fulfil certain functions in areas such as caring (Finch and Groves, 1983; Ungerson, 1987). Hence feminist policy analysts highlighted how social workers not only negatively focused on the conditions of women but also were dependent upon them to undertake tasks to support the welfare of others. Focusing on conditions of women meant they were seen as both the cause of the problem and the source of the solution.

In attending to the conditions of women, and acknowledging the condition of being a woman, feminist theory therefore provided a critique, but what were the solutions? The limitations of Marxist concentration on class and the economic system was seen merely to reflect and reinforce patriarchal underpin-nings. Hence some feminists established a radical perspective which identified the source of women's oppression as the social institution of gender. For social work, the recognition of sexual politics (Firestone, 1971; Millett, 1972) resonated because it emphasised the role of male power in interpersonal relationships within the family, which contributed to women's sense of personal and economic inferiority and helplessness. In practice, this analysis facilitated the identification of, and attempts to understand, domestic violence and sexual abuse. This led to an important strand of enquiry, the exploration of the condition of being a woman. Work in the area of domestic violence (Hanmer and Maynard, 1987), child abuse (Hudson, 1992) and women offenders (Carlen and Worrall, 1987) emphasised that there were oppressions and disadvantages experienced by women by virtue of their sex. This condition of being a woman, with assumptions of feminine behaviour, also led to an important critique of women and mental illness. Feminist critiques described how mental disorder was perceived as 'a female malady' (Showalter, 1987), illustrating how women's biology was seen to be the cause of their mental instability (Ussher, 1991). Attention to the condition of being a woman also challenged heterosexist assumptions of state services predicated on women being in relationships with men. The contribution of feminist theory to social work was to put women on the agenda.

Women-centred practice

Early recognition that women had been absent from social work discourse (Hale, 1983) led to approaches at the micro level which sought to enhance the lives of women. Raising consciousness, changing assumptions about, and perceptions of, women while acknowledging structural oppression were themes reflected in prescriptions for women-centred practice. These included codes of practice which recognised the power of the social worker in individual interpersonal relationships (Hanmer and Statham, 1988) or those which focused on constructing an anti-sexist environment and mode of service delivery (NAPO, 1990). However, maintaining a focus on the individual sometimes led to services that reinforced women in their role as mothers and/or carers, for example mother and toddler groups or prisoners' wives groups.

There were some who argued that feminists in social work could not combat the structural imbalances of state welfare systems which were imbued with individualised approaches which pathologised women (Wilson, 1980). Feminist social work, they argued, required women-only organisations. Indeed a rich stream of feminist social work did emerge with the establishment of women's refuges, rape crisis lines, well women clinics and other forms of women's self-help organisations. However, others thought it imperative that feminists remained within the statutory agencies and tried to change the culture of both the organisation and the practice to reflect feminist aims (Dominelli and McLeod, 1989).

This has happened more slowly than many would have wished. With the support of organisations such as CCETSW (Phillipson, 1991) feminism became a focus for study under the broad umbrella of anti-discriminatory practice. Attention to women and women's issues is gradually permeating the whole of the social work curriculum, but, as will be discussed below, feminist social work requires more than this.

Women-centred practice brought about other tensions. Balances of power inherent in traditional ways of working highlighted distinctions between workers and service users traditionally known as 'clients'. Feminism and social work were both accused of emanating from white, middle-class movements which ignored or denied the experiences of other women (hooks, 1984a). What is significant about the critique provided by Morris (1993) from the perspective of women with disabilities is that she points out how women who were deemed to be 'clients' or users of social services became invisible. They were defined in terms of their 'condition' but were not seen to experience the oppressions and discriminations of undisabled women (Morris, 1996). The same arguments can be made on behalf of older women (Orme, 2001). More significantly in social work, attention to the needs of one group, women carers, further oppressed and discriminated against women who required care, who were described as a burden. They were seen to constrain the lives of the women who provided care.

In the first edition of *Women and Social Work*, Hanmer and Statham (1988) drew attention to these tensions by urging women workers to identify commonalities and diversities; to acknowledge the differences in experience, but recognise that women workers and service users shared some of the same oppressions. But recognising commonality and diversity is not always helpful. It may reinforce notions that women are the source of, and solution to, the problems they experience. Acknowledging diversities between women and users, and arguing that these should be transcended, denies the power relationship between these groups of women (White, 1995). Also, while recognising that commonality is a way of expressing empathy (Hanmer and Statham, 1988), requiring workers to do so raises concerns over shared information. Lesbian women workers, in particular, may feel unable to disclose or share information about themselves for reasons to do with homophobia in the workplace.

Therefore, women-centred practice, while an important response to the conditions of women, did not necessarily challenge the source and cause of women's oppression.

The 'different voice' of women

A parallel development to women-centred practice was an exploration of the differences between women and men. This emerged from understandings of women's moral development explored by feminist psychologists (Gilligan, 1993). Claiming that women have developed an 'ethic of care' as opposed to the male 'ethic of justice' Gilligan argues that women therefore speak in 'a different voice'. This voice has been associated with women's facilitative nature in which they address relational aspects of problems rather than resorting to procedures, rules and rationality. It is argued that these feminine ways have traditionally been devalued. Indeed the very fact that social work as a profession drew on such qualities and was therefore a feminine profession had been the subject of criticism (Younghusband, 1951). The project for feminism was to valorise these qualities, and ensure that the different approaches permeated all services.

For example, feminist writing has challenged the male ethos of social work management, arguing that it can be more inclusive, collaborative and egalitarian (Coulshed and Mullender, 2000). Similarly, specific ways of intervention, based on feminist approaches to counselling (Chaplin, 1988), attempt to challenge and counteract power imbalances within the therapeutic relationship.

Another area in which the 'different voice' of women has been influential in social work is research. Based on assumptions that women have different ways of knowing (Hawkesworth, 1989; Belenky et al., 1997; Oakley, 1999), feminist theories have informed practice research. Feminist writing on epistemology and methodology (see, for example, Stanley, 1990) has invoked the notion of praxis. In social work this has led to methods of enquiry that have encouraged user participation and emancipatory research, and have linked knowledge production with bringing about change (Orme, 1997, Fawcett et al., 2000).

Another consequence of the 'different' voice has been to recognise the contribution that feminist social work makes to working with men. For example, early work on a feminist jurisprudence (Carlen, 1989) documents how women are adversely treated by the paternalism of the criminal justice system. In arguing for the appropriate treatment for women, Carlen recognises that dehumanising and punitive custodial sentences are not appropriate for women or men. For men to become less violent, there needs to be less violent treatment within the penal system.

These arguments have been further developed in writings on domestic violence where the emphasis initially and rightly was on having the problem recognised and making women safe. However, to ensure the long-term safety of all women it is necessary to widen the project. Work has to be undertaken with men to understand and halt the violent behaviour, not by the use of punitive measures but by pro-feminist ways of working (Orme et al., 2000).

Such approaches are not unproblematic. The urge to punish those men who have been violent to women and children and the tensions brought about by finite resources which precipitate the need to choose between services for women and those for men are not ducked by feminism. In putting them firmly on the agenda, feminist social work has not only been influential, but also subject to criticism.

Working with diversity

The developments in feminist social work, which acknowledge the imperative to recognise the heterogeneity of women's experiences and to address working with men, have been associated with the influence of postmodernism. The unitary category of women has been challenged by some feminist writers, who argue that essentialist notions of femininity reflected in Gilligan's writing constrain women to subordinate functions and prevent men from undertaking caring roles. Disabled, black and lesbian women have argued that to enable them to assert their rights there has to be recognition of diversity within the category 'women'. If this is so, then the false duality of women/men also has to be challenged. If there is no single category 'woman', there can be no single category 'man' (Butler, 1990). Such an analysis has created both a crisis and a development in feminist social work. Some see postmodernism as part of a (white) male academic backlash against feminist thought and action (Hester et al., 1996). Others see it as an opportunity for feminism to inform working with men, challenge masculinist assumptions and recognise the oppressions of patriarchy, rather than expecting women to change their own conditions (Cavanagh and Cree, 1996). These opportunities have also enabled pro-feminist men to explore ways in which they can work to challenge the oppression of women by men (Thompson, 1995b; Hearn, 1998; Christie, 2001).

Exploring gender as relational, recognising that women and men are constructed by certain aspects of their identity, challenges other dualities such as disabled/able-bodied; carer/cared for (Orme, 2001). Feminist social work therefore can work with all service users to challenge the way that their needs are constructed, interpreted and responded to.

Issues

The themes that have been identified in this account of the development of feminist social work raise a number of issues. The first is that critical debates with feminism and within feminist theory raise dilemmas about the way that the condition of being a woman is responded to. Should social workers see women as different, as having separate experiences, as being a special case, because of their biology, or because of the way that gender is socially constructed? If they do treat women in this way, then how can they argue for equality and equal treatment? Nowhere is this dilemma more apparent than in Welfare to Work policies that precipitate mothers into the workplace. Women are different and they experience different socio-economic conditions because of their child-bearing, but this should not deny them equality. Therefore while opportunities for women to enter the paid workforce are to be welcomed, such policies can only be effective if they provide an appropriate infrastructure of childcare and/or encourage and enable men to participate in childcare.

The second issue is that feminist social work has been criticised for not responding to the particular needs of women service users. To be effective it has to recognise the contradictions of women's lives and, through a process of individualisation, accept that being a woman (be that a black or disabled woman) is part of the person-in-environment perspective which is core to all social work practice. This is not difficult because it resonates with the feminist claim that the personal is political (Collins, 1986), that the environment includes the social construction of gender, of being a woman or a man. What has to be worked with is how individual women experience their situation. To tell a woman user that she is oppressed is no more liberating than labelling her as depressed, unless there are ways of changing the situation. Having recognised the dilemmas and clarified the accounts, it is also necessary to be open about the social control contained in the social work role. This control often emanates from both the dynamic of individual relationships and the legislative framework which reinforces gendered stereotypes or appears to circumscribe the work that has to be done. The challenge for feminist social work, therefore, is to acknowledge the operation of power within all relationships and influence the policy debates as well as work at the level of the individual.

However, this focus on the individual and the recognition of the diversity of women's experience, and the inclusion of men within the feminist social work project, is also problematic for some feminists. It is seen to lead to a deflection from focusing on the oppressions of women and to undermine research which has stressed the material realities of women's lives and men's behaviour in these (Hester et al., 1996). However, unless a dialogue occurs, unless work is done with men as users of services, as potential carers and as perpetrators of the abuse of women, there will be no challenge to constructions of masculine identity. Unless feminist theory and practice are used to undertake this challenge, there will be little change in the conditions and behaviours which women have had to tolerate.

What is important, therefore, is the way in which situations are worked with, the praxis that incorporates feminist analysis. It is appropriate for feminists to intervene to protect vulnerable people, whoever they may be. The notion of praxis requires feminists to be part of the debate about acceptable standards of conduct, ensuring that these are not constructed on stereotypical gendered lines and arguing for the inclusion of users, especially women who constitute the majority of users, in the decisions (Wise, 1990). In this way feminist social work will contribute to the transformation of social and structural relations.

CONCLUSION

Feminist thought in social work practice has played a vital role in recognising the conditions of women and their oppression and subjugation. It has moved from a woman-centred analysis that it is for women, by women and with women to a perspective that includes working with men. That is not to say that a woman-centred stance is not valid: women-only space is important, and women's thoughts and experiences should be actively heard. In working with women, feminist social work practitioners are only too aware that any one person's condition is influenced by the behaviour and expectations of others. For women users of social services, their lives are defined and constrained by malestream thinking and organisation and male behaviour. To focus solely on women, to attempt to empower them, leads to dilemmas, conflict and frustration, and can hold them responsible for change in their own circumstances and those of others. It concentrates on their feminine condition in a negative way and does not address other conditions which oppress them. Feminist praxis recognises the diverse experience of all users of social work services and seeks to challenge and transform policy, practice and the organisation of the service delivery which constrains people in gender-specific roles or oppresses them by the inappropriate exercise of power.

The themes explored in this chapter illustrate that more than most paradigms feminist social work has been reflexive in responding to the experiences and criticisms of those whose position it seeks to explore, explain and exhibit. It has striven to ensure that women are both made visible within the organisation of service provision and empowered by individual interpersonal interventions. This emphasis on the transformational is now evident in debates within feminist social work about working with men.

FURTHER READING

Cavanagh, K. and Cree, V.E. (eds) (1996) *Working With Men: Feminism and Social Work* (London, Routledge). A collection of practice accounts which explore the contribution that feminism has made to working with men.

Hanmer, J. and Statham, D. (1999) *Women and Social Work: Towards a Woman-centred Practice*, 2nd edn (London, Macmillan – now Palgrave Macmillan). This second edition of this introductory text continues to focuses on non-sexist women-centred practice, but emphasises more strongly diversities created by age, class, disability, employment, race and sexuality.

Orme, J. (2001) *Gender and Community Care; Social Work and Social Care Perspectives* (Basinsgtoke: Palgrave – now Palgrave Macmillan). Drawing on a range of feminist theory, this text explores how these theories help us to understand how women and men service users are constructed by policy and practice.

Anti-oppressive Practice

Beverley Burke and Philomena Harrison

Introduction

The complex nature of oppression is witnessed in the lives of people who are marginalised in this society. As social work practitioners, we have a moral, ethical and legal responsibility to challenge inequality and disadvantage. Historically, the profession, in attempting to understand, explain and offer solutions to the difficulties experienced by groups and individuals, has drawn from, among others, the disciplines of sociology, psychology, history, philosophy and politics. This multidisciplined theoretical framework, informed by anti-oppressive principles, provides social workers with a tool to understand and respond to the complexity of the experience of oppression.

This chapter explores how a theorised social work practice informed by anti-oppressive principles can be sensitively and effectively used to address the inequalities of oppression that determine the life chances of service users.

The writings of black feminists (hooks, 1981, 1984b, 1989, 1991; Lorde, 1984; Neale-Hurston, 1986; Morrison, 1987; Jordan, 1989; Hill-Collins, 1990; Russell, 1990; James and Busia, 1993) provides a rich literature that is theoretically based and informed by the disciplines of psychology, sociology, politics, history and anthropology. It incorporates existentialist ideas, liberatory educational principles, community activism and personal experiences provided by both autobiographical and fictional accounts. It thus expands understandings of oppression and lays the foundations for the exploration of the experience of power, powerlessness and oppression.

Black feminist thought is a dynamic perspective, derived from 'diverse lived experiences', that not only analyses human interactions based on principles of equality, but also considers the interconnections that exist between the major social divisions of class, race, gender, disability, sexuality and age as they impact on the individual, family and community.

Black feminist thought has helped us to understand ourselves as black women. It has enabled us to make sense of the patterns of domination and oppression which characterise our professional and personal lives. We hold the view that personal experiences are inextricably linked to and determined by social, cultural, political and economic relationships within specific geographical and historical situations. This process of location allows us to challenge those who see only our race, gender or class, failing to understand that it is the interconnections between the social divisions to which we belong that defines who we are (Lorde, 1984).

The finding of solutions to and explanations of oppressive situations and practices poses a real challenge for those committed to making a difference. A starting point would, therefore, have to be a clear understanding of what is meant by anti-oppressive practice.

What is anti-oppressive practice?

There are a number of definitions, ranging in complexity and length. Anti-oppressive practice has been debated by a number of writers, whose works are informed by differing perspectives (Thompson, 1993; Clifford, 1994a; Braye and Preston-Shoot, 1995; Dalrymple and Burke, 1995; Featherstone and Fawcett, 1995; Dominelli, 1996). However, for the transformative potency of anti-oppressive practice to be realised, the reader needs to be critically aware that the choice of words used to define reveals not only the value and ideological base of the definer, but also the nature of the practice that will emanate from that definition.

Anti-oppressive practice is a dynamic process based on the changing complex patterns of social relations. It is, therefore, important that a definition is informed by research within academic institutions, practitioner research and the views of service users. For the purposes of this chapter, we provide below a 'definition' (with all the attendant problems of defining) which incorporates points already discussed providing a framework to clarify and inform practice.

Clifford (1995: 65) uses the term 'anti-oppressive':

> to indicate an explicit evaluative position that constructs social divisions (especially 'race', class, gender, disability, sexual orientation and age) as matters of broad social structure, at the same time as being personal and organisational issues. It looks at the use and abuse of power not only in relation to individual or organisational behaviour, which may be overtly, covertly or indirectly racist, classist, sexist and so on, but also in relation to broader social structures for example, the health, educational, political and economic, media and cultural systems and their routine provision of services and rewards for powerful groups at local as well as national and international levels. These factors impinge on people's life stories in unique ways that have to be understood in their socio-historical complexity.

Within this definition, there is a clear understanding of the use and abuse of power within relationships on personal, family, community, organisational and structural levels. These levels are not mutually exclusive – they are interconnected, shaping and determining social reality. Clifford, informed by the writings of black feminist and other 'non-dominant perspectives' (Clifford, 1995), has formulated the following anti-oppressive principles, which provide the foundation for a social work assessment that is theorised and empowering:

- *Social difference.* Social differences arise because of disparities of power between the dominant and dominated social groups. The major divisions are described in terms of race, gender, class, sexual preference, disability and age. Other differences, such as those of religion, region, mental health and single parenthood, exist and interact with the major divisions, making the understanding and experience of oppression a complex matter.

- *Linking personal and political.* Personal biographies are placed within a wider social context and the individual's life situation is viewed in relation to social systems such as the family, peer groups, organisations and communities. For example, the problems associated with ageing are not solely due to the individual but should be understood in relation to the ageist ideologies, policies and practices that exist within the social environment in which the individual is located.

- *Power.* Power is a social concept which can be used to explore the public and private spheres of life (Barker and Roberts, 1993). In practice, power can be seen to operate at the personal and structural levels. It is influenced by social, cultural, economic and psychological factors. All these factors need to be taken into account in any analysis of how individuals or groups gain differential access to resources and positions of power.

- *Historical and geographical location.* Individual life experiences and events are placed within a specific time and place, so that these experiences are given meaning within the context of prevailing ideas, social facts and cultural differences.

- *Reflexivity/mutual involvement.* Reflexivity is the continual consideration of how values, social difference and power affect the interactions between individuals. These interactions are to be understood not only in psychological terms, but also as a matter of sociology, history, ethics and politics.

The above principles relate to each other, interconnecting and overlapping at all times. Working from a perspective that is informed by anti-oppressive principles provides an approach that begins to match the complex issues of power, oppression and powerlessness that determine the lives of the people who are recipients of social care services. An understanding of these principles brings with it a fundamental transformation in the relationship that exists between the assessment of a situation and the nature of the action that is required to change the existing state of affairs.

The driving force of anti-oppressive practice is *the act of challenging inequalities*. Opportunities for change are created by the process of the challenge. Challenges are not always successful and are often painful for the person or group being challenged or challenging. A challenge, at its best, involves changes at macro- and micro-levels. If anti-oppressive practice is to provide appropriate and sensitive services that are needs-led rather than resource-driven, it has to embody:

> a person centred philosophy; and egalitarian value system concerned with reducing the deleterious effects of structural inequalities upon people's lives; a methodology focusing on both process and outcome; and a way of structuring relationships between individuals that aims to empower users by reducing the negative effects of social hierarchies on their interaction and the work they do together. (Dominelli, 1994: 3)

Work in welfare organisations is constrained by financial, social, legislative and organisational policies. Social workers operating within such an environment will inevitably face conflicting and competing demands on their personal and professional resources. The use of anti-oppressive principles offers the worker a way of responding to and managing these sometimes hostile and disempowering situations which affect both worker and user.

The dynamic link between theory and practice will be demonstrated through the use of a case scenario, written in autobiographical form. It is through the action of practice that theories, principles and methods come alive. By reading the following scenario, you, the reader, are directly involved in a young black woman's 'lived experiences'. Through the very act of reading, you become both *participant* and *observer*. You begin to start the process of critical thinking, reflection and analysis of her life, bringing with you to the interpretation of her story your values, assumptions and practice wisdom. It is important to remember, when reading Amelia's story, that it contains the stories of others – her son, the professionals involved, her community networks and her family.

A decision was made by a social services department that changed the life of a family. A young, single, 19-year-old black woman was told that the care plan regarding her 20-month-old son was that of adoption. The decision was based on evidence from extended social work involvement, which was ultimately influenced by information obtained from reports written by a white male psychologist and a white female psychiatrist.

Amelia's story as told to a friend

> Leaving home at sixteen, I spent most of my time trying to find a place to live and make ends meet. I relied on shoplifting and my friends to survive. At seventeen I met a man who was twenty seven. We lived together; when I became pregnant, things began to change. He became violent towards me.
>
> I was placed in a hostel for mothers with children, I wasn't very happy at the hostel, I disliked the racist name calling – no one in charge did anything about it. Drugs were easily available. I tried heroin.
>
> My baby was born three months prematurely. While he was in hospital he nearly died, I was really frightened. I visited him every day for the two months he

was in hospital. I kept asking for social work help. I needed money to travel to and from the hospital and I needed someone to talk to. The nurses asked for help for me. I never got any.

I returned to the hostel, with my son. He became ill. I took drugs to help me to stay awake so that I could look after him. Everything seemed too much. When he was in hospital I told one of the nurses that I had 'tapped' him when he would not stop screaming. They told social services. So when I tried to leave the hospital with him I was stopped. My son was placed in respite care for a couple of weeks. I was told that I could have him back when I felt better.

When I wanted him back they said that they had to do an assessment to see if I was able to care for him. I began to scream and shout. I begged them to give my baby back, but they placed him with white foster carers; I did not agree, but there were no black foster carers. I saw him every day.

It was decided that I needed to have a psychological and psychiatric assessment. I felt that I needed someone to talk to. I know I am not mad. The social workers spent time with me and wrote a report saying I should have my son back. My son was put on a supervision order for a year.

I moved into a new house. I told my social worker that I really did not feel ready to live on my own. The social worker arranged for a childminder two days a week and a home help. I wanted a nursery place.

I was lonely in the new house. I went out a lot. I told someone I knew that I had tried six months earlier, while on drugs, to harm my son. She said we should tell the social services and they would help me sort it all out. I agreed, they took my son into care again.

A month went by. They were trying to find a place where I could live with my son and get the help I needed. They never really told me anything. I felt very frustrated. It was hard being without my son.

One day, after access, I did not return my son to the carer. I kept him overnight, they found me the next morning. They took him away. Now I can only see him for two hours a day at the foster carers, and at weekends.

I cannot think straight. I cannot be upset or depressed as this would go against me. All the time I was told that I was capable of looking after my son and that they were working on us being together. They knew I loved and wanted him very much. But now they have told me that they have plans for adoption. I am so angry and frightened, but I cannot be angry or this would upset the workers. My son has had so many changes.

I am not sure what to think or do. Should I start thinking about when I will not have him? I know that I need someone to talk to about all the things that have happened to me. But I cannot do this without my son. Why do they need to take him away when I know I can look after him with help. I do not know how I can fight any of this.

Theory into practice

Using anti-oppressive principles, which incorporates challenging as a central process, we will analyse Amelia's story, highlighting issues and dilemmas that workers face in attempting to empower a service user.

The anti-oppressive principle of *reflexivity* demands that workers continually consider the ways in which their own social identity and values affect the information they gather. This includes their understanding of the social world as experienced by themselves and those with whom they work.

Involvement in Amelia's life is not a neutral event. It is determined by the interaction between the personal biographies of the worker and Amelia, and will be expressed in the power relationships that arise from their membership of differing social divisions.

For example, a white male social worker brings to the situation a dynamic that will reproduce the patterns of oppression to which black women are subjected in the wider society. In this scenario, Amelia feels she is silenced. Her plea for 'someone to talk to', to be listened to and taken seriously, is neither understood nor acted upon. This is highlighted in the powerlessness expressed in the telling of her story.

The challenge to you, the worker, is to reflect on your social division membership, your personal and professional biography and the impact that this will have on your involvement with Amelia. Are you the right worker for her? If the answer is no, the challenge is not only to find a more appropriate worker but to look to ways in which you may minimise the potential for oppressive practice at the point of referral. In and through this process of thinking and reflecting, which should take place in supervision, team discussions and interactions with service users, you will begin to work in an anti-oppressive way.

Society is divided along the major divisions of race, class, gender, sexual preference, disability and age. There are also other divisions which occur as a result of inequality and discrimination, such as poverty, geographical location, mental distress and employment status. The *social difference* principle is based on an understanding of how the divisions interconnect and shape the lives of people.

Amelia is young, black, unemployed, female, of a particular class background, living in poverty and a single parent. Yet in the scenario, she is seen merely as a young woman suffering domestic violence and in need of accommodation. Her needs as a black woman from a particular background with a specific history are not fully considered. Amelia's experience of racism in the hostel compounded her overall experience of oppression, forcing her into independence before she was ready.

The challenge for you, the worker, is to understand both the specific and general nature of social division membership and how it may contribute to the individual's experience of oppression. As a worker, you must make a systematic analysis of the social division membership of all the individuals involved in Amelia's life and understand the relevance of this for your intervention.

It is important to locate both Amelia's and her son's life experiences and events within a *historical and geographical context*. Those experiences need to be chronologically charted and their relevance clearly understood and applied to Amelia's story. In doing that, you, the worker, will get an accurate picture of how events within the family, community and society have influenced Amelia's current situation. Amelia's story will have been influenced by previous specific historical and geographical factors.

As the worker, you need to be aware of how prevailing ideologies have influenced legislation, agency policy and practice relating to childcare, homelessness and parenting by single mothers. The challenge is to use that analysis to inform your assessment and decision-making. You need to question the agency's policies on work with homeless young women. Amelia's needs as a homeless, black young woman were never assessed with reference to research evidence which documents the oppression and lack of services faced by this specific user group.

The principle of historical and geographic context directs the worker to consider not only the individual worker's relationship with the service user, but also the team and agency practice. The following are some of the questions that need to be considered: 'How does a prevailing ideology of a mixed economy of care affect practice within the team?'; 'How does the team prioritise work with homeless young people?'; and 'How far has the historical development of service provision in the area determined current practices?' Such questions will help workers to understand what is constraining their practice. Anti-oppressive thinking moves the worker beyond the confines of agency policy and practice and directs the challenge more appropriately.

In understanding the *personal* as *political*, the everyday life experiences of individuals need to be located within social, cultural, political and economic structures which are historically and geographically specific. This process of location ensures that, in practice, the individual is not pathologised, and weight is given to the interconnections and interactions between that individual's story and the social systems they encounter.

Amelia is defined in terms of the domestic violence she has experienced. The assessment is not placed in a wider context, failing to make sense of Amelia's whole life experience. You, the worker, need to take into account the structural factors that contribute to womens' experience of violence and how, for Amelia, the dimension of race and her membership of other social divisions added other layers to her experience of oppression.

The social workers' decision in the scenario to formulate a care plan which put forward adoption as a solution to Amelia's problems needs to be analysed. Their decision appears to be highly influenced by the expert evidence which focused on Amelia's psychiatric and psychological functioning. How did these assessments inform the workers' analysis of Amelia's ability to parent adequately? Here, we see a failure to locate assessment evidence within a framework that takes into account all aspects of Amelia's existence – her gender, her race, her poverty, her single parenthood – as well as making reference to assessment evidence from other professionals.

The challenge to the worker is to examine the range of evidence used in decision-making, asking questions about why any one piece of evidence is given more weight than another. Does that weighting pathologise the individual by not taking into account the assessments made by other professionals, such as the health visitor and the foster carers. For example, was the support offered by the extended family and informal community support networks considered? By ignoring the impact of oppressive social values and policies in the decision-making process, the worker can further devalue the service user's capacity to function.

In addressing *power* and *powerlessness*, it is essential to understand how the differential access to power shapes and determines relationships on an individual, group, community, organisational and societal level. We get a glimpse of Amelia's feelings of powerlessness when she says, 'I do not know how I can fight any of this.' Central to her powerlessness is the lack of access to many social resources.

There is evidence in Amelia's story of her being denied access to the resources she feels will help her to parent effectively.

You, as the worker, need to take into account the professional and personal power (based on your particular social division membership) you hold. What power does the service user have from her previous life experiences?

How do you, as a worker, ensure that your assessment and intervention includes an analysis of power? The worker in this situation could have advocated on behalf of Amelia, working creatively to explore other options which would have supported her in her parenting. It appears that the workers ignored the personal strengths of Amelia, gained from her experiences of oppression, leading to practice which compounded her feelings of powerlessness. They failed to listen and work in partnership with Amelia.

The misuse of power by the worker culminates in a situation in which decisions can be made where the outcome labels Amelia as a non-deserving case. Amelia, however, is not alone in her powerlessness. There are clear differences of the power ascribed to the opinions of one professional group over another. It appears that extended social work practice had little impact on the overall decision regarding the future of the family. Explanations of Amelia's behaviour are reduced to the opinions of one professional group who are seen as 'expert', reducing complex explanations of her behaviour to psychology and psychiatry.

Social workers are well placed to make assessments that are theoretically informed, holistic, empowering and challenging. Anti-oppressive practice should not negate the risks posed to the child. Intervention based on anti-oppressive practice incorporates a risk and needs analysis of both mother and child.

To work effectively, it is important to have a perspective that:

- is flexible without losing focus;

- includes the views of oppressed individuals and groups;

- is theoretically informed;

- challenges and changes existing ideas and practice;

- can analyse the oppressive nature of organisational culture and its impact on practice;

- includes continuous reflection and evaluation of practice;

- has multidimensional change strategies which incorporate the concepts of networking, user involvement, partnership and participation;

- has a critical analysis of the issues of power, both personal and structural.

Anti-oppressive practice remains the focus of numerous debates regarding its utility and relevance to current practice situations (Nellis, 2000; Wilson and Beresford 2000; O'Hagan 2001). Service users, practitioners, students and academics continue to try to find ways of dealing with issues of oppression in the delivery of health and social care services. This has generated a number of theoretical positions which promote particular ways of working, such as 'critical practice' (Healy, 2000), 'emancipatory social work practice' (Pease and Fook, 1999) and 'culturally competent practice' (O'Hagan, 2001). Common to all these positions are the principles of anti-oppressive practice which we have explored in our chapter.

This chapter was originally written using Amelia's story. It is to her we have returned. She has tried to make sense of the social work intervention to which she was subject to and its impact on her and her child. In keeping with black, feminist and anti-oppressive principles, which advocate the use of narrative, we have updated this chapter using Amelia's reflections.

Amelia's reflections

It is now four years since I experienced difficulties in caring for my son. Following the care plan for adoption, and the court hearing, my mother took care of my son for the next two years. I now have full care of him without a care order.

Looking back, I would say that it is really important for the worker to look at you as a whole person. Not just focus on what you did and make you feel like a bad person. I knew I had done something wrong. I always wished they could have understood me as a young person, who was very confused. I was also black, a single parent and homeless.

I felt the workers needed to listen to my views more, and work with me. They were only OK with me when I agreed with their views. I needed to understand why they made certain plans for me and my son. I wanted them to be honest with me. I feel it is important for those who want to go into social work to have had some experience of life. I realise I still have a lot to learn, but I do know some things about myself and what I need.

The strength of anti-oppressive practice is that it combines the concepts of participation, partnership and empowerment, offering the potential for the service user's voice to be heard and acted upon. The challenge for practitioners is not to act as 'mere functionaries of agencies' (O'Sullivan, 1999: 35), following practice guidelines without questioning the underpinning knowledge and value base. It requires workers to be reflexive, informed and challenging in their practice.

Amelia asks for workers to understand her and her child's needs by locating her individual act within a social and political context, taking account of her many differences and how they contributed to her situation. In her reflections, Amelia asks for her voice to be heard and respected, not merely when it coincides with the workers professional views (Holland, 2000). Anti-oppressive practice extends the choices available for service users and can prepare workers and users to deal effectively with power differences by addressing the impact of oppression at both the micro- and macro-level.

If the principles of anti-oppressive practice are to move the practitioners' thinking beyond agency policy and practice and make a difference, then they need to invest time and energy in the application of those principles, enabling them to analyse situations systematically and think through the action that needs to be taken. Anti-oppressive practice then moves beyond descriptions of the nature of oppression to dynamic and creative ways of working.

The principles of reflexivity, social difference, historical and geographical location, the personal as political, power and powerlessness, and the act of challenging provide a framework which can be used to inform work with people in need.

FURTHER READING

Barn, R. (1993) *Black Children in the Public Care System* (London, Batsford). A research study which highlights the significance of race and racism on decisions made by social workers and on the care careers of black children.

Campion, M.J. (1995) *Who's Fit To Be a Parent?* (London, Routledge). This book, cutting across numerous professional boundaries and personal expertise on parenting, investigates what is deemed as fit parenting and how it is to be assessed.

Clifford, D. (1998) *Social Assessment Theory and Practice* (Aldershot, Ashgate). This book provides a theoretically informed anti-oppressive framework for undertaking assessments. Clifford looks at the personal, structural and methodological dynamics which impinge on the assessment process and demonstrates his ideas in relation to a practice example.

Humphries, B. (ed.) (1996) *Critical Perspectives on Empowerment* (Birmingham, Venture). Interrogates the concept of empowerment and raises questions about the political context in which debates about empowerment take place.

O'Hagan, K. (2001) *Cultural Competence in the Caring Professions* (London, Jessica Kingsley). A text that explores the ideas and definitions of 'culture' and 'cultural competence' and its relevance for health and social care practice.

Walker, A. (1983) *The Color Purple* (London, Women's Press). A first-person account of domination and abuse, it is also a story of recovery and the love and support that women can offer to each other.

Postmodern and Constructionist Approaches to Social Work

Nigel Parton

It is only in very recent years that postmodern and social constructionist perspectives have been drawn upon to think about, analyse and directly contribute to social work practice (see, for example, Howe, 1994; Parton 1994; Hall, 1997; Leonard, 1997; Meinert et al., 1998; Chambon et al., 1999; Jokinen et al., 1999; Pease and Fook, 1999; Fawcett et al., 2000; Healy, 2000; Parton and O'Byrne, 2000; Taylor and White, 2000). In many respects, the starting point has been the recognition that social work has recently been experiencing a major period of change and uncertainty in its organisation and day-to-day practice such that it seems qualitatively different from what went before, thus requiring new skills and new forms of knowledge in order to practise. Social work's engagement with postmodern and constructionist perspectives is a recognition that these changes and experiences are not particular to social work but reflect much wider transformations in Western societies and have been the subject of considerable and often heated debate within social theory. More particularly, the significance of postmodern perspectives is that they draw attention to a number of areas of social transformation in terms of:

- the increasing pace of change;

- the emergence of new complexities and forms of fragmentation;

- the growing significance of difference, plurality and various political movements and strategies, and the pervasive awareness of relativities;

- the opening up of individual 'choice' and 'freedom'; and

- the increasing awareness of the socially constructed nature of existence.

Perhaps most centrally, such perspectives have reactivated a question which has lain dormant in social theory for many years but which touches the heart of much social work – what kinds of human being have we become (Rose, 1996)?

At the outset, however, it is important to recognise that the term 'postmodern' has been hotly contested so that it is almost impossible to impose, by definitional fiat, an agreed set of terms for the debates (Turner, 1990). While the primary concern is to consider how far and in what ways 'current times' are different from what went before, a number of commentators have argued that it is inappropriate to periodise history in this way (Heelas et al., 1996), that the changes and breaks have been exaggerated (Clark, 1996) and that, rather than characterise the present in terms of the postmodern, it is better characterised as high or late modern (Giddens, 1990, 1991). It is for this reason that I have previously very consciously used parenthesis for the '(post)modern', pointing to a provisional and somewhat sceptical use of the term (Parton, 1994b), and have more recently argued that postmodern interpretations are in danger of not taking the situation of actually living human actors sufficiently seriously (Parton, 1998). Even so, the debates provide an important vehicle for developing our insights into the nature of the contemporary complexities, uncertainties and experiences, and for opening up new and creative ways of thinking and acting.

Certainly, reference to the postmodern is much older than the recent fashion in social theory might suggest and in art history and aesthetic theory goes back many years (Featherstone, 1988). The term 'postmodernism' was first used in the 1930s but became increasingly used in the areas of literature, architecture, philosophy and the arts more generally from the 1960s onwards (Turner, 1990; Smart, 1999). The perspective came to particular prominence with the publication of Lyotard's *The Postmodern Condition* in 1984. While perhaps 'postmodern' perspectives are united by a number of cultural projects which claim a commitment to heterogeneity, fragmentation and difference, it is perhaps their critiques of modernity which have proved most influential but contentious.

Modernity as a summary term is seen to refer to the cluster of social, economic and political systems which emerged in the West with the Enlightenment in the late eighteenth century. Unlike the premodern, modernity assumed that human order is neither natural nor God-given, but is vulnerable and contingent. However, by the development and application of science, nature could be subject to human control. The distinguishing features of modernity are seen to be: the understanding of history as having a definite and progressive direction; the attempt to develop universal categories of experience; the idea that reason can provide a basis for all activities and that the nation state could coordinate and advance such developments for the whole society. The guiding principle of modernity is the search to establish reliable foundations for knowledge. It aims to identify central truths about the world but also assumes that truth does not reside on the surface of things but is hidden by appearances. The two crucial elements of modernity in the post-Enlightenment period were thus seen as the progressive union of scientific *objectivity* and politico-economic *rationality* (Parton, 1994b).

In the modern 'frame' the goal is to produce knowledge about a chosen aspect of the physical or social world by which we can claim *greater certainty*. At that point we can confer a sense of truth about that knowledge, and also confer on the people producing knowledge (for example scientists or professionals) the status of holder-of-truth and expert about that aspect of the world. In short, the modernist equation is:

> *external reality – objective knowledge – certainty about that knowledge – claim to truth – expert status given to holder-of-truth/knowledge*. Modernist truth is indeed bound to certainty, external reality and objective knowledge for modernism both relies on (and produces) a clear splitting of the subject who wants to know and the object which is being observed for knowledge and truth. (Flaskas, 1997: 5, original emphasis)

Increasingly, however, there is a recognition that we now inhabit a world which has become disorientated, disturbed and subject to doubt. The pursuit of order and control, the promotion of calculability, belief in progress, science and rationality and other features which were so intrinsic to modernity are being undermined by a simultaneous range of unsettling conditions and experiences. In part this is related to the major social, economic and cultural transformations that have characterised recent times in terms of:

- globalisation;
- the increasing significance of the media and the widening networks of information technology, which transform and transmit knowledge;
- the changes in modes of consumption and production; and
- the increased awareness of risk and uncertainty.

Social work and the postmodern

Howe (1994) has usefully outlined the possible significance of such debates for social work. His central argument is that, if social work was a child of modernity, it now finds itself in a world uncertain of whether or not there are any deep and unwavering principles which define the essence of its character and hold it together as a coherent enterprise.

He suggests that not only can the emergence of social work from the mid-nineteenth century onwards be seen as a particular manifestation of the development of the modern, but also that the three traditional cornerstones of social work – *care, control* and *cure* – can be seen as particular manifestations of modernity's three great projects. He suggests that:

> in its own way social work has pursued the beautiful (aesthetics), the good (ethics) and the true (science) as it attempts to bring about a pleasing quality of life and a just society by using the insights of the social sciences. (Howe, 1994: 518)

Howe (1994) and Parton (1994) both suggest that the high point of modern social work in the UK came in the 1970s when major attempts were made to rationalise and reorganise social work's practices, skills and approaches. This was exemplified by the creation of unified social services departments and the generic social worker at the organisational and practice level and the search for a common base for social work (Bartlett, 1970) via the development of the systems approach (Pincus and Minahan, 1973) and integrated methods (Specht and Vickery, 1977).

However, Howe suggests that contemporary social work is, in many respects, experiencing a number of features which have been characterised as symptomatic of the postmodern condition. Modernism's promise to deliver order, certainty and security has been unfulfilled, and it is increasingly felt that there are no transcendental universal criteria of truth (science), judgement (ethics) and taste (aesthetics). The overriding belief in reason and rationality is disappearing as there is a collapse of consensus related to the 'grand narratives' and their articulation of progress, emancipation and perfection, and what constitutes the centres of authority and truth. The rejection of the idea that any one theory or system of belief can ever reveal the truth, and the emphasis on the plurality of truth and 'the will to truth', captures some of the essential elements associated with postmodern approaches.

Truth takes the guise of 'truth' centred neither in God's word (as in the premodern) nor in human reason (as in the modern), but is decentred and localised so that many 'truths' are possible, dependent on different times and places. Notions of 'truth' are thus related to context and are culture-specific so that there is a refusal to accept that some groups have a monopoly on what constitutes truth, beauty and the good. Relativities, uncertainties and contingencies are no longer seen as marginal and problems to be overcome as yet beyond the reach of reason, but as central and pervasive. In fact, the modern approach, rather than being humanitarian, progressive and emancipatory, is seen as invariably exploitative and repressive because of its failure to recognise difference and its reliance on totalising belief systems, be these patriarchal, capitalist or socialist.

The importance of discourse and language

These developments have contributed to new ways of understanding the self in context which question the central assumptions of human nature and models of the person encoded in professional knowledge and derived from the modernist projects of sociology and psychology. Language is seen as central:

> An understanding of the part that language plays in the formation of human selves, human thought and human subjectivity underpins the postmodern perspective. (Howe, 1994: 521)

Instead of being described as a tool that simply reflects objects, language is seen as mediating and constituting all that is 'known'. Reality is not just obtrusive, but is also embedded within interpretation and 'language games' (Lyotard, 1984), so that 'truth' is a product of language. We cannot transcend the influence of interpretation and assume that reality is simply waiting to be discovered; it is constituted and constructed within language.

If it is the way in which language is structured that provides us with the basis for our notion of selfhood, personal identity and the way in which we relate to social 'reality', a central part of such approaches is to look at the way language is structured, used and accomplished in any situation. It is in this sense that the notion of discourse becomes key. For while such approaches give particular weight to the linguistically constituted character of reality, it does not mean that discourses are 'mere words'. Discourses are structures of knowledge claims and practices through which we understand, explain and decide things. In constituting agents, they also define obligations and determine the distribution of responsibilities and authorities for different categories of person, such as parents, children, social workers, doctors, lawyers and so on. A discourse is best understood as a system of possibilities for knowledge and agency which makes some actions possible while precluding others. It is a system of possibility that allows us to produce statements which are either 'true' or 'false'.

Thus, whereas modernity assumes that increasing knowledge of the real world produces power, postmodernity reverses the formula, recognising that the formation of particular discourses creates contingent centres of power which define areas of knowledge and truth claims, and frameworks of explanation and understanding. Those with power can influence language and discourse and can therefore influence the way in which life is experienced, seen and interpreted. However, because there is a range of different contexts, cultures and discourses available at any one time and place, there is also a plethora of different meanings, knowledges and truths available and many experiences and interpretations of self and identity. Notions of plurality and difference are widespread. Thus we should proceed on the recognition that language does not simply reflect or mirror objects, events and categories existing in the social and natural world – it actively *constructs* those things. Words do not simply describe things, they *do* things and thus have social and political implications.

Implications for practice

However, it has been suggested that the implications for politics, policy and practice of such perspectives are at best ambiguous and at worst undermine many of the central values and principles of social work itself. Similarly, they may neglect the salience of issues of inequality in a simple celebration of difference. Postmodern perspectives have been criticised for being overly relativistic, nihilistic, negativistic and anarchistic, failing to recognise the importance of agency and resistance, and overturning the past in a way which does not take heed of the positive and progressive elements that have previously gone on under the umbrella of social work (Smith and White, 1997). Such criticisms indicate that social work must be wary of such perspectives, for it is essentially a practice where decisions have to be made and practitioners have to act. For while practitioners need to develop a critical reflexive awareness, they must also feel sufficiently confident to act. The contemporary challenge for social work is to take action, which demands that we have made up our mind, while being open minded.

In this respect, Rosenau (1992) provides an important contribution in characterising postmodern perspectives along a continuum from the *sceptic* to the *affirmative postmodernist*. While it is difficult to accommodate the sceptic perspective, with its nihilistic stance on truth and other absolutes, within social work, the emphasis of the affirmative postmodernist on 'truth redefinition' rather

than 'truth denying' is potentially much more suggestive. Rosenau's interpretation of an affirmative postmodern vision demonstrates that, while it cannot offer
truth, it is not without content. It is interpretative and its focus is receptivity,
dialogue, listening to and talking with the other. It reveals paradox, myth and
enigma, and it persuades by showing, reminding, hinting and evoking rather than
by constructing theories and approximating truth. It is suggested that our focus
should be narrative, fragmented fantasies and different stories. Social work takes
on the guise of persuasive fiction or poetry.

What such an approach demonstrates is that postmodern perspectives are not
necessarily bleak or anti-social work but provide novel and creative insights that
clearly talk to a number of themes and approaches which have been associated
with social work for much of its history. It almost suggests that social work could
be (re)interpreted as being postmodern all along. Many social workers will
identify with approaches which blur the difference between fact and fiction,
history and story, art and science (England, 1986), and which take the view that
what an individual perceives or experiences as her or his reality is *the* reality, but a
reality capable of change in an endless variety of ways.

There are now a number of attempts to develop and apply the positive elements
of such an approach explicitly to social work practice. In the process, a number of
themes and issues are illustrated which are of wide application and which can be
developed further in different contexts. *Uncertainty* is seen as central, for, as
Pozatek (1994: 399) suggests, 'the acknowledgement of uncertainty is an essential
element of the postmodern practice of social work' and such a position can push
workers to make the effort to understand a service user's experience. A position of
uncertainty is seen to represent a more respectful approach to cultural difference,
as certainty and objectivity are an illusion. Social workers should not expect,
therefore, to know in advance what the outcomes of interactions will be. They can,
at best, only trigger an effect. A position of uncertainty means that social workers
will approach each situation respectful of difference, complexity and ambiguity.
Words are understood by clients according to how they have constructed the
reality embodied in the interaction. It is thus essential for practitioners to be aware
of this and construct, through *dialogue* with the client, a shared understanding
and reality which they agree is a representation of their interaction. It is an
approach which recognises that *language* is crucial for constituting the experiences
and identity of both the self and the interaction, and which takes seriously the
diverse elements of power involved. It is similarly serious about notions of
partnership and *participation*, and potentially enables the views of service users to
be prioritised. This is not to say, however, that such issues are self-evident and clear
cut. A commitment to uncertainty, indeterminacy and unpredictability will
reinforce social workers' continual attempts reflexively to consider what they are
doing, why and with what possible outcomes.

Sands and Nuccio (1992) have similarly identified a number of themes central
to postmodern perspectives which can be drawn on in practice. Thus, rather than
think and act according to *logocentrism*, assuming that there is a singular fixed
logical order which is 'real' or 'true', practitioners need to recognise that there
are no essential meanings. *Definitions and interpretations are historically contingent and context bound and hence fluid*. Similarly, logocentric thought promotes

thinking in terms of binary opposites – male/female, black/white, adult/child, true/false – which are seen as mutually exclusive, categorical and hierarchical rather than interdependent. Such categories are usually embedded in language in a way which privileges some experiences and marginalises others. It is thus important explicitly to recognise the important, but fluid and changing nature of *difference*, so that the oppressed and devalued can have a voice and we can think and act in terms of both/and *relational* terms.

One way to recover suppressed meaning is through the key postmodern operation of *deconstruction* whereby phenomena are continually interrogated, evaluated, overturned and disrupted. Deconstruction is a way of analysing texts, language and narratives that is sensitive to contextual dimensions and marginalised voices. The process of deconstruction recognises that, while *multiple discourses* might be available, only a few are heard and are dominant, these being intimately related to the dominant powers/knowledges. When one deconstructs, one does not accept the constructs as given but looks at them in relation to their social, historical and political contexts. Constructs are 'problematised' and 'decentred'. Through deconstruction, the presumed fixity of phenomena is destabilised, and the perspective of the marginalised can be given voice. It involves, among other things, helping people to externalise the problem, examining its influences on their life, reconstructing and liberating themselves from it. The notion of *possibility* (O'Hanlon and Beadle, 1994) recognises that things can be changed. A vision of possibility can be used to mobilise people's potential and competence, and can empower them to reclaim and redefine who they are and how they want to act.

However, we should not assume that postmodern perspectives are concerned with giving suppressed subjects a voice in any simple way. The notion of *subjectivity* is itself complex. While, within a logocentric tradition, the individual is autonomous and (if healthy) integrated and has an essential subjectivity, identity, personality, this is not the case with postmodern perspectives. In the latter, subjectivity is precarious, contradictory and in process, constantly being reconstituted in discourses. Accordingly, the subject is multifaceted and speaks in many voices, depending on the sociocultural, historical and interpersonal contexts in which it is situated.

It is perhaps the emphasis on language and its intimate relationship with knowledge and power which provides the most distinctive message for practice arising from postmodern perspectives. A focus on social work as text, narrative and artistry, as opposed to social work as science, moves centre stage. Whereas science looks for explanations and causes, the story or narrative approach is intent on finding a *meaningful* account. As Howe (1993) has demonstrated, via his in-depth analysis of studies of what clients say about what they value from counselling and therapy, it is the latter which is important. Talking not only helps people to understand their experiences, but also allows them to control, reframe and move on. As Howe states:

> there are no objective fundamental truths in human relationships, only working truths. These decentred contingent truths help people make sense of and control the meaning of their own experience. This is how we learn to cope. (Howe, 1993: 193)

Such approaches emphasise *process* and *authorship*. An open-minded engagement with people's stories and the possibility of helping them to re-author their lives using more helpful stories can be both an empowering and respectful way of understanding situations and bringing about change.

Constructive social work

Recently these ideas have been built upon in terms of the development of *constructive social work* (Parton and O'Byrne, 2000). The term 'constructive social work' has been chosen for two reasons. First, to demonstrate a positive, strengths-based approach; and, second, to reflect the postmodern, discourse and social constructionist theoretical perspectives which inform it. The constructive approach, developed by Parton and O'Byrne, emphasises process, plurality of both knowledge and voice, possibility and the relational quality of knowledge. It is affirmative and reflexive and focuses on dialogue, listening to and talking with the other. Social work practice is seen as a specialised version of the process by which people define themselves, participate in their social worlds, and cooperatively construct social realities. It underlines both the shared building of identity and meaning that is the basis of effective practice, and the positive results for service users that stem from the approach.

Constructive social work is concerned with the narratives of solutions to problems, and with change; instead of providing the practitioner with information about the causes of problems, so that she or he can make an expert assessment and prescribe a 'scientific' solution, the service user is encouraged to tell the *story* of the problem in a way that *externalises* it, giving more control and agency and creating a new perspective on how to manage or overcome it. These *narratives* construct the future and anticipate change; questions encourage the service user to identify *exceptions* to the apparently overwhelming nature of problems – situations where she or he has done something that made a positive difference. Constructive social work develops techniques and thinking associated with 'solution-focused' (de Shazer, 1985, 1991, 1994; Miller, 1997), 'narrative' therapy (White and Epston, 1990; White, 1993), 'possibility' (O'Hanlon and Weiner-Davis, 1989; O'Hanlon, 1993; O'Hanlon and Beadle, 1994) and the 'strengths' (Saleeby, 1997) perspectives. The approach attempts to provide questions which elicit clear goals about what the service user wants, in their own words, and which involves her or him in doing something in the immediate future which can launch a new beginning. The practitioner's mode of address is one of 'curiosity and respectful puzzlement' (Parton and O'Byrne, 2000) at the service user's unique way of making things better, rather than expertise in fitting an intervention to a need. Service users are encouraged to repeat successes, to identify solutions as theirs, and as steps to the achievement of their own goals.

Service users are invited to tell their stories using the cultural resources of their communities – local language and interpretation of the problem and the origins of their oppression and exclusion. The language of oppression, domination, subjugation, enslavement and recruitment is used in order to try and establish how the problem is dominating the person. The service user is then encouraged to distance herself or himself from the problem and to give it an unpleasant name, using their own metaphors. It can then be 'externalised' and 'politicised' in terms of the forces operating against empowerment and achievement in society, in terms of style, appearance, class, gender, race, ability, family relationships or whatever. The approach aims to defeat the stereotypes of the blaming official organisations, and offers service users new ways of giving an account of their situation in which their agency becomes central, and they begin to take control. This reduces conflict between the practitioner and the service user and prepares the ground for cooperation in trying to reduce the influence of the problem, and constructing possibilities and solutions. None of this reduces the accountability for mistakes, offences or the abuse of others, although it may challenge beliefs about more fundamental issues of self-worth and potential for change. Thus, a key aspect of the approach is that it encourages service users to retell their stories in terms of courageous opposition to their disadvantages and heroic resistance to their problems.

CONCLUSION

What I have attempted in this chapter is to outline a number of approaches and perspectives which have emerged over recent years which explicitly draw on and use ideas and concepts associated with postmodernism and social constructionism. In doing so, a range of creative, critical and challenging possibilities have been opened up – not only in terms of how we can understand and analyse contemporary social work but also in providing positive contributions to practice itself. In doing so, such approaches can be seen as being particularly pertinent to developing and refining the notion of reflective practice. As Imogen Taylor has suggested, reflective practice and reflective learning may be conceptualised 'as a response to postmodernism, as a positive and creative approach to the prospect of living with contingency' (Taylor, I., 1996: 159). In a world of uncertainty and rapid change, reflective practice offers the possibility of developing strategies for learning how to learn and how to practise in a self-conscious way. The concern is less with developing our knowledge than with developing and deploying our capacities for reflexivity and action.

Dedication

This chapter was originally drafted and planned with Wendy Marshall, who died on 26 March 1997. It is dedicated to Wendy's memory and her considerable contribution to social work education and practice. She is much loved and missed.

NIGEL PARTON

FURTHER READING

Fawcett, B., Featherstone, B., Fook, J. and Rossiter, A. (eds) (2000) *Practice and Research in Social Work: Postmodern Feminist Perspectives* (London, Routledge). This wide-ranging and lively book considers a range of key issues and possibilities in response to the question of what it means, practically, to research and practise from a postmodern feminist point of view.

Leonard, P. (1998) *Postmodern Welfare: Reconstructing an Emancipating Project* (London, Sage). From a critical perspective founded in Marxism and feminism, this book draws on elements of postmodern deconstruction to consider the current state and future of social work and welfare more generally.

Parton, N. and O'Byrne, P. (2000) *Constructive Social Work: Towards a New Practice* (Basingstoke, Macmillan – now Palgrave Macmillan). This book provides a detailed critical approach to practice which explicitly draws on concepts and insights derived from social constructionism, postmodernism and narrative perspectives.

Pease, B. and Fook, J. (eds) (1999) *Transforming Social Work Practice: Postmodern Critical Perspectives* (St Leonards, Australia, Allen & Unwin). Drawing on a number of case studies, this edited collection explores ways of developing practice frameworks, paradigms and principles which take advantage of postmodern perspectives while not abandoning attempts to pursue human emancipation and social justice.

Taylor, C. and White, S. (2000) *Practising Reflexivity in Health and Welfare: Making Knowledge* (Buckingham, Open University Press). Drawing on social constructionism and discursive psychology, this book provides an in-depth analysis of the idea of professional reflexivity. It explores how knowledge is used in professional practice, and how it is made and generated in everyday encounters.

Social Work Practice

23

Social Work Processes

Robert Adams

Introduction

Efforts to arrive at a single, definitive statement about the ingredients of social work practice are likely to fail. The title of Martin Davies' book *The Essential Social Worker* (1994) might imply that there is an ineradicable core of social work roles and activities, but that book does not build on a general consensus about what constitute the essentials of social work. Part I of the present book illustrates the controversial and uncertain context in which social work is practised. Part II demonstrates the great diversity of approaches to practice, some of which contradict or conflict with each other. The postmodern scenarios depicted in Chapter 22 lie closer to Salman Rushdie's observation in *Midnight's Children* that 'reality is a question of perspective' (Rushdie, 1982: 165). Rushdie adds that the further you are from the present, the more concrete and plausible it seems, but the closer you get, the more incredible it becomes, a comment which applies with equal force to the past and the present of social work. From a distance, the outlines of the major areas of social work practice dealt with in this third part of the book – social work with children and families, adults and offenders – seem firm and clear, but a closer study of the detail of each area shows how uncertain and problem-ridden it is.

The content of the first two parts of this book might seem more problematic because their diversity of perspectives makes definition difficult and consensus impossible. In contrast, the practice considered in Part III could be regarded as the tangible reality and therefore as unambiguous. Donald Schön, writing about reflective practice, casts doubt on the accuracy of such a generalisation:

> In the varied topography of professional practice, there is a high, hard ground
> where practitioners can make effective use of research-based theory and
> technique, and there is a swampy lowland where situations are confusing 'messes'
> incapable of technical solution. The difficulty is that the problems of the high
> ground, however great their technical interest, are often relatively unimportant to
> clients or to the larger society, while in the swamp are the problems of greatest
> human concern. (Schön, 1983: 42)

Taking Schön's analogy a little further, this introductory chapter makes connections between the contexts, approaches and practical terrain of social work. In
following these connections through, some parts of the three following chapters
maintain the high ground of social work, while others negotiate its swamps. This
is complicated further by the fact that social work contexts and approaches are
subject to continuing and often rapid change. The first section of this chapter
examines some key features of the changing relationship between social work
practice and its contexts. The second section considers aspects of the changing
relationship between social work approaches and practice. The final section
brings together the implications of these for practice, focusing on the two
somewhat conflicting themes of managerialism and user empowerment; it
concludes by showing how practice-based research has attempted to address, and
in some ways transcend, these difficulties.

Changing contexts and social work practice

There is a lack of consensus about the conditions in which social work is practised
and understood. No single perspective exists, whether from the vantage point of
the professional, worker, officer, staff member, client, service user or offender,
from which to consider the core of the actual matters of practice. Since the late
1980s, this lack of consensus has been made more noticeable by many factors
dealt with in Part I of this book, chief among which are the development of
managerialism, the creation of a contract culture in the health and personal social
services (the impact of which is apparent especially in Chapter 25, on work with
adults), and the imposition on social work education and training of a
competence-based approach. These factors have changed the nature of customary
processes of practice, making them more procedurally governed and increasingly
subject to service specifications in novel contractual relationships between
commissioners, purchasers and providers. Staff training and appraisal focus
increasingly on competent performance rather than on the theory-based and
value-driven aspects of critically reflective and progressive practice.

Managerialism and managerialisms

'Managerialism' is the term used to refer to the inroads made by management
into professional autonomy and power. Clarke et al. (1994a: 6–7) argue that,
while professional ideology pushes practice towards empowering service users,
managerialist strategies locate professionals and service users, as consumers, in a
commercial relationship controlled by managers. Doray describes how, under

scientific management, workers became slaves to the machine and the production process (Doray, 1988: 2). But, of course, many modern managers are committed to bringing out the best in their workforce, using a whole battery of approaches to maximise output and productivity. Many managers in social services share common backgrounds, experiences and qualifications with members of their own workforce, which in theory equips them to anticipate and control their subordinate professionals. Lines of demarcation between health and social services professsionals break down or are repositioned as professionals develop new ways of working together. Clarke et al. (1994a: 4) point out that managerialisms are plural, in the sense that they take many different forms. The nature of these continually changes in different settings. The new managerialisms express aspects of the government's 'promotion and support of the values of entrepreneurialism and methods of business management' (Kelly, 1991: 178). The new managerialist agenda – ensuring effective control of the professionals by the managers – is policed by an ever-increasing array of procedures and standards, based on the prominent ideology of quality assurance, with reference to both the processes and the products of the professionals' work. This contrasts with the traditional centralised organisation, in which social work was judged largely by the extent to which, for example, staff kept within budgets. Lewis and Glennerster (1996: 141) acknowledge, in their evaluation of the implementation of community care in the 1990s, that its broader aspects have been pushed along by managerial rather than professional considerations.

However, not all versions of managerialism undermine professional social work. In fact, a notable feature of managerialism in the personal social services is the close interweaving with professional work achieved by some government-sponsored managerialist initiatives (Adams, 1998). The SSI, for example, mediates between state policies, the operations of local authorities and the professional practice of social work. The SSI has continued a working style evolved in the former Social Work Service of the Department of Health and Social Security in the 1970s. This, although responsible for implementing government policy, often responds sensitively to local practice issues. At the same time, commentators such as Shaw view the tight parameters of managerial control as dramatically curbing professional autonomy (Shaw, 1995: 132), for example in the support by the Chief Social Services Inspector of a shift to a working style where 'no individual fieldworker should be regarded as self-sufficient' (SSI, 1992: 13) (see in particular, Chapter 24 on social work with children and families).

A number of the trends occurring in the personal social services mirror wider, similar changes going on in the public sector as a whole: first, rather paradoxically, towards larger and more complex organisations managed by local and central government, and a trend towards a greater diversity, and a greater number, of smaller service-providing organisations in the voluntary and private sectors; second, towards a separation of senior management in the organisation purchasing services from the professionals who provide those services; third, towards more partnerships between public and private providers of services; fourth, towards the reduction of the size of the permanent service-providing workforce in the large local authority social work and social services departments of the 1970s, more staff being bought in on short and temporary contracts around a decreasing core of full-time, permanent officials.

Far from statutorily based social work remaining the backbone of the social services, programme cuts have reduced the capacity of social services departments to provide services themselves. The implementation of community care in the 1990s (see Chapter 25) has sharpened debates about whether social work has a future as an autonomous profession.

The contract culture

The introduction of internal markets in the health and social services sector since the 1990s represents the most radical change for half a century in the way in which services are organised and delivered (see Chapter 7 for more detailed discussion). The language and culture of contracts – commissioning and costing, service specification – is a reminder of the business culture being nurtured in the social services. Practitioners cannot insulate themselves from these changes, but they may attempt to preserve their professional integrity by distancing themselves as far as possible from any negative impact they may have. Tensions exist within social work practice, from the vantage point of different stakeholders, whether managers, practitioners or service users. These are not necessarily discrete but may overlap and on occasions conflict with each other. There are also tensions in the ways in which social workers engage with practice, given the policy, organisational and managerial pressures which exist.

The superimposition on the relationship between the social worker and the client of a contract between the local authority as purchaser and the providing agency or body has a significant effect on the interaction between them. The contract culture commonly displays deep-seated features of self-interest and individualism which are antithetical to mutual help, collaboration and cooperation.

It is possible to make a virtue out of necessity and claim that basing social work with people on a service specification with built-in targets, standards and performance criteria by which to judge them improves the quality of the work done. However, such work runs the risk of decisions about what to do and how to achieve it being shaped by financial rather than professional considerations (Adams, 1996b). For example, the widespread trend towards recommending residential care for older people was reported by the Audit Commission in 1996 to be due to the perverse incentive that it was cheaper for a local authority to place people in residential care because they qualified for state benefits, such as those in independent sector homes who qualified for the residential allowance (Audit Commission, 1996b, para. 70: 6). This was due to the pressure of shortages of community care resources rather than based on needs-led assessments and care and planning.

Competence-based approaches

Competence-based approaches (see Chapter 7 for discussion of the organisational context) have been likened to the driving test, which judges performance without regard to the process by which that level of expertise is reached. One such approach is embodied in the rules and requirements for the Dip SW (CCETSW, 1996), reflecting an emphasis on outcomes and performance. Of course, the development of a new, degree-linked three-year qualification in social work is still based on the notion of a list of occupational standards, although upgrading from a diploma to a degree is likely to strengthen the intellectual and theoretical underpinnings for the demonstration by students of expertise in practice. Such developments emphasise the ambiguous nature of competence-based approaches in social work. Undoubtedly they can strengthen practice and empower practitioners and services users. On the other hand, they may be regarded as a managerialist means by which managers control what their staff are doing. Dominelli (1996) argues that the adoption of a competence-based approach in social work contradicts the development of anti-oppressive practice.

There has been a widespread move in the health and social care field in the UK since the early 1980s towards developing occupational standards based on competence approaches. A competence-based approach involves assumptions about the appropriateness of identifying an inseparable common base of values, knowledge and skills. The value base of practice derives from the examination of the ethical dimension of practice. The base of knowledge for practice includes the wide range of aspects referred to in occupational standards. The use of the knowledge base includes not only the ability to repeat relevant memorised facts, but also a critical understanding which workers can apply to practice. For example, in drawing upon knowledge of the law, it is anticipated that the competent social worker will appreciate its problematic nature. Skills include such areas as engaging with people, assessing needs, planning, carrying out the work and evaluating work done. However, the location of such a competence-based approach in the contract culture implies that processes are regarded merely as an instrumental means by which to attain valued goals.

A competence approach uses task analysis to define what workers do. It is based on assessing what people do – and how they perform – rather than on their qualities or professional judgment and grasp of relevant issues. It involves three essential features. First, it rests on an assessment of what people actually do rather than on their critical understanding. Second, it builds on an analysis of people's existing jobs, matching personal specifications to lists of key roles which amount to occupational standards (Mangham and Silver, 1986). Boyatzis (1982), an influential advocate of a competence-based approach in management development, deduces necessary or desired qualities in performance at work from observing and measuring what workers do and distinguishes 'threshold' competences inherent in all competent performance from that level of competence demonstrated by the outstanding person (Salaman et al., 1994: 33–4). Third, it assumes a correlation between a person's actions, value commitment and critical awareness, with the crucial emphasis of judgments about professional expertise resting on performance.

Competence-based approaches are prone to six main criticisms:

1. They tend to focus on areas of expertise that are most appropriate in stable, bureaucratic work settings, rather than being directed towards future job requirements.

2. They encourage fragmentation, that is, a somewhat artificial atomisation of components of activities which could otherwise be viewed holistically.

3. They are convergent, in that they may bring about a narrowing of ideas consistent with outcome-based activity rather than encouraging divergent thinking and an emphasis on the value of the process of the activity accompanying creative practice.

4. They focus mainly or wholly on those easily measurable aspects of people's performance.

5. They concentrate on techniques and skills, and this relegates considerations of values, critical evaluation and the deployment of front-line knowledge, particularly at more advanced levels, into second place.

6. They emphasise students acquiring specified techniques rather than developing approaches based on critically reflective practice.

Hayman also argues that, apart from the risk that competences may reduce complex professional issues to banal simplifications (Hayman, 1993: 182), competences 'can become frozen in time' and produce technicians rather than professionals (Hayman, 1993: 181). They are fundamentally contradicted by the requirement that the critical professional should constantly re-evaluate accepted practice and thereby achieve 'a constant openness to redefining what competent, effective practice is'. Hayman concludes: 'It is hard to see how to devise competences that call themselves into question in this way' (Hayman, 1993: 181).

Where practice is complex, uncertain and inherently problematic, a purely empirically driven competence-based approach is less likely to produce an adequate analysis of key roles. There is not much encouragement for the kind of reflective practice to which Payne refers (Chapter 11). Where changes in the context of practice are very rapid, a purely descriptive approach, without consultation with relevant – probably diverse and possibly conflicting – interests in the field of practice, inevitably falls short of representing complex reality. In social work, a wide range of advice from different interests and groups would be necessary, including different stakeholder managers and professionals in the statutory, voluntary, private and informal sectors, as well as services users and carers. There is a risk that the empirical analysis of competence may neglect 'soft' personal qualities, such as 'assertiveness, impact, creativity, sensitivity and intuition [which] are difficult to measure under any circumstances' (Jacobs, 1989, quoted in Salaman et al., 1994: 35), in favour of hard areas of activity and skill, such as finance budgeting. Job analysis based on limited consultation may not exclude bad practice, based on a distorted or flawed value base.

Changing approaches and social work practice

Practice is an extremely complex activity, rooted in the contexts set out in Part I of this book and drawing on many of the approaches examined in Part II. All three interact, though. Contexts and approaches do not precede practice. All three are inseparable. This is one reason why the analysis of practice is so complex and demanding. There is no single version of practice for a given set of circumstances. The impact of the factors reviewed above varies greatly according to the approaches adopted in local settings.

Inseparable from their context, changing views about what constitutes the core of the practice of social work since the 1960s mirror wider debates about how professional social work's knowledge base has changed and how theory, practice and research into social work should be conceived. As Part II of this book shows, these debates have intensified since the 1960s as the legal basis and knowledge and value bases for social work have extended and become more complex and controversial.

Practice does not derive from an unchanging, agreed base of theories and knowledge. New social work approaches have tended to overlay rather than extinguish existing ideas about practice. Practice is a feature of constantly changing circumstances in which professionals and clients interact, and realities are fragmented and diverse, with few, if any fixed, unchanging or agreed points of reference. Until the 1950s, social work in Britain relied heavily on psychological and psychotherapeutic theories and researches with a bearing on work with individuals and groups, including families (Woodroofe, 1962). Influences from social psychology were evident in the growing popularity of groupwork and group-based approaches to work with families, including family therapy and group counselling (Brown, 1988; Whitaker, 1985). From the 1960s, social work was increasingly influenced by work in and with community groups engaged in social and political action and by sociology. Social administration and social policy informed social work practice and, along with sociology and criminology, supplied increasingly critical – that is, radical, feminist, Marxist – perspectives from the early 1970s. Concepts such as empowerment, which from the late 1980s found their way into the UK social work literature, derived much of their impetus from the social action movements and pressure group politics of the 1960s. By the 1990s, all the approaches examined in the chapters in Part II coexisted in social work. The use of this diversity of social work approaches in different circumstances is not precluded by the fact that some are at variance or even in conflict with each other.

Diverse notions of process

The considerable ambiguities inherent in notions of process in social work surface particularly at the interface with other professions, notably in health care. Social work has shifted since the 1980s towards multidisciplinary and multiprofessional working. Yura and Walsh (1967) used the term 'the nursing process' to encompass four component stages of nurses' work with patients – assessment, planning, implementation and evaluation – each of which had its own discrete processes. Conceptualisations of such processes vary greatly according to the model of nursing which is applied to practice (Aggleton and Chalmers, 1986). Traditionally, the nursing process informing what nurses and midwives did reflected a view of health care which was hospital-based and medically dominated. The growth of community care and the impact of hospital closure programmes in areas such as mental health and learning disability have contributed to a situation where more nurses now work outside than inside hospitals. Social perspectives on health care

are diminishing the professional distance between health visitors, occupational therapists, community nurses and social workers. The complementary roles of care assistants and health-care assistants are often blurred. Lewis and Glennerster (1996: 188) use as an example the blurring of roles of health and social care at the interface with service users. Some managers, for example, leave to the professional the negotiation of the demarcation of responsibilities concerning which worker makes the toast and who gives the insulin to the person on a home visit. We can add to this complicated set of issues which the professionals may have to resolve on the spot, at the interface with service users and carers, the debates about what is legitimate professional work. The blurring of the boundary around the traditional activities of doctoring and nursing reflects the increasing legitimacy within health care of professions allied to medicine and complementary health care. There are moves to legitimise oriental practice such as acupuncture as complementary to Western medicine (MacPherson and Kaptchuk, 1996). This emphasises a process orientation. In fact, it is arguable that such complementary therapies are more appropriate than, for example, surgery, for working with people in an ongoing process rather than at a fixed point of intervention such as an operation. The increasing tendency for professionals in the health and social services to work together heightens rather than resolves differences of professional ideologies, cultures and practices. The many problems of developing collaboration between disciplines, professions and health and social services organisations require careful attention in practice and cannot be resolved by a quick-fix approach.

Implications for practice

The final part of this chapter selects three of the main implications of the above discussion of contextual factors and changing approaches for social work practice. The first two of these concern the tensions between the 'upward' or organisationally 'inward' accountability of the social worker through the line manager to the state and the employing organisation, and the 'downward' or 'outward' accountability to the client or service user. The third area – the interface between research and practice – shows that, since both managers and service users have legitimate stakes in the practice of social work, there is merit in exploring ways of surmounting such tensions rather than fatalistically accepting them.

Engaging with managerialism

We saw earlier in this chapter how managerialisms tend to emphasise a sequence or cycle of activity, as conceptualised and laid down by line managers rather than professionals working within their own knowledge base. Thus, they tend to reflect legalistic and procedural imperatives. The language and culture of such perspectives on practice is administrative. They may also borrow from the industrial or commercial sectors. In the contract culture, products may be the focus, at the expense of production processes; financial and outcome-based performance indicators may predominate over qualitative evaluation. The significant impact of these factors on all the areas of social work covered in Chapters 24 to 26 is referred to now.

In childcare and family-based social work (Chapter 24), whereas the notion of stages bypasses more sophisticated concepts associated, for example, with intrapsychic change – whether development or decay – it cannot be dismissed as less useful. The collaborative arrangements between agencies set out in the publication *Working Together under the Children Act, 1989* (DoH, 1991b) date from the 1960s, although they have attracted higher-profile attention particularly since the inquiry into the death of Maria Colwell (DHSS, 1974) and, even more so, following the Cleveland Inquiry (DHSS, 1988). The useful summary of outcomes of 20 research studies in 1995 provided the occasion for the process of child protection to be set out in four stages: preinvestigation, first enquiry, family visit, and conference and registration (DoH, 1995a: 26). One of the most useful concepts associated with the child protection process is that of thresholds, often linked with particular actions performed by the practitioner, but in any case involving a specific decision being taken, as a consequence of which there is movement from one stage to the next (DoH, 1995a: 33). The separation of the stage of preinvestigation from first enquiry draws attention to the processes by which children for whom services are immediately forthcoming are distinguished from those referred for further investigation. Inevitably, proceduralism in childcare has the negative consequence of constraining, or even eroding, professional autonomy. The challenge for professionals is to use procedures as the basis for claiming the necessary resources to engage in progressive practice (Adams, 1998).

There is ambiguity over the circumstances in which processes of care management examined in Chapter 25 are driven by either professional or managerial imperatives. These are reflected in, but do not altogether originate in, the rationale for the care planning process. Notably, there is a similarity between the managerial sequence of planning, implementation and review in care management since the NHS and Community Care Act 1990 and various models of the therapeutic process.

Miller and Gwynne (1972) were subsequently attacked by advocates of non-oppressive work with people with impairments, for applying the metaphors of the industrial setting to the residential care of disabled people, likening it to processes of operating warehouse or greenhouse approaches to care.

Again, in criminal and youth justice, one consequence of the ironic convergence between radical and conservative views referred to in Chapter 26 is the development of systems-based approaches to the management of the processing of offenders. Such top-down approaches have been nourished by the same research which has stimulated an overhaul of traditional, functionalist criminologies. Critiques by sociologists of deviance of processes by which people become labelled as problems were applied first to social work with offenders and subsequently to work with other client groups, such as people with mental health problems. From the late 1960s, challenges to the welfare model in criminal and juvenile justice impacted upon criminology (Taylor et al., 1974) and then upon social work in the UK (Thorpe et al., 1980). Thorpe's work involving evaluating, among other things, key stages in the career processes of delinquents provided an influential critique of the failings of the Children and Young Persons Act 1969 and stimulated efforts to develop correctional curricula of sufficient rigour and attractiveness to the courts to enable young offenders to be diverted from custody. Latterly, Thorpe developed a similarly evaluative approach to other client groups (see the section on research viewpoints below), notably children in the child protection system (Thorpe, 1994).

Since the 1970s, in the fields of criminal and youth justice, the term 'process' has acquired added significance from the extensive literature based on research concerning offenders' progress through, or diversion from, criminal careers. Since that period, work with offenders has been concerned with managing the tension between the agencies and professions – among which social work is prominent – and processes of signification (Matza, 1969) or labelling (Becker, 1963), with the goal of minimising the penetration of individuals into the criminal and youth justice systems. Ironically, policies of delinquency management based on protecting the public by controlling youth justice systems (Audit Commission, 1996a) tend to manage the boundaries of intervention rather than developing a correctional curriculum which empowers young people. They may become intrusive, like tagging, or may even be overtly controlling (Adams et al., 1981: 22).

In probation work, the combined impact of the 1991 and 1993 Criminal Justice Acts and the 1994 Criminal Justice and Public Order Act (see Chapter 26), in England and Wales at any rate, has been to shift the balance of the work of probation officers towards buttressing correctional philosophies. The writing of presentence reports (PSRs) tends to focus on questions such as the seriousness of the offence and the risk to the public, to the near-exclusion of personal history or cultural and social factors contributing to criminality. The increasing prominence in probation practice of a focus on 'What Works', in terms of the relative effectiveness of different sentences and approaches to work with offenders, follows research reviews which emphasise psychological rather than social and environmental factors contributing to criminality, such as unemployment, poor housing, poverty and environmental degradation (McGuire, 1995).

Engaging with perspectives on empowering service users and carers

Since the late 1980s, principles and practices of empowerment have become prominent matters for debate among politicians, managers and professionals in the health and social services. However, empowering social work relates to traditions of activism and advocacy which are well established and not generally circumscribed by professional discourse and practice. In the 1980s, the growth of user-led and self-advocacy movements in the UK, notably among disabled people and people who had experienced hospital-based treatment for mental health problems, drew on, and gave additional impetus to, concepts of personal and community action with long traditions in many other countries (Wolfensberger, 1997). Conventional wisdom has it that these ideas were imported from the USA into social work in the UK (see Solomon, 1985; Adams, 1996b: 15; Payne, 1997: 275). The most dramatic signs of this change were the take-up in the personal social services in the UK from the late 1980s of the concept of empowerment and its incorporation into official guidance from the Department of Health concerning the implementation of the NHS and Community Care Act 1990. This comes close to Orem's (1985) self-care approach to nursing, which encourages a holistic view, focusing on empowering people, so that they can initiate and carry out their own strategies to maintain health and well-being.

Empowering practice has received most attention in the areas of childcare and community care, while in work with offenders it is the least developed and, not surprisingly, least well articulated in the, almost by definition, professionally dominated social work literature. Even in community care, however, the adherence of official guidance to rhetorical statements about empowering service users is surprising, since people may in practice complain of feeling disempowered by, marginalised by, or excluded from the ways in which professional services are provided for them. A further complication is that much of the literature on user empowerment contributes to the field of interprofessional communication or education for students rather than empowering clients (Adams, 1996b: 72–3).

Empowering practice is furthermore very often associated with 'bottom-up' processes of consciousness-raising or liberation as they affect individuals and groups, whereas a growing literature on anti-oppressive work (Ward and Mullender, 1991) proceeds at the same time from 'top-down', structural analyses of divisions and inequalities in societies. There is, therefore, some looseness of fit between these concepts and practices (Taylor et al., 1992; Servian, 1996).

However, commentators in the field of citizen participation are increasingly taking on board the need to link areas of anti-discrimination and anti-oppression with discourse on empowerment. Mullender and Ward locate their empowering practice in groupwork, outlining five stages of user-led groupwork, which they then augment into twelve stages as they apply anti-oppressive principles of practice (Mullender and Ward, 1991). The work of Beresford and Croft (1995) takes as axiomatic the link between issues concerning citizen participation in service planning, implementation and evaluation, and the case for extending human rights to all disempowered individuals and groups, including those excluded by virtue of such social problems as poverty or disability.

Engaging at the interface between practice and research

Tensions betwen managerial and user perspectives on social work processes are reflected in the diversity of approaches to research in practice. Research and practice go hand in hand, but, depending on its assumptions, research may either reinforce oppressive practice, or espouse the goal of empowerment (see Chapter 10). Research provides, among other things, an evaluation of services provided by the agency. Thorpe and Thorpe (1992: 24) offer a systems model for evaluating what happens to clients after they become clients, with reference to three components of the systems model:

> input – information available on records, for example, concerning how people became clients; process; and outcomes – information about the results of services in the short, medium and longer terms.

Thorpe and Thorpe (1992: 24) define process in these terms as 'a simple description of the services provided by the agency and the reasons why those services (as opposed to any other service) are supplied'. Whitaker and Archer (1989: 12–15) identify some shared features of the processes of research and practice in social work, notably those involved in activities such as collecting data and drawing conclusions. However (see Chapter 10), they use the variety of practice-based research carried out by post-qualifying social workers on practice-based research programmes at York to distinguish in some significant ways the research process from the process of practice (Whitaker and Archer, 1989: 75). Their observations also draw on some unpublished work by Dixon of Barnardo's (Dixon, 1984: 4) in which she draws parallels, paraphrased below, between processes of research and social work:

1. The social worker and the researcher are presented with a problem or question.

2. The social worker collects facts to illuminate the problem; the researcher carries out a literature search on the problem or question.

3. The social worker formulates a plan of action; the researcher designs a piece of research.

4. The social worker implements the plan, recording progress; the researcher implements the study by collecting and collating data.

5. The social worker reviews the work and may make fresh plans; the researcher analyses the data, draws conclusions and may make recommendations for further action.

Whitaker and Archer (1989: 13) identify important differences between research and practice: the pace of research is likely to be much slower than that of practice, with much more time, for example, spent reflecting on methodological issues and the interpretation of data; practitioners tend to receive feedback much more quickly than researchers, in terms of whether a particular action has been appropriate to a service.

The proximity of the research and practice processes is not just conceptual, but also interactive. Research and practice may coexist in a symbiotic relationship. Learning and insights from practice – the phrase Whitaker and Archer use is 'practice wisdom', while Parton (Chapter 22) refers to different forms of discourse – can form the basis for developing research, the equivalent term for this being 'academic wisdom'. The reverse is also true, of course. Research may produce new knowledge and stimulate fresh practice. Research may be regarded as integral to practice and useful to local policy developments (Whitaker and Archer, 1989: 13).

Many useful examples of empowering research approaches can be found in countries outside the UK. For example, empowerment evaluation, which originated in the USA, is an increasingly popular approach in many fields of the human services, including social work. It enables a creative convergence between empowering research and practice. Empowerment evaluation lies beyond collaborative evaluation and involves facilitating people to engage in what is essentially self-evaluation (Fetterman, 1996: 11). The worker plays a facilitating role as consultant, rather than acting as expert, during this process. This comprises what

Fetterman, a leading exponent, identifies as four steps: taking stock – the existing strengths and weaknesses of the situation; setting goals – people themselves deciding where they want to go in future; developing strategies – people choosing and developing the means of accomplishing their goals; and documenting progress – enabling people to use relevant, credible and rigorous means of evaluating their activities (Fetterman, 1996: 18–20).

But we do not need to go so far afield. New paradigm research, as developed by Reason and Rowan (1981), has a close affinity with the paradigm of empowerment which emerged in social work in the UK in the late 1980s (Adams, 1990, 1996a). New paradigm research is a cooperative approach to experiential enquiry, embodying a move to participatory and holistic knowing, critical subjectivity and knowledge in action. These are three key components in a fundamentally empowering approach, predating the use of the term 'empowerment' in social work, but which nevertheless has recognisable conceptual antecedents 'rooted in a new world-view which is emerging through systems thinking, ecological concerns and awareness, feminism, education, as well as in the philosophy of human inquiry' (Reason, 1988: 3). Reason refers to Rowan's (1981) argument that the orthodox scientific method alienates experimental subjects from the product of the research, from the work of the research, from other people and from themselves (Reason, 1988: 6). The process of cooperative research set out by Rowan in 1981 contrasts with the traditional experimental method and the implicitly professionally owned, practice-based model set out by Whitaker and Archer (1989). Reason defines the cooperative research process as follows:

Stage 1: A group of co-researchers and co-subjects meet to inquire into some aspect of their life and work.

Stage 2: The group take decisions about what research action to take into their lives and begin to record. This may involve 'self-observation, reciprocal observation of other members of the inquiry group, or other agreed methods of recording experience; it is primarily in the realm of practical knowledge' (Reason, 1988: 5).

Stage 3: The co-researchers engaged in this activity become fully immersed in their practice and may actually lose their distinct awareness of being engaged in an inquiry.

Stage 4: The co-researchers return to reflect and make sense of their experience. This may involve abandoning early assumptions and 'a whole range of both cognitive and intuitive forms of knowing; its expression may be primarily propositional, but may also involve stories, pictures, and other ways of giving voice to aspects of experience which cannot be captured in propositions. When this making sense has been completed, the co-researchers can consider how to engage on [sic] further cycles of inquiry' (Reason, 1988: 5).

The rigid segregation of stages in the above description does less than justice to Reason's point that movement between experience and reflection goes on; there are similarities between this flux and the existential process of reflective practice developed by Schön (1983) (see Chapter 11). Reflective practice emerges as less a technique and more a perspective, less a series of concrete actions and more a state of being. Thus, Schön uses the term 'reflection-in-practice' to convey the dynamism and holism of the concept. Interestingly, Krim, in Reason's 1988 edited collection of studies, explicitly refers to Schön's work (Krim, 1988: 145). Some useful similarities can be identified with personal consciousness-raising, group-based community action or community development perspectives. Reason writes of the cooperative inquiry process, which involves:

> establishing relationships of authentic collaboration and dialogue; ideally we care for each other, and approach each other with mutual love and concern. While not ignoring the necessity for direction and the role of expertise, we eschew unnecessary hierarchy and compulsive control. The emphasis on wholeness also means that we are not interested in either fragmented knowing, or theoretical knowing that is separated from practice and from experience. We seek a knowing-in-action which encompasses as much of our experience as possible. This means that aspects of a phenomenon are understood deeply because we know them in the context of our participation in the whole system, not as the isolated dependent and independent variables of experimental science. Our holistic concerns lead us to a form of theory-building and understanding which is descriptive and systemic, what Geertz (1973) would call a 'thick description', or Kaplan (1964) a 'concatenated' theory. The essential quality of a pattern model is that it creates a dense ... web of knowing. This kind of non-hierarchical thinking-in-action is quite foreign to formal Western thinking: we tend to see the world in terms of hierarchical cause-and-effect, rather than in networks of understanding. (Reason, 1988: 11)

Changes in the legal and policy basis for social work, and in approaches to practice and research, have sharpened rather than resolved fundamental clashes between traditional and critical perspectives on how social work practice should be described and evaluated. On one hand, as Heineman notes in a seminal article, there are traditionalists who may seek credibility by 'embracing an antiquated research model that philosophers of science and social scientists from other disciplines were abandoning', on the positivist assumption that 'core practice-related concepts can be defined by empirical or quantitative measures' (Heineman, 1981: 371). On the other hand, there is a growing cadre of commentators, practitioners and researchers, representing a diversity of perspectives but invariably united in their scepticism of the efforts of positivists to generate a 'scientifically determined knowledge base and research methods' (Reamer, 1993: 121) which are unique to social work. According to Reamer, much theorising and research based on positivist empiricial approaches is 'of relatively limited value and relevance to practitioners' (Reamer, 1993: 141).

Finding ways forward: sustaining critical practice in an era of diversity

So social work contexts, approaches and practices remain as controversial in the twenty-first century as they were in the 1970s and 80s. However, as the questions and assumptions associated with them have been subjected to more open and critical scrutiny, so the areas of debate have become more apparent. Social workers are engaged in complex webs of social and institutional relationships, embracing multiple accountabilities: to the state; to their employers who provide social work services; to colleagues; to professional values; and not least towards the client and the wider community. Within this history, diverse views of practice reflect broader debates about the nature of social work and its relationship with its contexts.

A delicate balance needs to be maintained between becoming enmeshed in the politics and practice of managerialism – challenging from the inside – and maintaining professional distance and developing areas of progressive, but fairly isolated, practice.

The coexistence of professional and managerial perspectives on the social work process is somewhat anomalous. However, there is no virtue in pretending that professional, managerial and research perspectives on process can be coalesced and their differences somehow dissolved. It is possible, however, that they may interact creatively. The most common approaches to practice have also become clear, and it may help to regard these as responses to the areas of uncertainty and debate that the first two parts of this book have highlighted, which have been revisited and to some extent reframed in this discussion of process in social work. We can use three terms to help to clarify the wide range of responses to these uncertainties and debates: *absolutism*, or retention of one perspective; *relativism* or a pluralistic tendency; and *transcendentalism*, or the attempt to find a meta-perspective which incorporates the desired features of others. Each of these simplifies and is thus inevitably untidy in some way, but the brief exposition of each of them perhaps helps to clarify the territory of this final part of the book.

'Absolutism' is a rather unsatisfactory term – in that it sounds extreme and authoritarian – but one which nevertheless conveys accurately the stance which ring-fences one perspective on theory, research and practice and, by definition, excludes all debate and serious consideration of other perspectives. Reamer, for example, implies that the social worker setting out to develop a behaviourally based theory of assessment and the social worker committed to developing a psychodynamically oriented treatment theory may be equally unable or unwilling to consider their work from a pluralistic viewpoint (Reamer, 1993: 152). The term 'relativism' may sound more dubious than words such as 'pluralism' or 'eclecticism' concerning the tendency towards practitioners being prepared to pick up a suitable approach in particular circumstances from a range of possibly divergent or even conflicting approaches. Reamer (1993: 149) acknowledges the comment by Wood (1990: 378) that competent social work depends on:

> the ability of practitioners to be polyocular – to have a variety of lenses through which to view their cases ... Indeed, in a given case – or even in one interview in a case – the competent practitioner may be utilising several different descriptive and prescriptive theories in rapid succession or even simultaneously.

However, a supermarket or 'pick-and-mix' approach is not implied as the optimum. Reamer is careful to point out that:

> Anarchy in research and extreme forms of relativism should be avoided; rather, social workers need to draw *systematically* on various research perspectives and techniques in order to produce the most lucid, illuminating, and compelling body of information required by varying practice circumstances. Thus, formal evaluation

> of a long-term residential program for emotionally disturbed adolescents may call for a combination of quantitative, empirically based, self-report data from checklists, questionnaire data, and academic performance data, *and* qualitative data based on extensive observation in several naturalistic settings. (Reamer, 1993: 149)

Unfortunately, though, the hierarchy of knowledges and power within qualitative and quantitative methodologies may operate to produce what Willis (1978), in his ground-breaking but controversial ethnography of boys making the transition from school to work in the 1970s, called 'mere methodological variety'. More significant, perhaps, this crititique of methodological soup-making may not tackle more insidious divisions and inequalities which have marginalised qualitative methodologies, for example, as a feature of a less desirable form of masculinity, of which Gherardi and Turner (1987) write in their ironically titled paper 'Real men don't collect soft data'.

There is no certain way of transcending the limitations of single-focus perspectives on social work practice and the dangers of extreme forms of pluralism or relativism. Many gaps and discontinuities exist between different ways of chunking up perspectives, theories and approaches to social work processes and practices, so it is unrealistic to expect that one approach can, as it were, provide a meta-framework for incorporating all the others.

Since the 1970s, accumulating experiences and research through theory and practice in the areas of empowerment and non-oppressive practice have emerged in key areas of social work. Three kinds of contribution are worth noting: creative (England, 1986), critical (Everitt et al., 1992; Everitt and Hardiker, 1996) and participatory (Reason and Rowan, 1981; Marsden and Oakley, 1990; Beresford and Croft, 1993; Marsden et al., 1994). England (1986) addresses the one-dimensionality of instrumentality expressed in the more rigid, skill-based approaches to competence by amplifying the many ways in which expressive aspects of practice contribute to a holistic approach. The approach of Everitt and colleagues is informed by Marxian and Hegelian notions of a dialectical process which creates synthesis from opposed interests. The creative approach suggests that beyond the dualism of positivism and anti-positivism lies a transcendent position which harnesses instrumental/technical and expressive/artistic components of theory and practice. The new paradigm approach of Rowan and Reason assumes that the differentials of interest and power between different stakeholders in research and practice can be reduced or even abolished by a collaborative strategy. This involves maximising the participation of service users, for example by meeting with them at the outset of any research process to elicit their own goals for the study and, in effect, recruiting them as co-researchers throughout the subsequent process. Marsden and Oakley (1990) and Marsden et al. (1994) use experience in social development projects from many parts of the world to caution against segregating academics, managers and professionals – and the research project – from the social development activity itself. In the UK, Beresford and Croft (1993) have used collaborative research in their examination of the feasibility of, and barriers to, citizen participation in the planning, delivery and management of local services.

It is doubtful whether the gulf between positivist and non-positivist perspectives can be abolished by treating them as possible contributors to a multimethod approach. We are left with a diversity of ideas and practices entirely consistent with the postmodern conditions described by Parton (Chapter 22). However, the developments referred to in the previous paragraphs are having a significant impact on theory, research and practice, in particular through emancipatory and participatory research projects focusing on the involvement of people in social services. These initiatives present three forms of challenge: first, to managerialism, which undermines professional autonomy and reduces professional decision-making to the gatekeeping of rationed services; second, to contribute to knowledge and theorising as activities owned equally by service users, professionals and academics; third, to empower people through developing participatory action which integrates both research and practice, by not separating the ownership of research from service development.

Professionals can use their practice as the basis for self-evaluation and reflections which in turn contribute to social work models and theories. One important question arising from the practitioner research programme at Stirling University was how to develop research-mindedness and a research culture in social work agencies (Fuller and Petch, 1995: 184). A questioning, self-questioning attitude to practice can encourage this, as much as formal evaluation and research programmes. The starting point for this is with a detailed, critical examination of a particular area of practice. Each of the three following chapters addresses this task by situating examples of practice in the context of current policy directions and research findings.

CONCLUSION

This chapter has set the scene for the detailed examination of practice in the three areas covered in the following chapters. It portrays the diversity of work with different individuals and groups of people and illustrates the inadequacy of any attempt to distil the essentials of social work into an artificially contrived, unified set of concepts. The integrity of the profession is likely to be better served by social work professionals and educators aspiring to a more sophisticated understanding of practice, located in its contexts and taking account of the complexity of professional values and approaches.

FURTHER READING

Farnham, D. and Horton, S. (eds) (1993) *Managing the New Public Services* (London, Macmillan – now Palgrave Macmillan). Deals critically with the nature and impact of managerialism in the public services, in a way which enables their general analysis to be applied easily to the personal social services.

Le Croy, C.W. (ed.) (1992) *Case Studies in Social Work Practice* (Pacific Grove, CA, Brooks/Cole). A collection of wide-ranging case studies in different settings, exemplifying a variety of therapeutic approaches to social work processes.

Marsden, D., Oakley, P. and Pratt, B. (eds) (1994) *Measuring the Process: Guidelines for Evaluating Social Development* (Oxford, INTRAC). A concise exposition of the process of empowering evaluation, viewed through a number of practical examples from different parts of the world.

Walsh, K., Deakin, N., Smith, P., Spurgeon, P. and Thomas, N. (1997) *Contracting for Change: Contracts in Health, Social Care, and Other Local Government Services* (Oxford, Oxford University Press). Chapter 1, especially pp. 17–21 on the personal social services, provides an excellent overview of assumptions embedded in the shift towards reinventing local government based on market principles.

Yelloly, M. (1995) 'Professional competence and higher education', in Yelloly, M. and Henkel, M. (eds) *Learning and Teaching in Social Work: Towards Reflective Practice* (London, Jessica Kinglsey). Explores the concept of competence as it applies in social work and relevant areas of higher education.

Social Work with Children and Families

Lorraine Waterhouse and Janice McGhee

Introduction

Social work with children and families raises public and professional concern. Inquiries into the fatal non-accidental injury and sexual abuse of children highlight the need for sound childcare decision-making and effective interagency and interdisciplinary collaboration, and for the child's best interests to have paramountcy at all times. From the mid-1970s in the UK, public accountability was demanded and influenced the shape of social work services with children and their families, giving rise to an emphasis on investigation and surveillance mediated through detailed procedural guidance in local authorities and other agencies. Since 1990, major changes in child and family law have been enacted throughout the UK, leading to a greater emphasis on parental responsibility and ascertaining children's views.

A major review of child protection practices in the UK (DoH, 1995b) introduced a radical reappraisal of childcare policy and practice. The importance of social work services supporting families to rear their children, working in partnership with parents and other adult carers and responding to child welfare as well as child protection needs has received renewed attention (DoH/DfEE/ Home Office, 2000). The challenge these goals bring is to change the public face of social work childcare services away from services of last resort to outreaching services which seek to work alongside families in improving the life chances of their children.

This chapter considers four aspects of social work with children and families which are important for understanding how social work might contribute to the health and development of children growing up in the UK today. These include information on the social circumstances of children and families, on some of the different settings and legislation which underpin childcare services, on approaches to working positively with children and families, and on the issues which must be faced if childcare social work is to move forward. The importance of linking social science and social work research to social work intervention in childcare is stressed. Childcare research provides social workers and their agencies with clear messages about where to focus their efforts. Social work has a vital contribution in practice to help children gain access to early years services, support parents and adult carers in developing their parenting skills and promote a range of flexible child welfare services for children and families, balancing the need for support and protection.

Social context

The Joseph Rowntree Inquiry (Hills, 1995) into the distribution of income and wealth in the UK found that children comprise 30 per cent of the poorest tenth of the population. Single parents and their children, who make up 6 per cent of the population, are significantly overrepresented in the poorest fifth. Not surprisingly, 70 per cent of the gross incomes of families in the poorest two-tenths of households come from social security benefits. The proportion of children living in relative poverty in the UK has increased threefold since 1980, and almost a third of children come from homes below the EC poverty line, households with less than half the national average income (Wilkinson, 1994). Between 1979 and 1989, the number of citizens living on the safety net was up by two-thirds and by a third for those living below the level which income support is intended to guarantee. Income inequality has been rising more rapidly in Britain than other Westernised countries with the exception of New Zealand.

Absolute poverty further blights the life chances of children (Bradshaw, 2001). Wilkinson (1994) points to the worrying effects which the widening differences in income distribution are having on the welfare and well-being of children and young people. Widening of income differences since 1985 appears to be matched by a marked slowing of the decline in national death rates for infants and children and an apparent decline in reading standards over the same period which are not adequately explained by differences in teaching methods. Between 1981 and 1991, mortality rates for adults in the prime parenting years widened (Wilkinson, 1994).

The rise in homelessness and the privations that this brings pose serious threats to the health and development of children and young people. It is estimated there are 33,000 children affected by homelessness in Scotland (Children in Scotland, 1995). The steady decline of public sector provision in favour of home ownership and the private rented sector is resulting in poorer standards of housing for families unable to compete in the new market economy. Ironically, the general rise in car ownership leaves the poorest families exposed to all the risks of pollution and road traffic accidents (still one of the highest causes of child mortality in the UK) without the benefits of good public transport, especially in rural areas.

The Rowntree Inquiry (Hills, 1995) and Wilkinson (1994) highlight the range of social problems associated with areas of low income and poverty. Problems in the poorest areas are found to have increased, with high rates of family break-up, high levels of crime, vandalism and youth unemployment, and growing numbers of children registered with local authorities as at risk of abuse. Hills (1995) identifies that, since the 1970s, council housing nationally has become concentrated on those with low incomes. This tenure policy locates council housing in particular estates and areas, creating a social polarisation on the ground. Lone parents surviving on the margins of society, high levels of crime and vandalism, sometimes involving very young children, poor education and some schools being rejected by the children as symbols of 'authority' are noted. Booth and Booth (1996) highlight that the most significant factors in a child's health and development is the uneven distribution of risk or exposure to adversity. Inequalities in health and education remain persistent for poor children (Howarth et al., 1999) and have long-term consequences (Gregg et al., 1999).

A study of children registered at risk in three local authorities in Scotland (Pitcairn and Waterhouse, 1996) found that the children were primarily children in need, only some of whom were in need of protection from physical or sexual abuse. The parents of the children were almost always unemployed and had been so for at least a year. Few left school with any educational qualifications. A significant number of fathers had been in trouble with the law as children and continuing into adulthood. Poor physical health was reported in the parents and children, with about half the women describing themselves as depressed. Alcohol and drug problems were in evidence. Children growing up against these odds may come to share some of the social adversity which characterises the biographies of their parents.

The impact of poor physical and mental health in children and parents set against a background of poverty and family disruption provides a disturbing threat to the safety, health and development of children known to social work services. Childcare social work intervention is largely targeted on estates and areas where the Joseph Rowntree Inquiry (Hills, 1995) identified a 'cycle of poor parenting'. This was characterised by an intergenerational lack of good experiences of parenting, often combined with youth. Few support networks or childcare facilities compounded isolation, which can lead to depression and health problems. These problems present major challenges to social work with children and families, requiring a focus on community as well as individual interventions.

The debate about providing for children as developed legislatively ignores the reality of the growing disparity in the material and social circumstances of children in the UK and the consequent impact that this has on a child's health and development. The impact of poor parenting is also attracting wider recognition (Quinton and Rutter, 1988) as a significant factor in the safety, health and development of children. Holman (1988) observed that similar expectations of parenting are placed on parents irrespective of their social circumstances and resources; certainly, in legal terms, the standard is an objective one of 'best interests' of the child.

Changing family patterns

The traditional view of the nuclear family, with mother at home caring for children and father as breadwinner in full-time employment, no longer describes the reality of family life. The changing nature of adult relationships and women's growing participation in the labour market have resulted in diverse family patterns. Rising divorce rates have resulted in larger numbers of lone parents and step-parenting. Childlessness, whether or not chosen, is an issue for many adults. The importance of developing services to meet the changing needs of families is vitally important (Lewis, 2000). Existing policies and frameworks do not always recognise the diversity of families living in the UK today. Black and minority ethnic people are often disadvantaged on social and economic indicators, especially in relation to employment, housing and childcare.

Understanding the changing patterns of partnership and the impact on parenting are central to the development of supportive social services for children and families. Utting (1995) observed that 40 per cent of marriages end in divorce, 20 per cent of families are headed by a lone parent and 8 per cent of dependent children live in step-families. However, step-families are not a new phenomenon, as Walker (1997) indicates: in the nineteenth century, two in every five children lost their father and almost the same proportion their mother by the age of 15 years. Step-families and lone-parent households were as common a feature of Victorian life as they are today, although death rather than divorce was the source of change. Divorce has a significant effect on parenting, with consequences for children related to their age, gender and post-divorce arrangements (Rodgers and Pryor, 1998). Parenting in the context of adoption, foster care or where a child may have a disability has particular features and additional aspects to be considered in the provision of services to children and families. Recognition of the impact of all types of family transitions on children are important to childcare professionals.

The status of children

The United Nations Convention on the Rights of the Child (UNCRC) was adopted in 1989 and ratified by the UK in 1991. The Convention contains 41 substantive articles which can be grouped around the four main themes of survival, development, protection and participation (Lindsay, 1992). Each state must, after ratification, report to the UN Committee on the Rights of the Child, the Convention thus providing a universal standard against which to measure progress in each of the broad areas outlined. Within the UK, the Department of Health has been given lead responsibility for overseeing progress on the implementation of the Convention. In 1994, they cited the Children Act 1989 as one major achievement by government in promoting the rights of children, and since then the Children (Scotland) Act 1995 and the Children (NI) Order 1995 have continued to build on this tradition. A Children's Commissioner has been appointed in Wales and the Scottish parliament is discussing a similar development.

The underlying principles stress the paramountcy of the child's welfare, the child's right to express his or her views, the child's right to be free from discrimination, inhumane treatment and all forms of physical, sexual or mental violence, and the child's right to information, education and health care (Lindsay, 1992). Putting these principles into practice is not straightforward. The UN Committee on the Rights of the Child (1995) criticised the UK government for its failure to address the economic rights of children, reflected in growing levels of child poverty, homelessness amongst young people and the treatment of young offenders, especially by placement in secure training units (Franklin and Franklin, 1996).

Despite the ratification by the UK of the UNCRC, Oppeneheim and Lister (1996) point to the longstanding marginalisation of children in political debates. When children do appear, they are often treated as objects of public attention rather than subjects who are able to contribute in a meaningful way to an understanding of the circumstances which directly affect them. There is growing concern that children and young people are increasingly marginalised from mainstream society. Despite the growing emphasis on the participation of children in decision-making, increasing numbers of children and young people are excluded from employment, housing and other material aspects of life.

Setting

The legal basis and organisational settings for social work with children and families differ between the constituent parts of the UK. The Children Act 1989 in England and Wales introduced major legislative reform; Scotland and Northern Ireland have recently adopted new children's legislation (Children (Scotland) Act 1995; Children (Northern Ireland) Order 1995). While the policy focus of all three is similar, being informed by the promotion of child welfare and having a common emphasis on children 'in need' (Cohen and Hagen, 1997), the legislative content varies to take account of longstanding organisational and legal differences in the delivery of childcare services. There is also a long tradition of charitable and voluntary organisations providing services to children and families (Children First, Barnardo's, National Children's Home (NCH), Save the Children Fund (SCF)).

The Children's Hearings System is the nexus for childcare decision-making in Scotland. The system was established under the Social Work (Scotland) Act 1968 as a direct result of the deliberations of the Kilbrandon Committee (Kilbrandon, 1964), which sought to find solutions to the rise in the rate of juvenile delinquency in post-war Scotland. Developments similar to Kilbrandon also arose in England and Wales with the production of the White Paper *Children in Trouble* (Home Office, 1968), which 'embodied the new thinking including the conflation of the previously separate 'delinquent' and 'deprived' category' (Frost and Stein, 1989) and provided the basis for some of the main provisions of the Children and Young Persons Act 1969. Northern Ireland was not affected by these major reforms, the Children and Young Persons Act (NI) 1968 still applying (Kelly and Pinkerton, 1996).

This legislative period in Scotland, England and Wales reflected a family-oriented approach where concern was focused on problems at the parenting level with an emphasis on prevention against a background of expansion of welfare and support services (Fox Harding, 1991a, 1991b; Packman and Jordan, 1991). However, key sections of the Children and Young Persons Act 1969 were never implemented, reflecting the beginning, as Frost and Stein (1989) argue, of a shift in the balance towards justice and away from welfare. The welfare principle has remained the key focus of childcare decision-making in relation to children in Scotland regardless of the reason for their referral to the Children's Hearings System, whether 'delinquent' or 'deprived'. The central philosophy of the hearings system has a clear welfare orientation, 'needs' rather than 'deeds' being the basis for decision-making and intervention.

The children's hearing is not a court but a tribunal serviced by lay people drawn from the community of the child, with a knowledge of family life. It aims to work in partnership with parents to identify needs and solutions in the best interest of the child, assuming that most parents will want the best for their children. The local authority is responsible for providing social interests reports to the hearing and the provision of social work services for the child and family if a supervision requirement is made. The intention of the legislation was to introduce a straightforward procedure, avoiding legal technicalities, with the lay panel taking appropriate action in the child's best interests (Lord Cameron in *McGregor* v. *D* [1977] SLT 182 at 185). The recent case of *S* v. *Miller and Lord Advocate* [2001] SLT 531 considered a human rights challenge to the system. The courts are only involved where the facts of a case are in dispute, for appeals and for dealing with serious offences. The hearings system was intended as an early intervention system for those children who would benefit from compulsory measures of care and protection, and as a diversion system for those children for whom more harm than good would be done by being drawn into a juvenile justice system.

Since its inception, the Children's Hearings System has given rise to debate about the balance to be struck between natural justice and the welfare of children (Adler, 1985; McGhee and Waterhouse, 1999). This was brought into public focus by the Orkney (Scottish Office, 1992a), and Fife (Scottish Office, 1992b) inquiries, and the decision in *O* v. *Rae* [1992] SCLR 318, which drew further attention to a children's hearing using information which could have founded a condition of referral but had not been tested before a sheriff. Criticisms as in Orkney (Scottish Office, 1992a) questioned the ability of hearings to deal with complex cases of child abuse, especially where allegations of child sexual abuse are to the fore. All legal fora appear to have difficulty in dealing with this issue (see *Re H (Minors) (Sexual Abuse: Standard of Proof)* [1996] 2 WLR 8). Recent studies have evaluated the effectiveness of the hearings system (Hallett et al., 1998; Waterhouse et al., 2000).

Childcare in Northern Ireland is part of the UK state system but has unique arrangements for the delivery of personal social work services. The Health and Personal Social Services (Northern Ireland) Order 1972 removed personal social services from local government control, making them part of the NHS (Kelly and Pinkerton, 1996). Since 1973, four integrated health and social service boards have been responsible for providing social work services within a regional strategic plan. The personal social services for each board have a particular responsibility with regard to children and young people, not unlike the Children's Hearings System in Scotland; lay representation is found on the area boards. This has potentially facilitated closer links between social services and health than elsewhere in the UK (Cohen and Hagen, 1997). Legislation in 1994 (Health and Personal Social Services (NI) Order) allowed health and social service boards to delegate responsibility for statutory childcare duties to self-governing Trusts (Cohen and Hagen, 1997).

Peyton (1997) argues that, despite organisational integration between health and social services, childcare services come second to the health agenda and acute sector spending. In order to improve the status of childcare, an interdepartmental project has been established to ensure coordinated implementation of the 1995 Children (NI) Order. A five-year package of financial investment geared mainly to the most vulnerable children in Northern Ireland (including children with disabilities) has been put in place. It remains to be seen whether this will change the emphasis within childcare in Northern Ireland from surveillance to support. Tensions have arisen, since the implementation of the 1995 Order, between a business culture and children's needs (Peyton, 1997). Attempts have been made to address the complex contracting process, and additional mechanisms for monitoring and setting standards, including joint assessments of local need and a joint childcare strategy, are being explored (Peyton, 1997). The Audit Commission Report (1994) in England and Wales identified that most commissioning health authorities have yet to assess the full needs of children in their areas for community child health services.

Despite these differing legal and organisational contexts, all social work services for children and families throughout the UK depend on a mix between statutory local authority services, the voluntary and private sector. Social services came of age during a political era of economic restraint without the benefit of already well established professional traditions. Social work services have remained selective to those families and children most in need, sitting uneasily against health and education with their universalist concerns. Recent legislation in different parts of the UK will lead to the establishment of commissions to regulate care services against national care standards; and councils to register staff in social care services (Care Standards Act 2000, Regulation of Care (Scotland) Act 2001).

Childcare policy and practice

Childcare social work has been highly concentrated on children in need, children in public care, children who offend and children in need of care and protection. Social work intervention may be on a compulsory or requested basis and may involve children being looked after away from home in foster or residential care either on a short- or long-term basis and in some instances permanently. There is a tension in practice between the provision of support where requested by families and the possibility of compulsory intervention. This highlights the context within which modern social work childcare practice operates, influencing the type of services provided and the approaches to social work intervention. The role of social work intervention in family life is the subject of continuing debate within government, among professionals and publicly in the media, especially in the context of child abuse. It is important to remember that child protection is only one aspect of childcare, albeit one which has been a major influence in shaping social work practice.

The management of child abuse in the UK has evolved since the mid-1970s to a national system of local area review committees to coordinate policy and interdisciplinary cooperation. All areas now have procedural guidelines for professions concerned with children's welfare, child protection registers to identify children at risk of harm and multidisciplinary case conferences led by social work/services departments as a forum to assess risk and formally identify children in need of registration. There is increasing cooperation between law enforcement, health and social work agencies, most recently exemplified by the move towards the joint interviewing of children and their parents by police officers and social workers. Procedural guidelines and numerous governmental circulars on child abuse have been the consequence of inquiries into the deaths of children at the hands of their parents or guardians (for example the Maria Colwell Inquiry; DHSS, 1974). The Cleveland (DHSS, 1988) and Orkney (Scottish Office, 1992a) Inquiries provided further impetus for the development of invest-igatory techniques in child sexual abuse to provide evidence admissible within an adversarial court system.

Government procedural guidance has increasingly shifted the emphasis in social work/services departments away from the universal principle of welfare established in the Kilbrandon and Seebohm committees to a focus in social work practice on the detection and identification of children at risk of physical and sexual abuse. Perhaps the most detrimental outcome of this shift to surveillance may be the stigma which families who are in receipt of social work childcare services are reported to experience (Farmer and Owen, 1995). The Department of Health's review of child protection studies (1995b) demonstrated that, for many families, their greatest fear was the possibility of the compulsory removal of their child into public care. The statistical analysis of pathways into public care for child protection referrals shows that removal of the child on initial investigation occurs for fewer than 1 per cent of all children referred. Furthermore, the numbers of children accommodated on a compulsory basis after a child protection conference are no greater than those on a voluntary basis (DoH, 1995b: 28).

Good childcare practice dictates an acknowledgement with families of the anxieties which child protection investigations raise. This is important to ensure the open communication required between practitioners and families so central to assessment and working together. The majority of families, however, who are investigated for apparently transgressive behaviour are poor and are, in the main, filtered out of the system, receiving no services or family support (Gibbons et al., 1995). Cleaver and Freeman (1995) found that these families were seldom advised of the outcome of the investigation, reinforcing their wariness of professional intrusion. This points to the importance of discussing outcomes with families providing an important opportunity to improve parent and professional relationships.

The Department of Health, in *Child Protection: Messages from Research* (1995a), encourages social work policy-makers to recast the problem of child abuse in ways which emphasise child welfare needs as the primary factor in determining the child's best interests. This has led to an increasing policy emphasis on prevention and support to families and 'children in need'. However, in a context of diminishing resources where local authorities may have insufficient means to meet their duties to children 'in need', the gateway to limited resources may become the legal or administrative procedures which define children as 'at risk'. Therefore, a child's chances of gaining access to resources may possibly be significantly increased through the imposition of a legal order.

Professionals involved in childcare decision-making are aware of this dilemma in practice, and it seems naive to assume that this will not influence their decisions. In an in-depth study of the way in which policies for children in need were defined and prioritised (Colton et al., 1995: 204), it was found, in two Welsh authorities, 'that social service departments in Wales are clearly concentrating their effort on children at risk of abuse and neglect'. However, managers ideally wished to place a greater emphasis on family support work to enable a corresponding reduction in the need for statutory intervention. Similarly, in a SSI Report (1996) of local authority services to families, in seven out of eight authorities inspected it was 'very difficult' to gain access to services unless child protection concerns were expressed. Clearly, children 'at risk' and their parents may be reassured and benefit from access to support services, which is a positive contribution to the welfare of children. It remains important in practice, however, not to label children as 'at risk' unnecessarily when they are 'in need', recognising the problem that this may pose for practitioners on a day-to-day basis in a context of scarce resources.

The following example illustrates this dilemma of balancing risk and need in day-to-day practice. The authors visited a lone mother whose partner had left the family home after hitting the younger of two children, who was 18 months old at the time. After a child protection investigation, it was clear that he would not be returning to the household, and the children were therefore not deemed to be at risk of abuse. However, at the home visit, the mother was clearly struggling to care adequately for her two children, the elder being seven years of age. There was a marked absence of play materials, hygiene standards were fairly low: for example the youngest child needed bathing and the nappy changing. This family were living in a deprived housing estate with few public amenities for either adults or children. It was clear that the mother was unable to provide sufficient stimulation for either child to enhance their development, as she herself recognised. Family support was needed and wanted by this mother to enhance the life chances of her children and to support her parenting of them. She was disappointed social work services appeared to be no longer interested in her or her children once the immediate source of risk – her partner – had left the household. Failing to address broader childcare needs leaves children vulnerable to further crises and poorer long-term outcomes for health and development.

Hallett (1993), comparing European and UK practices in relation to child protection, stresses the need to strike a balance between the paramountcy of the welfare of the child and the notion of justice within the wider community. This struggle is also played out in relation to children who offend. The law and social work practice have attempted to balance these competing claims against a growing background of public policy which seeks to isolate the young offender for the protection of the community.

Policy appears to be shifting from a concern with the social and personal needs of juvenile offenders to the frequency and nature of their offending.

Anderson and Kinsey (1993), while finding no significant social class differences in offending amongst young people, confirm that infrequent, non-serious offending is the norm rather than the exception for young people. Cleland (1995) suggests that increased public pressure to make children accountable for wrongdoing plus a growing concentration on victims' needs have contributed to the public focus shifting from the welfare of the child to the offending behaviour and its consequences. These are not necessarily mutually exclusive, but a balance needs to be struck between addressing offending behaviour and responding to the needs of children in trouble. Since the introduction of the Crime and Disorder Act 1998, youth justice policy in England and Scotland has diverged with an apparently greater focus on a 'just deserts' approach to child offending in England.

There is growing concern, however, about young people who persistently offend, with a belief that these youngsters tend to be specialist criminals. In their research, Hagel and Newburn (1994) identified 531 10–16-year-olds in two areas in England who had allegedly committed at least three offences in 1992. The most common were road traffic offences, theft from shops and car theft. Violent and/or sexual crimes were unusual, and drug-related offences were apparently rare. Few of the young people were employed, or in further education or training, and 50 per cent were already known to social services. Patterns of familial disruption characterised by alcohol and/or drug misuse as well as criminality within the family were reported. Adverse personal and social circumstances, rather than the nature of their offences, were the factors common to the children. Closeness of parental supervision and levels of parental expectation of behaviour regarding offending were more important predictors of offending behaviour (Farrington, 1993).

Support to families in their parenting responsibilities would appear to be a central concern for social work practice in relation to children who offend. Parenting education programmes are increasingly being utilised within practice for all ages of children. Furthermore, direct work with young offenders, especially to improve their social and personal skills, is relevant. Cognitive-behavioural techniques have been widely used and have proved effective in reducing offending behaviour. The importance of education is vital, truancy often being related to offending and poor educational attainment (Farrington, 1993).

A young man aged 20 years was convicted of assault and robbery with two older co-accused when he was aged 17 years. He was placed on probation for three years, this being his first offence and clearly related to his drug-taking behaviour. He had left school with no qualifications and had, for the most part, been unemployed following some youth training. He spent most of his time with other young men in similar circumstances, often sleeping for much of the day and meeting at night. He became involved on the fringes of a local older group of men who had criminal histories and were involved in a local drugs trade. In the course of the probation order, he was encouraged to resume physical fitness training, which he had had an interest in at one time. This was also partly a way to address his drug-taking, providing some substitute activity, and to offer opportunities to make new friends outside the drug scene. The social worker supervising the probation order supported his application to the local further education college to begin further training, and he gained recognised educational certificates equipping him to become a trainer. He subsequently went on to gain employment in the local authority's recreation department working with young people. In the final review of his probation order, he felt his life had been turned around and he had been given 'something to live for, a future'. Most importantly, his own sense of self-esteem and self-efficacy had been improved through discovering he was good at something.

Partnership, prevention and support in practice

Direct involvement of a social worker with a child and their family remains the major context in which childcare social work is practised in the UK. This may be on an voluntary or compulsory basis. There has also been a move towards specialism, with the development of dedicated children and families teams within social work/services departments. A growing recognition is being given to the importance of social work services working alongside health, education, social security and housing (Audit Commission, 1994). This may lead to a clearer articulation of policies and planning requirements for children and their families. It is clear that policy and practice are moving towards a renewed interest in partnership, prevention and early intervention, family support, and an emphasis on interagency coordination (Hallet and Birchall, 1995).

Partnership

The model of partnership between parents and professionals, as set out in guidance, is a cornerstone of the Children Act 1989 in England and Wales, the importance of which is emphasised by the Department of Health (1995b) in relation to child protection practice. Guidance in Scotland emphasises that parents should normally be responsible for the upbringing of their children and promotes a partnership model. Similarly, the Children (NI) Order 1995 promotes partnership with parents if children are in care and specifically requires consultation with parents and children about any decisions made. The Department of Health (1991b), in *Working Together under the Children Act 1989* made it clear that agencies should work in partnership with families in all childcare cases; Hill (2000) reviews the concept of partnership as a key principle in child and family social work.

Partnership in day-to-day practice means involving parents and, where appropriate, children in decisions about the welfare of the child, offering real choices to families, sharing information and keeping families informed about progress and procedures. Partnership involves the sharing of responsibility between professionals and families, and recognising the imbalance in power which the statutory role may bring. Clarity about social workers' powers and duties, especially in the context of child protection, is vital to open communication and equalising the power balance between the local authority and the parent. Cleaver and Freeman (1995) found, in their study of parental perspectives in cases of suspected child abuse, that parents, who later found that inquiries had been made prior to any exploration of concern directly with them, were subsequently alienated from the professionals who were trying to offer help or support. Furthermore, organisational change is likely to be necessary to ensure child-friendly procedures as well as practice and a move towards a more cooperative model of working with families. An open complaints procedure is a further important step (BAAF, 1996).

Thoburn et al. (1995) found a clear link between better outcomes for children and greater involvement of parents. With greater parental involvement, parenting arrangements for the children seemed to be more settled, links with parents and important adults were maintained, and progress was made in the child's health and development. In contrast, where there was a failure to work in partnership with parents, outcomes were less favourable. In these cases, parents were less involved and identified less with childcare decisions. Yet it was rare that the difficulties facing parents and their children were so severe as to preclude any working together.

The attitudes, skills and efforts of social workers were found to be critical in achieving participation in families where there were multiple problems. Creative thinking by practitioners to encourage participation in these worse-case scenarios was best supported when agency policies and procedures aimed for parental participation. Bell (1999) however, recognises that risk assessments may limit participative practice. Children, too, strongly welcomed involvement in decisions which affected their lives, as borne out by Thoburn et al. (1995), Roberts and Taylor (1996) and Thomas and O'Kane (1999).

A practical example concerns the admission of a young man into residential care as he had been consistently truanting and mixing with a group of older boys who were frequently involved in minor theft and drinking. The parents were initially relieved at his admission as they had found it difficult to control his behaviour, and this had resulted in physical aggression between father and son at times. However, after a short time, the parents began to feel distanced from their son and decisions being made about his education and future. Although they attended review meetings, they found it difficult to speak and felt they had very little influence over their son's life. The social worker and residential staff quickly became aware of this and utilised a number of strategies to ensure closer communication between all the parties and rebuild the parent–child relationship. Residential staff agreed to contact the parents on a daily basis to keep them in touch with their son's activities; furthermore, the social worker supported the parents in keeping directly in touch with their son's school to monitor his progress and attendance.

The aim was to support the parents in maintaining their parental responsibilities for their son even though he was not living with them. The young man became interested in golf, and his father was encouraged to take part with him, this joint activity becoming a positive focus in their relationship. At the same time, direct work was done with the parents in renegotiating their strategies for controlling and disciplining their son and developing more appropriate means of communicating with their son as he grew into adulthood. The father was helped by the social worker to explore his own childhood, which had been characterised by harsh parental discipline, causing him to fear and dislike his own father. He did not wish this to occur with his own son but had found it difficult to be open about his experiences and the effects on him.

Early years services

It has become increasingly clear that one of the most effective forms of primary prevention lies in early years services, particularly those encouraging parental involvement. Preschool education remains discretionary despite widespread recognition of its importance to future outcomes for children (Berrueta-Clement et al., 1984) and a significant growth in demand (including increasing women's employment and the wish to provide stimulating environments for children in the early years). Traditionally provided by the statutory and voluntary sectors, there has recently been a rapid growth in private nurseries and daycare centres, available at a cost to those families who can afford them. Britain still compares unfavourably with other European, notably Scandinavian, countries, the majority of whom provide high levels of preschool services (Cohen and Fraser, 1991).

A variety of services, including childminders, play groups, family centres, day nurseries and nursery schools, are available, but choice is largely restricted to those who can afford to pay (Jones and Bilton, 1994). Children from families on low incomes in the UK are most likely to be placed in local authority social work provision, which may set them apart from other children.

Black children, especially, are more likely to be referred to local authority childcare services for broader social and economic reasons. Barn (1990) found that black children were overrepresented in public care and little attention was paid to their specific needs. Black children were twice as likely as white children to be admitted into care within four weeks of referral, which indicates a shortfall in appropriate preventive work with black children and their families. Asian children are underrepresented in public care but also in relation to family-based services, especially for children with disability (Shah, 1992). It is clear that, in the planning and provision of social services to black children and their families, there has been a fundamental lack of systematic consideration of race and cultural pluralism in mainstream service provision and social work practice.

Headstart and Hi-Scope are particular forms of intervention and support to preschool children and their families which emphasise active learning by the child and the involvement of parents. Research provides evidence that these types of service are of particular benefit to the most disadvantaged children. Black children, when assessed some years after an early years intervention programme, appeared to secure the most benefit, especially in cognitive development (Mac-Donald and Roberts, 1995). Positive effects were also reported in mothers' attitudes towards their children's schoolwork and future aspirations (MacDonald and Roberts, 1995). In the short term, health promotion programmes concentrating on child development appear to contribute to reducing the likelihood of appearance on child protection registers (Barker et al., 1994).

The longer-term outcomes for children participating in these types of service is less clear. The most systematic study (Berrueta-Clement et al., 1984) of long-term benefits for children of high-quality preschool education concludes that cognitive and social development are enhanced. The Hi-Scope programme, which places particular emphasis on an active learning curriculum, appears to be associated with fewer arrests in adolescence and early adulthood and a lower percentage in receipt of social services at the age of 27 years (MacDonald and

Roberts, 1995). The Headstart programme, however, found that progress was not always maintained, especially in families facing extreme social adversity. Advantages initially gained could be lost within a few years as the child progressed into the formal school system.

The Hi-Scope curriculum has been widely adopted throughout the UK. Barnardo's, along with the Department of Health, has promoted its development. A Hi-Scope Institute was opened in London in 1990, with the aim of providing high-quality training and continuing support.

Social work needs to play an increasing role in early years services including initiatives such as Sure Start. The MARS project points to the success of an integrated approach. This project was jointly funded by Barnardo's and a local authority social work and education department in Scotland. Practitioners worked intensively with children and families deemed to be at high risk and in crisis, using traditional social casework methods. The intervention was found to prevent entry into public care and offset some of the harmful effects of poor parenting (Fuller, 1992). There is an increasing recognition of the importance of preschool education which involves parents and an ongoing development of family centres which seek to support parents and children.

Parenting

There are numerous organisations and services developing to support parents, such as Family Mediation, Parent Link/Parent Network and Adoption UK for adoptive and long-term foster carers. Parenting education programmes are being developed, as are associated home visiting programmes (Home-Start UK), often involving volunteers to provide practical support, advice and role models. The importance of interdisciplinary and interagency collaboration in supporting parents is emphasised in government policy (Audit Commission, 1994).

In practice, social workers can assist parents in bringing up their children by drawing on their knowledge of child development and effective parenting strategies. However, there may be conflicting views between parents and professionals on what constitutes 'good enough' parenting. The demands of parenting will also be influenced by general social expectations of parents and social workers in society.

There is evidence to suggest some intergenerational continuity in parenting, although the experience of poor parenting does not automatically result in parenting difficulties in the next generation (Quinton and Rutter, 1988). Findings suggest that people who have been brought up in institutional care, have experienced abuse or neglect in their own childhood or grew up in hostile discordant families are more likely to experience difficulties in parenting themselves (Quinton and Rutter, 1988). Critics of the notion of intergenerational continuity in parenting point to social class, rather than prior childhood experiences, as a key factor influencing parenting styles (Smith, 1991).

Parenting styles have been linked to children's behaviour and social development (Baumrind, 1971). The Department of Health review of research in relation to child protection (DoH, 1995b) highlights families where there is low warmth and high criticism towards children as most damaging to their development. Physical chastisement has been shown in non-abusing families to be routinely used as a method of behavioural control (Newson and Newson, 1976), and this may have reinforced the notion of a continuum of physical disciplinary strategies where, in an abusive situation, normal limits may have been exceeded. In practice, social workers are seeking to encourage parents to relate to their children with warmth, using effective disciplinary strategies to reduce discord. Parents can be helped by social workers to make links between their own past experiences of being parented and their present experiences of being a parent.

In Pitcairn and Waterhouse's (1996) study of parents whose children were registered as potentially at risk, difficulties in the control and management of the children clearly emerged. Surprisingly, the nature of these difficulties, as reported by the parents, reflected a failure to discipline the children consistently and routinely, even when the parents were clear that some intervention on their part was necessary. Lax disciplinary strategies appeared to predominate for parents, while the social workers' framework remained fixed on the idea that excessive discipline was central in parent–child relationships in the context of alleged abuse. Misunderstanding of this aspect of the problem may lead to inappropriate solutions which fail to influence the daily management of the child in a positive way, especially for parents overwhelmed by the demands of parenting young children. Information and strategies to manage difficult behaviour are increasingly available and provide a practical way forward.

Public care services

Providing a range of flexible public child welfare services is essential to the implementation of an effective childcare strategy. Residential childcare remains a major plank of children's services despite the shift since the mid-1970s towards family-based care, especially for young children. This change was partly influenced by Rowe and Lambert's (1973) study showing the failure on the part of some social workers to plan actively for children in public care. Policy, not uninfluenced by financial imperatives, shifted to either rehabilitation with the natural family or placement in a permanent substitute family. These developments led to some patchy results. The pressure to reduce the use of residential resources led to some of the most disturbed and troubled young people being looked after in residential care when either family care or family placement broke down.

This swing against residential care coincided with a reduction in financial and training investment, lowering the morale of childcare staff. Despite these difficulties, research by Fisher et al. (1986) and a Department of Health inspection (1994) found that young people and parents preferred residential care to foster care. Both the Utting Report on *Children in the Public Care* (1991) and Skinner (1992) strongly recommend the recognition of residential childcare as a positive choice, especially for young people who are unable to live at home and present challenging behaviour. Cliffe with Berridge (1991) and Hill and Aldgate (1996b) found that there was little choice of placement for children or parents, resource levels being limited in scale and range. The Department of Health in their summary of research findings for children looked after away from home set out 24 recommendations to support the development of effective residential care services (DoH, 1998a). Recent reports commissioned by the government have addressed the need to provide safeguards to protect children in public care (DoH, 1997; Kent 1997).

In practice, residential care remains an important resource for many young people. A key focus for social work practice is the maintenance of links between parents and children and between residential and field social workers (Millham et al., 1986). Hill and Aldgate (1996b) also point to the importance of actively involving young people in significant decisions and ensuring that meetings which concern their future are not overly adult-dominated. There is a responsibility incumbent on social work to provide safe environments for children in public care and to ensure that there is an adequate complaints procedure. Some local author-ities now employ Children's Rights Officers offering an independent service to children in public care. The need to promote educational opportunities for children in public care is a central practice concern.

More recent research outlines the poor educational outcome for many children in public care (Aldgate et al., 1993; Jackson, 1994; Fletcher-Campbell, 1997). The loss of schooling in children who are already facing adversity appears to have further negative consequences for later life chances. Quinton and Rutter (1988), looking at outcomes for young people raised in institutions, have shown the importance of positive school experiences in mediating adverse adult outcomes where home circumstances are characterised by poor relationships. Schooling is of central importance to children who come from already difficult backgrounds. This is particularly relevant for girls, where research has shown that choice of partner is likely to reflect their own circumstances of disadvantage and limit their horizons (Quinton and Rutter, 1988). Girls who come from backgrounds of family discord and have experienced institutional care are more likely to select deviant partners, perhaps as a well-intentioned but misguided escape from discordant relationships at home. Positive educational experience can, in effect, widen the choice of partner, research having shown that a supportive marital relationship is a protective factor against stressful experiences (Brown and Harris, 1978) and may support better child-rearing practice (Quinton and Rutter, 1988).

Young people in residential care generally report getting on well with staff while regretting the lack of continuity in relationships. They are looking for individualised care, privacy, attention and support with school work, control of bullying and wider peer contacts (Fletcher, 1993). Staff favouritism was disliked. There is increasing recognition of the importance of taking account of the views of children looked after by local authorities.

Family placement is another public childcare service. It includes short-term or long-term foster care and adoption for those children in need of permanent alternative care. Sellick (1996) found that 65 per cent of all children in local authority public care for one year were fostered. Most of the children spent very short periods in care, that is, less than 14 days for 50 per cent of the children. Concern continues about the number of children who are placed in short-term foster care at times of emergency without clear future childcare plans (Stone, 1995). Materials have been developed by the Department of Health (1995b) to aid planning and decision-making for 'looked-after' children. McAuley (1996), in her study of children placed in foster care, found that the majority of the children had experienced several previous care placements before long-term solutions were sought. Most of the children had experienced abuse and/or neglect. Despite these difficulties, regular access to birth parents and siblings was maintained. McAuley, like Millham et al. (1986) and Packman et al. (1986), stresses the importance of social workers helping children to maintain links with their families, friends and wider social networks. Children themselves are often the most vocal advocates for this continuing contact.

The family placement needs of black children have received greater attention in recent years, although much of the debate has centred around the debates between 'transracial' and 'same-race' placements, especially for children of mixed parentage (Caesar et al., 1993). However, while it is generally accepted that children may be best placed with families or in residential settings reflecting the ethnic background of their own parents, the experience of young people who have been placed transracially varies, and it is not necessarily always a damaging experience (Tizard and Phoenix, 1989). A full assessment of each child's needs should be made in decisions about family placement.

Increasingly the needs of young people leaving care are being recognised legislatively (see the Children (Leaving Care) Act 2000) and through a growing body of research (Ince, 1998; Barn, 1999; Stein, 2001).

Adoption is a childcare option for a small proportion of children who cannot live with their families. In a survey by Rowe et al. (1989) of placement patterns in six local authorities, only 0.8 per cent of children in care went on to be adopted. The pattern of adoption has changed radically in the past thirty years. Fewer babies are now available for adoption, reflecting changes in societal values relating to lone parenthood. There are increasing numbers of older children for whom adoption is sought; many of these children have special health or educational needs or have been removed from their families after contested proceedings, often against a background of abuse and neglect. Research focusing on disrupted family placements (Rowe and Thoburn, 1988; Borland et al., 1991) has shown that higher disruption rates are associated with increasing age at placement. In the case of children adopted as infants, there are still ongoing issues of explaining adoption, and of identity (Hoopes, 1990), which adoptive parents may also need support in approaching. The Department of Health has recently reviewed reseach into adoption (DoH, 1999a) recognising the continuing problems of some adopted children.

In the light of these changing patterns of adoption, there has been an increasing recognition of the need for continuing post-placement support for adoptive families beyond the initial adjustment period, especially in the context of the adoption of 'hard to place' children, (Macaskill, 1985; Yates, 1985; Rushton et al., 1993). Macaskill (1985) demonstrated that it was frequently after the first two years of placement that more complex difficulties were recognised. She further found that, even in the most stable placements, adopted children still tended to show vulnerability in the face of unexpected change or crisis.

It seems clear that, for children who have had poor early experiences, a secure home environment is not always sufficient to compensate for early difficulties. If there are further complexities in the adoption process, for example continuing birth family contact as in the case of 'open adoption', further social work support is likely to be necessary in the family's life.

A useful way of providing post-placement support to adoptive parents and foster carers was initiated by the British Agencies for Adoption and Fostering (BAAF) in Scotland. A series of training initiatives were organised for adoptive parents and foster carers, focusing on the types of difficulty that children and young people may bring to placement. The training courses were both knowledge- and skill-based in an attempt to increase understanding and equip people with possible methods of approaching these issues. Participants from all courses saw the opportunity to meet other parents with similar concerns and share experiences as helpful. The courses with more skills orientation were seen to offer parents practical ideas that they could use in looking after their adoptive or foster child. This may be a helpful and cost-effective way to offer support to adoptive parents and foster carers.

CONCLUSION

There is an urgent need to protect children from the worst consequences of social and economic change over the past two decades, to recognise that many children are growing up in poverty, and that children who come from poor families may also face additional adversities which threaten children's social development. Social adversity, such as poverty, is accumulative and harder to fight as parental reserves diminish. Changing family patterns mean that many children will experience disruption in their upbringing, and many women will be lone parents, at least for a part of their child-rearing years.

Children in need and their families run the risk of falling between the priorities of mainstream services and the highly selective provision of social work and social services departments (Wilkinson, 1994). The Audit Commission Report (1994) points to the importance of health, education and social work working together to develop a joint strategy for children's services. Encouragement is given to the three agencies to take a more equal share in the responsibility to provide for 'children in need'. Social work/services departments' duties to provide 'children's services plans' detailing policy and service links between health, education and social work are seen as the way forward in the UK. They have already been implemented in England and Wales and appeared in primary legislation in Scotland for the first time in 1997.

The Audit Commission (1994) called for a greater emphasis on family support services, drawing from a wide range of agencies in the community. Health services were seen to have a key role in improving the health of 'children in need'. Education was expected to accept joint ownership of the problem of disrupted education for 'looked-after' children. Family centres were proposed as a suitable focus for developing joint ventures between health, social work and education. These could act as an integrated base for child health clinics, peer support groups, preschool provision, and advice centres on housing and social security benefits. This recommendation remains timely when many of the preventive and early intervention strategies, such as Home-Start, play groups and youth work, are underresourced. At present, there is no infrastructure to ensure inter-agency and interdisciplinary collaboration in setting the aims, philosophy and principles for children's services in the UK.

Three implications stand out as central to the development of effective social work practice with children and families. The first concerns developing services which are available to all families in society who may be experiencing difficulties. The emphasis on child protection investigations within social services may have detracted from the promotion of wider preventive services where the primary emphasis is on support rather than surveillance alone. Child protection will always be central to social work because of the legislative and policy framework and a recognition that some parents are unable to care for and protect their own children. Social work practice with children and families should be proactive, involving local communities in the development of practical services, especially those which may support lone parents. This would allow social workers to work alongside the communities they are seeking to serve and may encourage families to turn to social work services for help, support and advice. Models of practice need a community orientation, which appears to have lost ground to models of individual surveillance and supervision. Set against the levels of poverty many families in the UK now face, the need for a community orientation has never been more pressing.

Second, social work practitioners have a key role in helping families to gain access to child welfare and educational services. The importance of early years services for the health and development of children cannot be overemphasised, nor can the significance of education in preparing children for the future. As many of the families in receipt of social work services are adversely affected by poverty, poor housing and unemploy-ment, such services are critical in improving the life chances of children in these circumstances. Such services can act as a protective factor for vulnerable children and point to social work not as a sole provider of services but as having a role in supporting parents and children to get the most out of current universal child welfare provision. While it is important that parents are encouraged to see the value of education for their children, parental attitude being an important factor in determining educational outcomes, it is equally incumbent on schools and social work services to reach out to parents and children in ways which let them participate and benefit from educational and social care systems.

Third, developing parenting programmes and providing direct support to families remains an important goal for social work practice. Research consistently points to the importance of 'good enough' parenting for the future development of children. Social work practitioners have a contribution to make alongside other disciplines in helping parents to gain the skills and resources they need to carry out their parental respons-ibilities. Research also suggests that the vast majority of parents want the best for their children, but some may not be able to provide it without public and professional support. In future, the emphasis needs increasingly to be on what social work services can offer children and families alongside the other major services of health, housing, education and income support.

There is a renewed interest in prevention, family support and early intervention. The Children Act 1989, the Children (Scotland) Act 1995 and the Children (NI) Order 1995 all focus on the importance of partnership between the family and the state and providing support to 'children in need'. Legislation alone is not the solution to the problems that children face in our society, nor does it represent child welfare policy, but is an attempt to set out principles and practice to regulate public and legal interventions in children's lives. General financial and economic policies will remain important, and services to support children and families will also require resources in cash and in kind.

Public confidence in social work services will only be achieved if our own institutions set an example of practice which promotes the health and development of children and their families. This can only be ensured if social work can provide a safe environment for children, a matter which has been called into question by public scandals since the 1980s over the institutional abuse of children in public care. Social work has to be clear that policies and practices are truly child-centred and work towards the best interests of children and their families.

FURTHER READING

DoH (1995) *Child Protection: Messages From Research* (London, HMSO). This book provides a review of over 20 child protection studies commissioned by the Department of Heath, drawing out direct lessons for practice in social work with children and families.

DoH (2001) *The Children Act Report 2000* (London: Department of Health). This provides an overview of the main changes resulting from the Children Act 1989.

Fahlberg, V. (1991) *A Child's Journey Through Placement* (London: BAAF). A very readable book which draws well on theory and research to highlight issues for the child looked after away from home. The strength of Fahlberg lies in her practical focus and ability to link theory to practice.

Hill, M. and Aldgate, J. (eds) (1996) *Child Welfare Services: Developments in Law, Policy, Practice and Research* (London, Jessica Kingsley). An excellent collection of essays which provides an extended view of some of the issues outlined in this chapter.

Waterhouse, L. (ed.) (1996) *Child Abuse and Child Abusers: Protection and Prevention* (London, Jessica Kingsley). A key reading for any social work student or practitioner who needs to understand the social, legal and professional context of child abuse.

25

Social Work with Adults

Neil Thompson

Introduction

Social work with adults is a vast topic covering a wide range of client groups, settings, problems, challenges, approaches, resources and rewards. This chapter is therefore necessarily selective and introductory in nature. What it is intended to provide is an overview of the context in which such work takes place, differences between client groups and settings, and common themes in terms of the roles and tasks expected of social workers undertaking work with adults.

Of course, social work with adults takes place in the context of a complex legislative and policy framework, one that underwent considerable change during the 1990s and continues to do so into the new millennium as a result of new legislation and changes of emphasis in political perspectives on the role of social welfare in modern society, as, for example, in an increasingly significant role for market forces. This policy framework will no doubt continue to evolve, so the discussions presented here should be seen in that context rather than as static entities that will not change over time.

Social work with children is often presented as if it were more skilled and more important than work with adults (Preston-Shoot and Agass, 1990). An important point to be emphasised in this chapter is the highly skilful nature of effective practice in social work with adults. To regard such work as routine, straightforward or unskilled is both inaccurate and unfair – inaccurate because it fails to take account of the challenges involved and the skills needed to rise to them; unfair because it undervalues the high-quality work of so many practitioners involved in adult services. The myth of social work with adults being the poor relation of childcare work is, therefore, something that will be challenged and 'debunked' in this chapter.

As we shall see, social work with adults is extremely diverse. However, this is not to say that there are no common themes. One such theme, and a very important one at that, is the importance of seeking to empower people, to support them constructively in their efforts to retain as much control as possible over their lives, to remain as independent and autonomous as possible, and to remove or avoid barriers to enjoying a quality of life free from distress, disadvantage and oppression. This theme should therefore be borne in mind in considering the discussions that follow.

The context for practice is the first set of issues to be addressed. This involves outlining the different sets of people or 'client groups' that are included under the umbrella term of 'social work with adults'. Following on from this, I shall explore the significance of 'systematic practice' with adults and, in so doing, emphasise the importance of being clear about what we are doing and why. Next comes a discussion of the life course and an examination of the significance of life stages for adults as well as for children, and for families as well as individuals. This paves the way for an exploration of the roles and tasks required of social workers in their work with adults, a discussion of many of the duties involved in such work. Space does not permit a critical analysis of, or commentary upon, these roles and tasks, but this is not to say that they are unproblematic or not open to criticism. Indeed, it could be seen as a general rule of professional practice that no method, technique or approach to intervention should be accepted uncritically at face value. This is partly what is meant by critically reflective practice. Finally, the conclusion seeks to draw together the main threads of the chapter and present an overview of the principles of good practice.

Before launching into the main substance of the chapter, it is also worth noting that this chapter addresses adults as direct service users in their own right. It does not, therefore, refer to the work undertaken with adults in a childcare context (as parents, for example) nor as offenders within the criminal justice system.

The context for practice

Work with adults encompasses a number of client groups and a wide variety of settings. Figure 25.1 summarises the situation in terms of the main elements, but this is of course by no means comprehensive.

Such groups have a great deal in common but also significant differences. I shall comment here on some of the aspects that apply to specific groups and will return to the question of commonalities below under the heading of roles and tasks.

Older people

A fundamental basis for social work with older people must be the need to work consistently within a context of anti-ageist practice in order to ensure that the steps taken by the worker, or others involved in the process of helping, act against the predominant tendencies to demean, marginalise and disempower older

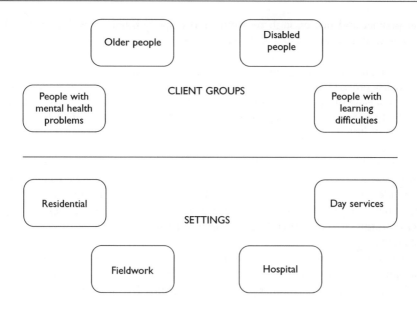

Figure 25.1 Client groups and settings

people without in any way reinforcing or condoning such tendencies. This involves recognising older people as a group who are subject to discrimination and oppression.

One particular example of ageist ideology is the tendency for older people to be excluded at times from the category of social work with adults. For example, services are often organised under the headings of services for children and families, services for adults, and services for 'the elderly', as if older people were not adults (Midwinter, 1990). It is therefore important to assert the right of older people to be included within the category of 'adults'.

Work with older people includes the assessment of need and provision (either directly or through purchasing from other sources) of appropriate services, advocacy and mediation, and counselling and other problem-solving methods. However, it should be noted that ageist attitudes and structures can lead to the first item on this list becoming more or less the only item on the list for some practitioners or agencies, a point to which I shall return below.

People with physical disabilities

There are strong parallels here with the discussion above of social work with older people, in so far as disabled people also constitute a group who face discrimination and oppression (Oliver, 1990). A major factor in this regard is the importance of moving away from a medical model in which disability is confused with a form of illness, with the result that staff tend to focus too much on care and doing things for people, and not enough on rights and empowerment (a theme that will be explored more fully below). As Oliver (1996: 76–7) comments:

> discrimination against disabled people is institutionalised throughout society and ... welfare provision has compounded rather than alleviated that discrimination ... The fact remains that providing welfare services on the basis of individual need has aided the process of excluding disabled people from society rather than facilitated their inclusion.

Like older people, adults with disabilities can also face 'infantilisation' (Hockey and James, 1993). That is, they too are often treated as if they were children, for example when they are not fully consulted about steps that are being taken on their behalf or services that are being provided. Recognising disabled people's status as full citizens is therefore an important part of social work with this group of adults.

Work with disabled people includes the assessment of need and the provision of appropriate services, as well as a range of other activities geared towards reducing risk, maximising independence and improving quality of life.

People with learning difficulties

The fact that we use terms such as 'learning difficulties' or 'learning disability' is in itself quite significant. It reflects the struggle that we have had in trying to move away from problematic terms such as 'mental handicap' or 'mental deficiency', terms that are profoundly stigmatising and unduly negative. Indeed, this is a criticism that can be levelled at traditional forms of practice with this client group – that it has tended to focus too much on the negatives and has thereby neglected the strengths and positive characteristics of people who have learning difficulties.

Support services for adults with learning difficulties include the promotion of employment, education and leisure opportunities, often as part of a programme of developing independence and life skills.

People with mental health problems

As with disabled people, a major feature of social work with people with mental health problems is the significance of the medical model, an approach which, although quite a dominant discourse in terms of influencing health and social welfare practice, can be seen to be quite destructive as a result of the disempowerment it engenders. The notion of 'mental illness' is one that brings with it considerable stigma as well as a number of other potentially problematic implications:

- Power is vested in members of the medical profession who do not necessarily have the appropriate training or experience for dealing with complex psychological processes and the sociopolitical context in which they occur.

- It implies that the remedies to the problems encountered lie primarily with the experts, and thus undermines self-determination and authenticity.

- By focusing on biologically based issues of 'illness', it fails to take adequate account of cultural and structural factors such as ethnicity, race, class and gender. It therefore runs the risk of exacerbating existing patterns of discrimination and oppression.

The work undertaken with people with mental health problems includes the assessment of need and the provision of appropriate services, statutory duties under the Mental Health Act 1983 and related statutory provisions, and other activities geared towards reducing risk of harm, maximising independence and improving quality of life.

These categories are, of course, not mutually exclusive, as people can and do belong to more than one category at a time. For example, an older person may also be disabled, or a person with learning difficulties may also have mental health problems (depression, for example). This situation can at times lead to organisational difficulties, including conflict between specialist teams as to who is the most appropriate person to deal with a particular situation. At times, this may emerge as an example of territoriality, two or more individuals or teams competing with each other to play a lead role. At other times, the opposite may occur, a particular client finding that he or she is falling between two stools, with both service areas arguing that the other is the more appropriate. In view of the problems that such situations can cause, it is vitally important not to lose sight of the fact that each client is an individual in his or her own right and is not simply a representative of an abstract category. At all times, it is important to remember that the individual is precisely that – a *unique individual* with needs and rights – and should therefore not lose out as a result of the inability of teams to work effectively together where administrative or organisational categories overlap or conflict. A category should be an aid to understanding and helping people rather than a barrier to doing so.

This issue of 'territoriality' and boundary disputes is also an important consideration in relation to multidisciplinary collaboration. An important part of good practice in this respect is the ability to work cooperatively and constructively with colleagues from other disciplines without entering into unprofessional forms of behaviour that have more to do with professional rivalry than professional good practice. Difficult though it may be at times, it is vitally important that, where possible, professionals from different disciplines work together rather than against each other, so that the focus is clearly on the service user's needs and circumstances.

In addition to the above client groups, it is important to recognise a further category of people whose needs, rights and wishes also have to be taken into consideration, regardless of which of the particular groups is being dealt with. I am referring to carers – the friends, relatives, neighbours and others who provide day-to-day practical and emotional care. Carers have a right, under the Carers (Representation and Services) Act 1995, to have an assessment of their ability to provide care. Consequently, it is very important that carers are part of the picture in working with any adult client group.

In work with all the client groups mentioned here, the common theme remains that of empowerment, working positively towards independence and autonomy while challenging factors, such as discrimination and oppression, that stand in the way of progress.

Systematic practice

One of the dangers that busy practitioners face is that of losing track of what they are trying to achieve or how they are going to achieve it – this is the problem of 'drift'. A proposed 'antidote' to drift is that of *systematic practice*. This can be seen to comprise two elements: working within the parameters of a clear and identifiable process, and retaining a clear focus on what is happening and why.

The phenomenon of drift is a well-known concept in childcare social work, as evidenced by the emphasis, especially in child protection, on clear planning, defined goals and comprehensive or holistic assessment (DoH, 1988). The extent to which such clarity and focus are carried through into the hurly-burly of the pressures of practice is something that probably varies considerably, but at least the emphasis is there in the policy and theory base, a base that provides a platform on which to build good practice. My argument in this chapter is that good practice in social work with adults should also be based on clear planning, defined goals and holistic assessment – in short, systematic practice.

In order to facilitate clarifying what is involved in systematic practice, I shall divide the discussion into two sections. The first addresses the importance of the social work process, with its focus on a clear, coherent and logical progression through a set of stages, each stage helping to provide guidelines for what the agenda for practice should be. The second relates to the vital role of clarity of focus, and it is in this section that I describe what I shall refer to as the three key questions of systematic practice.

The social work process

There are various conceptions of 'the social work process' (see Chapter 23), but the one I present here consists of five stages within an 'iterative' framework (a term I explain below). These stages are as follows:

1. *Assessment*. This initial stage of the process involves gathering information about the situation in order to establish, as far as possible, the nature, extent and seriousness of the problems to be addressed, the needs of the people concerned, the risk factors involved, the strengths and resources available to the individual, family or group and so on. However, the gathering of information is not enough on its own – such information has to be interpreted so that it can be of use in understanding the situation and planning a response to it. Assessment therefore consists of:

   - gathering relevant information;
   - constructing a 'picture' of the situation;
   - considering possible courses of action;
   - deciding upon the course(s) of action to be pursued.

There is inevitably a subjective element to assessment, but this is not to say that the worker should not endeavour to be as objective as possible. Indeed, the principle of working in partnership should help to guard against personal bias, as it necessarily involves taking account of the perspectives of all concerned and not simply the worker's.

2. *Intervention.* While assessment involves working together to recognise the problems be addressed and identifying possible solutions, the intervention stage involves implementing one or more courses of action geared towards resolving or ameliorating the situation. A number of potential approaches to intervention are available to guide and inform practice, either as direct forms of intervention or as parts of a 'mix-and-match' approach based on experience and practice wisdom. It is important to recognise, as I shall emphasise below, that intervention should amount to much more than simply providing (or commissioning) services.

3. *Review.* Circumstances can and do change, and mistakes can be made at the assessment. It is therefore necessary to review our work from time to time in order to be able to respond appropriately to changing circumstances and to be able to rectify mistakes made in the assessment or fill in gaps in our understanding of the situation.

4. *Ending.* This stage of the process is one that is often neglected, both in practice and in the supporting literature base. This is a significant deficiency, as the ending stage can be a crucial one in ensuring that any good done is not undone by a mishandled ending of a piece of work (for example by allowing it to 'fizzle out' without the loose ends being tied up carefully). The skills involved in effective and appropriate endings are ones that are well worth the investment of time and effort to develop them.

5. *Evaluation.* This is another stage in the process that tends to be neglected. It is not unusual to hear busy practitioners state that they do not have time to evaluate their work. While this seems understandable on the surface, a closer examination reveals a significant flaw in the logic. Evaluation involves examining our practice so that we can learn from our mistakes and build on our successes. It is therefore a very worthwhile investment of time that can save considerable time and energy in the medium and long term. Neglecting to evaluate our work involves running the risk of repeating mistakes and failing to capitalise on the lessons to be learned from earlier successes. It is therefore a waste of time *not* to evaluate our practice.

The process is an *iterative* one. That is, it is not a mechanical, linear progression from one stage to the next. Systematic practice is not a rigid prescription for practice but rather a flexible framework to facilitate clarity and focus. An iterative process involves 'looping', returning to an earlier stage in the process as and when required, as Figure 25.2 illustrates.

It should also be recognised and emphasised that each of the five stages should operate on the basis of partnership. That is, each stage should be a shared endeavour rather than a one-sided process in which the powerful 'expert'

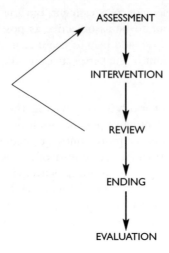

Figure 25.2 The social work process

diagnoses the problem and prescribes the solution, with little or no reference to the relatively powerless person or persons concerned – in short, a partnership model is to be preferred to a medical model. As Knibbs (1994: 19) puts it: 'professionals should be on tap not on top'. A clear benefit of working in partnership is that it promotes:

- working relationships based on openness and trust;
- opportunities for empowerment;
- shared responsibility for outcomes so that no individual is scapegoated for failures or receives undue credit for successes; and
- the avoidance of dependency.

Partnership has achieved the status of something of a 'buzz word' in recent years, but this should not be allowed to detract from its role as an essential part of good practice if we are to avoid paternalistic and disempowering forms of practice.

Clarity of focus

A helpful way of developing and maintaining clarity of focus is to use a framework of three key questions. These questions make it easier to keep track of what we are doing and why. The three questions are:

1. What are you trying to achieve?
2. How are you going to achieve it?
3. How will you know when you have achieved it?

The first question refers to the process of clarifying the aims of the intervention – the needs, problems and rights to be addressed. It is not always possible to be precise about these, but the more clarity that can be gained the better, so that the focus of work does not become sidetracked. By establishing, through a process based on partnership, the overall aims and specific objectives of intervention, a firm basis for collaboration can be achieved. This can bring the benefits of reassurance for the client, confidence for the worker and clarity of purpose for both parties.

The second question refers to the courses of action decided upon with a view to achieving the objectives agreed in response to question 1. In other words, the answer to the first question determines the destination we wish to arrive at, while question 2 is intended to clarify the route to be taken to get there – the steps that need to be taken to achieve our ends. In this respect, the process has much in common with task-centred practice (Doel and Marsh, 1992; see also Chapter 17). However, where it differs is that the process I am describing here may involve identifying the specific tasks that need to be achieved, but it does not have to; the process of intervention may take a number of other forms (service provision, advocacy, counselling or other problem-solving activities).

The third question is perhaps the most difficult to respond to, and is, unfortunately, one that is often neglected in practice. Answering the question 'How will you know when you have achieved it?' involves considering in advance what success will look like and how we will recognise that we have arrived at our destination. This does not mean that we should attempt to use a (pseudo)-scientific approach with precise, measurable indicators of success. Such an approach does not sit comfortably with the complexities and subtleties of social work practice, but this is not to say that it is not possible to measure or identify success – we just have to be more flexible and creative in our methodology. For example, as I. Shaw (1996: 21) points out, it is possible, and quite appropriate, to draw on 'humanist' forms of evaluation of practice which are:

> likely to adopt qualitative methods of inquiry and to stress the importance of discovering the meaning of events to the participants. Hence 'process' and the way in which meanings are constructed through negotiation are likely to figure largely.

The benefits of taking the trouble to seek to answer question 3 are:

- It helps to ensure that questions 1 and 2 have been answered appropriately. That is, if the answers to the earlier questions are too vague, unclear or ambiguous, it will be very difficult to answer question 3.

- It acts as a source of motivation for client and worker alike by providing a vision of how much better the situation could possibly be.

- It allows greater workload control as it avoids time and effort being wasted by pursuing inappropriate courses of action or continuing with intervention when it is no longer necessary or appropriate to do so. That is, it helps to prevent drift.

Systematic approaches to practice offer clarity and focus but without rigidity or tying people down to a particular method or technique of intervention. As such, then, the effort required to develop the necessary skills can be seen as a very worthwhile investment of personal resources. Systematic practice is not intended as a rigid, pseudoscientific approach to practice but rather as a structured framework which:

- provides focus and guidance but not at the expense of flexibility;

- enhances professional credibility by giving clients and carers a degree of confidence in the worker;

- acts as a firm basis for partnership;

- contributes positively to the avoidance of vagueness and drift;

- provides the basis for a coherent process of positive intervention; and

- facilitates the review and evaluation of work undertaken.

The life course

It is well established that child development is an important part of the know-ledge base that childcare workers need in order to practise in an informed way, with an understanding of the context of the child's thoughts, feelings and actions in relation to the stage of development within the life course that he or she has reached. However, what is not so well established is the significance of the life course for adults as well as children (see Chapter 8).

Perhaps the most salient example of the significance of the life course for work with adults is in relation to working with older people. Old age can be seen as the final stage in the life course (Sidell, 1993; Corr et al., 1996). An important aspect of the life course is the predominance and influence of age-related expectations. This arises from the fact that age is not only a biological marker, but also a social division, an example of the many ways in which society is subdivided into more or less privileged groups (in much the same way as are class, race and gender). Age is used as a means of attaching significance to people and allocating power and life chances. Consequently, children and older people are assigned fewer rights and less power than young adults. As noted earlier, older people may even at times be excluded from the category of 'adults'.

Age-related expectations, when applied rigidly, become manifestations of ageism – the social division of age being used to marginalise and disempower older people. Our understanding of age-related expectations should therefore play a part in recognising and challenging ageist stereotypes. Consequently, we should not seek to explain people's behaviour by reference to their age – 'What do you expect at your age?' – as this runs the risk of relying on ageist assumptions or overgeneralisations.

Within the life course, there are a number of transitions to be encountered and dealt with, some of which are the recognised 'developmental crises' associated with ego psychology (Erikson, 1977), which contain within them an element of predictability: leaving the parental home and establishing an independent lifestyle; the menopause/mid-life crisis; retirement and so on. Other transitions involve the less predictable but nonetheless common experiences of grieving and significant losses (see the discussion below of loss and grief). An understanding of the significance and impact of such transitions should be a basic part of the social worker's repertoire of competence, for, without this, there is a danger that assessments may be significantly off-target and that interventions may be not only ineffective, but also positively harmful.

Similarly, while the importance of life stages needs to be considered in general, situations where they are different from the general picture also need to be taken into account. That is, such life stages are socially constructed and are therefore subject to considerable variation according to culture and other such social factors. It is important that they are not seen as biological stages that have to be experienced in a particular way. Such an approach would be ethnocentric and totally insensitive to issues of disability and sexual identity, for example. It is worth considering these questions under three headings: race, culture and language; disability; and sexual identity.

Race, culture and language

The life course is commonly depicted as if it were primarily or exclusively a question of biology. However, this is too narrow a perspective that fails to take account of the various processes – psychological, social, political and ontological – that are part and parcel of the life course. It is therefore necessary to take into consideration religious and cultural norms, values and folkways in understanding a person's 'trajectory' through the life course. The cultural and linguistic context of a person's lifeworld will, of course, have a major bearing on his or her perception of the world, the meanings attached to life events and experiences, the values that guide action and so on. A person's experience of the life course will therefore be largely shaped by his or her cultural and linguistic background (see Chapters 8 and 21).

However, while the importance of such ethnically and linguistically sensitive practice has to be recognised, it should not be allowed to overshadow the need to develop, in addition, forms of anti-racist practice. That is, while ethnically sensitive practice recognises the importance of cultural differences, anti-racist practice goes a step further in recognising the significance of assumed cultural (or 'racial') superiority. The significance of racism in the lives of black people will, of course, have an influence on their experiences of the life course and the various points of transition it involves (Robinson, 1995; see also Chapter 8).

Disability

One criticism of much of the literature on the life course is that it adopts an able-bodied perspective – that is, it fails to consider the life course experiences of people with a disability. The 'developmental milestones' of a person with one or more physical impairments may well be significantly different from those associated with non-disabled people. Conventional approaches can therefore contribute to the view that disabled people are not just different from non-disabled people but are actually inferior to them by virtue of the fact that they do not 'live up to' the developmental norms expected (Abberley, 1993). This is the equivalent of ethnocentric forms of racist thinking in which other cultures are seen as not only different, but also inferior (Ahmad, 1990).

Sexual identity

Davies (1996) points out that the stages of the life course are usually conceived in heterosexist terms – that is, they take heterosexual identity development as the desirable norm to be aimed for. Similarly, it can be argued that, for gay men and lesbians, there are two further stages in the life course. The first is that of 'coming out', bringing that identity into the public domain, and the second that of opting for a lifestyle (Plummer, 1981). Such transitions are not usually addressed in the mainstream literature on human development.

In some ways, perhaps, the most significant aspect of the life course is its ending. Issues of death, dying and bereavement can be seen as important factors in the ways in which they have a bearing on life. Death is, after all, a significant part of life. As Frank (1991) puts it:

> Death is no enemy of life; it restores our sense of the value of living. Illness restores the sense of proportion that is lost when we take life for granted. To learn about value and proportion we need to honor illness, and ultimately to honor death. (p. 120, cited in Corr et al., 1996)

It is therefore fair to say that loss and grief play a key role in our life experiences and should therefore be taken into account in our practice as social workers. An awareness of, and sensitivity to, issues of grief and loss can therefore be seen as fundamental aspects of good practice (Thompson, 2002).

Another aspect of the life course to be taken into account is that it is not simply individuals who go through life course transitions. The concept of 'life course', although not an entirely unproblematic one, can also be seen to apply at a familial or social network level. This is the case in two ways:

1. Life course development affects not only specific individuals, but also the whole family (or social group) in which each individual lives. For example, the situation of an older person reaching the stage where they may have to give up their home is one that will affect a number of people within the family or social network, rather than just the individual concerned.

2. Families also go through a form of life course, in the sense that there will be different stages in terms of the challenges they face, the resources they can draw upon and the losses and gains they face. For example, the situations faced by a family with young children are likely to be very different from those faced by a family where the children have grown up and moved out. Once again, it should be emphasised that the life course is not simply a matter of biological

development, despite the fact that many texts on developmental psychology give this impression.

Roles and tasks

Social workers engaged in work with adults are charged with a number of roles and tasks. We do not have space to explore these in the detail they merit, so it would be unrealistic to attempt to. I shall therefore restrict myself to outlining the key elements of such work, thereby laying the foundations for further learning and development.

The first element to consider is that of assessment. As outlined above, this involves gathering relevant information, forming an overview of the situation, identifying possible solutions or responses and determining the best way forward. There are various stages and levels of assessment, ranging from initial 'screening' to comprehensive analyses of very complex situations (Seed and Kaye, 1994). There are (at least) two potential problems associated with assessment practice, each representing the extremes of a continuum (Figure 25.3). The first is the tendency sometimes apparent for a very narrow perspective to be adopted, focusing primarily or exclusively on client need without taking sufficient account of a range of wider factors (see the discussion of care management below). The second, but less common, problem is that of gathering more information than is necessary for present purposes, thereby risking an infringement of civil liberties as well as a waste of time brought about by creating a situation of information overload. Good practice in assessment can therefore be seen to rely on achieving a constructive balance between the two destructive extremes illustrated in Figure 25.3.

Effective and appropriate assessment has a crucial role to play in 'setting the scene' for subsequent intervention. A mistake or oversight at the assessment stage can lead to significant difficulties later as services or other interventions may be misdirected or even wholly inappropriate. The price to be paid for mistakes or 'corner-cutting' at the assessment stage can therefore be very high indeed. This is particularly the case in relation to anti-discriminatory practice. For example, to make a racist assumption at the assessment stage may mean that subsequent actions have a profoundly racist impact.

In addition to assessment, consideration needs to be given to planning. Complex situations require careful planning in order to prevent inappropriate responses or simplistic, ill-conceived answers that run the risk of making the situation worse. Planning begins from the moment of referral and continues through assessment and subsequent interventions. In this respect, planning is not

Figure 25.3 The information balance

a stage of the social work process per se, but instead a continuous aspect of practice. Indeed, it can be seen as an essential element of *reflective practice* in which routinised, uncritical practice is to be avoided.

If practice is to be systematic and effective, it needs to be goal-oriented; that is, there needs to be clarity about what is to be achieved. Consequently, practice needs to be *future-oriented* – constantly having an eye to the future and the steps that need to be taken to move towards the desired future outcomes. In this respect, planning has a key role to play.

Planning is also important in a broader sense. Above and beyond individual cases or pieces of work, there are broader patterns to be discerned and accounted for. That is, planning can and should relate to these broader patterns of need (particularly unmet need), service availability and shortfall, demographic or other changes (in relation to minority ethnic groups, for example), training require-ments and so on. To a certain extent, this broader level of planning is the respons-ibility of managers and policy-makers, but this is not to say that practitioners should not operate on this territory at all. Practitioners have an important role to play in such planning in terms of:

- contributing to the policy monitoring and development role by providing information through the appropriate channels in order to ensure, as far as possible, that the process is informed by the perspective of staff involved directly in practice;

- recognising patterns in their own practice, for example in identifying oppor-tunities for groupwork or other collaborative efforts with colleagues or partner agencies.

Planning, then, is more than the process that applies on an individual basis to managing particular cases or pieces of work.

Care management is a relatively new element to consider, but nonetheless an important one. The development of care management in the UK owes much to the implementation of the NHS and Community Care Act 1990, an Act which places a responsibility on local authorities to assess the needs of those members of the community who may require community care services. Care management therefore refers to the process of constructing a 'package' of care services designed to maintain the person in the community and thus avoid the need for residential care. As Orme and Glastonbury (1993: 187) put it, care management is:

> The label given in the UK to the task of organising and overseeing the provision of a care package for a client who has been assessed, and whose needs are consid-ered of sufficient priority to warrant the allocation of services.

In principle, care management should provide an effective system for identi-fying and, as far as possible, meeting the needs of those members of the community who are in need of care services. However, one danger with this system is that it can easily become a form of service brokerage in which there is a narrow focus on needs and the services that may be able to meet them, without adequate consideration of:

- the factors that give rise to those needs (loss and grief, low self-esteem/internalised oppression, relationship difficulties, discrimination, debt and so on);

- the strengths that people bring to their particular situations and their overall circumstances;

- the importance of rights, and the problems and injustices that can occur when rights are not upheld.

A key concept in relation to care management is that of the purchaser–provider split. This refers to the organisational practice of dividing the traditional social work role in two, care managers taking primary responsibility for purchasing or commissioning services, while a range of others in statutory, voluntary and private organisations have the task of providing such services. Care management is, in this context, therefore largely a process of commissioning services, hence the danger that other social work issues may be neglected or marginalised through an over-emphasis on service brokerage at the expense of the broader processes of problem-solving, safeguarding rights, building on strengths, working towards social justice and so on. Care management should therefore be seen as a part of the overall social work role rather than as a substitute for it. While seeking to meet someone's practical care needs within an organised and coordinated framework is clearly an important social work function, we should not make the mistake of limiting our vision of the social work task to this. This is for (at least) three reasons:

1. Failing to address broader issues may mean that, despite the provision of a substantial package of services, the client's quality of life may remain at a low level because more profound needs have not been addressed, rights have been overlooked or strengths have not been recognised and consolidated.

2. Failure to address broader issues or deeper needs (for example in relation to self-esteem) or to safeguard rights can render intervention ineffective, thereby wasting precious resources that could have been more appropriately directed to other clients.

3. A narrow focus on service brokerage can remove much of the job satisfaction of social work, thereby acting as a demotivating factor and a possible source of low morale.

Advocacy and mediation can also be seen as parts of the social worker's repertoire in working with adults. Social workers may, at times, be called upon to act as an advocate or mediate on behalf of a client or group of clients. This involves representing a person's or group's interests in circumstances where they are not able to do so themselves or where the support of a social worker may be of partic-ular value. Phillipson (1993: 182–3) describes advocacy in the following terms:

> The general understanding of advocacy is that it is concerned with the balance of power between the client as a member of a minority or other disenfranchised group and the larger society. From the advocate's point of view, the client's

problems are not seen as psychological or personal deficits but rather as stemming or arising from discrimination as regards social and economic opportunities. Therefore, techniques of intervention, rather than focusing solely on the relief of individual clients, should challenge those inequalities within the system which contribute to or which cause difficulties for the ... person.

Advocacy can therefore be an important form of empowerment in which relatively powerless individuals or groups are supported in their attempts to influence or challenge more powerful elements in society, such as official agencies. For a more detailed discussion of advocacy, see Bateman (1995).

Mediation is a process that has much in common with advocacy but is also crucially different. It parallels advocacy in so far as it tends to involve a process of negotiation, but differs in so far as mediation involves adopting a neutral role between two opposing parties (members of a family, for example) rather than taking up the case of one party against another. At times, particularly in very complex situations, the processes of advocacy and mediation can overlap, perhaps with very problematic results, as the worker loses clarity over his or her role. It is therefore important, if not essential, to maintain a clear focus in undertaking advocacy or mediation in order to ensure that the roles do not become blurred and therefore potentially counterproductive. For example, a mediator who 'takes sides' is likely to lose all credibility, as is an advocate who seeks to adopt a neutral position.

Responding to abuse is a further important part of social work with adults. Social workers have not only a 'duty of care', but also one of protection in certain circumstances, particularly protection from abuse. The most well-documented aspect of the abuse of adults is that of elder abuse, a phenomenon that was neglected for a long time but which is now beginning to attract a great deal more attention, both in the literature base (Pritchard, 1992; Bennett and Kingston, 1993; Eastman, 1994; Biggs et al., 1995) and in emerging policy and practice. However, other groups of adults, of course, are also prone to abuse and exploitation, so it would be a mistake to focus exclusively on elder abuse. The potential for abuse is one that has to be borne in mind in working with any client group.

Responding to abuse can be difficult, complex and harrowing work, so it is not surprising that some people feel anxious or even reluctant when it comes to dealing with such issues. However, we should not see such work in an entirely negative light, as it is both very important work in terms of the harm that can be done if it is not undertaken properly, or not followed through at all, and can also be very rewarding in terms of job satisfaction. The time and effort required to develop the skills and knowledge required for responding to abuse are therefore a very worthwhile investment.

A further important element is that of counselling, although it is perhaps worth drawing a distinction between counselling and psychotherapy. The latter involves attempting to make major and sometimes radical changes to a person's psychological functioning and is generally well beyond the scope of a social worker in terms of both the expertise and time commitment required. The former, in contrast, involves helping clients to clarify their thoughts and feelings on their current circumstances, or a particular aspect of them, with a view to identifying and implementing possible ways forward. This is a skilled activity for which specialist training can be helpful. However, a qualified social worker should be equipped to undertake at least the basics of counselling.

It is worth stressing that counselling is not simply a matter of giving people the opportunity to talk about their situation or 'ventilate' their feelings, although these can be important elements of successful counselling. As Burks and Stefflre (1979) comment, counselling is:

> designed to help clients to understand and clarify their views of their lifespace, and to learn to reach their self-determined goals through meaningful, well-informed choices and through resolution of problems of an emotional or interpersonal nature. (p. 14, quoted in McLeod, 1993: 1–2)

Counselling can at times be of tremendous benefit in helping to set people free from the barriers and restrictions that are preventing them from taking control of their lives and resolving the difficulties they face. In short, counselling can be empowering.

Social work is rightly included under the heading of the 'caring professions', but this is not to say that control is not also part of the social worker's duties. Indeed, it is often necessary to exercise control in order to care. Much of the control element of social work derives from the legal context and the statutory interventions that social workers are obliged to make under certain circumstances. Space does not permit a detailed account of these interventions, but we should at least note that social workers engaged in work with adults may be at times involved in statutory interventions that may entail a client being deprived of his or her liberty because of a danger to self or to others (for example under the Mental Health Act 1983).

Social action is perhaps an unfashionable approach in this day and age. However, 'unfashionable' should not be equated with 'non-existent'. Social action involves tackling problems at a broader level than the individual or family (Barber, 1991). This entails working in and with communities to identify problems affecting a range of people and exploring possible solutions that can be implemented by the community as a whole or by certain groups of people within the community. There are a range of schemes and projects that come under the heading of 'social action', for example community law centres, 'drop-in' resources or 'one-stop' shops where a range of community services are offered.

Social action can also involve taking up a political campaign, for example protesting against a particular plan or proposal or applying pressure to an organisation to influence policy or campaign for a particular service to be provided. The approach is, therefore, one that is often characterised by conflict. Nonetheless, such conflict can often be constructive and productive, especially if skilfully and creatively handled.

User involvement can also be seen as an aspect of social action. This involves taking whatever steps are possible to help clients to gain a voice in terms of assessment, service delivery, the processes of intervention, review, ending and evaluation, as well as the broader processes of policy formulation, implementation, monitoring and evaluation (see Beresford and Croft, 1993; Beresford and Harding, 1993).

In addition to these elements, we also need to consider working in partnership as a form of practice in its own right. The point has already been made that good practice needs to be premised on partnership rather than the traditional model of the social worker as expert who 'diagnoses' the problem and 'prescribes' a 'cure'. A participative approach has far more to offer than a medicalised one in which barriers are erected between worker and client (Croft and Beresford, 1994). Wineman's (1984: 80) explanation of the need for 'two-way' approaches to practice is worth quoting in full:

> Professionals are taught to remain detached, not to become 'overinvolved', not to get too 'emotional', certainly not to look to a client as a source of help. But one-way helping necessarily creates a power imbalance, and it communicates to the 'client' that s/he does not have the strengths and skills that it takes to be a source of support – or at the very least fails to actively recognize and affirm those strengths and skills. It thus cements the image of the 'client' as 'sick' and deficient. Two-way helping can create the shared power of mutual definition; can create a realistic perception of people as encompassing various combinations of strength and weakness, competence and troubles; can dignify and affirm people who have previously been defined in terms of their problems, deficiencies and 'pathologies' by also looking to them as sources of support and defining them as people with something to give as well as to receive.

However, it also needs to be recognised that working in partnership is a skilled activity. It involves communication, assertiveness and negotiation skills so that the possibilities for effective collaboration can be maximised.

Another broad approach is that of problem-solving. This is something of an umbrella term that describes a range of interventions geared towards resolving one or more difficulties. This may relate to practical problems, for example through adjustments made to the physical environment or the provision of aids that remove difficulties or enhance quality of life. However, problem-solving can be on a much broader basis, incorporating emotional, psychological, inter-personal and social problems. The breadth of this approach can act as a counter-balance to the narrow 'brokerage' approach associated with care management, as mentioned above.

Problem-solving involves working in partnership to:

- identify those aspects of a person's life or current circumstances (or those of a family, group or community) that are problematic;

- generate a range of possible solutions;

- evaluate the options; and

- choose and implement the most appropriate solution.

The question of 'generating a range of possible solutions' is an important part of the process in so far as problem-solving is not simply a process of *finding* the right answer, as if there were one definitive answer to each problem encountered. It is more accurately represented as a process of *constructing* one or more solutions and considering the strengths and weaknesses, advantages and disadvantages of each option. This, then, makes it necessary to work in partnership so that the clients play an active part in dealing with their own problems. This enables them to share ownership of the proposed solution and be empowered by the process, whereas an approach in which the social worker plays 'the expert' and prescribes a 'cure' is far more likely to encourage dependence (and recriminations if the proposed solution is not entirely successful).

Problem-solving is not an 'exclusive' approach. It is a framework that can be used in tandem with one or more other approaches (care management, counselling and so on).

Working together in a group context also offers considerable scope for addressing problems and unmet needs, safeguarding rights, enhancing quality of life and promoting empowerment (see Douglas, 1983; Preston-Shoot, 1987; Mullender and Ward, 1991; Brown, 1992). As Brown (1994: 34) comments:

> The essence of groupwork is the benefit that can be gained from being together with several other people who share something in common with you.

Groups can exist in relation to a geographical community (for example older people at a residential home), in relation to a particular set of issues (social skills development for people with learning difficulties, for example) or in other such areas in which a communal approach can have benefits for all concerned. Having the opportunity to express feelings in a safe, supportive and responsive environment, to discuss common problems and identify ways in which they might be tackled can be a very constructive and empowering experience.

However, it should also be noted that groupwork can have destructive outcomes, leaving people feeling distressed and disempowered. It is a highly skilled form of practice, so it should not be entered into lightly, without being carefully planned and without the support of more experienced groupworkers.

I earlier identified empowerment as an overarching theme, but it too can be seen as an element of practice in its own right. As with partnership, empowerment has achieved the status of a buzz word, an overused word that is in danger of losing its meaning, potency and value (Gomm, 1993). Nonetheless, the concept of empowerment remains a central one. It can be defined as:

> the means by which individuals, groups and/or communities become able to take control of their circumstances and achieve their own goals, thereby being able to work towards themselves and others to maximise the quality of their lives. (Adams, 1996a: 80)

The notion of social work practice 'giving' power to clients should not be interpreted simplistically as handing power to clients as if it were a commodity to be passed from one person to another. Power is not a 'zero-sum' concept – that is, social workers can empower others without necessarily being disempowered themselves (that is, losing control over their own circumstances), as if there were a finite sum of power that has to be shared or divided up. Indeed, as Adams (1996a) affirms, it is necessary for social workers to be empowered if they are to empower others.

Empowerment can be seen as both a specific strategy (or set of strategies) for increasing clients' control over their lives (through advocacy, for example) and an aspect of all practice – that is, all forms of good practice should be geared in some way towards helping people to increase their level of control. This is consistent with the discussion below of emancipatory practice and those above of partnership and participation.

Finally, emancipatory practice needs to be recognised as a central theme of social work with adults. In view of the fact that discrimination operates at personal, cultural and structural levels, good practice is not simply a matter of avoiding discriminatory actions, attitudes or language in our own work. It also involves the need to tackle discrimination in the work of others, in the cultural norms, values, stereotypes and assumptions that surround us and in the structural patterns and power relations that sustain them. Social work with adults therefore needs to be premised, first, on the recognition of the forms of discrimination to which adult client groups are subject, for example ageism and disablism, in addition to those that apply across the board, such as sexism, racism and heterosexism; and second, on a commitment to challenging these forms of discrimination in order to reduce, eliminate or counteract the oppression that such discrimination engenders.

Developing emancipatory practice involves challenging traditional assumptions about 'women's place', about racial superiority, about older people being 'past it', about disabled people being 'incapable' and so on. The process therefore involves 'unlearning' taken-for-granted assumptions and maintaining a focus on the need to counter discrimination wherever it is encountered.

CONCLUSION

Developing good practice

As we have seen, social work with adults is diverse, complex and challenging. In this final section, I shall try to pull together the main themes and issues by teasing out what I see as the principles of good practice. These are not intended as simple formulae to be followed unthinkingly or uncritically. Social work is far too complex for such simple prescriptions to be of any value – indeed, such an uncritical approach can be dangerous. Instead, these guidelines are intended as themes to be considered, debated and used as a stimulus to developing critically reflective practice. They should therefore be seen as the beginning or further step in a process of developing high-quality practice, rather than as a short cut.

1. *Systematic practice, based on clarity, focus and partnership, is the foundation of good practice.* Being clear, at all times, about what we are trying to achieve and how we are hoping to achieve it is a fundamental part of good practice in so far as it helps to prevent a drift, vagueness and wasted efforts.

2. *Assessment should not be narrow and service-oriented.* It is not simply a question of assessing need but rather of assessing circumstances, and such circumstances should include strengths as well as weaknesses, rights as well as needs.

3. *Interventions should not be routine or unimaginative.* Social work is a demanding job, so developing routines can be one way of coping with its pressures. However, where practice has become too heavily reliant on routines, opportunities for progress are likely to be missed through a failure to practise creatively.

4. *Social work with adults needs to be both ethnically sensitive and anti-racist.* Practice involves working with people from a range of ethnic backgrounds, some of which are regarded by many as inferior to dominant white cultures. Good practice therefore needs to recognise the specific customs, values and so on of the specific group being worked with at any one time (ethnically sensitive practice), while also taking account of, and responding to, the experiences of racism that so many members of minority ethnic communities are likely to have had (anti-racist practice).

5. *Good practice must be emancipatory practice.* Racism is not, of course, the only form of oppression that social workers are likely to encounter in their work with adults. Sexism, ageism, disablism, heterosexism and so on are also almost certain to feature in the day-to-day interactions of social work practice. It is important, therefore, that assumptions made and actions taken contribute to the undermining of such forms of oppression, rather than adding to them or condoning them.

Social work with adults is often regarded as less important, prestigious and rewarding than childcare work. It is to be hoped that the discussions in this chapter have helped to debunk the myth that adult services work is unskilled, unchallenging and unrewarding. Working with adults can be just as demanding as working with children and can also offer similar levels of stimulation, job satisfaction and opportunities for personal and professional development.

FURTHER READING

Oliver, M. (1996) *Understanding Disability: From Theory to Practice* (London, Macmillan – now Palgrave Macmillan). Oliver's book explores some of the shortcomings of traditional approaches to social work with disabled people.

Payne, M. (1995) *Social Work and Community Care* (London, Macmillan – now Palgrave Macmillan). This book provides a clear and useful overview of community care issues in relation to adults.

Thompson, N. (1995a) *Age and Dignity: Working with Older People* (Aldershot, Arena). A useful exploration of working with older people within a framework of anti-ageist practice is contained in this book.

Thompson, N. (2000) *Understanding Social Work: Preparing for Practice* (Basingstoke, Palgrave – now Palgrave Macmillan). This includes discussion of the importance of systematic practice.

Social Work with Offenders

David Smith

Introduction

Social work with offenders has a long history, as long as that of social work itself. Reformatory schools for juvenile offenders were established by legislation in the 1850s and 60s, the first of a long line of residential care institutions claiming to promote the well-being of young people in trouble and prevent them from being contaminated by older, less tractable criminals (Carlebach, 1970). The year 1876 is often taken as the point at which the probation service was born, on the initiative of the Church of England Temperance Society (Bochel, 1976; Haxby, 1978). Probation entered the statute books in 1907, with the Probation of Offenders Act, and the special needs of juvenile offenders for 'rescue' as well as punishment were formally acknowledged by the creation of the juvenile court in the following year (Gelsthorpe and Morris, 1994). However, despite this venerable lineage, the status and purposes of social work with offenders have been and continue to be the subject of political and professional debate, and although social work has long had a recognised place within the criminal justice system, this place has rarely been central or entirely secure: the image of the probation service 'moving centre-stage' which representatives of the Home Office frequently evoked in the early 1990s (Raynor et al., 1994) was probably less characteristic of the general ministerial view of the service than was the well-attested puzzlement of one new Home Office minister of the late 1980s, who asked whether the probation service was, after all, quite a well-established organisation (rather than an unwanted child of the 1960s).

The last decade of the twentieth century produced a flood of criminal justice legislation with implications for social work with offenders; starting under a

Conservative government, this showed no signs of abating when Labour came to power in 1997. The Labour legislation in general followed and developed the logic of the Conservatives' policies on criminal justice, with a strong emphasis on rigorous supervision, the management of risk, surveillance (increasingly involving electronic monitoring or 'tagging') and enforcement of court orders and licences after release from prison. There were, however, differences between the new government's position and that of its immediate predecessor, notably in the emphasis placed on the importance of interagency cooperation and 'partnerships', especially in work with young offenders (Smith, 2000a). At the same time there were less publicised initiatives in the field of crime and criminality prevention, and community development, which opened out new possibilities for social work outside the formal criminal justice system.

Attention to the policy and legislative context of practice is inevitable, because social work with offenders is both made possible and constrained by the law within which it operates and the associated guidelines, instructions and, from the early 1990s, National Standards. The first section of the chapter, therefore, sets the scene by outlining in broad terms the important strands of recent criminal justice policy and their implications for social work practice. The chapter then discusses, in turn, some important contemporary themes in work with juvenile and adult offenders. The next section considers the place of social work agencies in broader, community-based strategies on crime, in particular their potential contribution to 'community safety' (Home Office, 1991). Finally, the chapter argues for a more inclusive view of what counts as 'effective' practice than has featured in most recent debates. An attempt is made throughout to include Scotland within the scope of the discussion, since policy and practice in Scotland differ instructively from the pattern in England and Wales.

The policy background

Criminal justice policy is more liable to sudden, politically motivated changes of direction than is social policy in other fields, because of the high level of public concern and anxiety about crime and the fascination that crime and its control exert upon the media (Downes and Morgan, 1994). It is, therefore, remarkable that, from 1980 (to go back almost to the start of the long period of Conservative government which ended in 1997) until early 1993, Home Office policy was as generally consistent as it was. It is possible to trace a fairly coherent line of development through successive policy statements, Criminal Justice Acts and the practice guidelines associated with them, which was broken only in 1993. In that year, Kenneth Clarke, then Home Secretary, announced that the recently implemented Criminal Justice Act of 1991 required substantial modification. His successor, Michael Howard, quickly and enthusiastically confirmed that the policies of the previous years were to be abandoned. David Faulkner, who, as a senior civil servant at the Home Office, had been closely identified with the changes of the 1980s (Rutherford, 1996), wrote regretfully in the *Guardian* that the change of line was 'probably the most sudden and the most radical which has ever taken place in this area of public policy' (Faulkner, 1993). As Hough (1996: 192) notes, while 'in strictly legal terms' the changes to the 1991 Act looked minor, 'they were symbolically substantial, being widely interpreted as a rejection of the sentencing philosophy underlying the 1991 Act'. This rejection was a radical reversal of the previous official view: that prison could be 'an expensive way of making bad people worse' (Home Office, 1990: 6). Instead, Michael Howard announced that 'Prison works', as a means of incapacitating offenders and therefore protecting the public. His view was apparently shared by Jack Straw, Home Secretary from 1997–2001.

The 1980s

What were the main elements of the policy pursued in England and Wales during the 1980s, which, according to McIvor (1996), were still being maintained, perhaps precariously, in Scotland in the mid-1990s? Three important and interrelated themes appeared right at the start, in the 1980 White Paper *Young Offenders* (Home Office, 1980). Despite its anti-welfarist rhetoric and its reinstatement of punishment as the main aim of sentencing for juveniles as well as adults (Blagg and Smith, 1989), there was embedded in the White Paper a strong statement in favour of diversion – of cautioning rather than prosecuting juvenile offenders whenever possible. This represented one side of the process which Bottoms (1977) called 'bifurcation', and which he correctly predicted would be an important principle of criminal justice policy in the coming years. Bifurcation entails distinguishing sharply between serious and less serious offences – usually interpreted as offences against the person and offences against property. In general, it prescribes that imprisonment should be reserved for those who have committed the most serious offences and that the others (the great majority of known offenders) should be dealt with – if they cannot be kept out of the system altogether – by less punitive, less intrusive and less expensive measures, such as fines and the range of 'community penalties'.

The preference for cautioning minor juvenile offenders, vigorously advocated by the Home Office in the 1980s (Evans and Wilkinson, 1990), also reflected the influence of the labelling perspective, in an unusually clear example of sociological theory influencing policy (Smith D., 1995). The 1980 White Paper accepted that, for juveniles, involvement in the criminal justice system was likely to be inherently damaging and should be avoided whenever possible. A second consistent theme of the policy of the 1980s was therefore a radical scepticism about the capacity of any measure available to the criminal justice system to make a positive difference to an offender (a position often summed up in the phrase 'Nothing works' (Raynor et al., 1994; McGuire, 1995)). A third theme, implicit in the 1980 White Paper but increasingly explicit in the following years, was that of 'just deserts' or proportionality – the principle that the sentence should reflect the seriousness of the offence.

The themes of bifurcation and just deserts both appeared in the legislation which followed the White Paper, the Criminal Justice Act of 1982. This was greeted gloomily by social workers and their allies in the liberal penal reform lobby because of its reassertion of punishment as a relevant aim of the juvenile justice system, its association with the 'short sharp shock' regime in detention centres, and its effect of making the juvenile justice system more closely resemble the adult one; and early research (Burney, 1985) seemed to bear out their misgivings. However, the Act also contained the first serious attempt to use legislation to restrict the discretion of sentencers, particularly in relation to the use of custody. In doing so, it opened out an opportunity for social workers to increase their influence on criminal justice decision-making, by greatly widening the statutory place of presentence reports (then called social inquiry reports). Briefly, the Act required sentencers, in all but exceptional circumstances, to consult a social inquiry report before sending anyone under the age of 21 to custody. It also stipulated that a custodial sentence could only be justified on the basis of the seriousness of the offence, the public's need for protection, or the offender's inability or unwillingness to comply with a non-custodial measure. These 'criteria for custody', which were reinforced in the Criminal Justice Act 1988, formed the basis of the more radical and thorough-going effort to restrict custodial sentencing in the Criminal Justice Act 1991.

The Criminal Justice Act 1991

The 1991 Act followed the anti-custodial, bifurcatory logic of its predecessors, but its radical extension of it, and its particular version of just deserts, were to prove too much for some members of its judicial and political constituency. The Act extended the requirement to consider a presentence report for all offenders, and its criteria for custody laid greater stress on the seriousness of the offence (which could be combined with only one other offence to produce a total 'volume' of seriousness). It also took bifurcation a stage further by restricting the public protection criterion to violent and sexual offences (Cavadino and Dignan, 1992), and replaced the criterion of unwillingness or inability to respond to a community penalty by the defendant's refusal of consent. The Act encouraged a view of sentences as falling into three broad bands, the lowest of which consisted of nominal and financial penalties (discharges, fines and so on). The next band, which the court should only consider if the offence (or a combination of two offences) was 'serious enough', contained the range of community penalties – supervision and probation orders with or without additional conditions, community service and the new 'combination order', which included elements of both community service and probation. The final band was that of custody, which courts should consider only if the offence was 'so serious' that, on just deserts grounds (or public protection grounds for violent and sexual offences), only a custodial sentence would be sufficient.

The Act introduced two other changes which had a direct impact on social work agencies and which, unlike its attempt to restrict the use of custody, survived subsequent legislation. First, it abolished parole in the form in which it had existed since the Criminal Justice Act of 1967. Parole meant that probation officers had to supervise in the community many more serious or persistent offenders than they had been used to dealing with, and it carried with it an expectation that their supervision would be correspondingly more intensive and more concerned with public protection. Early research on the outcomes of parole suggested that it was successful, producing lower than predicted rates of reconviction (Nuttall et al., 1977), although the supervision of parolees was not in practice strikingly different from that of probationers (Morris and Beverley, 1975). By the late 1980s, however, the system was widely thought to be in need of reform, to reduce the gap between the sentences imposed and the time actually served in prison, which had widened over the years as a result of various tinkerings with the original system. Following the recommendations of the Carlisle Committee (Home Office, 1988a), the 1991 Act substituted for parole a system of automatic conditional release (ACR) for all prisoners sentenced to over 12 months but less than four years. The scope of discretionary conditional release (DCR), the new version of parole, was restricted to longer-term prisoners.

This change quickly had the effect of increasing the proportion of people on probation officers' caseloads who had not in any sense consented to be supervised by the service and with whom, therefore, it might be difficult to agree a basis for social work intervention. Another consequence was the decline of voluntary aftercare – support for released prisoners with no statutory obligation to keep in contact with the probation service (Maguire et al., 2000). The first two years of ACR were evaluated for the Home Office (Maguire et al., 1996; Maguire and Raynor, 1997): the system was thought to be fairer than parole by most parties, including offenders, and outcomes in terms of completed licences and reoffending rates appeared encouraging, but there was little consensus about the purposes of ACR; the expectations imposed by National Standards were thought to be impossible to meet; and there was little connection between 'sentence planning' within prison and supervision after release. The researchers concluded that the system would work better if it allowed more scope for the professional judgment and discretion of probation officers rather than relying on a rigid set of rules on the conduct of supervision.

Second, the 1991 Act abolished the juvenile court and replaced it by the Youth Court. The most obvious change was in the scope of the new court's jurisdiction. While the juvenile court dealt with offenders up to and including the age of 16, the Youth Court also dealt with 17-year-olds. This change was broadly in line with the Act's overall interest in reducing the use of custody, in this case by extending to 17-year-olds the benefits of the 'welfarist' tradition of the juvenile court. There seems little doubt that this aim lay behind the Act's linking of 16- and 17-year-olds as 'near adults' (NACRO, 1991) and its requirement that sentencers should make a judgment on their maturity before deciding whether they should be sentenced as if they were adults or juveniles.

Developments in Scotland

In Scotland, the Children's Hearing System, established by the Social Work (Scotland) Act of 1968 to deal with offenders up to the age of 16 on the same welfarist principles as other children in difficulties, has been jealously maintained as a distinctive feature of the Scottish legal system (Kelly, 1996). It has been safeguarded by the lower salience of law and order as a political issue in Scotland (McIvor, 1996) and by the strong commitment to the system of those who work within it. As a result, work with juvenile offenders in Scotland remained largely immune from the policy pressures described above, and even intensive programmes for the most persistent juvenile offenders can still operate on the basis of voluntary attendance (Lobley et al., 2001). In contrast, services for 'adult' offenders (aged 16 and over) tended to be relatively neglected in the years following the 1968 Act. This had abolished the probation service as a separate agency, which meant that adult offenders were in competition for the services of social work departments with other client groups more obviously deserving of help. In recognition of this imbalance, the Scottish Office took over full responsibility for funding community service in 1989 and for the whole range of services for adult offenders in 1991 (McIvor, 1996). This enabled greater specialisation in work with adult offenders, and the revival of activity in this field was supported by the introduction of National Standards (Social Work Services Group, 1991) noticeably more favourable to the values and methods of social work than were the Home Office's first version of National Standards for probation (Home Office, 1992), let alone the subsequent versions (Home Office, 1995, 2000a), with their emphasis on the strict enforcement of orders and the management of risk. Nevertheless, and despite some important legal differences (including, during the 1990s, a greater scope for discretionary release from prison), social work with adult offenders in Scotland came to resemble practice south of the border more closely than before, while work with juveniles continued to be carried out in a legal context which enabled it to proclaim without embarrassment the virtues of help and support as valid aims of practice.

After the 1991 Act

The relevant parts of the Criminal Justice Act 1991 were implemented in October 1992. Almost immediately, there came a chorus of complaint from powerful and authoritative figures, among them the Lord Chief Justice. It was claimed that the Act had been introduced without proper consultation and that its provisions to restrict the use of custody were illogical and unworkable (Feaver and Smith, 1994). The government hastened to amend it, by the Criminal Justice Act of 1993, amid increasingly extravagant declarations of the virtues of a punitive criminal justice policy – which, in a sign of what was to come, went largely unopposed by the Labour opposition. The 1993 Act, reversing the 1991 Act's attempt to restrict the use of custody, allowed courts to combine as many offences as they wished to arrive at a total measure of seriousness, and to treat a previous criminal record as an aggravating factor. The 1991 Act was further eroded by the 1994 Criminal Justice and Public Order Act, which removed the general requirement to consider a presentence report before imposing a custodial sentence. The Crime (Sentences) Act 1997 effectively completed the Conservatives' reversal of their own previous policy, with its provision for statutory minimum sentences for some repeat offenders; it also removed the requirement that offenders should consent to the imposition of a community penalty (probation order, community service order or combination order).

These measures led directly to a rapid increase in the prison population, setting a trend which continued into the twenty-first century. The Home Office (1993) found that, in the first few months after the implementation of the 1991 Act, it was beginning to achieve the desired effect: less use was being made of custodial sentences, and the prison population was falling. This nascent trend was reversed, however, even before the 1993 Act became law, as sentencers attended to the change of political line, and the next three years saw the fastest ever rise in the proportionate use of custodial sentences (Greenhorn, 1996). In 1993 the average daily prison population in England and Wales was 44,552; in 2000 it was 64,402 (lower than in 1998, as a result of the early release of some prisoners under electronically monitored home detention curfews, introduced by the 1998 Crime and Disorder Act). On 31 August 2001 the population in prison was 67,054 (all figures from the prison service website and from www.homeoffice.gov.uk/rds/prisons1.html). The rhetoric of the 1991 Act may not have been much to social workers' taste, with its talk of just deserts and probation as a form of punishment in the community, but in view of what subsequently happened it became easier to identify its virtues.

New Labour and criminal justice

The Labour government that came to power in 1997 maintained its predecessor's enthusiasm for new criminal justice legislation and related initiatives, covering both young and adult offenders, and containing major implications for social work practice. In the adult field, the Criminal Justice and Court Services Act of 2000 abolished local probation services and established a National Probation Service with 42 regions, coterminous with police force areas. It renamed probation orders 'community rehabilitation orders', community service orders 'community punishment orders', and combination orders (logically) 'community punishment and rehabilitation orders'. In section 53 it contained a provision, yet to be implemented, that the default sentence for people convicted of a breach of any of these community penalties should be imprisonment, a measure likely to lead to a further dramatic increase in the prison population. These changes to the context of probation work fell short of realising the worst fears of some practitioners, that the probation and prison services would be amalgamated in a single correctional service, a possibility considered but rejected by the wide-ranging *Prisons – Probation Review* (Home Office, 1998). The government was nevertheless committed to the promotion of much closer working links between the two services, as was clear from its revision of National Standards (Home Office, 2000a), and to the strict enforcement of orders (offenders are allowed only one 'unacceptable' failure to comply with the requirements of an order in any twelve-month period before action for breach). The 2000 Act also allowed for a further extension of electronic monitoring of orders and licences, which was to be piloted in three areas from the autumn of 2001. In the same year the Home Office published a review of the sentencing framework established by the 1991 Act (Home Office, 2001). It recommended that a main element of the framework be formally discarded, and that sentences should increase in severity in cases of repeated offending; it also recommended that all released prisoners should be subject to a period of statutory supervision. The document acknowledged that the proposals on sentencing could drive the prison population still further upwards if there were not some reduction in sentencers' use of imprisonment for less serious offences committed by less persistent offenders.

The Labour government was still more active in relation to young offenders. Its first policy statement on this, *No More Excuses* (Home Office, 1997), appeared only a few months after its election. The paper introduced a number of themes which were to recur in subsequent legislation and policy initiatives. Principal among these was that there were to be no more excuses either for young people's offending or for the failures of the youth justice system to respond to it effectively. This meant not just that the system should become more efficient – that delays between arrest and sentence should be minimised, for example – but that the policy of diversion should be finally abandoned. Instead, children and young people had a positive right to a quick and effective response to their offending (Goldson, 2000). Cautions were to be replaced by a system of reprimands and formal warnings (at most one of each for any young person). Under the 1999 Youth Justice and Criminal Evidence Act, young people convicted in court for the first time were normally to be made subject to a 'referral order', which was effectively to replace the conditional discharge; an active form of intervention was to replace minimum intervention. Referral orders (Haines, 2000) contained elements of restorative justice and the involvement of lay people that might have made them attractive to social workers, but the fear of net-widening – drawing young people needlessly into a punitive system – tended to outweigh appreciation of these positive innovations in the professional and academic communities.

The new government's main legislative effort on young offenders was the 1998 Crime and Disorder Act. This was greeted with almost universal hostility by social workers and commentators sympathetic to social work and its values (see the chapters in Goldson, 1999), because the dominant elements in the Act were interpreted as punitive and repressive, not only of children but of their parents. The Act went further than any previous legislation in making it possible for courts to lock chidren up, and its implementation was accompanied by the arrival of the first Secure Training Centre for children under 14 (Secure Training Centres were created by the 1994 Criminal Justice and Public Order Act). For older young offenders, the Act introduced the detention and training order, which sought to concieve of a period in custody and a period on licence as a single sentence. It abolished the presumption of '*doli incapax*' – incapable of crime – for children aged 10–13; henceforth they were not to be thought of as any less responsible for their actions than older children. It introduced a wide range of new orders to supplement the existing supervision orders and, for those aged 16–17, probation and community service orders – action plan orders, anti-social behaviour orders, child safety orders, reparation orders; it also gave local authorities powers to introduce child curfews, and, for the parents of young offenders, created a power to make training in parenting compulsory (parenting orders). Under the 2000 Criminal Justice and Court Services Act, any of the new orders, and the post-release part of a detention and training order, could in principle be supported by the use of electronic monitoring.

The hostile, even despairing, response of many commentators was understandable. But there were elements of the government's policy, and even parts of the Act itself, that suggested that the government's approach was not based solely on an ideologically driven desire to show how tough it was on crime. All the new orders were initially introduced on a 'pilot' basis, with built-in evaluation, suggesting that the government was serious about pursuing policies that were evidence-based and in line with – in the contemporary jargon – 'What Works'. The Act also departed from the tenor of Conservative legislation in its emphasis on the importance of 'partnership' in dealing with young people's offending, and in its interest in preventive work. It required the police and local authorities to establish crime and disorder partnerships and to conduct crime and disorder 'audits', from which a strategy for the prevention of youth crime was to be developed. It also established Youth Offending Teams (YOTs), again initially on a pilot basis (Holdaway et al., 2001), which were an attempt to promote coordinated, 'joined-up' policies and practices for young people in trouble, and included not only social workers, probation officers and the police but staff from education departments and health authorities. To promote consistency and the spread of what it regarded as good practice, the Act created a new agency, the Youth Justice Board (YJB), with a substantial budget and the power to take initiatives not requiring new legislation. One of the new orders introduced by the Act, the drug treatment and testing order (available for adult as well as young offenders, and requiring the offender's consent), was a genuinely innovative measure that allowed a flexible response to problem drug use among offenders: while it entailed a high level of surveillance, it allowed practitioners to recognise that users of illegal drugs were unlikely to be able to achieve instant abstinence, and – through provision for regular reviews of progress – involved sentencers in the process of treatment and change (Turnbull et al., 2000). All these elements of the Act suggested a more holistic understanding of the problem of young people's offending than is implied by a simply punitive response.

Other New Labour initiatives on crime and criminality prevention were less publicised, possibly because they lent themselves less obviously to incorporation in a rhetoric of discipline, enforcement and punishment (Toynbee and Walker, 2001). These reflected the government's interest in improving conditions in the poorest areas of the country, and amounted to an almost covert redistribution of resources (open redistribution through progressive taxation being regarded as politically unacceptable). Examples of such initiatives are the New Deal for Communities programme, intended to revitalise poor post-industrial neighbourhoods with high levels of crime and disorder, the establishment of Education Action Zones, and the reformulation of youth and community work as 'Connexions', with the specific aim of guiding young 'drop-outs' back into mainstream educational and vocational services. All these measures were concrete examples of what the government's commitment to 'social inclusion' could mean in practice. Perhaps most significant for social work was the Sure Start programme. Comprising 250 schemes in the most deprived and poorest electoral wards, Sure Start provided a range of resources, including intensive health visiting and preschool education, for mothers-to-be and mothers of young children. It provided a good example of evidence-based policy, since its components were those which American research suggested were likely to be most fruitful in reducing delinquency and other social harms over the long term (for a summary, see Nuttall, 1998). It was also the opposite of the 'quick fix' often demanded in crime reduction, which makes such visible changes as closed circuit TV (CCTV) cameras and other measures to increase surveillance and security so attractive to officials who need to be seen to be doing something about crime: Sure Start could only demonstrate results after about fifteen years. It is therefore an unusual example of a long-term effort at reducing the risk of crime and delinquency, and, because it uses social rather than situational methods, it provides an opportunity for the deployment of social work skills and values in the crime reduction field. Related programmes and a national childcare strategy confirmed the Labour government's intention to be much more active than its predecessor in supporting parents, and, in the Care Leavers Act 2000 and the 'Quality Protects' programme (DoH, 1998c), there were signs that children unable to live at home might also benefit from a policy of social inclusion.

The balance sheet

Under the Labour governments from 1997, then, there were examples of changes from the policies of the immediately preceding Conservative govern- ment as well as – perhaps more obviously – instances of continuity. The changes included a revival and indeed an intensification of the commitment to improved interagency cooperation which had been a prominent theme of Home Office policy in the late 1980s and early 1990s; this was exemplified by the creation of YOTs, the statutory requirement for crime and disorder partnerships, the creation of the YJB, the encouragement of closer working between the probation and prison services, and the interdisciplinary staffing of Sure Start programmes and related initiatives. Crime, especially youth crime, was no longer treated solely as a symptom of individual or familial wickedness or weakness, but as the product of an interplay of personal, family, social and environmental factors, including poverty and educational disadvantage. There was a further change of emphasis in the government's determination to promote evidence-based practice and encourage its dissemination through new agencies that provided central direction and control – the YJB and the National Probation Directorate.

In other ways, however, the direction of previous policy was maintained and in some cases followed with still more enthusiasm. Examples of such continuity included the government's lack of interest (with some qualifications) in reducing the use of custody for either young or adult offenders; indeed, a new emphasis on the need for custodial regimes to be positive and constructive encouraged the belief that prisons and similar institutions could be vehicles for constructive change, not just for punishment and containment. Again, in its emphasis on the need for community penalties and licences to be strictly supervised and rigorously enforced, the government maintained the position of its predecessor, and indeed strengthened it. The encouragement of electronic monitoring – in Scotland as well as England and Wales – as a means of enhancing the effectiveness of super- vision threatened by 2001 to make curfews and other forms of control, such as voice verification, routine elements of orders and licences, despite the ambiguity of the evidence on their effectiveness (especially over periods of several months) and the doubts expressed by some about the impact of the dramatic increase in private sector involvement in the delivery of sentences that such an expansion entailed (Lobley and Smith, 2000; Dodgson et al., 2001). The emphasis on control and discipline applied equally to young offenders, most strikingly in the

Intensive Supervision and Surveillance Programme (ISSP) announced in 2001 by the YJB. The guidance to magistrates on the Board's website explained that the programme would provide for a minimum of 25 hours a week of contact time with offenders for three months, and that the programme – normally to be implemented as part of a supervision order – was designed for persistent young offenders who had been charged or warned for offending on four or more occasions in the previous 12 months, and had previously been sentenced to a community penalty or to custody. For the programme to be feasible, it had to be possible to monitor offenders for 24 hours a day, through electronic monitoring or voice verification. The intensity and duration of supervision under the ISSP was claimed by the Board to be justified by evidence on effectiveness, but the basis for this claim is not clear: evidence from an evaluation of a Scottish programme requiring a similar amount of contact suggests that a high failure rate is probable (Lobley and Smith, 1999).

The Labour government's policies, then, both created new opportunities for social work with offenders or potential offenders in a preventive and developmental context and maintained an emphasis on risk management (Kemshall, 1998), enforcement and surveillance that threatened to leave little room in the context of the formal criminal justice system for the help, care and support that social workers have traditionally sought to provide to offenders, albeit usually in the context of legally enforceable orders. A broad commitment to social inclusion was accompanied by specific measures that seemed likely to increase the exclusion of known offenders, most obviously by the ultimately exclusionary device of custody. The National Probation Directorate and the YJB were both, among other things, designed to ensure that the scope for deviation by probation officers and social workers from nationally prescribed forms of practice was strictly limited. It is, however, worth remembering in this context that the relationship between legislation, policy and practice is not a simple one: it is usual to think of legislation as marking the beginning of something new, but in some cases it may be better to think of it as representing the end of a process (Smith, 1984; Gelsthorpe and Morris, 1994), the high-water mark of a particular strand of thinking, after which a reaction is to be expected. The fate of the 1991 Act can be viewed in this way, as can that, twenty years before, of the 1969 Children and Young Persons Act. The first version of this chapter, written in 1997, included a hopeful speculation that the same might turn out to be true of the 1997 Crime (Sentences) Act. It did not. It is nevertheless also worth remembering that social work practice itself was among the major influences on policy until the early 1990s: the 1982 Criminal Justice Act built on existing probation practice in extending the range of conditions which could be attached to probation orders (Raynor, 1985); the Home Offfice (1988b) explicitly endorsed developments in juvenile justice social work and encouraged the application of the same principles to adult offenders (Blagg and Smith, 1989); and social workers were among the advocates of a move 'back to justice' (or to just deserts) in the late 1970s and early 1980s (Morris et al., 1980). Social workers had a substantial influence on policy throughout the 1980s, even though the results were not always quite what they would have wished; they should therefore not despair of having some influence in future.

Working with young offenders

In their summary of developments in juvenile justice in England and Wales since the 1969 Children and Young Persons Act, Cavadino and Dignan (1992) suggest that a period of 'system disaster' (1969–82) was followed by a period of 'systems management', and that, during the latter period, it was plausible to claim that juvenile justice underwent a 'successful revolution'. The aims of this section are: first, briefly to summarise what the main elements of that revolution were and assess how far the claim of success is justified; and second, to discuss what seem to be the most important issues facing social work with young offenders in the early twenty-first century and what lessons could be drawn from the experience of the 1980s.

In spirit if not in the detail of its letter, the 1969 Children and Young Persons Act was broadly in line with the Social Work (Scotland) Act of 1968, but its effects were very different. During the 1970s, instead of becoming more welfare-oriented, the juvenile justice system became more dedicated to punishment; instead of an enhanced role for social work, the decade saw a reduction in social work's involvement with juvenile offenders and in its credibility and status. The use of community-based supervision declined while the use of custody massively increased, from 6 per cent of sentences in 1970 to 12 per cent of sentences in 1978 (Cavadino and Dignan, 1992: 206). The proportion of care orders overall declined (a sign of reduced faith in social work), while the number of children in secure accommodation increased from 150 in 1971 to well over 500 in 1981 (Muncie, 1984). What is strange, in retrospect, is that it took until the end of the 1970s for anyone to recognise that the juvenile justice system had not fallen victim to 'an unconscionable softness' (Cavadino and Dignan, 1992: 205), but rather to an unprecedented harshness.

One of the first and most influential critiques of what had gone wrong was Thorpe et al.'s (1980) advocacy of targeted community-based resources which would provide intensive forms of supervision, with a focus on offending as the reason for social workers' involvement, for serious or persistent offenders, combined with what came to be known as 'systems management'. The latter entailed understanding the 'tariff' of sentencing in local juvenile justice systems and trying to manage it by consistent efforts to divert all but the most persistent offenders, through liaison with the police to increase cautioning, and recommending non-interventionist, or minimally interventionist, measures for juveniles, at the early stages of a career in the courts. The argument was that well-intentioned recommendations for supervision and care for minor or transient offenders could quickly lead to the exhaustion of welfare measures in cases where offending turned out to be persistent, thus easing the passage into custody. The naiveté of social workers was thus held partly responsible for the 'system disaster'. These arguments were reinforced by central government initiatives, including the support for cautioning and the restrictions on the use of custody described above. The Department of Health also announced, in January 1983, that £15 million would be made available to voluntary organisations to develop 'intermediate treatment' facilities which would allow a higher proportion of persistent offenders to remain in the community. The intention was to shift the balance of community resources from ill-defined 'preventive' work to more focused and specialised services for young people at risk of care or custody (Bottoms et al., 1990). There is also no doubt that the arguments of Thorpe and his colleagues resonated with the concerns of many practitioners and local managers. For managers, there was the promise of a reduction in the costs of residential care (largely discredited since the mid-1970s as a means of reducing delinquency (Cornish and Clarke, 1975)); for practitioners, there was a new rationale for social work's presence in juvenile justice and a new hope that it could be made effective.

During the 1980s, social workers specialising in juvenile justice developed a distinct and theoretically coherent form of practice which combined a consistent commitment to diversion and minimum intervention with increasingly sophist-icated face-to-face work with the most persistent juvenile offenders. They also developed an unmistakable sense of comradeship and shared purpose, exemplified in the formation of what became the National Association for Youth Justice. There were critics, of course, of the 'minimalist radicalism' of the system management approach and the alleged 'Pavlovian behaviourism' of offending-focused work (Pitts, 1988). Some practitioners certainly embraced a more rigorous version of the 'justice model' ('Do as little as possible because anything you do is likely to be harmful') than Thorpe et al. (1980) had ever imagined (Raynor, 1993; Smith, D., 1995): paradoxically, some of the most assured and confident social work practice, and some of the most effective in pure 'systems management' terms, was based on the conviction that social work had been shown not to 'work'.

By the start of the 1990s, there were some signs that the enthusiasm and commitment which had fired the energies of social work in juvenile justice were beginning to wane. Local authorities were increasingly conscious of other prior-ities and the need to provide resources to more 'deserving' client groups under the NHS and Community Care Act 1990, with its emphasis on ensuring value for money and staying within budgets. The attractions of allowing the prison service to bear the burden of dealing with recidivist young offenders started to become more apparent. The 1991 Criminal Justice Act's abolition of the juvenile court threatened to disrupt established relations between social workers and courts and required the renegotiation of responsibilities between social services departments and the probation service. From 1993 on, as described above, the coherence of policy began to break up, and youth justice social workers found themselves in a less politically supportive environment than they had been used to. At least in some areas, the coherence of practice was also threatened, as tasks such as acting as an 'appropriate adult' under the Police and Criminal Evidence Act 1984 came to demand more of workers' time, and new areas of practice began to develop in response to anxieties about the adequacy of existing services, such as the growth of (highly labour-intensive) remand fostering and remand management schemes (NACRO, 1996). To some extent, youth justice workers were the victims of their own achievements. The very success of diversion meant that some well-resourced youth justice centres, including those in 'custody-free zones' (Rutherford, 1986), looked rather short of customers by the early 1990s, and this attracted the suspicious attention of hard-pressed staff in social services departments. Should they not be working with more young offenders, if the local authority was to get value for money? By the mid-1990s, even the best projects were under pressure to dilute the principles of diversion and offending-focused practice. By 'best' is meant projects that were well resourced and had skilled and experienced staff, with a high level of contact and credibility with other agencies, and skills in managing conflicts of interest (Blagg et al., 1988). Such projects adopted an activist, interventionist style in court, providing clear, well-focused presentence reports that promised nothing that could not be performed; and their direct work with young people was flexibly structured, attentive to the young people's needs, and delivered in an environment that conveyed a sense of care, comfort and safety. The creation of YOTs and the other innovations of the 1998 Crime and Disorder Act brought a revival of resources, but in a context that seriously constrained practice that did not embody the new principles of early intervention, close surveillance and rigorous enforcement.

Meanwhile in Scotland

The different political climate in Scotland allowed social work with young offenders to continue to develop in a very different legal context. Almost incomprehensibly to the newly arrived visitor from south of the border, and in stark contrast with the assumptions behind the Intensive Supervision and Surveillance Programme, work with even the most persistent offenders can still be carried out on a voluntary basis, with the full support of the relevant agencies. This is the case, for example, with the Freagarrach Project in central Scotland, which works with the most persistent juvenile offenders in the region (Lobley et al., 2001). The absence of statutory constraints and the willingness of others in the system, including the police and the Reporter to the Children's Hearings, to allow the project to experiment and manage the young people's problems in flexible and creative ways make for a striking contrast with even the best practice now to be found in England and Wales. While all projects cannot be equally successful (Lobley and Smith, 1999), the policy context in Scotland remains one that places the welfare of young people, including young offenders, at its core. An advisory group reviewed youth crime policies in 2000 and recommended that the scope of the Children's Hearing System be extended to cover 16- and 17-year-old offenders (Scottish Executive, 2000a); its recommendations were accepted by the Scottish Executive, and plans for implementation were developed during 2001. The system was thus destined to become more, not less, welfare-oriented, in dramatic contrast with trends south of the border.

Working with adult offenders

The main agency involved (in England and Wales) in work with adult offenders – the probation service – officially shed its long-established links with social work in the late 1990s, at least as far as qualifying training was concerned (Dews and Watts, 1994), and become something other than a social work agency. What that something will be is still not completely clear, but there is no doubt that the probation service is now expected to be much more concerned with risk management and the supervision and enforcement of community penalties, and much less concerned with helping, supporting and rehabilitating offenders than in the past. There is, however, a paradox here, because at the very time when it was losing the confidence of ministers, as penal policy shifted in the ways described above, the probation service was beginning to regain confidence in itself and its capacity to help offenders to change. Social work, or something very like it, was beginning to look as if it 'worked', just as policy-makers had decided that social work was the last thing they wanted.

The origins of the gloomy faith that 'nothing works' have often been described (for example, Raynor et al., 1994; McGuire, 1995), and there is no need to repeat the story here. Suffice it to say that pessimism as well as optimism can be naive, and the widespread belief that nothing made any difference to offenders' likelihood of reoffending, which characterised the probation service and other agencies between, roughly, 1975 and 1990, was no more rational than the earlier belief that it was somehow obvious that well-intentioned and hard-working people would produce the desired results. Nevertheless, the jolt which the probation service felt from the negative findings of the IMPACT experiment (Folkard et al., 1976), which seemed to show that 'intensive treatment' was less effective than everyday probation supervision, provoked some probably overdue new thinking about the aims and purposes of probation. One of the first and most impressive examples of this was the 'non-treatment paradigm' of Bottoms and McWilliams (1979). They argued that treatment on the medical model was neither ethically nor empirically defensible. In place of treatment, they argued for the provision of 'appropriate help'; in place of expert diagnosis by the probation officer, they proposed a shared assessment of needs and problems; and in place of the 'client's dependent need' (of which the client might be perfectly unconscious), they suggested that the basis for social work intervention should be a collaboratively defined task.

In reviewing the non-treatment paradigm fifteen years later, Raynor and Vanstone (1994) argued that research on effectiveness since 1979 meant that its proposals for replacing the medical model needed to be revised. Thus 'appropriate help', which for Bottoms and McWilliams meant that the client should determine what was to count as helpful, was glossed by Raynor and Vanstone (1994: 402) as 'help consistent with a commitment to the reduction of harm': there are limits to the extent to which client choice can be allowed to determine the nature of social work intervention. Similarly, 'shared assessment' might become 'explicit dialogue and negotiation offering opportunities for informed consent to involvement in a process of change', and the collaboratively defined task was qualified as one which is 'relevant to criminogenic needs and potentially effective in meeting them' (1994: 402). Raynor and Vanstone argued that it was now possible to specify reasonably closely what kinds of work were most likely to be effective in reducing the risk of reoffending and that it followed that to practise in ways which were less likely to be effective was not only wasteful but unethical. The conclusions of the relevant research (McIvor, 1990) can be summarised as follows: other things being equal, work is more likely to be successful if it:

● matches the intensity of intervention with the risk presented by the offender;

● is carried out in the community rather than in an institution;

- focuses on crime-related needs and problems;

- uses methods which are active and participatory;

- recognises the variousness of offenders' problems;

- aims to improve offenders' coping skills;

- has a cognitive-behavioural basis;

- maintains 'programme integrity' (that is, employs methods which are relevant to its stated aims);

- uses properly trained staff who are supported by their agency; and

- is systematically monitored and evaluated.

Set out like this, the list may strike many readers as uncontentious, but the idea that 'something works', that we can more or less specify what this is, and that probation officers might try to adapt their practice accordingly, has not been universally welcomed in the service (for example, Neary, 1992). There may have been some bleak comfort in the belief that nothing worked.

It is also important not to oversell the evidence of effectiveness. The most careful British evaluation of a programme consciously set up to meet the criteria for effectiveness outlined above – the STOP (Straight Thinking on Probation) programme in Mid-Glamorgan – showed promising rates of reconviction for those who had completed the programme one year on, but found that the two-year reconviction rates were no better than predicted (Raynor and Vanstone, 1996; for the reconviction predictor, see Lloyd et al., 1994). The authors suggest that the relatively disappointing two-year results (which were still better than those for a comparison group who had received custodial sentences) might reflect the lack of reinforcement of what had been learned during the programme in one-to-one supervision and the absence of any 'after-care' which would have allowed offenders to return to the programme for further support. The evidence on effectiveness was also limited in scope, since it referred mainly to groupwork programmes with fairly persistent offenders; individual work received less research attention (Underdown, 1996), although some research suggested that the qualities and methods of work associated with a reduced level of offending were similar to those associated with effective social work (Rex, 1999).

In respect of groupwork, the Home Office, and later the National Probation Directorate, took the view that the research findings were clear and decisive enough to justify a highly prescriptive approach to practice (Chapman and Hough, 1998; Underdown, 1998), implemented through a strongly managerial approach. An accreditation panel was established to review all programmes, in the community and in prisons, and bestow or withhold approval according to the panel's assessment of how closely they matched the model derived from effectiveness research. 'Pathfinder' projects were supported by the Home Office with a view to identifying and disseminating the crucial elements of best practice. Probation officers' training, while still located in universities, was subject to tight curricular requirements designed to promote the official version of effectiveness and exclude other forms of practice. It is arguable, however, that the official line on effectivenss is based on an overoptimistic interpretation of the research findings and a simplistic view of their implications for practice. The managerial insistence that programmes should adopt a prescribed content and a standard structure focused entirely on *what* was delivered, and not *how*, although, for example, the evaluation of the Freagarrach project suggested that the way a service is delivered matters, as well as its content: workers' ability to convey care, concern and respect is likely to be a prerequisite for effective learning and cognitive change. Arguably, too, the narrow focus of much of the effectiveness research led to a neglect of 'What Works', or might work, in other aspects of work with offenders. For example, the collection edited by Drakeford and Vanstone (1996) includes discussions of the possibilities of working for change within the criminal justice system and the implications for practice of poverty, unemployment and housing and health problems, all familiar to practitioners as common features of the lives of offenders (Stewart et al., 1994). The following section suggests how social work with offenders might be conceived more broadly, to include social change as well as individual change among its aims, and the conclusion argues for a correspondingly larger view of what should count as effective practice.

Social work and community safety

During the 1990s, in discussions of the aims and purposes of social work with offenders, it became usual to find some reference to victims, actual or potential, and to the responsibilities of social work towards them and towards the communities in which they and the offender-clients of social work live. Successive reports of the British Crime Survey (for example Mirrlees-Black et al., 1996) showed that, for most offences, the victimisation risks are highly concentrated in areas where the poorest and most vulnerable of the population are disproportionately likely to live, and ethnographic work has vividly conveyed the extent of the social and personal damage which high crime rates can cause (Robins, 1992; Campbell, 1993). It is inconceivable, in the light of this knowledge, that social workers should be indifferent to the implications of their work with offenders for the local public – the community of which offenders themselves must be counted as members (Currie, 1988) – and, indeed, the principle that part of the probation service's brief should be 'wider work in the community' featured in the first systematic attempt by the Home Office to define national objectives for the service (Home Office, 1984).

These considerations, and the idea that if something works it is arguably unethical to do something else, have informed recent thinking about what the values of probation practice might be. Nellis (1995a) suggested that the traditional 'personalist' values of social work, such as respect and care for persons, were inadequate as a basis for social work with offenders and that they should be augmented by more social values, including that of community safety (see also James, 1995; Nellis, 1995b; Spencer, 1995). One approach to practice that attempted to move beyond an exclusive concentration on individual offenders was informed by the idea of restorative justice, in the form of victim–offender mediation (Smith et al., 1988; Marshall and Merry, 1990), or as a means of involving members of local communities who had been affected by an offence in its resolution (Celnick, 1985). Despite a waning of government support from the mid-1980s, the practice of victim–offender mediation was maintained into the 1990s, for example as an element of 'caution plus' schemes for juveniles, in which form it won praise from the Audit Commission (1996a) as a positive and economical alternative to prosecution. By the early 1990s, a new theoretical basis for restorative justice had emerged in John Braithwaite's account of 'reintegrative shaming' (Braithwaite, 1989), which implies a more communitarian, less private form of restorative justice than mediation involving only the victim and offender. At first in New Zealand and then in Australia and elsewhere (Braithwaite and Mugford, 1994; Braithwaite, 1995), the family group conference became the model for practitioners interested in a more positive and less stigmatising response to offending, particularly by juveniles.

A family group conference is a vehicle for a ceremony of reintegration as opposed to one of degradation (Braithwaite and Mugford, 1994). The offender and his or her supporters meet the victim and his or her supporters, in the presence of a mediator who will try to guide the meeting towards a responsible reconciliation (McElrea, 1994). Ideally, the offender is shamed not by any deliberate process of humiliation or public denunciation but by being confronted with the victim's suffering and the hurt the offence has caused to his or her own family and friends. Any attempt to add to the shame inherent in the situation would be redundant and probably harmful (Smith et al., 1988). The offender's action is condemned, not the offender him- or herself ('He's a good lad really, although he made a bad mistake'), a principle that reflects the involvement of Quaker and other Christian groups in victim–offender mediation (Burnside and Baker, 1994). The aim is to reach an agreed means of putting right the wrong done by the offence, in which the offender and his or her supporters enter into various commitments intended to ensure that the offending is not repeated. In the process, both victim and offender lose the special outcast status bestowed by their relationship to the offence and are reintegrated as full participating members of the community. Critics have pointed to both conceptual and practical problems in the model (for example, Morris et al., 1993; Blagg, 1997), and the 1980s' projects demonstrated that practitioners need to be clear about their aims, and that successful mediation is a highly skilled activity. All the same, the revival of interest in (and official support for) restorative justice, now provided with a more secure theoretical and empirical foundation, provides an opportunity for social work with offenders to discover a new sense of direction and purpose.

'Community safety' (Home Office, 1991) has been criticised for being an unhelpfully vague term (Pease, 1994), but is now current not just in criminal justice agencies but increasingly in local authorities, and expresses a broad aspiration towards a social good from which few people would dissent. Despite official encouragement over recent years, social work agencies have not always found it easy to identify a distinctive niche in multi-agency initiatives on the prevention of crime (Sampson and Smith, 1992). But the reality of the 'attrition rate', which suggests that only about 2 per cent of crimes with a personal victim produce an offender available to be sentenced (Barclay, 1993), is a reminder of the relative unimportance of questions about sentencing compared with questions about crime prevention, and social work will risk marginalisation if it fails to engage in work on community safety. Social work agencies can bring to community safety programmes knowledge, skills and values without which these programmes would be impoverished. For example, social workers, by virtue of their structural position in the criminal justice system, have long experience of working cooperatively with other agencies and should have the skills to ensure that multi-agency initiatives avoid the pitfalls which lead to failure and frustration – such as a lack of a clear focus, inadequate resources, the absence of authoritative support, uneven levels of commitment, unrealistic expectations and so on (Geraghty, 1991; Raynor et al., 1994: 129–30). Social workers should also have faith in their own knowledge of offenders' lifestyles, the features of their daily experience which are criminogenic, and their patterns of offending – and be willing to share this knowledge and its implications for community safety programmes (Laycock and Pease, 1985). The values associated with social work, including a commitment to the social integration and inclusion of offenders, can also be an important influence on thinking and practice in community safety: purely 'situational' measures aimed at increasing physical security and/or surveillance are not only less effective than was once hoped (Smith, D., 1995), but are also potentially socially divisive and unjust. The voice of social work also needs to be heard to reduce the risk that community safety will slide towards punitiveness and repression (eviction orders, curfews and the like), without any compensating social measures such as support for parents under stress, the provision of services for young people at risk of delinquency and marginalisation, and efforts to reduce school exclusions (Graham and Bowling, 1995). As we saw, Sure Start and related social programmes provide a forum for new developments in social work practice and for a social work agenda that is radically different from that being promoted in the formal criminal justice system.

Community safety is one of a range of activities in which social work agencies must, of necessity, work in partnership with others. Reflecting the emphasis of policy, much work on partnerships has focused on the probation service's relationship with the voluntary or 'independent sector' (Smith et al., 1993; James and Bottomley, 1994; Cross, 1997; Rumgay, 2000). There is a good argument, however, that partnership with other public sector agencies and services is more important if a strategic commitment to community safety is to be more than a rhetorical gesture. The involvement of health services in YOTs is a positive indication that the importance of social work to health issues has been officially recognised: social workers are in contact not only with mentally disordered offenders and those with problems related to drug or alcohol abuse, but, for example, with many young men at high risk of harm from drug misuse, HIV infection and suicide (Farrar, 1996). Another example of imaginative thinking (and action) on partnerships across the public sector is the strategy for young people at risk developed in central Scotland, of which the Freagarrach Project was 'the tip of the iceberg' (Lobley et al., 2001). The strategy was designed to maximise diversion from the formal system of most juvenile offenders: police officers were encouraged to deal informally with minor offenders and to try to encourage them to participate in some positive recreational pursuit, and the police gave Freagarrach access to an information system (updated weekly) which allowed the project to identify the most serious or persistent offenders at any one time and thus offer the project's services to the intended target group. Education departments supported the strategy by providing places in a special unit for young people at Freagarrach, trying to reduce the level of exclusions from school by using special needs teachers to train their colleagues in mainstream education in the management of challenging behaviour, and seconding two teachers to work in the Reporter's Department, where they would be able to intervene quickly and effectively in school-related problems. Reporters and Children's Panel members supported Freagarrach by recognising that very persistent young offenders were unlikely to stop offending overnight. Social work contributed by seconding staff to Freagarrach, encouraging an inclusive style of practice in residential care, and maintaining a flow of appropriate referrals. What was achieved in central Scotland was not unlike what is envisaged for YOTs in England and Wales, and might provide a model for their efforts to develop a coherent cross-agency policy on young offenders.

CONCLUSION

Towards a wider conception of effectiveness

Much of the recent research on effectiveness has been limited by its relative or complete neglect of the ways in which offenders' performance on specific programmes may depend upon aspects of their lives which such programmes are powerless to influence. Thus, while it is widely recognised that most offenders known to social work agencies suffer from a range of stresses and difficulties, mostly associated with poverty and marginalisation, little is known about what works best in interventions designed to help them manage these problems (Stewart et al., 1994). As Thurston (1997) notes, the debate has also tended to neglect issues of gender and masculinity, whose relevance to criminality is empirically and theoretically well established (Newburn and Stanko, 1994). The contribution of social work to community safety will also need to be informed by questions and answers about what counts as effectiveness in, for example, interagency and partnership work, and in crime prevention initiatives generally, in respect of which there is little agreement about what the relevant measures of performance should be (Tilley, 1995). This is not meant as the familiar academic plea for more research, although it is certainly true that social work with offenders went underresearched for too long, largely because it was assumed that the (negative) answers were already known. Nor is it meant to imply that everything can be measured or subjected to a key performance indicator. It is, rather, to argue that the sheer scope of social work with offenders should be more fully recognised when questions are asked about its effectiveness, and that evaluative research should be more than a technical exercise in identifying the outcomes of specific programmes. As evaluation moves into unmapped areas, it will require an extension of the intellectual curiosity and theoretical awareness which have distinguished social work with offenders since the start of the 1980s. Having outgrown both naive optimism and naive pessimism, we can begin to try to answer such questions as: why are males much more likely to offend persistently and seriously than females, and what does this imply for social work practice? Why are some courts more ready to listen to social workers than others? Is this a quality of the courts or the social workers? Are the theoretical claims for restorative justice and reintegrative shaming borne out in practice? What is it that social work has distinctively to contribute to making community safety programmes work? Is our intuition that some social workers are better than others correct? What makes them better, and what can we learn from them? Some of the answers may be uncomfortable for some social workers, but then social work with offenders has never been the right job for those in search of a comfortable life.

FURTHER READING

These are all edited collections that give the reader access to a range of topics and intellectual approaches.

Bottoms, A.E., Gelsthorpe, L. and Rex, S. (eds) (2001) *Community Penalties: Change and Challenges* (Cullompton, Willan). An up-to-date, authoritative and varied collection.

Drakeford, M. and Vanstone, M. (eds) (1996) *Beyond Offending Behaviour* (Aldershot, Arena). A challenging and critical collection, with useful practice-based comments by the editors on each chapter.

Duff, P. and Hutton, N. (eds) (1999) *Criminal Justice in Scotland* (Aldershot, Dartmouth). Covers a wide variety of topics and provides some insight into how and why things are different in Scotland.

Goldson, B. (ed.) (1999) *Youth Justice: Contemporary Policy and Practice* (Aldershot, Ashgate). Critical essays on various aspects of a rapidly changing scene.

McGuire, J. (ed.) (1995) *What Works: Reducing Reoffending* (Chichester, Wiley). A handy collection bringing together evidence on effectiveness and suggesting how different forms of practice could be evaluated.

Concluding Comment: Past, Present and Future of Social Work

Robert Adams, Lena Dominelli and Malcolm Payne

Now, then and when: the need for critical practice

As we practise and study social work, we are in the 'now'. Inevitably, we are conscious that the present builds on the past and looks to the future. This is because both in practice and in understanding social work, as a profession and as an activity, we cannot deny what has formed our 'now'. Also, since all social work has purposes, it must look forward. Building on the past means changing some of it; because to build is to change, However, building always implies that the foundations and layout of the past form our present. Perhaps you have played one of the computer games that involves building cities, hospitals or theme parks for simulated people to live, work and play in. In these games, current pressures always make it difficult to find the time to change the basic road system, or the building structures, so we are always constrained by previous decisions. On the other hand, concentrating on planning a more organised future means that current crises may overwhelm us. Historians can point to the ancient field boundaries and streets that affect the layout of our modern towns, while strategic planners have to be sure that they work from the strengths and weaknesses in the present situation, rather than being unrealistic about where they start from.

In the same way, we have somehow to manage the present within our practice, while keeping a strategy in mind for future change and dealing with the constraints and opportunities of the past that structure our present efforts. This chapter – and this book – moves beyond acknowledging the importance of the past for our present efforts, beyond the constraints of the present, beyond prescriptions for the future and proposes that if we are going to take action within our practice we must always maintain a critical view of the past, present and future of social work. This affects the professional and agency context of our practice and the practice itself. A critical view of past, present and future is essential to good practice because of the way they interact. We must be able to think out when we must keep the past or change it, when we must focus on the present or avoid its constraints and when we must reach out for the future or move cautiously towards it.

This book has, therefore, highlighted how the nature of social work always presents problems and issues to be considered and debates about contexts for practice (Part I) and approaches to practice (Part II) remain unresolved and unfinished. Part III, though, shows that issues and uncertainties provide both opportunities for creative practice and contexts that control, constrain and shape our practice. Many of the chapters have been concerned in one way or another with the twin, but sometimes opposed, themes of continuity and change. We are likely to see some of these continuities and changes as positive, others as negative, others again as not entirely one or the other. Our position in discussions and controversies about them depends on our political stance and value position. Some aspects of our values are entirely personal, others cannot be dissociated from our practice and that of others.

The values associated with social work, explored in Part I, are particularly associated with its traditions and distinctiveness. They introduce moral, social and political dimensions to every aspect of theory and practice. Equally, they are constant guides to present actions, because they have continuing relevance to every decision we make. Then again, they condition the future because our values influence the choices that we make about our purposes.

We cannot forget either the past of social work or that of the people we encounter while we practice. Part I shows that how social work was formed creates and constructs our present practice and organisation. The theories considered in Part II show how different ideas can transform those contexts to provide alternative ways of practising. The constant linkage and interaction between past, present and future in this book draws attention to the ways in which hopes and plans for the future continually alter our present interpretation of the constraints and possibilities to be found in the past. Although the past is amenable to examination, this is inevitably coloured by our interpretations of it. Similarly, the future is still in our minds because it lies in our ideas and plans. The crucial aspect of linking past and future, therefore, is our interpretations, which are always of the 'now' but inevitably interact with the past and our ideas for the future.

Thus, there can never be certainty and clarity of past, present or future, because the past is indistinct and overlaid by interpretation, we are bound up in the currency of the present and the future is yet to be. We can see that various factors influence these different aspects of time. But the direction that social work takes in the future is not determined by the past. Those involved can shape it in the present. The dominant ideas about the direction of health and welfare policies and practices are subject to change. We can take action individually and collectively, campaign, protest and resist where we regard it as necessary. We can all act to contribute to the development of future values, approaches and practice. Some of us may become carers or users of services and we have power to act in those capacities as well.

At the outset of this chapter, we have to acknowledge that even what we think of as the past – set in concrete as a student once described it – cannot be taken for granted. That so-called concrete is a subject for endless debate. What is it? What is it composed of? Is it as solid, unchanged and unchanging as it seems? How was it formed? Can we ever be certain we have described it adequately and comprehensively?

Views of histories

> Reality is a question of perspective; the further you get from the past, the more concrete and plausible it seems – but as you approach the present, it inevitably seems more and more incredible. (Rushdie, 1982: 165)

With these words, referred to more briefly in Chapter 23, Salman Rushdie's novel about the emergence of Indian independence from the preceding history of civil disturbances delicately reminds us of the intrinsic paradoxes in the way we regard our past and our present. Some aspects of social work, such as civil disturbances, concern those aspects of people's lives which arouse strong feelings and views. It is often politicised, debated and controversial. Other aspects of social work are no less problematic, because they are hidden and concern people who commonly are neglected or ignored. So we can add to the paradoxes identified by Rushdie four further barriers between us and the so-called authentic account of the past and present of social work.

The first barrier is that our views of the past are framed by our assumptions and values. Just as people selecting a frame for a picture impose on it a particular set of assumptions and affect the way it is viewed, so our history is affected by how we frame it. It is easy to take history for granted as evolutionary and developmental, because we can understand how a particular decision came to be taken. That histories can be regarded from different perspectives is particularly relevant in social work. A brother shoves his sister and causes her to fall downstairs. Which is 'true'? Is it the brother's explanation of the 'accident', or the sister's view that the shove was 'intentional' because she won an argument, or their father's interpretation of high spirits, or the mother's interpretation of the boy's lack of physical control? Behind those potential explanations are views of the world and the past, present and future: of the relations between the sexes and how they arise from gendered assumptions about how boys and girls should behave. Perhaps most families nowadays would not openly say that the father should always be right, but interpersonal relationships in a family, based on historical assumptions, might still linger in how people actually behave. Whose history comes to dominate? It might be the mother's because she manages the family's daily life, or the father's because of his physical power. If a social worker comes to investigate, she will select for her record particular explanations, and her selection will determine whether this incident contributes to the family being put on the 'at-risk' register. However, that history will not prevent the sister who fell down the stairs relying on her own view of history in deciding how to deal with her brother, her parents and the social worker in future.

Similarly, for social work as a profession and activity, different views of the past and present of social work lead to distinctive portrayals of its nature and contexts in social policy and the social sciences. Liberal views might see it as a contributor to the stability of the state and emphasise the consciences of philanthropists and reformers as the main motivators for progress. Alternative views might adopt a range of socialist and radical perspectives, arguing the inadequacy of progressive zeal and humanitarian enlightenment as an explanation, regarding social work as a contributor to curbing the discontent of the lower classes, including the 'underclass', and contributing to the oppression and control of those classes by the state. Counter views from those in the 'new' social movements might bring into the analysis the understandings and experiences of people receiving services, such as survivors of mental health treatment or people with disabilities, for whom state control and intervention through social work and allied professions provide the stimulus for resistance, challenging oppression and endorsing empowerment. Postmodern views might interpret social work in any particular historical context as the product of the interaction of all these aspects of social work's position in society. These varied conceptions of social work lead to different emphases being put on different aspects and issues.

The second barrier between our present interpretations of the past and the events that comprise those interpretations is that our past is comprised of histories not history. There is no single, agreed history. There are histories. At school, some of us were taught 'the history' of a country with reference to its rulers. Nowadays, pupils are encouraged to put themselves into the position of various people occupying different strata of past societies and, using historical data – some based on diaries and reminiscences – imagine their histories. Social work history is often taught as a triumphant progression from uncertain beginnings to the achievement of its widely recognised role in most welfare states. This makes us despondent about present criticisms of present changes, which seem to move away from the welfare state and question the value of social work. However, there are many incidents which were setbacks in that progression, and different countries treat social work in different ways and organise it in varied structures and subject it to different regulatory regimes. We can see our present position as the beginnings of a downturn, which will lead to the displacement of social work's values in our country, or as one of the setbacks to be overcome, perhaps with the example of people from other countries. We can see the welfare state as a necessary condition of social work flourishing and defend it at all costs, or as a temporary phase of the international economy whose destruction will lead to social work arising in another form, perhaps the social development that has been so useful in developing countries.

The third barrier between our present and our histories is that we are constantly revising these. Histories are provisional, not definitive. Our knowledge of the past of social work is not complete. As new findings emerge, we have to revise our view of the past. This process is replicated when as a social worker we deal with a case and different points of view lead us to revise our assessment of it. It is also true of wider histories. For example, most histories of social work (for example Woodroofe, 1962) focus on the role of the nineteenth-century Charity Organisation Society (COS) as an origin for a set of social work methods that remain popular today. However, Laybourn's (1997) work on guilds of help suggests that there are alternative sources of practice to be uncovered. Why were they not obviously part of our histories already? It may be because the COS was based in the capital city and was run by people from social elites, whose historians dominated early interpretations of social work, while guilds of help started in the provinces and were influenced by municipal and local reformers. Similar points can be made abut the silencing of the impact of the Settlement Movement on the profession. These other explanations provide examples of how power and influence can create particular versions of history. Some of the great revelations about the past of the way children and families have been treated by social work agencies have arisen from uncovering the memories of ordinary people, rather than through official records, which are another form of power. For example, the remarkable work by a student at Nottingham University with Philip Bean followed a chance meeting with a former child of Barnardo's and led to the dramatic exposure of the enforced migration to Australia up to the 1970s of tens of thousands of Barnardo's children and the subsequent abuse of many of them (Bean and Melville, 1990).

Finally, the fourth barrier comes from our realisation that writing history retrospectively, and from people's own accounts, is intrinsically problematic. It may seem obvious but it is still important to note that just as histories written at the time in, say, a diary, may lack the broader perspective of what was going on in the organisation or society, histories written in retrospect cannot be segregated from the hindsight of the backward-looking writer. So, history-taking – as any social worker who has had to interview a person at depth and use this as the basis for an account of their life knows – is notoriously difficult. A good example of these problems is the use of oral history, which is history written in the light of interviewing numbers of people involved in an event or experience. The spirit of Mass Observation in Britain during World War II contributed to Harrison's impressive book *Living Through the Blitz* (Harrison, 1976). Its author pointed out that, although distinctive and unique, oral testimony is not necessarily more authentic than other records. People interviewed afterwards were prone to polish their memories as they told and retold the dramatic bits, responding, perhaps, to the astonishment of their audiences.

So, history-taking and history-making is no more straightforward than any other aspect of our construction of our experiences and perceptions of our pasts and presents. These are points well taken in social work, where we use the skills of interviewing to inform judgements about placing children and adults in households, residential homes and foster homes, and where inquiries and investigations are reliant largely on oral testimony, sometimes years after the alleged event.

Milestones in the past of social work

The past of social work may be problematic but it is marked by a number of events of significance. As we noted above, the significance of these events is likely to be debated endlessly. Not least, events which had earth-shaking significance at the time may have faded into obscurity twenty years later.

It is worth posing the question: what do those who have lived and worked through a particular era now regard as a milestone when they recall it? Everybody's memories will give a different emphasis. We can appreciate this by recalling some of the factors that may be important to social workers who lived through recent periods.

Social workers working in the 1970s, around the time that many current student social workers were born, are likely to recall the impact on policy and practice of the rediscovery of poverty in the early 1960s, the Seebohm Report (1968) and the Children and Young Persons Act 1969. The creation of social services departments and introduction of generic social workers, economic recession and debates about the impact of youth unemployment, long-term unemployment and the social workers' strikes over declining services in local authority budget cuts of the late 1970s will still be real to them.

Social workers active in the 1980s are likely to recall the impact of Conservative government throughout the decade, Thatcherism, the New Right. They might be aware of the Black Report (DHSS, 1980) giving evidence of persistent inequalities in health, which, however, was not broadcast by the Conservative government at the time. Debates developed about whether the universalistic welfare state would be dismantled, the introduction of the contract culture in local government service provision, marketisation, privatisation, the new importance of the voluntary, private and informal sectors in health and welfare provision, the Children Act 1989 and the NHS and Community Care Act 1990.

Social workers in the 1990s may identify in particular the impact of quality assurance, standards and inspection in health and social services. The change of government to New Labour from 1997, the reality of political devolution in Scotland, Wales and Northern Ireland and the growing impact on the UK of legislation in the European Union are all important markers of this period. Trends towards globalisation, changing government policy affecting pensions, social security and benefits for lone parents and disabled people, public private partnerships, the Human Rights Act 1998, legislation in criminal and youth justice and controversies concerning the treatment of refugees and asylum-seekers all had their impact on social work.

Continuities and changes

Many of these events in the past continue to have an impact today. Legislative and policy changes are highlighting the diversity of social work in different settings, but this arises in the context of basic service organisations, social services departments, that recall the experiences of the social workers from the 1970s. The pattern of community care services bears the hallmarks of the marketisation of the 1980s. Child protection work has developed from the early child abuse scandals of the 1970s, through the rise of concern about sexual abuse in the 1980s, and the reform of relations between parents and children attempted by the implementation of the Children Act 1989 in the 1990s.

Yet these arrangements for delivering social work and social services have continued to change. Social services departments are now rarely generic, and more often divided into childcare and adult services divisions. These aspects of service are being realigned with other services, in community mental health trusts, in stronger alliances with the NHS for adult and community care services and the education services for children.

The present also brings changes of its own period. Global changes are emphasising commonalities shared by social workers and social work organisations in different countries. The problems besetting people persist – poverty, criminal violence in the home, sexism, racism, discrimination against disabled people, older people, children, migrants and refugees. However, there are new attempts to devise responses to these longstanding problems. For example, the Connexions service, including personal advisers with roles similar to social work, attempts to respond to alienation and exclusion for unemployed young people by supporting their transition from school to adult life. An old problem, a new service, drawing upon elements of past experience looks forward to new plans, and provides a slightly changed environment for social work to operate in.

Future prospects for social work

These changes that social work is undergoing are never-ceasing, but are the context in which we look to the future. They raise questions: Will social work have a place in health and social care? Will social work lose ground to other professions or new creations such as personal advisers? Will social work gain in importance in particular areas such as mental health and childcare? Despite the fact that social work is in a state of flux and social workers who remain in the job are disillusioned, as Vivienne Cree (Chapter 2) notes, it is probably an exaggeration to describe social work as in a state of crisis.

Nevertheless, we know from crisis theory that change offers both opportunities and risks. Becoming more closely involved in health care and education services offers the chance to increase the concern of health care services for the social needs of patients, for a wider range of social explanations and knowledge to influence the health care. There may be advantages in being more closely associated with a more universal and less stigmatised service than social care has become. On the other hand, social explanations and needs may lose ground to more powerful medical models or educational priorities. The skills and commitment of social workers as they take up new roles in new settings offer the chance for every worker to have an impact, to make a difference not only to the lives of the people whom they work with, but also to the impact that social work might have on the societies in which we live.

Towards a critical view of the past, present and future of social work

We have emphasised in this chapter that it is important to develop a questioning attitude to the past and present and not to take for granted views handed to us as authoritative. The past may be changed in its impact by our present interpretations of it. Our present may have an impact on the future, by the plans we make and our commitment to change.

This is the point at which we leave you, the reader, and invite you to join us in the next stage of the journey – from critical debates about approaches to social work practice, to engaging critically in practice. We undertake this in the companion book to this one: *Critical Practice in Social Work* (Adams et al., 2002).

Bibliography

AASW (2000) *National Code of Ethics*, Australian Association of Social Workers http://www.aasw.asn.au/servicing/index.html.

Abberley, P. (1993) 'Disabled people and "normality"', in Swain, J., Finkelstein, V., French, S. and Oliver, M. (eds) *Disabling Barriers – Enabling Environments* (London, Sage).

Adams, A. (2000) 'Introduction: The challenge of globalisation', in Adams, A., Erath, P. and Shardlow, S. (eds) *Fundamentals of Social Work in Selected European Countries*, Lyme Regis, Russell House Publishing.

Adams, R. (1990) *Self-help, Social Work and Empowerment* (London, Macmillan – now Palgrave Macmillan).

Adams, R. (1994) *Skilled Work with People* (London, Collins).

Adams, R. (1996a) *Social Work and Empowerment*, 2nd edn (London, Macmillan – now Palgrave Macmillan).

Adams, R. (1996b) *The Personal Social Services: Clients, Consumers or Citizens* (London, Longmans).

Adams, R. (1998) *Quality Social Work* (London, Macmillan – now Palgrave Macmillan).

Adams, R. and O'Sullivan, T. (1994) *Social Work With and Within Groups* (Birmingham, BASW Trading).

Adams, R., Allard, S., Baldwin, J. and Thomas, J. (eds) (1981) *A Measure of Diversion? Case Studies in Intermediate Treatment* (Leicester, National Youth Bureau).

Adler, R. (1985) *Taking Juvenile Justice Seriously* (Edinburgh, Scottish Academic Press).

336

Aggleton, P. and Chalmers, H. (1986) *Nursing Models and the Nursing Process* (London, Macmillan – now Palgrave Macmillan).

Ahmad, B. (1990) *Black Perspectives in Social Work* (Birmingham, Venture).

Ahmed, S. (1986) 'Cultural racism in work with Asian women and girls', in Ahmed, S., Cheetham, J. and Small, J. (eds) *Social Work with Black Children and Their Families* (London, Batsford).

Ahmed, S., Cheetham, J. and Small, J. (eds) (1986) *Social Work with Black Children and their Families* (London, Batsford).

Ainsworth, M.D., Blehar, M.C., Walters, E. and Wall, S. (1978) *Patterns of Attachment: Psychological Study of the Strange Situation* (Hillsdale, NJ, Lawrence Erlbaum).

Aldgate, J., Heath, A., Colton, M. and Simm, M. (1993) 'Social work and the education of children in foster care', *Adoption and Fostering*, 17(3): 25–34.

Allan, M., Bhavnani, R. and French, K. (for the Department of Health Social Services Inspectorate) (1992) *Promoting Women: Management Development and Training for Women in Social Services Departments* (London, HMSO).

Allen, I. (ed.) (1988) *Hearing the Voice of the Consumer* (London, Policy Studies Institute).

Altrichter, H., Posch, P. and Somekh, B. (1993) *Teachers Investigate their Work: An Introduction to the Methods of Action Research* (London, Routledge).

AMA (1993) *Local Authorities and Community Development: A Strategic Opportunity for the 1990s* (London, Association of Metropolitan Authorities).

Amato-von Hemert, K. (1994) 'Should social work education address religious issues? Yes!', *Journal of Social Work Education*, 30(1): 7–11.

Anderson, L. and Kinsey, R. (1993) *Cautionary Tales, A Study of Young People and Crime in Edinburgh* (Edinburgh, Criminal Research Unit, Scottish Office).

Andrew, F. (1996) *Not Just Black and White: An Exploration of Opportunities and Barriers to the Development of Black Managers in Public Services* (London, Office for Public Management, 252B Gray's Inn Road, London WC1 8JT).

Anwar, M. (1976) *Between Two Cultures* (London, CRC).

Appleyard, B. (1993) 'Why paint so black a picture?', *Independent*, 4 August.

Askham, J., Henshaw, L. and Tarpey, M. (1993) 'Policies and perceptions of identity', in Evandrou, M. and Arber, S. (eds) *Ageing, Independence and the Life Course* (London, Jessica Kingsley).

Atkinson, D.R. and Hackett, G. (1995) *Counseling Diverse Populations* (Madison, Brown & Benchmark).

Audit Commission (1994) *Seen But Not Heard: Co-ordinating Community Child Health and Social Services for Children in Need* (London, HMSO).

Audit Commission (1996a) *Misspent Youth* (London, Audit Commission).

Audit Commission (1996b) *Balancing the Care Equation: Progress with Community Care* (London, HMSO).

BAAF (1996) *The Children (Scotland) Act 1995: A Training Programme* (London, British Agencies for Adoption and Fostering).

BAC (1985) *Counselling: Definitions and Terms in Use with Expansion and Rationale* (Rugby, British Association for Counselling).

Badham, B. (ed.) (1989) '"Doing something with our lives when we're inside": self-directed groupwork in a youth custody centre', *Groupwork*, **2**(1): 27–35.

Bailey, R. (1988) 'Poverty and social work education', in Becker, S. and MacPherson, S. (eds) *Public Issues, Private Pain: Poverty Social Work and Social Policy* (London, Social Services Insight).

Bailey, R. and Brake, M. (eds) (1975) *Radical Social Work and Practice* (London, Edward Arnold).

Bakhurst, D. and Sypnowich, C. (eds) (1995) *The Social Self* (London, Sage).

Ball, C., Preston-Shoot, M., Roberts, G. and Vernon, S. (1995) *Law for Social Workers in England and Wales* (London, Central Council for Education and Training in Social Work).

Balloch, S, and Taylor, M. (2001) *Partnership Working: Policy and Practice* (Bristol, Policy Press).

Bamford, T. (1990) *The Future of Social Work* (London, Macmillan – now Palgrave Macmillan).

Banks, S. (1995) *Ethics and Values in Social Work* (London, Macmillan – now Palgrave Macmillan).

Banks, S. (1996) 'Youth work, informal education and professionalisation: the issues in the 1990s', *Youth and Policy*, **54**: 13–25.

Banks, S. (2001) *Ethics and Values in Social Work* , 2nd edn (Basingstoke, Palgrave – now Palgrave Macmillan).

Barber, J.G. (1991) *Beyond Casework* (London, Macmillan – now Palgrave Macmillan).

Barclay Committee (1982) *Social Workers: Their Role and Tasks* (London, Bedford Square Press).

Barclay, G.C. (ed.) (1993) *Digest 2: Information on the Criminal Justice System in England and Wales* (London, Home Office).

Barker, R. and Roberts, H. (1993) 'The uses of the concept of power', in Morgan, D. and Stanley, L. (eds) *Debates in Sociology* (Manchester, Manchester University Press).

Barker, W.E., Anderson, R.A. and Chalmers, C. (1994) *Health Trends over Time and Major Outcomes of the Child Development Programme* (Bristol, Early Childhood Development Unit and Belfast, Eastern Health and Social Services Board).

Barn, R. (1990) 'Black children in local authority care: admission patterns', *New Community*, **16**(2): 229–46.

Barn, R. (1993) *Black Children in the Public Care System* (London, Batsford).

Barn, R. (ed.) (1999) *Working with Black Children and Adolescents in Need* (London: BAAF).

Bartlett, H. (1970) *The Common Base of Social Work Practice* (Washington, DC, National Association of Social Workers).

Basu, M. (1997) *The Challenge of Local Feminisms: Women's Movements in Global Perspective.* (Boulder, CO, Westview Press.)

BASW (1975) *A Code of Ethics for Social Work* (rev. 1986 and 1996) (Birmingham, British Association of Social Workers).

BASW (1979) *Clients are Fellow Citizens* (Birmingham, British Association of Social Workers).

Bateman, N. (1995) *Advocacy Skills: A Handbook for Human Service Professionals* (Aldershot, Arena).

Baty, P. (1997) 'Anita takes the plunge in Bath', *Times Higher Education Supplement*, 3 January, p. 5.

Baumrind, D. (1971) 'Current patterns of parental authority', *Developmental Psychology Monographs* 4, **1**(2).

Bean, P. and Melville, J. (1990) *Lost Children of the Empire* (London, Unwin Hyman).

Beck, A.T. (1976) *Cognitive Therapy and the Emotional Disorders* (New York, International Universities Press).

Beck, A.T. and Emery, G. (1985) *Anxiety Disorders and Phobias: A Cognitive Perspective* (New York, Basic Books).

Beck, U. (1992) *Risk Society. Towards a New Modernity* (London, Sage).

Becker, S. (1988) 'Poverty awareness', in Becker, S. and MacPherson, S. (eds) *Public Issues, Private Pain: Poverty Social Work and Social Policy* (London, Social Services Insight).

Becker, S. and MacPherson, S. (1986) *Poor Clients: The Extent and Nature of Financial Poverty Amongst Consumers of Social Work Services* (Nottingham, Nottingham University Benefits Research Unit).

Becker, S. and MacPherson, S. (1988) *Public Issues, Private Pain: Poverty Social Work and Social Policy* (London, Social Services Insight).

Beckford Report (1985) *A Child in Trust* (Wembley, London Borough of Brent).

Belenky, M., Clinchy, B.M., Goldberger, N.R. and Tarule, J.M. (1997) *Women's Ways of Knowing: The Development of Self, Voice, and Mind*, 2nd edn (New York, Basic Books).

Bell, M. (1999) 'Working in partnerhip in child protection: the conflicts', *British Journal of Social Work*, **29**(3): 437–55.

Bennett, G. and Kingston, P. (1993) *Elder Abuse: Concepts, Theories and Interventions* (London, Chapman & Hall).

Bensted, J., Brown, A., Forbes, C. and Wall, R. (1994) 'Men working with men in groups: masculinity and crime', *Groupwork*, 7(1): 37–49.

Benzeval, M., Judge, K. and Whitehead, M. (eds) (1995) *Tackling Inequalities in Health: An Agenda for Action* (London, King's Fund).

Beresford, P. and Croft, S. (1993) *Citizen Involvement: A Practical Guide for Change* (London, Macmillan – now Palgrave Macmillan).

Beresford, P. and Croft, S. (1995) 'It's our problem too!: Challenging the exclusion of poor people from poverty discourse', *Critical Social Policy*, **44/45**: 75–95.

Beresford, P. and Harding, T. (1993) *A Challenge to Change* (London, National Institute for Social Work).

Beresford, P. and Trevillion, S. (1995) *Developing Skills for Community Care* (Aldershot, Arena).

Berrueta-Clement, J.R., Schweinart, L.J., Barnett, W.C., Epstein, A.S. and Weikart, D.P. (1984) *Changed Lives: The Effects of the Perry Preschool Program in Youths through Age 19* (Ypsilanti, High Scope Press).

Biehal, N. (1993) 'Participation, rights and community care', *British Journal of Social Work*, **23**(5): 443–58.

Biehal, N., Clayden, J., Stein, M. and Wade, J. (1992) *Prepared for Living? A Survey of Young People Leaving the Care of Three Local Authorities* (London, National Children's Bureau).

Biestek, F.P. (1961) *The Casework Relationship* (London, Allen & Unwin).

Biggs, S., Phillipson, C. and Kingston, P. (1995) *Elder Abuse in Perspective* (Buckingham, Open University Press).

Black Assessors (1994) DipSW 'Consultation a Sham', *Community Care*, October, pp. 13–18.

Blagg, H. (1997) 'A just measure of shame? Aboriginal youth and conferencing in Australia', *British Journal of Criminology*, **37**(4): 481–501.

Blagg, H. and Smith, D. (1989) *Crime, Penal Policy and Social Work* (Harlow, Longman).

Blagg, H., Pearson, G., Sampson, A., Smith, D. and Stubbs, P. (1988) 'Interagency cooperation: rhetoric and reality', in Hope, T. and Shaw, M. (eds) *Communities and Crime Reduction* (London, HMSO).

Blakemore, K. and Boneham, M. (1994) *Age, Race and Ethnicity* (Buckingham, Open University Press).

Blom Cooper, L. (1985) *A Child in Trust* (London, London Borough of Brent).

Bochel, D. (1976) *Probation and After-care: Its Development in England and Wales* (Edinburgh, Scottish Academic Press).

Bolger, S., Corrigan, P., Docking, J. and Frost, N. (1981) *Towards Socialist Welfare Work* (London, Macmillan – now Palgrave Macmillan).

Booth, H. and Mallon, M. (1994) *Return Ticket* (Harpenden, Lennard Publishing).

Booth, T. and Booth, W. (1996) 'Parental competence and parents with learning difficulties', *Child and Family Social Work*, 1(2): 82–6.

Borland, M., O'Hara, G. and Triseliotis, J. (1991) *The Outcome of Permanent Family Placements in Two Scottish Local Authorities* (Scottish Office, Central Research Unit).

Bosanquet, B. (ed.) (1895) *Aspects of the Social Problem* (London, Macmillan – now Palgrave Macmillan).

Bosanquet, B. (1901) 'Meaning of social work', *International Journal of Ethics*, 11, p. 297.

Bosanquet, H. (1906) *The Family* (London, Macmillan – now Palgrave Macmillan).

Bottoms, A.E. (1977) 'Reflections on the renaissance of dangerousness', *Howard Journal of Criminal Justice*, 16, pp. 70–96.

Bottoms, A.E. and McWilliams, W. (1979) 'A non-treatment paradigm for probation practice', *British Journal of Social Work*, 9(2): 159–202.

Bottoms, A.E., Brown, P., McWilliams, B., McWilliams, W. and Nellis, M. (1990) *Intermediate Treatment and Juvenile Justice* (London, HMSO).

Boud, D. and Knights, S. (1996) 'Course design for reflective practice', in Gould, N. and Taylor, I. (eds) *Reflective Learning for Social Work* (Aldershot, Arena).

Bourn, D.F. (1993) 'Over-chastisement, child non-compliance and parenting skills: a behavioural intervention by a family centre worker', *British Journal of Social Work*, 23: 481–9.

Bowes, E. (1998) *Away From Home* (London, Labos Housing Association and Lemos & Crane).

Bowl, R. (1985) *Changing the Nature of Masculinity – A Task for Social Work* (Norwich, University of East Anglia, Social Work Monographs).

Bowlby, J. (1969) *Attachment and Loss*, vol. 1: *Attachment* (New York, Basic Books).

Bowlby, J. (1979) *The Making and Breaking of Affectional Bonds* (London, Tavistock).

Bowlby, J. (1988) *A Secure Base: Clinical Applications of Attachment Theory* (London, Routledge).

Boyatzis, R.E. (1982) *The Competent Manager: A Model for Effective Performance* (Chichester, Wiley).

Bradshaw, J. (ed.) (2001) *Poverty: The Outcomes for Children*. Occasional Paper 26 (London, Family Policy Studies Centre).

Bragg, M. (1996) *Reinventing Influence: How to Get Things Done in a World Without Authority* (London, Pitman Press).

Braithwaite, J. (1989) *Crime, Shame and Reintegration* (Cambridge, Cambridge University Press).

Braithwaite, J. (1995) 'Reintegrative shaming, republicanism and policy', in Barlow, H.D. (ed.) *Crime and Public Policy: Putting Theory to Work* (Boulder, CO, Westview Press).

Braithwaite, J. and Mugford, S. (1994) 'Conditions of successful reintegration ceremonies: dealing with juvenile offenders', *British Journal of Criminology*, **34**(2): 139–71.

Brandon, D. (1995) *Advocacy: Power to People with Disabilities* (Birmingham, Venture Press).

Braye, S. and Preston-Shoot, M. (1990) 'On teaching and applying the law in social work: it is not that simple', *British Journal of Social Work*, **20**(4): 333–53.

Braye, S. and Preston-Shoot, M. (1995) *Empowering Practice in Social Care* (Buckingham, Open University Press).

Braye, S. and Preston-Shoot, M. (1997) *Practising Social Work Law*, 2nd edn (London, Macmillan – now Palgrave Macmillan).

Braye, S. and Preston-Shoot, M. (1999) 'Accountability, administrative law and social work practice: redressing or reinforcing the power imbalance?' *Journal of Social Welfare and Family Law*, **21**(3): 235–56.

Braye, S. and Preston-Shoot, M. (2001) 'Social work practice and accountability', in Cull, L.-A. and Roche, J. (eds) *The Law and Social Work: Contemporary Issues for Practice* (Basingstoke, Palgrave – now Palgrave Macmillan).

Brearley, J. (1991) 'A psychodynamic appraoch to social work, in Lishman, J. (ed.) *Handbook of Theory to Practice Teachers in Social Work* (London, Jessica Kingsley).

Brearley, J. (1995) *Counselling and Social Work* (Buckingham, Open University Press).

Breton M. (1994) 'On the meaning of empowerment and empowerment oriented social work practice', *Social Work with Groups*, **17**(3): 23–38.

Brewer, C. and Lait, J. (1980) *Can Social Work Survive?* (London, Temple Smith).

Brewster, R. (1992) 'The new class? Managerialism and social work education and training', *Issues in Social Work Education*, **11**(2): 81–93.

Briggs, S. (1995) 'From subjectivity towards realism: child observation and social work', in Yelloly, M. and Henkel, M. (eds) *Learning and Teaching in Social Work: Towards Reflective Practice* (London, Jessica Kingsley).

Broad, B. and Fletcher, C. (eds) (1993) *Practitioner Social Work Research in Action* (London, Whiting & Birch).

Broadbent, J., Dietrich, M. and Laughlin, R. (1993) *The Development of Principal-Agent Contracting and Acceptability Relationships in the Public Sector: Conceptual and Cultural Problems* (Sheffield, Sheffield University).

Brook, E. and Davis, A. (eds) (1985) *Women, the Family and Social Work* (London, Tavistock).

Brooks, G., Pugh, A.K. and Schagen, I. (1996) *Reading Performance at Nine* (Buckingham, NFER/Open University).

Brown, A. (1979) *Groupwork* (London, Heinemann).

Brown, A. (1986) *Groupwork*, 2nd edn (Aldershot, Gower).

Brown, A. (1992) *Groupwork*, 3rd edn (Aldershot, Ashgate).

Brown, A. (1994) 'Groupwork in Britain', in Hanvey, C. and Philpot, T. (eds) *Practising Social Work* (London, Routledge).

Brown, A. (1996) 'Groupwork into the future: some personal reflections', *Groupwork* 9(1): 80–96.

Brown, A. and Bourne, I. (1996) *The Social Work Supervisor: Supervision in Community, Day Care and Residential Settings* (Buckingham, Open University Press).

Brown, A. and Clough, R. (eds) (1989) *Groups and Groupings: Life and Work in Day and Residential Centres* (London, Tavistock/Routledge).

Brown, G.W. and Harris, T. (1978) *Social Origins of Depression: A Study of Psychiatric Disorder in Women* (London, Tavistock).

Brown, H.C. (1996) 'The knowledge base of social work', in Vass Vass, A.A. (ed.) *Social Work Competences: Core Knowledge, Values and Skills* (London, Sage).

Brown, R. (1988) *Group Processes: Dynamics Within and Between Groups* (Oxford, Blackwell).

Bryan, B., Dadzie, S. and Scafe, S. (1985) *The Heart of the Race: Black Women's Lives in Britain* (London, Virago).

Bullock, R., Little, M. and Millham, S. (1993) *Going Home: The Return of Children Separated from their Families* (Dartmouth, Dartington Social Research Unit).

Bullock, R., Little, M. and Mount, K. (1999) *Research in Practice: Experiments in Development and Information Design* (Dartington, Dartington Social Research Unit).

Bulman, C. and Burns, S. (2000) 'Preface' in Burns, S. and Bulman, C. (eds) *Reflective Practice in Nursing: The Growth of the Professional Practitioner*, 2nd edn (Oxford: Blackwell Science).

Bulmer, M. (1982) *The Uses of Social Research: Social Investigation in Public Policy-Making* (London, Allen & Unwin).

Bunyan, A. (1987) '"Help, I can't cope with my child": a behavioural approach to the treatment of a conduct disordered child within the natural home setting', *British Journal of Social Work*, 17: 237–56.

Burgess, R. (ed.) (1993) *Educational Research and Evaluation for Policy and Practice* (London, Falmer Press).

Burke, P. and Cigno, K. (1996) *Support for Families: Helping Children with Learning Disabilities* (Aldershot, Avebury).

Burke, P. and Cigno, K. (2000) *Learning Disabilities in Children* (Oxford, Blackwell Science).

Burkitt, I. (1991) *Social Selves: Theories of the Formation of the Personality* (London, Sage).

Burks, H.M. and Stefflre, B. (1979) *Theories of Counseling*, 3rd edn (New York, McGraw-Hill).

Burney, E. (1985) *Sentencing Young People* (Aldershot, Gower).

Burnside, J. and Baker, N. (eds) (1994) *Relational Justice: Repairing the Breach* (Winchester, Waterside Press).

Butler, J. (1990) *Gender Trouble: Feminism and the Subversion of Identity* (London, Routledge).

Butler, S. (1994) '"All I've got in my purse is mothballs!", The Social Action Women's Group', *Groupwork*, 7(2): 163–79.

Butler, S. and Wintram, C. (1991) *Feminist Groupwork* (London, Sage).

Bywaters, E. and McLeod, E. (2001) 'The impact of New Labour health policy on Social Services: a new deal for service users' health?', *British Journal of Social Work* 31(4): 579–94.

Cabinet Office/Office of Public Service and Science/Office of Science and Technology (1993) *Realising Our Potential: A Strategy for Science, Engineering and Technology*, Cm 2250 (London, HMSO).

Caddick, B. (1991) 'Using groups in working with offenders: a survey of groupwork in the probation services of England and Wales', *Groupwork*, 4(3): 197–216.

Caesar, G., Parchment, M. and Berridge, D. (1993) *Black Perspectives on Services for Children and Young People in Need and their Families* (London, National Children's Bureau/Barnardos).

Campbell, B. (1993) *Goliath: Britain's Dangerous Places* (London, Methuen).

Cannan, C. (1992) *Changing Families, Changing Welfare* (Hemel Hempstead, Harvester Wheatsheaf).

Cannan, C (1994/95) 'Enterprise culture, professional socialisation and social work education in Britain', *Critical Social Policy*, 42: 5–19.

Cannan, C., Berry, L. and Lyons, K. (1992) *Social Work and Europe* (London, Macmillan – now Palgrave Macmillan).

Carlebach, J. (1970) *Caring for Children in Trouble* (London, Routledge & Kegan Paul).

Carlen, P. (1989) 'Feminist jurisprudence – or women-wise penology?', *Probation Journal*, 36(3).

Carlen, P. and Worrall, A. (eds) (1987) *Gender, Crime and Justice* (Buckingham, Open University Press).

Carmichael, K. (1974) 'The relationship between social work departments and the DHSS: the use of the Social Work (Scotland) Act', in Adler, M.E. (ed.) *In Cash or In Kind* (Edinburgh, Social Administration Department, Edinburgh University).

Carnall, C. (1990) *Managing Change in Organizations* (Englewood Cliffs, NJ, Prentice Hall).

Carter, P., Jeffs, T. and Smith, M.K. (1995) *Social Working* (Basingstoke, Macmillan – now Palgrave Macmillan).

Carter, R.T. (1991) 'Racial identity attitudes and psychological functioning', *Journal of Multicultural Counseling and Development*, **19**: 105–15.

Cavadino, M. and Dignan, J. (1992) *The Penal System: An Introduction* (London, Sage).

Cavanagh, K. and Cree, V.E. (eds) (1996) *Working with Men: Feminism and Social Work* (London, Routledge).

CCETSW (1991) *DipSW: Rules and Requirements for the Diploma in Social Work*, CCETSW Paper 30, 2nd edn (London, Central Council for Education and Training in Social Work).

CCETSW (1995) *Assuring Quality: in the Diploma in Social Work – 1: Rules and Requirements for the DipSW* (revised) (London, Central Council for Education and Training in Social Work).

CCETSW (1996) *Assuring Quality: in the Diploma in Social Work – 1: Rules and Requirements for the DipSW* (second revision) (London, Central Council for Education and Training in Social Work).

Celnick, A. (1985) 'From paradigm to practice in a special probation project', *British Journal of Social Work*, **15**(2): 223–41.

Central Statistical Office (1995) *Social Focus on Women* (London, HMSO).

Chambers, R. (1995) 'Paradigm shifts and the practice of participatory research and development', in Nelson, N. and Wright, S. (eds) *Power and Participatory Development: Theory and Practice* (London, Intermediate Technology Publications).

Chambon, A., Irving, A. and Epstein, C. (eds) (1999) *Reading Foucault for Social Work* (New York, Columbia University Press).

Chapillon, L. (1996) 'A behaviour management group for parents in a family centre', *Behavioural Social Work Review*, **17**: 22–30.

Chapman, T. and Hough, M. (1998) *Evidence-based Practice: a Guide to Effective Practice* (London, Home Office).

Charles, N. and Kerr, N. (1985) *Attitudes towards the Feeding and Nutrition of Young Children*, Research Report 4 (London, Health Education Council).

Cheetham, J., Ahmed, A. and Small, J. (1986) *Black Children and their Families* (London, Routledge).

Cheetham, J., Fuller, R., McIvor, G. and Petch, A. (1992) *Evaluating Social Work Effectiveness* (Buckingham, Open University Press).

Children in Scotland (1995) *Scotland's Families Today* (Edinburgh, HMSO).

Christie, A. (2001) *Men and Social Work: Theories and Practices* (Basingstoke, Palgrave – now Palgrave Macmillan)

Cigno, K. (1988) 'Consumer views of a family centre drop-in', *British Journal of Social Work*, **18**: 361–75.

Cigno, K. (1993) 'Changing behaviour in a residential group setting for elderly people with learning difficulties', *British Journal of Social Work*, **23**: 629–42.

Cigno, K. (1995) 'Helping to prevent abuse: a behavioural approach with families', in Wilson, K. and James, A. (eds) *The Child Protection Handbook* (London, Baillière Tindall).

Cigno, K. (1998) 'Intervention in group care for older people', in Cigno, K. and Bourn, D. (eds) *Cognitive-behavioural Social Work in Practice* (Aldershot, Ashgate).

Cigno, K. and Bourn, D. (eds) (1998) *Cognitive-behavioural Social Work in Practice* (Aldershot, Ashgate).

Cigno, K. and Wilson, K. (1994) 'Effective strategies for working with children and families: issues in the provision of therapeutic help', *Practice*, **6**: 285–98.

Clark, C. (1995) 'Competence and discipline in professional formation', *British Journal of Social Work*, **25**: 563–80.

Clark, C.L. (2000) *Social Work Ethics: Politics, Principles and Practice* (Basingstoke, Palgrave – now Palgrave Macmillan).

Clark, J. (1994) 'Should social work education address religious issues? No!', *Journal of Social Work Education*, **30**(1): 12–17.

Clark, J. (1996) 'After social work', in Parton, N, (ed.) *Social Theory, Social Change and Social Work*, (London, Routledge).

Clarke, D. (1992) *Women at Work: The Essential Guide for the Working Woman* (Shaftesbury, Element).

Clarke, J. and Newman, J. (1997) *The Managerialist State* (London, Sage).

Clarke, J. (ed.) (1993) *A Crisis in Care? Challenges to Social Work* (Milton Keynes, Sage and Open University).

Clarke, J. (1998) 'Doing the right thing? Managerialism and social welfare', in Abbott, P. and Meerabeau, L. (eds) *The Sociology of the Caring Professions* (London, UCL Press).

Clarke, J., Cochrane, A. and McLaughlin, E. (1994a) 'Introduction: why management matters', in Clarke, J., Cochrane, A. and McLaughlin, E. (eds) *Managing Social Policy* (London, Sage).

Cleaver, H. and Freeman, P. (1995) *Parental Perspectives in Cases of Suspected Child Abuse* (London, HMSO).

Clegg, S.R. (1990) *Modern Organizations: Organization Studies in the Post-modern World* (London, Sage).

Cleland, A. (1995) 'Legal solutions for children; comparing Scots law with other jurisdictions', *Scottish Affairs*, **10**, Winter, pp. 6–24.

Cliffe, D. with Berridge, D. (1991) *Closing Children's Homes: An End to Residential Child Care?* (London, National Children's Bureau).

Clifford, D.J. (1994) Critical life histories: a key anti-oppressive research method, in Humphries, B. and Truman, C. (eds) *Rethinking Social Research* (Aldershot, Avebury).

Clifford, D.J. (1995) 'Methods in oral history and social work', *Journal of the Oral History Society*, **23**(2).

Cockburn, C. (1991) *In the Way of Women: Men's Resistance to Sex Equality in Organisations* (London, Macmillan – now Palgrave Macmillan).

Cohen, B. and Fraser, N. (1991) *Children in a Modern Welfare System: Towards a New National Policy* (London, Institute for Public Policy Research).

Cohen, B. and Hagen, U. (eds) (1997) *Children's Services: Shaping up for the Millenium: Supporting Children and Families in the UK and Scandinavia* (Edinburgh, Stationery Office).

Cohen, S. (1975) 'It's all right for you to talk: political and sociological mani-festos for social work action', in Bailey, R. and Brake, M. (eds) *Radical Social Work and Practice* (London, Edward Arnold).

Cole-Hamilton, I. and Lang, T. (1986) *Tightening Belts* (London, London Food Commission).

Coleman, G. (1991) *Investigating Organisations: A Feminist Approach* (Bristol, University of Bristol, School for Advanced Urban Studies).

Collins, B. (1986) 'Defining feminist social work', *Social Work*, May–June, pp. 214–19.

Collins, P.H. (1990) *Black Feminist Thought* (London, Routledge).

Collinson, D.L. and Hearn, J. (1996) *Men as Managers, Managers as Men* (London, Sage).

Colton, M., Drury, C. and Williams, M. (1995) 'Children in need: definition, identification and support', *British Journal of Social Work*, **25**(6): 711–28.

Community Care (1996) 'Cradle to Grave Campaign' (November/December).

Connell, R.W. (1995) *Masculinities* (London, Routledge).

Constable, R. and Metha, U. (1993) *Education for Social Work in Eastern Europe* (Vienna, International Association of Schools of Social Work).

Constantine, M.C., Richardson, T.Q., Benjamin, E.M. and Wilson, J.W. (1998) 'An overview of Black racial identity theories: Limitations and considerations for future theoretical conceptualizations', *Applied and Preventive Psychology*, 7: 95–9.

Cordon, J. (1980) 'Contracts in social work practice', *British Journal of Social Work*, **10**: 143–62.

Cordon, J. and Preston-Shoot, M. (1987) 'Contract or con trick? A reply to Rojek and Collins', *British Journal of Social Work*, **17**: 535–43.

Cordon, J. and Preston-Shoot, M. (1988) 'Contract or con trick? A postscript', *British Journal of Social Work*, **18**(6): 623–34.

Cornish, D.B. and Clarke, R.V.G. (1975) *Residential Treatment and its Effects on Delinquency*, Home Office Research Study 32 (London, HMSO).

Corr, C.A., Nabe, C.M. and Corr, D.M. (1996) *Death and Dying, Life and Living* (New York, Brooks/Cole).

Corrigan, P. and Leonard, P. (1978) *Social Work under Capitalism* (London, Macmillan – now Palgrave Macmillan).

Coulshed, V. (1991) *Social Work Practice: An Introduction* (London, Macmillan – now Palgrave Macmillan).

Coulshed, V. and Mullender, A. (2000) *Management in Social Work*, 2nd edn (Basingstoke, Palgrave – now Palgrave Macmillan).

Cowburn, M. and Modi, P. (1995) 'Justice in an unjust context: implications for working with adult male sex offenders', in Ward, D. and Lacey, M. (eds) *Probation: Working for Justice* (London, Whiting & Birch).

Cox, M. (1998) 'Whistleblowing and training for accountability', in Hunt, G. (ed.) *Whistleblowing in the Social Services. Public Accountability and Professional Practice* (London, Arnold).

Cree, V.E. (1995) *From Public Streets to Private Lives. The Changing Task of Social Work* (Aldershot, Avebury).

Cree, V.E. (1996) 'Why do men care?' in Cavanagh, K. and Cree, V.E. (eds) *Working with Men* (London and New York, Routledge).

Cree, V.E. (2002) 'Social work and society', in Davies, M. (ed) *Blackwell Companion to Social Work*, 2nd edn (Oxford, Blackwell).

Cree, V.E. and Macaulay, C. (eds) (2001) *Transfer of Learning in Professional and Vocational Education* (London, Routledge).

Croft, S. and Beresford, P. (1994) 'A participatory approach to social work', in Hanvey, C. and Philpot, T. (eds) *Practising Social Work* (London, Routledge).

Crompton, M. (1992) *Children and Counselling* (London, Edward Arnold).

Cross, B. (1997) 'Partnership in practice: the experience of two probation services', *Howard Journal of Criminal Justice*, **36**(1): 62–79.

Cross, W.E. (1971) 'The negro to black conversion experience: towards the psychology of black liberation', *Black World*, **20**: 13–27.

Cross, W.E. (1980) 'Models of psychological nigrescence: a literature review', in Jones, R. L. (ed.) *Black Psychology*, 2nd edn (New York, Harper & Row).

Cross, W.E. (1991) *Shades of Black: Diversity in African American Identity* (Philadelphia, Temple University Press).

Cross, W., Parham, T, and Helms, J. (1998) 'Nigrescence revisited: theory and research', in Jones, R.L. (ed.) *African American Identity Development* (Hampton, VA, Cobb & Henry).

Crow, G. and Allen, G. (1994) *Community Life* (Hemel Hempstead, Harvester Wheatsheaf).

Cullen, C., Campbell, M., Connelly, D., Hutton, B., Beattie, K. and Robb, G. (1995) *Approaches to People with Challenging Behaviour* (learning pack) (St Andrews, University of St Andrews).

Culyer, A.A. (chair) (1994) *Supporting Research and Development in the NHS: A Report to the Minister for Health by a Research and Development Task Force* (London, HMSO).

Cumming, E. and Henry, W.E. (1961) *Growing Old: The Process of Disengagement* (New York, Basic Books).

Currie, E. (1988) 'Two visions of community crime prevention', in Hope, T. and Shaw, M. (eds) *Communities and Crime Reduction* (London, HMSO).

Dalal, F. (1988) 'The racism of Jung', *Race and Class*, **29**(3): 1–22.

Dale, J. and Foster, P. (1986) *Feminists and State Welfare* (London, Routledge & Kegan Paul).

Dalrymple, J. and Burke, B. (1995) *Anti-oppressive Practice: Social Care and the Law* (Buckingham, Open University Press).

d'Ardenne, P. and Mahtani, A. (1989) *Transcultural Counselling in Action* (London, Sage).

d'Ardenne, P and Mahtani, A. (1999) *Transcultural Counselling in Action*, 2nd edn (London: Sage).

Davies, B. (1975) *The Use of Groups in Social Work Practice* (London, Routledge & Kegan Paul).

Davies, D. (1996) 'Homophobia and heterosexism', in Davies, D. and Neal, C. (eds) *Pink Therapy: A Guide for Counsellors Working with Lesbian, Gay and Bisexual Clients* (Buckingham, Open University Press).

Davies, D. and Neal, C. (eds) (1996) *Pink Therapy: A Guide for Counsellors Working with Lesbian, Gay and Bisexual Clients* (Buckingham, Open University Press).

Davies, M. (1985) *The Essential Social Worker*, 2nd edn (Aldershot, Gower).

Davies, M. (1994) *The Essential Social Worker*, 3rd edn (Aldershot, Arena).

Davies, M. (ed.) (2002) *The Blackwell Companion to Social Work*, 2nd edn (Oxford, Blackwell).

Davies, N. (1997) *Dark Heart* (London, Chatto & Windus).

Davis, A. and Wainwright, S. (1996) 'Poverty work and the mental health services', *Breakthrough*, **1**(1): 47–56.

Deacon, B. (1992) *The New Eastern Europe* (London, Sage).

de Beauvoir, S. (1974) *The Second Sex* (trans. Pashley, H.M.) (New York, Vintage Books).

Delgado, M. (2000) *Community Social Work Practice in an Urban Context: The Potential of a Capacity-enhancement Perspective* (Oxford: Oxford University Press).

de Shazer, S. (1985) *Keys to Solutions in Brief Therapy* (New York, W.W. Norton).

de Shazer, S. (1988) *Clues: Investigating Solutions in Brief Therapy* (New York, W.W. Norton).

de Shazer, S. (1991) *Putting Difference to Work* (New York, W.W. Norton).

de Shazer, S. (1994) *Words Were Originally Magic* (New York, W.W. Norton).

Dews, V. and Watts, J. (1994) *Review of Probation Officer Recruitment and Qualifying Training* (London, Home Office).

DHSS (1974) *Report of the Committee of Inquiry into the Care and Supervision Provided in Relation to Maria Colwell* (London, HMSO).

DHSS (1980) *Inequalities in Health: A Report of a Research Working Group* (chaired by Sir Douglas Black) (London, DHSS).

DHSS (1988) *Report of the Inquiry into Child Abuse in Cleveland* (Butler-Schloss Report) Cmnd 412 (London, HMSO).

DHSS (1999) *Opportunity For All: Tackling Poverty and Social Exclusion*, Cm 4445 (London, Stationery Office)

Dixon, N. (1984) Research and Planning in Barnardo's (unpublished paper) (Ilford, Essex, Barnardo's).

Dodgson, K., Goodwin, P., Howard, P., Llewellyn-Thomas, S., Mortimer, E., Russell, N. and Weiner, M. (2001) *Electronic Monitoring of Released Prisoners: An Evaluation of the Home Detention Curfew Scheme*, Home Office Research Study 222 (London, Home Office).

Doel, M. (1994) 'Task-centred work', in Hanvey, C. and Philpot, T. (eds) *Practising Social Work* (London, Routledge).

Doel, M. and Lawson, B. (1986) 'Open records: the client's right to partnership', *British Journal of Social Work*, 16(4): 407–30.

Doel, M. and Marsh, P. (1992) *Task-centred Social Work* (Aldershot, Ashgate).

Doel, M. and Sawdon, C. (1999) *The Essential Groupworker*, (London, Jessica Kingsley).

Doel, M. and Shardlow, S.M. (1998) *The New Social Work Practice* (Aldershot, Arena).

DoH (1988) *Protecting Children: A Guide for Social Workers Undertaking a Comprehensive Assessment* (London, HMSO).

DoH (1989) *Homes are for Living In* (London, HMSO).

DoH (1991a) *Care Management and Assessment: Practitioners Guide* (London, HMSO).

DoH (1991b) *Working Together under the Children Act, 1989* (London, HMSO).

DoH (1992) *Committed to Quality: Quality Assurance in Social Services Departments*, (London, HMSO).

DoH (1993) *Guidance on Permissible Forms of Control in Children's Residential Care* (London, HMSO).

DoH (1994) *The Children Act 1989: Contact Orders Study* (London, HMSO).

DoH (1995a) *Child Protection: Messages from Research* (London, HMSO).

DoH (1995b) *Looking After Children: Good Parenting, Good Outcomes* (London, HMSO).

DoH (1996) *Building Bridges: A Guide to Arrangements for Inter-agency Working for the Care and Protection of Severely Mentally Ill People* (Yorkshire, Department of Health).

DoH (1998a) *Caring for Children Away from Home: Messages from Research* (Chichester, Wiley and Sons).

DoH (1998b) *Modernising Social Services: Promoting Independence, Improving Protection, Raising Standards*, Cm 4169 (London, Stationery Office).

DoH (1998c) *Quality Protects: Framework for Action and Objectives for Social Services for Children* (London, Department of Health Social Care Group/Stationery Office).

DoH (1999a) *Adoption Now: Messages from Research* (Chichester, Wiley and Sons).

DoH (1999b) *National Service Framework for Mental Health. Modern Standards and Service Models for Mental Health*, LAC(99)34 (London, Stationery Office).

DoH (2000a) *No Secrets: Guidance on Developing and Implementing Multi-Agency Policies and Procedures to Protect Vulnerable Adults from Abuse* (London, Stationery Office).

DoH (2000b) *Reforming the Mental Health Act* (London, Stationery Office).

DoH (2000c) *A Quality Strategy for Social Care* (London, Department of Health).

DoH (2000d) *The NHS Plan* (London, Department of Health).

DoH (2001a) *Valuing People. A New Strategy for Learning Disability for the 21st Century* (London, Stationery Office).

DoH (2001b) *Personal Social Services Staff of Social Services Departments at 30 September 2000*, Bulletin 2001/16 (London, Department of Health).

DoH (2001c) *The Children Act Now: Messages from Research* (London, Stationery Office).

DoH (2001d) *National Service Framework for Older People*, LAC(2001)12, (London, Stationery Office).

DoH/DfEE/Home Office (2000) *Framework for the Assessment of Children in Need and their Families* (London, Stationery Office).

DoH/Home Office/DfEE (1999) *Working Together to Safeguard Children. A Guide to Inter-agency Working to Safeguard and Promote the Welfare of Children* (London, Stationery Office).

DoH/SSI (1991a) *The Right to Complain: Practice Guidance on Complaints Procedures in Social Services Departments* (London, HMSO).

DoH/SSI (1991b) *Women in Social Services: A Neglected Resource* (London, HMSO).

DoH/SSI (1991c) *Practitioners and Managers' Guide to Care Management and Assessment* (London, HMSO).

Dominelli, L. (1988) *Anti-racist Social Work* (London, Macmillan – now Palgrave Macmillan).

Dominelli, L. (1990) *Women and Community Action* (Birmingham, Venture Press).

Dominelli, L. (1990–91) '"What's in a name?" A comment on "Puritans and paradigms"', *Social Work and Social Sciences Review*, 2(3): 231–5.

Dominelli, L. (1993) *Social Work: Mirror of Society or its Conscience?* (Sheffield, Department of Sociological Studies).

Dominelli, L. (1994) 'Anti-racist social work education', Paper given at the 27th Congress of the International Association of Schools of Social Work, Amsterdam, July.

Dominelli, L. (1996) 'Deprofessionalising social work: anti-oppressive practice, competencies and post-modernism', *British Journal of Social Work*, **26**: 153–75.

Dominelli, L. (1997a) *Sociology for Social Work* (London, Macmillan – now Palgrave Macmillan).

Dominelli, L. (1997b) *Anti-racist Social Work* (Basingstoke, Palgrave – now Palgrave Macmillan).

Dominelli, L. (2000) 'Empowerment: help or hindrance in professional relationships' in Ford, D. and Stepney, P. (ed.) *Social Work Models, Methods and Theories: A Framework for Practice* (Lyme Regis: Russell House Publishing).

Dominelli, L. (2002) 'Feminist theory' in Davies, M. (ed.) *The Blackwell Companion to Social Work*, 2nd edn (Oxford, Blackwell).

Dominelli, L. and Hoogvelt, A. (1996) 'Globalisation and the technocratisation of social work', *Critical Social Policy*, **47**(2): 45–62.

Dominelli, L. and McLeod, E. (1989) *Feminist Social Work* (London, Macmillan – now Palgrave Macmillan).

Doray, B. (1988) *From Taylorism to Fordism: A Rational Madness* (London, Free Association Books).

Douglas, T. (1978) *Basic Groupwork* (London, Tavistock).

Douglas, T. (1983) *Groups: Understanding People Gathered Together* (London, Tavistock).

Douglas, T. (1986) *Group Living: The Application of Group Dynamics in Residential Settings* (London, Tavistock).

Douglas, T. (1993) *A Theory of Groupwork Practice* (London, Macmillan – now Palgrave Macmillan).

Downes, D. and Morgan, R. (1994) '"Hostages to fortune"? The politics of law and order in post-war Britain', in Maguire, M., Morgan, R. and Reiner, R. (eds) *The Oxford Handbook of Criminology* (Oxford, Clarendon Press).

Downie, R.S. (1989) 'A political critique of Kantian ethics in social work: a reply to Webb and McBeath', *British Journal of Social Work*, **19**(6): 507–10.

Downie, R.S. and Telfer, E. (1969) *Respect for Persons* (London, Allen & Unwin).

Downie, R.S. and Telfer, E. (1980) *Caring and Curing* (London, Methuen).

Drakeford, M. (1994) 'Groupwork for parents of young people in trouble', *Groupwork*, 7(3): 236–47.

Drakeford, M. and Vanstone, M. (eds) (1996) *Beyond Offending Behaviour* (Aldershot, Arena).

Dryden, W. and Feltham, C. (1992) *Brief Counselling: A Practical Guide for Beginning Practitioners* (Buckingham, Open University Press).

Dryden, W., Charles-Edwards, D. and Woolfe, R. (eds) (1989) *Handbook of Counselling in Great Britain* (London, Routledge).

DSS (1998) *A New Contract for Welfare*, Cm 3805 (London, Stationery Office).

DSS (1999) *Opportunity for All: Tackling Poverty and Social Exclusion*, Cm 4445 (London, Stationery Office).

Durrant, P. (1997) 'Mapping the future? A contribution from community social work in the community care field', in Cannan, C. and Warren, C. (eds) *Social Action with Children and Families* (London, Routledge).

Dwivedi, K.N. (1996) 'Introduction' in Dwivedi, K.N. and Varma, V.P. (eds) *Meeting the Needs of Ethnic Minority Children: A Handbook for Professionals* (London, Jessica Kingsley).

Eastman, M. (ed.) (1994) *Old Age Abuse*, 2nd edn (London, Chapman & Hall).

Economic and Social Research Council (1996) 'Council to review priorities', *Social Sciences*, **32**.

Egan, G. (1994) *The Skilled Helper*, 5th edn (Pacific Grove, CA: Brooks/Cole).

Ellis, K. (1993) *Squaring the Circle: User and Carer Participation in Needs Assessment* (York, Joseph Rowntree Foundation).

England, H. (1986) *Social Work as Art: Making Sense of Good Practice* (London, Allen & Unwin).

Epstein, L. (1992) *Brief Treatment and a New Look at the Task-centered Approach* (New York, Macmillan).

Eraut, M. (1994) *Developing Professional Knowledge and Competence* (London, Falmer Press).

Erikson, E. (1965) *Childhood and Society* (Harmondsworth, Penguin).

Erikson, E. (1977) *Childhood and Society* (London, Fontana).

Erikson, E.H., Erikson, J.M. and Kivnick, H.Q. (1986) *Vital Involvement in Old Age: The Experience of Old Age in our Time* (New York, W.W. Norton).

Erikson, H. (1964) 'Memorandum on identity and Negro youth', *Journal of Social Issues*, **20**(4): 29–42.

Erikson, H. (1968) *Identity: Youth and Crisis* (London, Faber).

Evans, R. and Wilkinson, C. (1990) 'Variations in police cautioning policy and practice in England and Wales', *Howard Journal of Criminal Justice*, **29**: 155–76.

Everitt, A. (1995) 'Monitoring and evaluation: towards a culture of lying?', Paper given to NCVO Annual Research Conference, London, September.

Everitt, A. and Hardiker, P. (1996) *Evaluating for Good Practice* (London, Macmillan – now Palgrave Macmillan).

Everitt, A., Hardiker, P., Littlewood, J. and Mullender, A. (1992) *Applied Research for Better Practice* (Basingstoke, Macmillan – now Palgrave Macmillan).

Falloon, I.R.H. (1988) *Handbook of Behavioural Family Therapy* (London, Guilford Press).

Falloon, I.R.H., Laporta, M., Fadden, G. and Graham-Hole, V. (1993) *Managing Stress in Families: Cognitive and Behavioural Strategies for Enhancing Coping Skills* (London, Routledge).

Family Rights Group (1994) *Family Group Conferences* (London, Family Rights Group).

Farmer, E. and Owen, M. (1995) *Child Protection Practice: Private Risks and Public Remedies* (London, HMSO).

Farrar, M. (1996) 'Probation in the community', Paper presented to the First Annual Colloquium of the Probation Studies Unit, Centre for Criminological Research, University of Oxford, 16–17 December.

Farrington, D. (1993) 'Juvenile delinquency', in Coleman, J. (ed.) *The School Years* (London, Routledge).

Faulkner, D. (1993) 'All flaws and disorder', *Guardian*, 11 November.

Faulkner, D. (1995) 'The Criminal Justice Act, 1991: policy, legislation and practice', in Ward, D. and Lacey, M. (eds) *Probation: Working for Justice* (London, Whiting & Birch).

Fawcett, B., Featherstone, B., Fook, J. and Rossiter, A. (eds) (2000) *Practice and Research in Social Work: Postmodern Feminist Perspectives* (London, Routledge).

Featherstone, B. and Fawcett, B. (1995) 'Power, difference and social work: an exploration', *Social Work Education*, **15**(1).

Featherstone, M. (1988) 'In pursuit of the post modern: an introduction', *Theory, Culture and Society*, **5**(2–3): 195–216.

Feaver, N. and Smith, D. (1994) 'Editorial introduction', Special issue on probation. *British Journal of Social Work*, **24**(4): 379–86.

Feltham, C. (1995) *What is Counselling?* (London, Sage).

Feltham, C. and Dryden, W. (1993) *Dictionary of Counselling* (London, Whurr).

Fennell, G., Phillipson, C. and Evers, H. (1988) *The Sociology of Old Age* (Milton Keynes, Open University Press).

Fernando, S. (1991) *Mental Health, Race and Culture* (London, Macmillan – now Palgrave Macmillan).

Fetterman, D.M. (1996) 'Empowerment evaluation: an introduction to theory and practice', in Fetterman, D.M., Kaftarian, S.J. and Wandersman, A. (eds) *Empowerment, Evaluation: Knowledge and Tools for Self-Assessment and Accountability* (London, Sage).

Fimister, G. (ed.) (2001) *Tackling child Poverty in the UK: An End in Sight* (London, CPAG).

Finch, J. and Groves, D. (eds) (1983) *A Labour of Love: Women, Work and Caring* (London, Routledge & Kegan Paul).

Firestone, S. (1971) *The Dialectic of Sex* (London, Jonathan Cape).

Fischer, J. (1974) 'Is casework effective? A review', *Social Work*, **1**: 107–10.

Fischer, J. (1978) *Effective Casework Practice: An Eclectic Approach* (New York, McGraw-Hill).

Fisher, M., Marsh, P., Phillips, D. and Sainsbury, E. (1986) *In and Out of Care: The Experience of Children, Parents and Social Workers* (London, Batsford).

Flaskas, C. (1997) 'Reclaiming the idea of truth: Some thoughts on theory in response to practice', *Journal of Family Therapy*. **1**a(1): 1–20.

Fleet, F. (2000) 'Counselling and contemporary social work, in Stepney, P. and Ford, D. (eds) *Social Work Models, Methods and Theories: A Framework for Practice* (Lyme Regis: Russell House Publishing).

Fleming, J. and Ward, D. (1996) 'The ethics of community health needs assessment: searching for a participant centred approach', in Parker, M. (ed.) *Ethics and Community* (Preston, Centre for Professional Ethics, University of Central Lancashire).

Fletcher, B. (1993) *Not Just a Name: The Views of Young People in Foster and Residential Care* (London, National Consumer Council/Who Cares? Trust).

Fletcher-Campbell, F. (1997) *The Education of Children who are Looked After* (Slough, National Foundation for Educational Research).

Folkard, M.S., Smith, D.E. and Smith, D.D. (1976) *IMPACT Volume II: The Results of the Experiment*, Home Office Research Study 36 (London, HMSO).

Foster, G. (1996) *Getting What You Want: A Short Guide to Career Development for Senior Women Managers* (London, National Institute for Social Work).

Foucault, M. (1977) *Discipline and Punish* (London, Allen Lane).

Fox Harding, L.M. (1991a) 'The Children Act in context: four perspectives in child care law and policy (1)', *Journal of Social Welfare and Family Law*, **3**: 179–93.

Fox Harding, L.M. (1991b) 'The Children Act in context: four perspectives in child care law and policy (2)', *Journal of Social Welfare and Family Law*, **4**: 299–316.

Frank, A.W. (1991) *At the Will of the Body: Reflections on Illness* (Boston, Houghton Mifflin).

Franklin, A. and Franklin, B. (1996) 'Growing pains: the developing children's rights movement in the UK', in Pilcher, J. and Wagg, S. (eds) *Thatcher's Children? Politics, Childhood and Society in the 1980s and 1990s* (London, Falmer Press).

Franklin, B. (1989) 'Wimps and bullies: press reporting of child abuse', in Carter, P., Jeffs, T. and Smith, M. (eds) *Social Work and Social Welfare Yearbook I* (Milton Keynes, Open University Press).

Freeman, I., Morrison, A., Lockhart, F. and Swanson, M. (1996) 'Consulting service users: the views of young people', in Hill, M. and Aldgate, J. (eds) *Child Welfare Services: Developments in Law, Policy, Practice and Research* (London, Jessica Kingsley).

Freeman, J. (ed.) (undated) *The Tyranny of Structurelessness* (Dark Star Press) (first US publication 1970).

Freire, P. (1972) *The Pedagogy of the Oppressed* (Harmondsworth, Penguin).

Freud, S. ([1913]1950) *Totem and Taboo* (Harmondsworth, Penguin Freud Library 13).

Freud, S. (1915) 'Thoughts for the times on war and death', *Imago*, **4**(1): 1–21, trans. J. Strachey in *The Standard Edition of the Complete Psychological Works of Sigmund Freud*, vol. 14 (London, Hogarth Press).

Freud, S. (1930) 'Civilization and its discontents', in Strachey, J. (ed.) (trans. Rivière, J.) *The Standard Edition of the Complete Works of Sigmund Freud*, vol. 21 (London, Hogarth Press).

Frith, U. (1989) *Autism: Explaining the Enigma* (Oxford, Blackwell).

Frosh, S. (1987) *The Politics of Psychoanalysis* (London, Macmillan – now Palgrave Macmillan).

Frost, N. and Stein, M. (1989) *The Politics of Child Welfare: Inequality, Power and Change* (Hemel Hempstead, Harvester Wheatsheaf).

Frost, N. and Stein, M. (1990) 'The politics of the Children Act', *Childright*, July/August, p. 1.

Fuller, R. (1992) *In Search of Prevention* (Aldershot, Avebury).

Fuller, R. and Petch, A. (1995) *Practitioner-research: The Reflective Social Worker* (Buckingham, Open University Press).

Gambe, D., Gomes, J., Kapur, V., Rangel, M. and Stubbs, P. (1992) *Improving Practice with Children and Families* (Leeds, Central Council for Education and Training in Social Work).

Gambrill, E. (1983) *Casework – a Competency-based Approach* (Englewood Cliffs, NJ, Prentice-Hall).

Gambrill, E. (1986) 'Social skills training with the elderly', in Hollin, C.R. and Trower, P. (eds) *Handbook of Social Skills Training*, vol. 1 (Oxford, Pergamon).

Gambrill, E. (1997) *Social Work Practice: A Critical Thinkers' Guide* (New York, Oxford University Press).

Gardiner, H.W. (1994) 'Child development', in Adler, L.L. and Gielen, U.P. (eds) *Cross-cultural Topics in Psychology* (New York, Praeger).

Gelsthorpe, L. and Morris, A. (1994) 'Juvenile justice 1945–1992', in Maguire, M., Morgan, R. and Reiner, R. (eds) *The Oxford Handbook of Criminology* (Oxford, Clarendon Press).

Gendreau, P. and Andrews, D.A. (1990) 'Tertiary prevention: what the meta-analyses of the treatment programme literature tell us about 'what works', *Canadian Journal of Criminology*, **32**: 173–84.

Gendreau, P. and Ross, R. (1987) 'Revisitation of rehabilitation: evidence from the 1980s', *Justice Quarterly*, **4**: 349–406.

George, E., Iveson, C. and Ratner, H. (1990) *Problem to Solution: Brief Therapy with Individuals and Families* (London, Brief Therapy Press).

George, M. (1996) 'Figure it out', *Community Care*, 1–7 August, pp. ii–v.

Geraghty, J. (1991) *Probation Practice in Crime Prevention*, Crime Prevention Unit Paper 24 (London, Home Office).

Geva, J. and Weinman, M.L. (1995) 'Social work perspectives in organ procurement', *Health and Social Work*, **20**(4): 241–320.

Gherardi, S. and Turner, B. (1987) *Real Men Don't Collect Soft Data* (Trento, Quaderno Dipartimento di Politica Sociale, Università di Trento).

Gibbons, J., Gallagher, B., Bell, C. and Gordon, D. (1995) 'Development after physical abuse in early childhood: a follow up study of children on protection registers', *Child Protection: Messages from Research* (London, HMSO).

Giddens, A. (1990) *The Consequences of Modernity* (Cambridge, Polity Press).

Giddens, A. (1991) *Modernity and Self Identity: Self and Society in the Late Modern Age* (Cambridge, Polity Press).

Gilder, G. (1984) *Wealth and Poverty* (New York, Basic Books).

Gilligan, C. (1993) *In a Different Voice*, 2nd edn (Harvard University Press).

Ginsburg, N. (1997) 'Housing', in Walker, A. and Walker, C. (eds) (1997) *Britain Divided: The Growth of Social Exclusion in Britain 1979–1997* (London, Child Poverty Action Group).

Goldson, B. (2000) 'Wither diversion? Intervention and the new youth justice', in Goldson, B. (ed.) *The New Youth Justice* (Lyme Regis, Russell House).

Goldson, B. (ed.) (1999) *Youth Justice: Contemporary Policy and Practice* (Aldershot, Ashgate).

Gomm, R. (1993) 'Issues of power in health and welfare', in Walmsley, J., Reynolds, J., Shakespeare, P. and Woolfe, R. (eds) *Health, Welfare and Practice: Reflecting on Roles and Relationships* (London, Sage).

Gorman, K. (2001) 'Cognitive behaviourism and the Holy Grail: the quest for a universal means of managing offender risk', *Probation Journal*, **48**: 3–9.

Gould, N. (1990) 'A political critique of Kantian ethics: a contribution to the debate between Webb and McBeath, and Downie', *British Journal of Social Work*, **20**(3): 495–9.

Gould, N. (1996) 'Using imagery in reflective learning', in Gould, N. and Taylor, I. (eds) *Reflective Learning for Social Work* (Aldershot, Arena).

Gouldner, A. (1970) *The Coming Crisis of Western Sociology* (London, Heinemann).

Graham, H. (1992) 'Feminism and social work education' *Issues in Social Work Education*, **11**(2): 48–62.

Graham, J. and Bowling, B. (1995) *Young People and Crime*, Home Office Research Study 145 (London, Home Office).

Greenfield, P. and Cocking, R. (1994) 'Preface', in Greenfield, P. and Cocking, R. (eds) *Cross-Cultural Roots of Minority Child Development* (Hillsdale, NJ, Lawrence Erlbaum).

Greenhorn, M. (1996) *Cautions, Court Proceedings and Sentencing: England and Wales 1995*, Home Office Statistical Bulletin 16/96 (London, Home Office).

Greer, P. (1994) *Transforming Central Government: The New Steps Initiative* (Buckingham, Open University Press).

Gregg, P., Harkness, S. and Machin, S. (1999) *Child Development and Family Income* (York: YPS).

Griffiths, Sir Roy (1988) *Community Care: Agenda for Action* (London, HMSO).

Grimwood, C. and Popplestone, R. (1993) *Women, Management and Care* (London, Macmillan – now Palgrave Macmillan).

Grossman, K., Grossmann, K.E., Spangler, S., Suess, G. and Unzner, L. (1985) 'Maternal sensitivity and newborn attachment orientation responses as related to quality of attachment in northern Germany', in Bretherton, I. and Waters, E. (eds) *Growing Points of Attachment Theory: Monographs of the Society of Research in Child Development*, **50**(1–2) Serial No 209.

Guy, P. (1994) 'A general social work council – a critical look at the issues', *British Journal of Social Work*, **24**(3): 261–71.

Hadley, R. and Clough, R. (1996) *Care in Chaos* (London, Cassell).

Hagel, A. and Newburn, T. (1994) *The Persistent Offender* (London, Policy Studies Institute).

Haines, K. (2000) 'Referral orders and youth offender panels: restorative approaches and the new youth justice', in Goldson, B. (ed.) *The New Youth Justice* (Lyme Regis, Russell House).

Hale, J. (1983) 'Feminism and social work practice', in Jordan, B. and Parton, N. (eds) *The Political Dimensions of Social Work*, (Oxford, Blackwell).

Hall, C. (1997) *Social Work as Narratives. Storytelling and Persuasion in Professional Texts* (Aldershot, Ashgate).

Hallett, C. (1993) 'Child protection in Europe: convergence or divergence?', *Adoption and Fostering*, **17**(4): 27–32.

Hallett, C. and Birchall, E. (1992) *Coordination in Child Protection* (London, HMSO).

Hallett, C., and Murray, C., with Jamieson, J. and Veitch, B. (1998) *The Evaluation of Children's Hearings in Scotland*. vol. 1 *Deciding in Children's Interests* (Edinburgh, Scottish Office Central Research Unit).

Handler, J. (1968) 'The coercive children's officer', *New Society*, 3 October.

Handy, C. (1990) *The Age of Unreason* (London, Arrow).

Hanmer, J. and Maynard, M. (1987) *Women, Violence and Social Control* (London, Macmillan – now Palgrave Macmillan).

Hanmer, J. and Statham, D. (1988) *Women and Social Work: Towards a Woman-centred Practice* (London, Macmillan – now Palgrave Macmillan).

Hanmer, J. and Statham, D. (1999) *Women and Social Work: Towards a Woman-centred Practice*, 2nd edn (London, Macmillan – now Palgrave Macmillan).

Harding, S. (ed.) (1987) *Feminism and Methodology* (Milton Keynes, Open University Press).

Harrison, A., Wilson, M., Pine, C., Chan, S. and Buriel, R. (1990) 'Family ecologies of ethnic minority children', *Child Development*, **61**: 347–62.

Harrison, T.H. (1976) *Living through the Blitz* (London, Collins).

Harrison, W.D. (1991) *Seeking Common Ground: A Theory of Social Work in Social Care* (Aldershot, Avebury).

Hart, E. and Bond, M. (1995) *Action Research for Health and Social Care: A Guide to Practice* (Buckingham, Open University Press).

Harwin, J. (1990) 'Parental responsibilities in the Children Act 1989', in Manning, N. and Ungerson, C. (eds) *Social Policy Review 1989–1990* (London, Longman).

Hawkesworth, M.E. (1989) 'Knower, knowing, known: feminist theory and claims of truth', *Signs: Journal of Women in Culture and Society*, **14**(31): 533–57.

Hawxhurst, D. and Morrow, S. (1984) *Living Our Visions: Building Feminist Community* (Tempe, AZ, Fourth World).

Haxby, D. (1978) *Probation: A Changing Service* (London, Constable).

Hayman, V. (1993) 'Re-writing the job: a sceptical look at competences', *Probation Journal*, **40**(4): 180–3.

Healy, K. (2000) *Social Work Practices: Contemporary Perspectives on Change* (London, Sage).

Heap, K. (1985) *The Practice of Social Work with Groups* (London, Allen & Unwin).

Hearn, J. (1998) *The Violences of Men* (London, Sage).

Hearn, J. and Parkin, W. (1995) *Sex at Work: The Power and Paradox of Organisation Sexuality* (rev. edn) (London, Prentice Hall/Harvester Wheatsheaf).

Heelas, P., Lash, S. and Morris, P. (eds) (1996) *Detraditionalization: Critical Reflections on Authority and Identity* (Oxford, Blackwell).

Heineman, M. (1981) 'The obsolete scientific imperative in social work research', *Social Service Review*, **55**(3): 371–96.

Herbert, M. (1987a) *Conduct Disorders of Childhood and Adolescence: A Social Learning Perspective*, 2nd edn (Chichester, Wiley).

Herbert, M. (1987b) *Behavioural Treatment of Children with Problems: A Practice Manual*, 2nd edn (London, Academic Press).

Hester, M., Kelly, L. and Radford, J. (eds) (1996) *Women, Violence and Male Power*, (Buckingham, Open University Press).

Hill, M. (2000) 'Partnership reviewed: Words of caution, words of encouragement' *Adoption and Fostering*, **24**(3): 56–68.

Hill, M. and Aldgate, J. (eds) (1996a) *Child Welfare Services: Developments in Law, Policy, Practice and Research* (London, Jessica Kingsley).

Hill, M. and Aldgate, J. (1996b) 'The Children Act, 1989 and recent developments in research in England and Wales', in Hill, M. and Aldgate, J. (eds) *Child Welfare Services: Developments in Law, Policy, Practice and Research* (London, Jessica Kingsley).

Hill, S. (1999) *African American Children: Socialization and Development in Families* (California, Sage).

Hill-Collins, P. (1990) *Black Feminist Thought – Knowledge, Consciousness, and the Politics of Empowerment* (London, Unwin Hyman).

Hills, J. (1995) *Joseph Rowntree Foundation Inquiry into Income and Wealth*, vol. 2 (York, Joseph Rowntree Foundation).

Hochschild, A.R. (1975) 'Disengagement theory: a critique and proposal', *American Sociological Review*, **40**: 553–69.

Hockey, J. and James, A. (1993) *Growing Up and Growing Old: Ageing and Dependency in the Life Course* (London, Sage).

Holdaway, S., Davidson, N., Dignan, J., Hammersley, R., Hine, J. and Marsh, P. (2001) *New Strategies to Address Youth Offending: The National Evaluation of the Pilot Youth Offending Teams*, Home Office Occasional Paper 69 (London, Home Office).

Holland, S. (2000) 'The asssessment relationship: interactions between social workers and parents in child protection assessments', *British Journal of Social Work*, **30**: 149–63.

Hollin, C.R. and Trower, P. (eds) (1986) *Handbook of Social Skills Training*, vol. 1 (Oxford, Pergamon).

Hollin, C.R., Epps, K.J. and Kendrick, A.J. (1995) *Managing Behavioural Treatment* (London, Routledge).

Hollis, F. (1972) *Casework: A Psychosocial Therapy*, 2nd edn (New York, Random House).

Hollis, M. and Howe, D. (1987) 'Moral risks in social work', *Journal of Applied Philosophy*, **4**: 123–33.

Hollis, M. and Howe, D. (1990) 'Moral risks in the social work role: a response to Macdonald', *British Journal of Social Work*, **20**(6): 547–52.

Holman, B. (1988) *Putting Families First* (London, Macmillan – now Palgrave Macmillan).

Holman, R. (1983) *Resourceful Friends* (London, Children's Society).

Holman, R. (1993) *A New Deal for Social Welfare* (Oxford, Lyon Publishing).

Holmans, A. (1996) 'Meeting housing needs in the private rented sector', *Housing Review* 1996/7 (York, Joseph Rowntree Foundation).

Home Office (1968) *Children in Trouble*, White Paper, Cmnd 3601 (London, HMSO).

Home Office (1980) *Young Offenders*, Cmnd 8045 (London, HMSO).

Home Office (1984) *Probation Service in England and Wales: Statement of National Objectives and Priorities* (London, Home Office).

Home Office (1988a) *The Parole System in England and Wales: Report of the Review Committee*, Cm 532 (London, HMSO).

Home Office (1988b) *Punishment, Custody and the Community*, Cm 424 (London, Home Office).

Home Office (1990) *Crime, Justice and Protecting the Public*, Cm 965 (London, HMSO).

Home Office (1991) *Safer Communities: The Local Delivery of Crime Prevention through the Partnership Approach, the Morgan Report* (London, Home Office).

Home Office (1992) *National Standards for the Supervision of Offenders in the Community* (London, Home Office).

Home Office (1993) *Monitoring of the Criminal Justice Act 1991: Data from a Special Data Collection Exercise*, Home Office Statistical Bulletin 25/93 (London, Home Office).

Home Office (1995) *National Standards for the Supervision of Offenders in the Community* (London, Home Office).

Home Office (1997) *No More Excuses: A New Approach to Tackling Youth Crime in England and Wales*, Cm 3809 (London, Stationery Office).

Home Office (1998) *Prisons – Probation Review: Final Report* (London, Home Office).

Home Office (2000a) *National Standards for the Supervision of Offenders in the Community* (London, Home Office).

Home Office (2000b) *What Works: First Report from the Joint Prison Probation Accreditation Panel* (www.homeoffice.gov.uk).

Home Office (2001) *Making Punishments Work: Review of the Sentencing Framework for England and Wales* (The Halliday Report) (London, Home Office).

hooks, B. (1981) *Ain't I a Woman: Black Women and Feminism* (London, Pluto Press).

hooks, B. (1984a) 'Feminism: a movement to end sexist oppression', in Philips, A. (ed.) *Feminism and Equality* (Oxford, Blackwell).

hooks, B. (1984b) *Feminist Theory – from Margin to Center* (Boston, South End Press).

hooks, B. (1989) *Talking Back: Thinking Feminist, Thinking Black* (Boston, South End Press).

hooks, B. (1991) *Yearning: Race, Gender and Cultural Politics* (London, Turnaround).

Hoopes, J.L. (1990) 'Adoption and identity formation', in Brodzinsky, D.M. and Schechter, M.D. (eds) *The Psychology of Adoption* (Oxford, Oxford University Press).

Horne, M. (1999) *Values in Social Work* (Aldershot, Ashgate).

Hough, M. (1996) 'People talking about punishment', *Howard Journal of Criminal Justice*, **35**(3): 191–214.

Houston, G. (1984) *The Red Book of Groups* (London, Rochester Foundation).

Howard, M. (1997) 'Cutting social security', in Walker, A. and Walker, C. (eds) *Britain Divided: The Growth of Social Exclusion in Britain 1979–1997* (London, Child Poverty Action Group).

Howarth, C., Kenway, P., Palmer, G. and Street, C. (1998) *Monitoring Poverty and Social Exclusion: Labour's Inheritance* (New Policy Institute/Joseph Rowntree Foundation).

Howarth, C., Kenway, P., Palmer, G. and Miorelli, R. (1999) *Monitoring Poverty and Social Exclusion 1999* (York, Joseph Rowntree Foundation).

Howe, D. (1987) *An Introduction to Social Work Theory*, Community Care Practice Handbooks (Aldershot, Arena).

Howe, D. (1989) *The Consumers' View of Family Therapy* (Aldershot, Gower).

Howe, D. (1993) *On Being a Client: Understanding the Process of Counselling and Psychotherapy* (London, Sage).

Howe, D. (1994) 'Modernity, postmodernity and social work', *British Journal of Social Work*, **24**(5): 513–32.

Howe, D. (1995) *Attachment Theory for Social Work Practice* (London, Macmillan – now Palgrave Macmillan).

Howe, D., Brandon, M., Hinings, D. and Schofield, G. (1999) *Attachment Theory, Child Maltreatment and Family Support* (London, Macmillan – now Palgrave Macmillan).

Hudson, A. (1992) 'The child sex abuse "industry" and gender relations in social work', in Langan, M. and Day, L. (eds) *Women, Oppression and Social Work: Issues in Anti-Discriminatory Practice* (London, Routledge).

Hudson, B.L. (1982) *Social Work with Psychiatric Patients* (London, Macmillan – now Palgrave Macmillan).

Hudson, B.L. and Macdonald, G. (1986) *Behavioural Social Work: An Introduction* (London, Macmillan – now Palgrave Macmillan).

Hughes, C. (1995) 'Really useful knowledge: adult education and the Ruskin Learning Project', in Mayo, M. and Thompson, J. (eds) *Adult Learning, Critical Intelligence and Social Change* (Leicester, National Institute for Adult and Continuing Education).

Hutton, W. (1996) *The State We're In* (rev. edn) (London, Vintage).

Iannello, K. (1992) *Decisions without Hierarchy: Feminist Interventions in Organization Theory and Practice* (New York, Routledge).

IFSW (1994) *The Ethics of Social Work: Principles and Standards* (International Federation of Social Workers, http://www.ifsw.org/publications/4.4.pub.html).

Ince, L. (1998) *Making It Alone: A Study of The Care Experiences of Young Black People* (London, BAAF).

Iwaniec, D. (1995) *The Emotionally Abused and Neglected Child: Identification, Assessment and Intervention* (Chichester, Wiley).

Iwaniec, I., Herbert, M. and McNeish, A.S. (1985a) 'Assessment and treatment of failure-to-thrive children and their families: Part I. Psychosocial factors', *British Journal of Social Work*, **15**: 243–59.

Iwaniec, I., Herbert, M. and McNeish, A. S. (1985b) 'Social work with failure-to-thrive children and their families: Part II. Behavioural social work intervention', *British Journal of Social Work*, **15**: 375–98.

Ixer, G. (1999) 'There's no such thing as reflection', *British Journal of Social Work* **29**(4): 523–37.

J.M. Consulting Ltd (1999) *Review of the Delivery of the Diploma in Social Work for the Department of Health*.

Jackson, M., Kolody, B. and Wood, J.L. (1982) 'To be old and black: the case for double jeopardy on income and health', in Manuel, R.C. (ed.) *Minority Ageing* (Westport, CT, Greenwood Press).

Jackson, S. (1994) 'Educating children in residential and foster care'. *Oxford Review of Education*, Special Issue: 'The Education of Children in Need', **20**: 267–81.

Jacobs, M. (1988) *Psychodynamic Counselling in Action* (London, Sage).

Jacobs, P. and Landau, S. (1967) *The New Radicals* (London, Pelican).

Jacobs, R. (1989) 'Getting the measure of management competence', *Personnel Management*, **21**(6): 32–7.

James, A.L. (1995) 'Probation values for the 1990s – and beyond?', *Howard Journal of Criminal Justice*, **34**(4): 326–43.

James, A.L. and Bottomley, A.K. (1994) 'Probation partnerships revisited', *Howard Journal of Criminal Justice*, **33**(2): 158–68.

James, S.M. and Busia, A.P.A. (eds) (1993) *Theorizing Black Feminisms: The Visionary Pragmatism of Black Women* (Routledge, London).

Jannson, B. (1994) *Social Policy: From Theory to Policy Practice* (Pacific Grove, CA, Brooks/Cole).

Jehu, D. (1967) *Learning Theory and Social Work* (London, Routledge & Kegan Paul).

Jokinen, A., Juhila, K. and Pösö, T. (eds) (1999) *Constructing Social Work Practices* (Aldershot, Ashgate).

Jones, A. and Bilton, K. (1994) *The Future Shape of Children's Services* (London, National Children's Bureau).

Jones, C. (1978) An analysis of the development of social work education and social work 1869–1977. Unpublished PhD thesis, University of Durham.

Jones, C. (1983) *State Social Work and the Working Class* (London, Routledge & Kegan Paul).

Jones, C. (1993) 'Distortion and demonisation: the Right and anti-racist social work education', *Social Work Education*, **12**(12): 9–16.

Jones, C. (1994) Dangerous Times for British Social Work Education. Paper presented at the 27th Congress of the International Association of Schools of Social Work, Amsterdam, 11–15 July.

Jones, C. (1996a) 'Anti-intellectualism and the peculiarities of British social work', in Parton, N. (ed.) *Social Theory, Social Change and Social Work* (London, Routledge).

Jones, C. (1996b) 'Dangerous times for British social work education', in Ford, P. and Hayes, P. (eds) *Educating for Social Work: Arguments for Optimism* (Aldershot, Avebury).

Jones, C. (1996c) 'Regulating social work: a review of the review', in Jackson, S. and Preston-Shoot, M. (eds) *Social Work Education in a Changing Policy Context* (London, Whiting & Birch).

Jones, C. (1997) 'Social work and poverty', in Davies, M. (ed.) *Blackwell's Companion to Social Work* (Oxford, Blackwell).

Jones, C. (2001) 'Voices from the front line: state social workers and New Labour', *British Journal of Social Work*, **31**(4): 547–62.

Jones, C. and Novak T. (1999) *Poverty, Welfare and the Disciplinary State* (London, Routledge).

Jones, M.A. (1985) *A Second Chance for Families: Five Years Later: a Follow Up Study of a Program to Prevent Foster Care* (New York, Child Welfare League of America).

Jones, S. and Joss, R. (1995) 'Models of professionalism', in Yelloly, M. and Henkel, M. (eds) *Learning and Teaching in Social Work: Towards Reflective Practice* (London, Jessica Kingsley).

Jordan, B. (1990) *Social Work in an Unjust Society* (Hemel Hempstead, Harvester Wheatsheaf).

Jordan, B. (2000) *Social Work and the Third Way. Tough Love as Social Policy* (London, Sage).

Jordan, J. (1989) *Moving Towards Home: Political Essays* (London, Virago).

Jung, C. (1950) 'On the psychology of the Negro', in McGuire, W. (ed.) *Collected Works of Carl Jung*, vol. 18 (Princeton, NJ, Princeton University Press).

Kahan, B. (ed.) (1989) *Child Care Research, Policy and Practice* (London, Hodder & Stoughton).

Kant, I. (1785) 'Groundwork of the metaphysic of morals', in Paton, H.J. (ed.) (1948) *The Moral Law* (London, Routledge).

Katz, J. (1978) *White Awareness* (Oklahoma City, University of Oklahoma Press).

Kelly, A. (1991) 'The "new" managerialism in the Social Services', in Carter, P., Jeffs, T. and Smith, M. (eds) *Social Work and Social Welfare Yearbook 3* (Milton Keynes, Open University Press).

Kelly, A. (1996) *Introduction to the Scottish Children's Panel* (Winchester, Waterside Press).

Kelly, D. and Warr, B. (1992) *Quality Counts: Achieving Quality in Social Care Services* (London, Whiting & Birch).

Kelly, G. and Pinkerton, J. (1996) 'The Children (Northern Ireland) Order, 1995', in Hill, M. and Aldgate, J. (eds) *Child Welfare Services: Developments in Law, Policy, Practice and Research* (London, Jessica Kingsley).

Kelly, T. (1962) *A History of Adult Education in Great Britain from the Middle Ages to the Twentieth Century* (Liverpool, Liverpool University Press).

Kempson, E. (1996) *Life on a Low Income* (York, Joseph Rowntree Foundation).

Kempson, E. (1997) 'Privatisation of utilities', in Walker, A. and Walker, C. (eds) (*Britain Divided: The Growth of Social Exclusion in Britain 1979–1997* (London, Child Poverty Action Group).

Kemshall, H. (1998) *Risk in Probation Practice* (Aldershot, Ashgate).

Kemshall, H. and Pritchard, J. (1996) *Good Practice in Risk Assessment and Risk Management* (London, Jessica Kingsley).

Kent, R. (1997) *Children's Safeguards Review* (London, Stationery Office).

Kilbrandon, L. (1964) *Children and Young Persons, Scotland*, Cmnd 2306 (Edinburgh, HMSO).

King, M. (ed.) (1999) *Moral Agendas for Children's Welfare* (London, Routledge).

King, M. and Trowell, J. (1992) *Children's Welfare and the Law: The Limits of Legal Intervention* (London, Sage).

Knibbs, S. (1994) 'User-run services', *Community Care*, 26 May.

Kolb, D.A. (1984) *Experiential Learning: Experience as the Source of Learning and Development* (Englewood Cliffs, NJ, Prentice Hall).

Konopka, G. (1990) 'Thirty-five years of group work in psychiatric settings', *Social Work With Groups*, **13**(1): 13–16.

Kotter, J. (1996) *Leading Change* (Boston, Harvard Business School Press).

Kotter, J. and Schlesinger, L. (1979) 'Choosing strategies for change', *Harvard Business Review*, March/April, pp. 106–14.

Krim, R. (1988) 'Managing to learn: action inquiry in city hall', in Reason, P. (ed.) *Human Inquiry in Action: Developments in New Paradigm Research* (London, Sage).

Krueger, R. (1994) *Focus Groups: A Practical Guide for Applied Research* (Newbury Park, CA, Sage).

Kurland, R. and Salmon, R. (1993) 'Groupwork versus casework in a group', *Groupwork*, 6(1): 5–16.

Labour Party (1997) *Manifesto* (London, Labour Party).

Langan, M. and Day, L. (eds) (1992) *Women, Oppression and Social Work: Issues in Anti-Discriminatory Practice* (London, Routledge).

Langan, M. and Lee, P. (1989) *Radical Social Work Today* (London, Routledge).

Law Commission (1995) *Mental Incapacity: Summary of Recommendations*, Consulting paper 231 (London, HMSO).

Laybourn, K. (1997) 'The guild of help and the community response to poverty 1904–c.1914', in Laybourn, K. (ed.) *Social Conditions, Status and Community 1860–c. 1920*, (Stroud, Sutton).

Laycock, G. and Pease, K. (1985) 'Crime prevention within the probation service', *Probation Journal*, **32**: 43–7.

Lee, J. (1994) *The Empowerment Approach to Social Work Practice* (New York, Columbia University Press).

Lee, J.A.B. (2000) *The Empowerment Approach to Social Work Practice: Building the Beloved Community* (New York, Columbia University Press).

Leonard, P. (1973) 'Professionalism, community action and the growth of social service bureaucracies', *Sociological Review Monographs*, No. 20.

Leonard, P. (1976) 'The function of social work in society', in Timms, N. and Watson, D. (eds) *Talking about Welfare* (London, Routledge & Kegan Paul).

Leonard, P. (1997) *Postmodern Welfare: Reconstructing an Emancipatory Project* (London, Sage).

Lewis, C. (2000) *A Man's Place in the Home: Fathers and Families in the UK* (Foundations Review) (York, Joseph Rowntree Foundation).

Lewis, J. (1996) 'What does contracting do to voluntary agencies?', in Billis, D. and Harris, M. (eds) *Voluntary Agencies: Challenges of Organisation and Management* (Basingstoke, Macmillan – now Palgrave Macmillan).

Lewis, J. and Glennerster, H. (1996) *Implementing the New Community Care* (Buckingham, Open University Press).

Lindow, V. and Morris, J. (1995) *Service User Involvement* (York, Joseph Rowntree Foundation).

Lindsay, M. (1992) *An Introduction to Children's Rights*, Highlight No. 113 (London, National Children's Bureau).

Lishman, J. (1994) *Communication in Social Work* (Basingstoke, Macmillan – now Palgrave Macmillan).

Lishman, J. (2000) *Evidence for Practice: The Contribution of Competing Research Methodologies* ESRC Funded Seminar Series on Theorising Social Work, Seminar 4, Cardiff 'What Works as Evidence for Practice? The Methodological Repertoire in an Applied Discipline' NISW Website (London, NISW).

Lloyd, C., Mair, G. and Hough, M. (1994) *Explaining Reconviction Rates: A Critical Analysis*, Home Office Research Study 136 (London, HMSO).

Lobley, D. and Smith, D. (1999) *Working with Persistent Juvenile Offenders: An Evaluation of the Apex CueTen Project* (Edinburgh, Scottish Office).

Lobley, D. and Smith, D. (2000) *Evaluation of Electronically Monitored Restriction of Liberty Orders* (Edinburgh, Scottish Executive).

Lobley, D., Smith, D. and Stern, C. (2001) *Freagarrach: An Evaluation of a Project for Persistent Juvenile Offenders* (Edinburgh, Scottish Executive).

Local Government Management Board and Association of Directors of Social Services (1993) *Social Services Workforce Analysis 1992: Workforce Survey Main Report* (London, Local Government Management Board).

Loney, M. (1983) *Community Against Government: The British Community Development Projects, 1968–1978: A Study of Government Incompetence* (London, Heinemann).

Looney, J. (1988) 'Ego development and black identity', *Journal of Black Psychology*, **15**(1): 41–56.

Lorde, A. (1984) *Sister Outsider* (New York, The Crossing Press).

Lorenz, W. (1994) *Social Work in a Changing Europe*, London, Routledge.

Low Pay Unit (1996) 'Coming apart at the seams', *New Review*, **42**: 8–10.

Lymbery, M. (2001) 'Social work at the crossroads', *British Journal of Social Work*, **31**(3): 369–84.

Lyotard, J.F. (1984) *The Postmodern Condition: A Report on Knowledge* (Manchester, Manchester University Press).

Macaskill, C. (1985) 'Post-adoption support: is it essential?', *Adoption and Fostering*, **9**(1): 45–9.

McAuley, C. (1996) 'Children's perspectives on long-term foster care', in Hill, M. and Aldgate, J. (eds) *Child Welfare Services: Developments in Law, Policy, Practice and Research* (London, Jessica Kingsley).

McBrian, J. and Felce, D. (1992) *Working with People who have a Severe Learning Difficulty and Challenging Behaviour: A Practice Manual* (Clevedon: British Institute for Learning Disabilities).

Macdonald, G. (1990a) 'Allocating blame in social work', *British Journal of Social Work*, **20**(6): 525–46.

Macdonald, G. (1990b) 'Moral risks? A reply to Hollis and Howe', *British Journal of Social Work*, **20**(6): 553–6.

Macdonald, G. (1994) 'Developing empirically-based practice in probation', *British Journal of Social Work*, **24**: 405–27.

MacDonald, G. and Roberts, H. (1995) *What Works in the Early Years?* (Ilford, Barnardo's).

Macdonald, G., Sheldon, B. with Gillespie, J. (1992) 'Contemporary studies of the effectiveness of social work', *British Journal of Social Work*, **22**: 615–43.

McElrea, F. (1994) 'Justice in the community: the New Zealand experience', in Burnside, J. and Baker, N. (eds) *Relational Justice: Repairing the Breach* (Winchester, Waterside Press).

McGhee, J. and Waterhouse, L. (1999) 'Comparative juvenile justice policy: the alliance between Scotland and the State of Massachusetts revisited' *Children and Youth Services Review*, **21**(11/12).

McGuire, J. (ed.) (1995) *What Works: Reducing Reoffending: Guidelines from Research and Practice* (Chichester, Wiley).

McIvor, G. (1990) *Sanctions for Serious or Persistent Offenders: A Review of the Literature* (Stirling, University of Stirling, Social Work Research Centre).

McIvor, G. (1996) 'Recent developments in Scotland', in McIvor, G. (ed.) *Working with Offenders*, Research Highlights in Social Work, 26 (London, Jessica Kingsley).

McLaughlin, E. and Muncie, J. (1994) 'Managing the criminal justice system', in Clarke, J., Cochrane, A. and McLaughlin, E. (eds) *Managing Social Policy* (London, Sage).

McLeod, E. (1993) *An Introduction to Counselling* (Buckingham, Open University Press).

McMurran, M. and Hollin, C.R. (1993) *Young Offenders and Alcohol-related Crime*, (Chichester, Wiley).

MacPherson, H. and Kaptchuk, T.J. (eds) (1996) *Acupuncture in Practice: Case History Insights from the West* (Edinburgh, Churchill Livingstone).

Macpherson, W. (1999) *The Stephen Lawrence Inquiry* (London, Stationery Office).

Maguire, M. and Raynor, P. (1997) 'The revival of throughcare: rhetoric and reality in automatic conditional release', *British Journal of Criminology*, 37(1): 1–14.

Maguire, M., Perroud, B. and Raynor, P. (1996) *Automatic Conditional Release: The First Two Years*, Home Office Research Study 156 (London, Home Office).

Maguire, M., Raynor, P., Vanstone, M. and Kynch, J. (2000) 'Voluntary aftercare and the probation service: a case of diminishing responsibility', *Howard Journal of Criminal Justice*, 39(3): 234–48.

Main, M. and Solomon, J. (1986) 'Discovery of an insecure disorganised/disoriented attachment pattern,' in Yogman, M. and Brazelton, T. (eds) *Affective Development in Infancy* (Norwood, NJ, Ablex).

Main, M., Kaplan, N. and Cassidy, J. (1985) 'Security in infancy, childhood and adulthood', in Bretherton, I. and Walters, E. (eds) *Growing Points of Attachment Theory and Research: Monographs of the Society for Research in Child Development 50* (1–2, Serial No. 209).

Mama, A. (1995) *Beyond the Masks* (London, Routledge).

Mangham, I.L. and Silver, M.S. (1986) *Management Training: Context and Practice* (London, ESRC and DTI).

Marchant, H. and Wearing, B. (eds) (1986) *Gender Reclaimed: Women in Social Work* (Sydney, Hale & Iremonger).

Marris, P. (1974) *Loss and Change* (London, Routledge & Kegan Paul).

Marsden, D. and Oakley, P. (eds) (1990) *Evaluating Social Development Projects* (Oxford, Oxfam).

Marsden, D., Oakley, P. and Pratt, B. (eds) (1994) *Measuring the Process: Guidelines for Evaluating Social Development* (Oxford, INTRAC).

Marsh, P. (1991) 'Task-centred practice', in Lishman, J. (ed.) *Handbook of Theory for Practice Teachers in Social Work* (London, Jessica Kingsley).

Marsh, P. and Fisher, M. (1992) *Good Intentions: Developing Partnerships in Social Services* (York, Joseph Rowntree and *Community Care*).

Marsh, P. and Triseliotis, J.P. (1996) *Ready to Practise?: Social Workers and Probation Officers: Their Training and First Year in Work* (Aldershot, Avebury).

Marshall, T.F. and Merry, S. (1990) *Crime and Accountability* (London, HMSO).

Martin, L. (1994) 'Power, continuity and change: decoding black and white women managers' experience in local government', in Tanton, M. (ed.) *Women in Management: A Developing Presence* (London, Routledge).

Martyn, H. (ed.) (2001) *Developing Reflective Practice: Making Sense of Social Work in a World of Change* (Bristol, Policy Press).

Mattinson, J. (1975) *The Reflection Process in Casework Supervision* (London, Institute of Marital Studies).

Matza, D. (1969) *Becoming Deviant* (Englewood Cliffs, NJ, Prentice Hall).

Maxime, J. (1986) 'Some psychological models of black self-concept', in Ahmed, S., Cheetham, J. and Small, J. (eds) *Social Work with Black Children and their Families* (London, Batsford).

Maxime, J. (1993) 'The therapeutic importance of racial identity in working with black children who hate', in Varma, V. (ed.) *How and Why Children Hate* (London, Jessica Kingsley).

May, T. and Anniston, J. (1998) 'De-professionalization of probation officers', in Abbott, P. and Meerabeau, L. (eds) *The Sociology of the Caring Professions* (London, UCL Press).

Mayer, J.E. and Timms, N. (1970) *The Client Speaks* (London, Routledge & Kegan Paul).

Maynard, M. (1994) 'Methods, practice and epistemology: the debate about feminism and research', in Maynard, M. and Purvis, J. (eds) *Researching Women's Lives from a Feminist Perspective* (London, Taylor & Francis).

Mayo, M. (1994a) *Communities and Caring* (London, Macmillan – now Palgrave Macmillan).

Mayo, M. (1994b) 'Community work', in Hanvey, C. and Philpot, T. (eds) *Practising Social Work* (London, Routledge).

Meinert, R., Pardeck, J.T. and Kreuger, L. (2000) *Social Work. Seeking Relevancy in the Twenty-First Century* (New York, Haworth Press).

Meinert, R.G., Pardeck, J.T. and Murphy, J.W. (eds) (1998) *Postmodernism, Religion and the Future of Social Work* (New York, Haworth Press).

Midwinter, E. (1990) 'An ageing world: the equivocal response', *Ageing and Society*, **10**.

Miller, E.J. and Gwynne, G.V. (1972) *A Life Apart* (London, Tavistock).

Miller, G. (1997) *Becoming Miracle Workers: Language and Meaning in Brief Therapy* (New York, Aldine de Gruyter).

Millett, K. (1972) *Sexual Politics* (London, Abacus).

Millham, S., Bullock, R., Hosie, K. and Haak, M. (1986) *Lost in Care* (Aldershot, Gower).

Mintzberg, H. (1989) 'The structuring of organizations', in Asch, D. and Bowman, C. *Readings in Strategic Management* (London, Macmillan – now Palgrave Macmillan).

Mirrlees-Black, C., Mayhew, P. and Percy, A. (1996) *The 1996 British Crime Survey: England and Wales*, Home Office Statistical Bulletin 19/96 (London, Home Office).

Mirza, H. (1992) *Young, Female and Black* (London, Routledge).

Mitchell, J. (1974) *Feminism and Psychoanalysis* (London, Allen Lane).

Morgan, D. (1988) *Focus Groups as Qualitative Research* (London, Sage).

Morris, A., Giller, H., Szwed, E. and Geach, H. (1980) *Justice for Children* (London, Macmillan – now Palgrave Macmillan).

Morris, A., Maxwell, G.W. and Robertson, J.P. (1993) 'Giving victims a voice: a New Zealand experiment', *Howard Journal of Criminal Justice*, **32**(4): 304–19.

Morris, C. (1964) 'The future of the social services', *Almoner*, **17**(3).

Morris, J. (1991) *Pride Against Prejudice: Transforming Attitudes to Disability* (London, Women's Press).

Morris, J. (1993) 'Feminism and disability', *Feminist Review*, **43**: 57–70.

Morris, J. (1996) 'Gender and disability' in Wain, J., Finkelstein, V., French, S. and Oliver, M. (eds) *Disabling Barriers – Enabling Environments* (London, Sage in association with the Open University).

Morris, J. (1997) 'Care or empowerment? A disability rights perspective', *Social Policy and Administration*, **31**(1): 54–60.

Morris, P. and Beverley, F. with Vennard, J. (1975) *On Licence: a Study of Parole* (Chichester, Wiley).

Morrison, T. (1987) *Beloved* (London, Picador).

Mulhall, S. and Swift, A. (1995) 'The social self in political theory: the communitarian critique of the liberal subject', in Bakhurst, D. and Sypnowich, C. (eds) *The Social Self* (London, Sage).

Mullender, A. (1996a) *Rethinking Domestic Violence: The Social Work and Probation Response* (London, Routledge).

Mullender, A. (1996b) 'The empowerment framework', in Berkowitz, N. (ed.) *Humanistic Approaches to Health Care: Focus on Social Work* (Birmingham, Venture Press).

Mullender, A. and Ward, D. (1991) *Self-directed Groupwork: Users Take Action for Empowerment* (London, Whiting & Birch).

Muncie, J. (1984) *'The Trouble with Kids Today': Youth and Crime in Post-War Britain* (London, Hutchinson).

Munday, B. and Lane, D. (1998) *The Old and the New – Changes in Social Care in Central and Eastern Europe* (Canterbury, European Institute of Social Services, University of Kent).

Murray, C. (1984) *Losing Ground: American Social Policy, 1950–80* (New York, Basic Books).

Murray, C. (1990) *The Emerging British Underclass* (London, Institute for Economic Affairs).

Murray, C. (1994) *Underclass: The Crisis Deepens* (London, Institute for Economic Affairs).

NACRO (1991) *Training Materials for the 1991 Criminal Justice Act* (London, National Association for the Care and Resettlement of Offenders).

NACRO (1996) *Remand Fostering*, NACRO Briefing, December (London, National Association for the Care and Resettlement of Offenders).

NAPO (1990) 'Working with women: an anti-sexist approach', in *Practice Guidelines*, edited by Probation Practice Committee (London, National Association of Probation Officers).

NASW (1996) *Code of Ethics*, 2nd edn, (Silver Spring, MD, National Association of Social Workers) http://www.naswdc.org/code.htm.

National Association of Race Equality Advisers (1993) *Black Community Care Charter* (Birmingham, NAREA, c/o Race Relations Unit, Central Executive Department, Congreve House, 3 Congreve Passage, Birmingham, B3 3DA).

National Urban League (1964) *Double Jeopardy, the Older Negro in America Today* (New York, National Urban League).

NCH Action for Children (1991) *Poverty and Nutrition* (London, NCH Action for Children).

Neale-Hurston, Z. (1986) *Their Eyes Were Watching God* (London, Virago).

Neary, M. (1992) 'Some academic freedom', *Probation Journal*, **39**, pp. 200–2.

Nellis, M. (1995a) 'Probation values for the 1990s', *Howard Journal of Criminal Justice*, **34**(1): 19–44.

Nellis, M. (1995b) 'The "third way" for probation: a reply to Spencer and James', *Howard Journal of Criminal Justice*, **34**(4): 350–3.

Nellis, M. (2000) 'Taking oppression seriously: A critique of managerialism in social work/probation', in Paylor, I, Froggett, L. and Harris, J. (eds) *Reclaiming Social Work: The Southport Papers*, vol. 2 (Birmingham, Venture Press).

Nelson, N. and Wright, S. (eds) (1995) *Power and Participatory Development: Theory and Practice* (London, Intermediate Technology Publications).

Newburn, T. and Stanko, E.A. (eds) (1994) *'Just Boys Doing Business?'*, *Men, Masculinities and Crime* (London, Routledge).

Newman, T., Oakley, A. and Roberts, H. (1996) 'Weighing up the evidence', *Guardian*, 10 January, p. 9.

Newson, J. and Newson, E. (1976) *Seven Years Old in the Home Environment* (London, Allen & Unwin).

NISW (1992) *General Social Services Council Consultation Papers* (London, National Institute for Social Work).

NISW (1995a) *Working in the Social Services*, Policy Briefings, No. 10 (London, National Institute for Social Work).

NISW (1995b) *Managing Innovation and Change*, Policy Briefings, No. 11 (London, National Institute for Social Work).

NISW (1996) *Social Exclusion, Civil Society and Social Work* Policy Briefings, No. 18 (London, National Institute for Social Work).

Noonan, E. (1983) *Counselling Young People* (London, Tavistock/Routledge).

Nuttall, C.P., Barnard, E.E., Fowles, A.J., Frost, A., Hammond, W.H., Mayhew, P., Pease, K., Tarling, R. and Weatheritt, M. (1977) *Parole in England and Wales*, Home Office Research Study 30 (London, HMSO).

Nuttall, C.P. (director) (1998) *An Assessment of Evidence on Ways of Dealing with Offending Behaviour*, Home Office Research Study 187 (London, Home Office).

Oakley, A. (1999) 'People's ways of knowing: gender and methodology', in Hood, S., Mayal, B. and Oliver, S. (eds) *Critical Issues in Social Research: Power and Prejudice* (Buckingham, Open University Press).

Oakley, A. and Williams, A.S. (eds) (1994) *The Politics of the Welfare State* (London, University of Central London Press).

Office for National Statistics (2000) *Social Inequalities* (London, Stationery Office).

Office for Public Management (1994) *From Margin to Mainstream: User and Carer Involvement in Community Care, Local Authorities Changing Themselves – Manager's Manual* (London, Office for Public Management).

Office of Science and Technology (1994) *The Forward Look of Government-funded Science, Engineering and Technology* (London, HMSO).

O'Hagan, K. (ed.) (1996) *Competence in Social Work: A Practical Guide for Professionals* (London, Jessica Kingsley).

O'Hagan, K. (2001) *Cultural Competence in the Caring Professions* (London, Jessica Kingsley).

O'Hanlon, B. (1993) 'Possibility theory', in Gilligan, S. and Price, R. (eds) *Therapeutic Conversations* (New York, Norton).

O'Hanlon, B. and Beadle, S. (1994) *A Field Guide to Possibility Land* (Omaha, Possibility Press).

O'Hanlon, B. and Weiner-Davis, M. (1989) *In Search of Solutions* (New York, Norton).

Oliver, J.P.J. and Hudson, B.L. (1998) 'Behavioural work, crisis intervention and the mental health call-out', in Cigno, K. and Bourn, D. (eds) *Cognitive-behavioural Social Work in Practice* (Aldershot, Ashgate).

Oliver, J.P.J., Huley, P.J. and Butler, A. (1989) *Mental Health Casework: Illuminations and Reflections* (Manchester, Manchester University Press).

Oliver, M. (1990) *The Politics of Disablement: A Sociological Approach* (London, Macmillan – now Palgrave Macmillan).

Oliver, M. (1996) *Understanding Disability: From Theory to Practice* (London, Macmillan – now Palgrave Macmillan).

Oppenheim, C. (1997) 'The growth of poverty and inequality', in Walker, A. and Walker, C. (eds) (1997) *Britain Divided: The Growth of Social Exclusion in Britain 1979–1997* (London, Child Poverty Action Group).

Oppenheim, C. and Harker, L. (1996) *Poverty: The Facts*, 3rd edn (London, Child Poverty Action Group).

Oppenheim, C. and Lister, R. (1996) 'The politics of child poverty 1979 to 1995', in Pilcher, J. and Wagg, S. (eds) *Thatcher's Children? Politics, Childhood and Society in the 1980's and 1990's* (London, Falmer Press).

Orem, D. (1985) *Nursing Concepts of Practice* (New York, McGraw-Hill).

Orme, J. (1997) 'Research into practice', in McKenzie, G., Powell, J. and Usher, R. (eds) *Understanding Research: Perspectives on Methodology and Practice* (Hove, Falmer Press).

Orme, J. (2001) *Gender and Community Care: Social Work and Social Care Perspectives* (Basinsgtoke: Palgrave – now Palgrave Macmillan).

Orme, J., Dominelli, L. and Mullender, A. (2000) 'Working with violent men from a feminist social work perspective', *International Social Work*, **43**(1): 89–105.

Orme, J. and Glastonbury, B. (1993) *Care Management* (London, Macmillan – now Palgrave Macmillan).

O'Sullivan, T. (1999) *Decision Making in Social Work* (London, Macmillan – now Palgrave Macmillan).

Packman, J. and Jordan, B. (1991) 'The Children Act: looking forward, looking back', *British Journal of Social Work*, **21**: 315–27.

Packman, J., Randall, J. and Jaques, N. (1986) *Who Needs Care? Social Work Decisions about Children* (Oxford, Blackwell).

Pahl, J. (1992) 'Force for change or optional extra? The impact of research on policy in social work and social welfare', in Carter, P., Jeffs, T. and Smith, M.K. (eds) *Changing Social Work and Welfare* (Buckingham, Open University Press).

Parham, T.A. (1989) 'Cycles of psychological nigrescence', *Counseling Psychologist*, **17**(2): 187–226.

Parham, T.A. and Helms, J. (1985) 'Relation of racial identity to self-actualization and affective states of black students', *Journal of Counseling Psychology*, **28**(3): 250–6.

Parker, R. (1990) *Safeguarding Standards* (London, National Institute for Social Work).

Parker, R.A., Ward, H., Jackson, S., Aldgate, J. and Wedge, P. (eds) (1991) *Looking After Children: Assessing Outcomes in Child Care* (London, HMSO).

Parmar, P. (1981) 'Young Asian women: a critique of the pathological approach', *Multi-Racial Education*, **9**(3): 19–29.

Parton, N. (1994) 'The nature of social work under conditions of (post)modernity', *Social Work and Social Sciences Review*, **5**(2): 93–112.

Parton, N. (ed.) (1996) *Social Theory, Social Change and Social Work*, London, Routledge.

Parton, N. (1998) 'Advanced liberalism, (post)modernity and social work: Some emerging social configurations', *Social Thought*, **18**(3): 71–88.

Parton, N. and O'Byrne, P. (2000) *Constructive Social Work: Towards a New Practice* (Basingstoke, Palgrave – now Palgrave Macmillan).

Patel, N. (1990) *A 'Race Against Time?' Social Services Provision to Black Elders* (London, Runnymede Trust).

Patel, N., Naik, D. and Humphries, B. (eds). (1998) *Visions of Reality: Religion and Ethnicity in Social Work* (London, Central Council for Education and Training in Social Work).

Payne, H. and Littlechild, B. (2000) *Ethical Practice and the Abuse of Power in Social Responsibility* (London, Jessica Kingsley).

Payne, M. (1991) *Modern Social Work Theory: A Critical Introduction* (London, Macmillan – now Palgrave Macmillan).

Payne, M. (1992) 'Psychodynamic theory within the politics of social work theory', *Journal of Social Work Practice*, **6**(2): 141–9.

Payne, M. (1995) *Social Work and Community Care* (London, Macmillan – now Palgrave Macmillan).

Payne, M. (1996a) *What is Professional Social Work?* (Birmingham, Venture).

Payne, M. (1996b) 'The politics of social work theory and values', in IFSW, IASSW and HKSWA (eds) *Participating in Change – Social Work Profession in Social Development:* Proceedings of the Joint World Congress of the International Federation of Social Workers and the International Association of Schools of Social Work (Hong Kong, HKSWA, IASSW and IFSW).

Payne, M. (1997) *Modern Social Work Theory*, 2nd edn (London, Macmillan – now Palgrave Macmillan).

Payne, M. and Shardlow, S. (eds) (2002) *Social Work in The British Isles* (London, Jessica Kingsley).

Pearson, G. (1983) 'The Barclay Report and community social work: Samuel Smiles revisited?', *Critical Social Policy*, **2**: 73–86.

Pearson, G., Treseder, J. and Yelloly, M. (1988) *Social Work and the Legacy of Freud* (London, Macmillan – now Palgrave Macmillan).

Pearson, R.E. (1990) *Counseling and Social Support: Perspectives and Practice* (London, Sage).

Pease, B. and Fook, J. (eds) (1999) *Transforming Social Work Practice: Postmodern Critical Perspectives* (London, Routledge).

Pease, K. (1994) 'Crime prevention', in Maguire, M., Morgan, R. and Reiner, R. (eds) *The Oxford Handbook of Criminology* (Oxford, Clarendon Press).

Penna, S. and O'Brien, M. (1996) 'Postmodernism and social policy: a small step forwards?', *Journal of Social Policy*, **25**(1): 39–61.

Perlman, H.H. (1957) *Social Casework: a Problem-solving Process* (Chicago, University of Chicago Press).

Pernell, R.B. (1986) 'Empowerment and social group work', in Parnes, M. (ed.) *Innovations in Social Group Work: Feedback from Practice to Theory* (New York, Haworth Press).

Perrott, S. (1994) 'Working with men who abuse women and children', in Lupton, C. and Gillespie, T. (eds) *Working with Violence* (London, Macmillan – now Palgrave Macmillan).

Peters, M.F. (1985) 'Racial socialization of young black children', in McAdoo, H. and McAdoo, J. (eds) *Black Children: Social, Educational and Parental Environments* (Newbury Park, CA, Sage).

Peters, T. and Waterman, R. (1982) *In Search of Excellence* (London, Harper & Row).

Peyton, L. (1997) 'Reorganisation; trends and issues in Northern Ireland', in Cohen, B. and Hagen, U. (eds) *Children's Services: Shaping up to the Millennium* (Edinburgh, HMSO).

Phillips, M. (1993) 'An oppressive urge to end oppression', *Observer*, 1 August.

Phillips, M. (1994) 'Illiberal liberalism', in Dunant, S. (ed.) *The War of the Word: The Political Correctness Debate* (London: Virago).

Phillipson, C. (1993) 'Approaches to advocacy', in Johnson, J. and Slater, R. (eds) *Ageing and Later Life* (London, Sage).

Phillipson, J. (1988) 'The complexities of caring: developing a feminist approach to training staff in a residential setting', *Social Work Education*, 7(3): 3–6.

Phillipson, J. (1991) *Practising Equality: Women, Men and Social Work* (London, Central Council for Education and Social Work).

Phinney, J. (1990) 'Ethnic Identity in Adolescents and Adults: Review of Research', *Psychological Bulletin* **108**: 499-514.

Pietroni, M. (1995) 'The nature and aims of professional education for social workers; a postmodern perspective', in Yelloly, M. and Henkel, M. (eds) *Learning and Teaching in Social Work: Towards Reflective Practice* (London, Jessica Kingsley).

Pincus, A. and Minahan, A. (1973) *Social Work Practice: Model and Method* (Itasca, IL, Peacock).

Pinker, R. (1993) 'A lethal kind of looniness', *Times Higher Educational Supplement*, 10 September.

Pinkney, S. (1998) 'The reshaping of social work and social care', in Hughes, G. and Lewis, G. (eds) *Unsettling Welfare: The Reconstruction of Social Policy* (London, Routledge).

Pitcairn, T. and Waterhouse, L. (1993) 'Evaluating parenting in child physical abuse', in Waterhouse, L. (ed.) *Child Abuse and Child Abusers: Protection and Prevention* (London, Jessica Kingsley).

Pitcairn, T. and Waterhouse, L. (1996) 'Evaluating parenting in child physical abuse' in Waterhouse, L. (ed.) *Child Abuse and Child Abusers: Protection and Prevention*, 2nd edn (London, Jessica Kingsley).

Pitts, J. (1988) *The Politics of Juvenile Crime* (London, Sage).

Plomin, R. (1994) *Genetics and Experience: The Interplay Between Nature and Nurture* (Thousand Oaks, CA, Sage).

Plummer, K. (1981) 'Going gay: identities, life cycles and lifestyles in the male gay world', in Hart, J. and Richardson, D. (eds) *The Theory and Practice of Homosexuality* (London, Routledge).

Popple, K. (1995) *Analysing Community Work* (Buckingham, Open University Press).

Pottage, D. and Evans, M. (1994) *The Competent Workplace: The View from Within* (London, National Institute for Social Work).

Powell, F. (2001) *The Politics of Social Work* (London, Sage).

Pozatek, E. (1994) 'The problem of certainty: clinical social work in the post modern era', *Social Work*, **39**(4): 396–403.

Preston, P. (1996) 'When focus groups can be hocus-pocus', *Guardian*, 15 November.

Preston-Shoot, M. (1987) *Effective Groupwork* (London, Macmillan – now Palgrave Macmillan).

Preston-Shoot, M. (2000a) 'What if? Using the law to uphold practice values and standards', *Practice*, **12**(4): 49–63.

Preston-Shoot, M. (2000b) 'Making connections in the curriculum: law and professional practice', in Pierce, R. and Weinstein, J. (eds) *Innovative Education and Training for Care Professionals: A Providers' Guide* (London, Jessica Kingsley).

Preston-Shoot, M. (2000c) 'Clear voices for change: messages from disability research for law, policy and practice', in Cooper, J. (ed.) *Law, Rights and Disability* (London, Jessica Kingsley).

Preston-Shoot, M. (2001) 'A triumph of hope over experience? On modernising accountability in social services – the case of complaints procedures in community care', *Social Policy and Administration*, **35**(6): 701–15.

Preston-Shoot, M. and Agass, D. (1990) *Making Sense of Social Work: Psychodynamics, Systems and Practice* (London, Macmillan – now Palgrave Macmillan).

Preston-Shoot, M., Roberts, G. and Vernon, S. (1998a) 'Social work law: from interaction to integration', *Journal of Social Welfare and Family Law*, **20**(1): 65–80.

Preston-Shoot, M., Roberts, G. and Vernon, S. (1998b) 'Working together in social work law', *Journal of Social Welfare and Family Law*, **20**(2): 137–50.

Preston-Shoot, M., Roberts, G. and Vernon, S. (2001) 'Values in social work law: strained relations or sustaining relationships?' *Journal of Social Welfare and Family Law*, **23**(1): 1–22.

Priestley, P., McGuire, J., Flegg, D., Hemsley, V. and Welham, D. (1978) *Social Skills and Personal Problem Solving: A Handbook of Methods* (London, Tavistock).

Pringle, K. (1992/93) 'Child sexual abuse perpetrated by welfare personnel and the problem of men', *Critical Social Policy*, **12**(3): 4–19.

Pritchard, J. (1992) *The Abuse of Elderly People: A Handbook for Professionals* (London, Jessica Kingsley).

Professional Social Work (1996) 'Parliamentary concern about social work stress', *Professional Social Work*, August, pp. 1–2.

Pugh, D. (1993) 'Understanding and managing organizational change', in Mabey, C. and Mayon-White, B. (eds) *Managing Change* (London, Paul Chapman).

Quinton, D. and Rutter, M. (1988) *Parenting Breakdown: The Making and Breaking of Intergenerational Links* (Aldershot, Avebury).

Rafferty, A.M. and Traynor, M. (1997) 'Quality and quantity in research policy for nursing', *NTresearch*, **2**(1): 16–27.

Rahman, M., Palmer, G., Kenway, P. and Howarth, C. (2000) *Monitoring Poverty and Social Exclusion 2000* (Joseph Rowntree Foundation).

Raynor, P. (1985) *Social Work, Justice and Control* (Oxford, Blackwell).

Raynor, P. (1993) 'System purists, client refusal and gatekeeping: is help necessarily harmful?', *Social Action*, **1**: 4–8.

Raynor, P. and Vanstone, M. (1994) 'Probation practice, effectiveness and the non-treatment paradigm', *British Journal of Social Work*, **24**(4): 387–404.

Raynor, P. and Vanstone, M. (1996) 'Reasoning and rehabilitation in Britain: the results of the straight thinking on probation (STOP) programme', *International Journal of Offender Therapy and Comparative Criminology*, **40**(4): 272–84.

Raynor, P., Smith, D. and Vanstone, M. (1994) *Effective Probation Practice* (London, Macmillan – now Palgrave Macmillan).

Reamer, F.G. (1990) *Ethical Dilemmas in Social Service*, 2nd edn (New York, Columbia University Press).

Reamer, F.G. (1993) *Philosophical Foundations of Social Work* (New York, Columbia University Press).

Reason, P. (ed.) (1988) *Human Inquiry in Action: Developments in New Paradigm Research* (London, Sage).

Reason, P. and Rowan, J. (eds) (1981) *Human Inquiry: A Sourcebook of New Paradigm Research* (Chichester, Wiley).

Rees, S. (1991) *Achieving Power: Practice and Policy in Social Welfare* (London, Allen & Unwin).

Reid, B. (1994) 'The mentor's experience – a personal perspective', in Palmer, A., Burns, S. and Bulman, C. (eds) *Reflective Practice in Nursing: The Growth of the Professional Practitioner* (Oxford, Blackwell).

Reid, W.J. (2000) *The Task Planner: An Intervention Resource for Human Service Planners* (New York: Columbia University Press).

Reid, W.J. (2001) 'The role of science in social work: The perennial debate', *Journal of Social Work*, 1(3): 273–94.

Reid, W.J. and Epstein, L. (1972) *Task-centered Casework* (New York, Columbia University Press).

Reid, W.J. and Shyne, A.W. (1969) *Brief and Extended Casework* (New York, Columbia University Press).

Rex, S. (1999) 'Desistance from offending: experiences of probation', *Howard Journal of Criminal Justice*, 38(4): 366–85.

Rickford, F. (2001) 'Going through the motions?', *Community Care*, 20–26 September, pp. 18–19.

Ritchie, J., Dick, D. and Lingham, R. (1994) *Report of the Inquiry into the Care and Treatment of Christopher Clunis* (London, HMSO).

Roberts, J. and Taylor, C. (1996) 'Sexually abused children and young people speak out', in Waterhouse, L. (ed.) *Child Abuse and Child Abusers: Protection and Prevention* (London, Jessica Kingsley).

Roberts, R. (1990) *Lessons from the Past: Issues for Social Work Theory* (London, Tavistock/Routledge).

Robins, D. (1992) *Tarnished Vision: Crime and Conflicts in the Inner City* (Oxford, Oxford University Press).

Robins, S. (1990) *Organization Theory: Structure, Design and Applications*, 3rd edn (Englewood Cliffs, NJ, Prentice Hall).

Robinson, L. (1995) *Psychology for Social Workers: Black Perspectives* (London, Routledge).

Robinson, L. (2000) 'Racial identity attitudes and self-esteem of black adolescents in residential care: an exploratory study', *British Journal of Social Work*, 30: 3–24.

Rochdale County Council (1986) *Report of Chief Executive to Social Services Committee, Study of Needs and Circumstances of Elderly Asians in Rochdale* (Rochdale, Rochdale Metropolitan Borough Council).

Rochford, G. (1991) 'Theory, concepts, feelings and practice: the contemplation of bereavement within a social work course', in Lishman, J. (ed.) *Handbook of Theory to Practice Teachers in Social Work* (London, Jessica Kingsley).

Rodgers, B. and Pryor, J. (1998) *Divorce and Separation: The Outcomes for Children* (York, Joseph Rowntree Foundation).

Roediger, D.R. (1991) *The Wages of Whiteness* (London, Verso).

Rogers, C. (1980) *A Way of Being* (Boston, Houghton Mifflin).

Rogers, C.R. (1942) *Counseling and Psychotherapy* (Boston, Houghton Mifflin).

Rojek, C. and Collins, S. (1987) 'Contract or con trick?', *British Journal of Social Work*, **17**: 199–211.

Rojek, C. and Collins, S. (1988) 'Contract or con trick revisited: comments on the reply by Corden and Preston-Shoot', *British Journal of Social Work*, **18**(6): 611–22.

Rojek, C., Peacock, G. and Collins, S. (1988) *Social Work and Received Ideas* (London, Routledge).

Rollnick, S. and Miller, W.R. (1995) 'What is motivational interviewing?', *Behavioural and Cognitive Psychotherapy*, **23**: 325–34.

Rose, N. (1996) 'Authority and the genealogy of subjectivity', in Heelas, P., Lash, S. and Morris, P. (eds) *Detraditionalization: Critical Reflections on Authority and Identity* (Oxford, Blackwell).

Rosenau, P.M. (1992) *Post-modernism and the Social Sciences: Insights, Inroads and Intrusions* (Princeton, NJ, Princeton University Press).

Ross, R.R., Fabiano, E. and Ross, R. (1989) *Reasoning and Rehabilitation: A Handbook for Teaching Cognitive Skills* (Ottawa, Cognitive Centre).

Rowan, J. (1981) 'A dialectical paradigm for research', in Reason, P. and Rowan, J. (eds) *Human Inquiry: A Sourcebook of New Paradigm Research* (Chichester, Wiley).

Rowe, J. and Lambert, L. (1973) *Children Who Wait* (London, Association of British Adoption Agencies).

Rowe, J. and Thoburn, J. (1988) 'A snapshot of permanent family placement', *Adoption and Fostering*, **12**(3): 29–34.

Rowe, J., Hundleby, M. and Garnett, L. (1989) *Child Care Now* (London, British Agencies for Adoption and Fostering).

Royal Commission on Long Term Care for the Elderly (1999) *With Respect to Old Age*, Cm 4192-I (London, Stationery Office).

Rumgay, J. (2000) *The Addicted Offender: Developments in British Policy and Practice* (Basingstoke, Palgrave – now Palgrave Macmillan).

Rushdie, S. (1982) *Midnight's Children* (London, Pan).

Rushton, A., Quinton, D. and Treseder, J. (1993) 'New parents for older children: support services during eight years of placement', *Adoption and Fostering*, **17**(4): 39–45.

Russell, S. (1990) *Render Me My Song: African-American Women Writers from Slavery to the Present* (London, Pandora Press).

Rutherford, A. (1986) *Growing out of Crime* (Harmondsworth, Penguin).

Rutherford, A. (1996) *Transforming Criminal Policy* (Winchester, Waterside Press).

Rutherford, J. (1992) *Men's Silences: Predicaments in Masculinity* (London, Routledge).

Rutter, M. (1991) 'A fresh look at maternal deprivation,' in Bateson, P. (ed.) *The Development and Integration of Behaviour* (Cambridge, Cambridge University Press).

Rutter, M. and Smith, D. (eds) (1995) *Psychosocial Disorders in Young People: Time Trends and their Causes* (Chichester, Wiley).

Salaman, G., Adams, R. and O'Sullivan, T. (1994) *Managing Personal and Team Effectiveness Book 1: Managing Competently* (Milton Keynes, Health and Social Services Management Programme, Open University).

Saleeby, D. (ed.) (1997) *The Strengths Perspective in Social Work Practice*, 2nd edn (New York, Longman).

Salzberger-Wittenberg, I. (1970) *Psycho-analytic Insight and Relationships: A Kleinian Approach* (London, Routledge & Kegan Paul).

Sampson, A. and Smith, D. (1992) 'Probation and community crime prevention', *Howard Journal of Criminal Justice*, 31(2): 105–19.

Sands, R.G. and Nuccio, K. (1992) 'Postmodern feminist theory and social work', *Social Work*, 37(6): 489–94.

Sanfacon, A. (2001) How social workers address ethical dilemmas. Unpublished PhD research paper (Leicester, De Montfort University).

Sapsford, R. and Abbott, P. (1992) *Research Methods for Nurses and the Caring Professions* (Buckingham, Open University Press).

Schofield, G. (1996) 'Inner and outer worlds in child and family social work', Working paper (Norwich, Centre for Research on the Child and Family, University of East Anglia).

Schön, D.A. (1983) *The Reflective Practitioner: How Professionals Think in Action* (New York, Basic Books).

Schön, D.A. (1987) *Educating the Reflective Practitioner* (San Francisco, Jossey-Bass).

Schorr, A. (1992) *The Personal Social Services: An Outsider's View* (York, Joseph Rowntree Foundation).

Scott, M. (1989) *A Cognitive-behavioural Approach to Clients' Problems* (London, Tavistock/Routledge).

Scott, M.J., Stradling, S.J. and Dryden, W. (1995) *Developing Cognitive-behavioural Counselling* (London, Sage).

Scottish Executive (2000a) *It's a Criminal Waste: Stop Youth Crime Now* (Edinburgh, Scottish Executive).

Scottish Executive (2000b) *The Way Forward for Care: A Policy Position Paper* (Edinburgh, Tactica Solutions)

Scottish Office (1992a) *The Report of the Inquiry into the Removal of Children from Orkney in February 1991* (the Clyde Report) (Edinburgh, HMSO).

Scottish Office (1992b) *Inquiry into Child Care Policies in Fife* (the Kearney Report) (Edinburgh, HMSO).

Scottish Office (1999) *Aiming for Excellence*, Cm 4288 (Edinburgh, Scottish Office).

Scrutton, S. (1989) *Counselling Older People: A Creative Response to Ageing* (London, Edward Arnold).

Secker, J. (1993) *From Theory to Practice in Social Work: The Development of Social Work Students' Practice* (Aldershot, Avebury).

Seebohm Committee (1968) *Report of the Committee on Local Authority and Allied Social Services* (London, HMSO).

Seed, P. and Kaye, G. (1994) *Handbook for Assessing and Managing Care in the Community* (London, Jessica Kingsley).

Segall, M.H., Dasen, P.R., Berry, J.W. and Poortinga, Y.H. (1990) *Human Behaviour in Global Perspective* (New York, Pergamon).

Segall, M.H., Lonner, W.J. and Berry, J.W. (1998) 'Cross-cultural psychology as a scholarly discipline: on the flowering of culture in behavioral research', *American Psychologist*, **53**(10): 1101–10.

Seligman, M.E.P. (1975) *Helplessness* (San Francisco, Freeman).

Sellick, C. (1996) 'Short-term foster care in research in England and Wales', in Hill, M. and Aldgate, J. (eds) (1996a) *Child Welfare Services: Developments in Law, Policy, Practice and Research* (London, Jessica Kingsley).

Senge, P., Kleiner, A. and Roberts, C. (1994) *The Fifth Discipline: Strategies and Tools for Building a Learning Organisation* (London, Nicholas Brealey).

Senior, P. (1993) 'Groupwork in the probation service: care or control in the 1990s', in Brown, A. and Caddick, B. (eds) *Groupwork with Offenders* (London, Whiting & Birch).

Servian, R. (1996) *Theorising Empowerment: Individual Power and Community Care* (Bristol, Policy Press).

Shah, R. (1992) *The Silent Minority: Children with Disabilities in Asian Families* (London, National Children's Bureau).

Shakespeare, P., Atkinson, D. and French, S. (eds) (1993) *Reflecting on Research Practice: Issues in Health and Social Welfare* (Buckingham, Open University Press).

Shakespeare, T. (1996) 'Rules of engagement doing disability research', *Disability and Society*, **11**(1): 115–19.

Shardlow, S.M. (1992) 'Abstracts (Philosophy)', *British Journal of Social Work*, **22**(5): 588–92.

Shaw, I. (1995) 'The quality of mercy: the management of quality in the personal social services, in Kirkpatrick, I. and Martinez Lucio, M. (eds) *The Politics of Quality in the Public Sector* (London, Routledge).

Shaw, I. (1996) *Evaluating in Practice* (Aldershot, Arena).

Shaw, M. (1996) 'Out of the quagmire: community care-problems and possibilities for radical practice', in Cooke, I. and Shaw, M. (eds) *Radical Community Work* (Edinburgh, Moray House Publications).

Shaw, I. and Lishman, J. (eds) (1999) *Evaluation and Social Work Practice* (London, Sage).

Sheldon, B. (1982) *Behaviour Modification: Theory, Practice and Philosophy* (London, Tavistock).

Sheldon, B. (1994) 'Social work effectiveness research: implications for probation and juvenile justice', *Howard Journal of Criminal Justice*, **33**(3): 218–35.

Sheldon, B. (1995) *Cognitive-behavioural Therapy: Research, Practice and Philosophy* (London, Routledge).

Sheldon, B. and Chilvers, R. (2000) *Evidence-based Social Care. A study of Prospects and Problems* (London, Russell House).

Sheppard, M. (1995) *Care Management and the New Social Work: A Critical Analysis* (London, Whiting & Birch).

Shera, W. and Wells, L.M. (eds) (1999) *Empowerment Practice in Social Work.* (Toronto, Canadian Scholars Press).

Showalter, E. (1987) *The Femal Malady: Women, Madness and English Culture 1830–1980* (London, Virago)

Sibeon, R. (1991) 'Sociological reflections on welfare politics and social work', *Social Work and Social Sciences Review*, **3**(3): 184–203.

Sidell, M. (1993) 'Death, dying and bereavement', in Bond, J., Coleman, P. and Peace, S. (1993) *Ageing in Society: An Introduction to Social Gerontology*, 2nd edn (London, Sage).

Simons, K. (1992) *'Sticking Up For Yourself'*, *Self-advocacy and People with Learning Difficulties* (York, Joseph Rowntree Foundation).

Simpkin, M. (1989) 'Radical social work: lessons for the 1990s', in Carter, P., Jeffs, T. and Smith, M. (eds) *Social Work and Social Welfare Yearbook 1* (Milton Keynes, Open University Press).

Sinclair, R., Garnett, L. and Berridge, D. (1995) *Social Work Assessment with Adolescents* (London, National Children's Bureau).

Sinfield, A. (1969) *Which Way for Social Work?*, Fabian Tract 393 (London, Fabian Society).

Sinha, D. (1983) 'Cross-cultural psychology: a view from the Third World', in Deregowski, J.B., Dziurawier, S. and Annis, R.C. (eds) *Explorations in Cross-Cultural Psychology* (Lisse, Swets & Zeitlinger).

Skellington, R. with Morris, P. (1992) *'Race' in Britain Today* (London, Sage).

Skinner, A. (1992) *Another Kind of Home* (London, HMSO).

Smale, G. (1993) *Managing Change through Innovation: Workbook* (London, National Institute for Social Work, Practice and Development Exchange).

Smale, G. and Tusan, G., with Biehal, N. and Marsh, P. (1993) *Empowerment, Assessment, Care Management and the Skilled Worker* (London, HMSO).

Smart, B. (1999) *Facing Modernity. Ambivalence, Reflexivity and Morality* (London, Sage).

Smith, C. and White, S. (1997) 'Parton, Howe and postmodernity: a critical comment on mistaken identity', *British Journal of Social Work*, **27**(2): 275–96.

Smith, D. (1984) 'Law and order: arguments for what?', *Critical Social Policy*, **11**: 33–45.

Smith, D. (1992) 'Puritans and paradigms: a comment', *Social Work and Social Sciences Review*, **3**(2): 99–103.

Smith, D. (1995) *Criminology for Social Work* (London, Macmillan – now Palgrave Macmillan).

Smith, D. (2000a) 'Corporatism and the new youth justice', in Goldson, B. (ed.) *The New Youth Justice* (Lyme Regis, Russell House).

Smith, D. (2000b) *The Limits of Positivism Revisited*, ESRC Funded Seminar Series on Theorising Social Work, Seminar 4, Cardiff, 'What Works as Evidence for Practice? The Methodological Repertoire in an Applied Discipline', NISW website (London, NISW).

Smith, D., Blagg, H. and Derricourt, N. (1988) 'Mediation in South Yorkshire', *British Journal of Criminology*, **28**(3): 378–95.

Smith, D., Paylor, I. and Mitchell, P. (1993) 'Partnerships between the probation service and the independent sector', *Howard Journal of Criminal Justice*, **32**(1): 25–39.

Smith, G., Smith, T. and Wright, G. (1997) 'Poverty and schooling: choice, diversity or division?', in Walker, A. and Walker, C. (eds) *Britain Divided: The Growth of Social Exclusion in Britain 1979–1997* (London, Child Poverty Action Group).

Smith, J. (chair) (1994) *A Wider Strategy for Research and Development relating to Personal Social Services*, Report to the Director of Research and Development, Department of Health, by an Independent Review Group (London, HMSO).

Smith, P.K. (1991) *The Psychology of Grandparenthood: An International Perspective* (London, Routledge).

Smith, T. (1995) 'Children and young people – disadvantage, community and the Children Act, 1989', in Henderson, P. (ed.) *Children and Communities* (London, Pluto), pp. 54–69.

Social Trends (1996) (London, HMSO).

Social Work Services Group (1991) *National Objectives and Standards for Social Work Services in the Criminal Justice System* (Edinburgh, Scottish Office).

Solomon, B.B. (1985) 'Community social work practice in oppressed minority communities', in Taylor, S.H. and Roberts, R.W. (eds) *Theory and Practice of Community Social Work* (New York, Columbia University Press).

Sone, K. (1995) 'Get tough', *Community Care*, 6–12 March, pp. 16–18.

Specht, H. and Vickery, A. (eds) (1977) *Integrating Social Work Methods* (London, Allen & Unwin).

Spencer, J. (1995) 'A response to Mike Nellis: probation values for the 1990s', *Howard Journal of Criminal Justice*, **34**(4): 344–9.

Spencer, M.B. (1988) 'Self-concept development', in Slaughter, D.T. (ed.) *Black Children in Poverty: Developmental Perspectives* (San Francisco, Jossey-Bass).

Spender, D. (1980) *Man Made Language* (London, Routledge & Kegan Paul).

SSI (1991a) *Care Management and Assessment* (London, HMSO).

SSI (1991b) *Care Management and Assessment: Managers Guide* (London, HMSO).

SSI (1992) *Concerns for Quality: The First Annual Report of the Chief Inspector Social Services Inspectorate 1991/2* (London, HMSO).

SSI (1996) *Children in Need: Report of the SSI National Inspection of Family Support Services 1993/1995* (Leeds, Department of Health).

Stanley, L. (ed.) (1990) *Feminist Praxis: Research Theory and Epistemology in Feminist Sociology* (London, Routledge).

Statham, D. (1978) *Radicals in Social Work* (London, Routledge & Kegan Paul).

Stein, M. (2001) *Helping Care Leavers: Problems and Strategic Responses* (London, Department of Health).

Stein, M. and Carey, K. (1986) *Leaving Care* (Oxford, Blackwell).

Stevenson, O. (1988) 'Law and social work education: a commentary on the "Law Report"', *Issues in Social Work Education*, **8**(1): 37–45.

Stevenson, O. (1994) 'Social work in the 1990s: empowerment – fact or fiction?' in Page, R. and Baldock, J. (eds) *Social Policy Review 6* (Canterbury, Social Policy Association).

Stevenson, O. and Parsloe, P. (1993) *Community Care and Empowerment* (York, Joseph Rowntree Foundation and *Community Care*).

Stewart, J., Smith, D. and Stewart, G. (1994) *Understanding Offending Behaviour* (Harlow, Longman).

Stone, J. (1995) *Making Positive Moves: Developing Short-Term Fostering Services* (London, British Agencies for Adoption and Fostering).

Stubbs, P. (1988) The reproduction of racism in state social work. Unpublished PhD thesis, University of Bath.

Sue, D.W. and Sue, D. (1990) *Counselling the Culturally Different* (New York, Wiley).

Sutton, C. (1994) *Social Work, Community Work and Psychology* (Leicester, British Psychological Society).

Sutton, C. (1999) *Helping Families with Troubled Children: a Preventive Approach* (Chichester, Wiley).

Sutton, C. (2000a) 'Cognitive-behavioural theory: relevance for social work', *Cognitive Behavioural Social Work Review*, **21**: 22–46.

Sutton, C. (2000b) *Child and Adolescent Behaviour Problems. A Multidisciplinary Approach to Assessment and Intervention* (Leicester, British Psychological Society).

Tannen, D. (1996) *Talking from 9 to 5: How Men's and Women's Conversational Styles Affect Who Gets Heard, Who Gets Credit and What Gets Done at Work* (London, Virago).

Taylor, B.J. (2000) *Reflective Practice: A Guide for Nurses and Midwives,* (Buckingham, Open University Press).

Taylor, C. and White, S. (2000) *Practising Reflexivity in Health and Welfare: Making Knowledge* (Buckingham, Open University Press).

Taylor, G. (1996) 'Ethical issues in practice: participatory social research and groups', *Groupwork*, **9**(2): 110–27.

Taylor, I. (1996) 'Reflective learning, social work education and practice in the 21st century', in N. Gould and I. Taylor (eds) *Reflective Learning for Social Work* (Aldershot, Arena).

Taylor, I., Walton, P. and Young, J. (1974) *The New Criminology* (London, Routledge & Kegan Paul).

Taylor, M., Hoyes, L., Lart, R. and Means, R. (1992) *User Empowerment in Community Care: Unravelling the Issues,* Studies in Decentralisation and Quasi-Markets 11 (Bristol, School for Advanced Urban Studies University of Bristol).

Taylor-Brown, J. (ed.) (2000) *Reducing Domestic Violence: What Works?* (London, Home Office).

Taylor-Gooby, P. (1994) 'Postmodernism and social policy: a great leap backwards?', *Journal of Social Policy*, **23**(3): 385–405.

Thobani, M. (1995) 'Working for equality in the London Borough of Hounslow', in Itzin, C. and Newman, J. (eds) *Gender, Culture and Organizational Change: Putting Theory into Practice* (London, Routledge).

Thoburn, J., Lewis, A. and Shemmings, D. (1995) *Paternalism or Partnership? Family Involvement in the Child Protection Process* (London, HMSO).

Thomas, E.J. (ed.) (1974) *Behaviour Modification Procedure: A Sourcebook* (Chicago, Aldine).

Thomas, N. and O'Kane, C. (1999) 'Experiences of decision-making in middle childhood; the example of children 'looked after' by local authorities' *Childhood*, **6**(3): 369–87.

Thompson, N. (1993) *Anti-Discriminatory Practice* (London, Macmillan – now Palgrave Macmillan).

Thompson, N. (1995a) *Age and Dignity: Working with Older People* (Aldershot, Arena).

Thompson, N. (1995b) 'Men and anti-sexism', *British Journal of Social Work*, **25**: 459–75.

Thompson, N. (1996a) *People Skills: A Guide to Effective Practice in the Human Services* (London, Macmillan – now Palgrave Macmillan).

Thompson, N. (1996b) 'Opening the floodgates', *Professional Social Work*, November, p. 4.

Thompson, N. (ed.) (2002) *Loss and Grief: A Guide for Human Services Practitioners* (Basingstoke, Palgrave – now Palgrave Macmillan)

Thompson, N. and Thompson, S. (2001) 'Empowering older people', *Journal of Social Work* 1(1): 61–76.

Thompson, N., Stradling, S., Murphy, M. and O'Neill, P. (1996) 'Stress and organizational culture', *British Journal of Social Work*, 26(5): 647–65.

Thorpe, D. (1994) *Evaluating Child Protection* (Buckingham, Open University Press).

Thorpe, D. and Thorpe, S. (1992) *Monitoring and Evaluation in the Social Services* (Brighton, Pavilion).

Thorpe, D.H., Smith, D., Green, C.J. and Paley, J.H. (1980) *Out of Care: The Community Support of Juvenile Offenders* (London, Allen & Unwin).

Thurston, R. (1997) 'Review', *Vista: Perspectives on Probation*, 2(3): 200–2.

Tilley, N. (1995) *Thinking about Crime Prevention Performance Indicators*, Crime Prevention and Detection Series, Paper 57 (London, Home Office).

Timms, N. (1983) *Social Work Values: An Enquiry* (London, Routledge & Kegan Paul).

Tizard, B. and Phoenix, A. (1989) 'Black identity and transracial adoption', *New Community*, 15(3).

Tober, G. (1991) 'Motivational interviewing with young people', in Miller, W. and Rollnick, S. (eds) *Motivational Interviewing: Preparing People to Change* (New York, Guilford Press).

Tober, G. (1998) 'Learning theory, addiction and counselling', in Cigno, K. and Bourn, D. (eds) *Cognitive-behavioural Social Work in Practice* (Aldershot, Ashgate).

Tolson, E.R., Reid, W.J. and Garvin, C.D. (1994) *Generalist Practice: A Task Centred Approach* (New York, Columbia University Press).

Thompson, N. (1995) 'Men and anti-sexism', *British Journal of Social Work*, 25: 459–75.

Townsend, P., Phillimore, P. and Beattie, A. (1988) *Health Deprivation: Inequality and the North* (London, Croom Helm).

Toynbee, P. and Walker, D. (2001) *Did Things Get Better?* (Harmondsworth, Penguin).

Tronick, E.Z., Morelli, G.A. and Ivey, P.K. (1992) 'The Efe forager infant and toddlers pattern of social relationships: multiple and simultaneous', *Developmental Psychology*, 28: 568–77.

Trowell, J. (1995) 'Working together in child protection, some issues for multi-disciplinary training from a psychodynamic perspective', in Yelloly, M. and Henkel, M. (eds) *Learning and Teaching in Social Work: Towards Reflective Practice* (London, Jessica Kingsley).

Turnbull, P.J., McSweeney, T., Webster, R., Edmunds, M. and Hough, M. (2000) *Drug Treatment and Testing Orders: Final Evaluation Report*, Home Office Research Study 212 (London, Home Office).

Turner, B.S. (1990) 'Periodisation and politics in the postmodern', in Turner, B.S. (ed.) *Theories of Modernity and Post Modernity* (London, Sage).

Turner, M. (1995) 'Supervising', in Carter, P., Jeffs, T. and Smith, M. K. (eds) *Social Working* (Basingstoke, Macmillan – now Palgrave Macmillan).

Twelvetrees, A. (1991) *Community Work* (London, Macmillan – now Palgrave Macmillan).

Twigg, J. (ed.) (1992) *Carers: Research and Practice* (London, HMSO).

UN Committee on the Rights of the Child (1995) *The Concluding Observations of the Committee on the Rights of the Child: United Kingdom of Great Britain and Northern Ireland*, in Consideration of Reports Submitted by State Parties Under Article 44 of the Convention Eighth Session (Geneva, United Nations).

Underdown, A. (1996) 'Practice and method', paper presented to the First Annual Colloquium of the Probation Studies Unit, Centre for Criminological Research, University of Oxford, 16–17 December.

Underdown, A. (1998) *Strategies for Effective Offender Supervision: Report of the HMIP What Works Project* (London, Home Office).

Ungerson, C. (1987) *Policy is Personal: Sex, Gender and Informal Care Work* (London: Tavistock)

Ussher, J. (1991) *Women's Madness: Misogyny or Mental Illness* (Hemel Hempstead: Harvester Wheatsheaf)

Utting, W. (1989) 'Foreword', in Kahan, B. (ed.) *Child Care Research, Policy and Practice* (London, Hodder & Stoughton).

Utting, W. (1991) *Children in the Public Care* (London, HMSO).

Utting, W. (1993) 'Foreword', in Ellis, K. *Squaring the Circle: User and Carer Participation in Needs Assessment* (York, Joseph Rowntree Foundation).

Utting, W. (1995) *Family and Parenthood: Supporting Families, Preventing Breakdown* (York, Joseph Rowntree Foundation).

Vanstone, M. (1995) 'Managerialism and the ethics of management', in Hugman, R. and Smith, D. (eds) *Ethical Issues in Social Work* (London, Routledge).

Vass, A.A. (1996) *Social Work Competences: Core Knowledge, Values and Skills* (London, Sage).

Veal, A.J. (1992) *Research Methods for Leisure and Tourism: A Practical Guide* (Harlow, Longman/ILAM).

Vernelle, B. (1994) *Understanding and Using Groups* (London, Whiting & Birch).

Wainwright, D. (1996) 'The political transformation of the health inequalities debate', *Critical Social Policy*, **49**(16): 4.

Walker, A. and Walker, C. (eds) (1997) *Britain Divided: The Growth of Social Exclusion in Britain 1979–1997* (London, Child Poverty Action Group).

Walker, J. (1995) 'Counselling in a social services area office: the practice behind the thoery', in Carter, P., Jeffs, T. and Smith, M. K. (eds) *Social Working* (Basingstoke, Macmillan – now Palgrave Macmillan).

Walker, J. (1997) 'Partnership and parenting', in Davies, M. (ed.) *The Blackwell Companion to Social Work* (Oxford, Blackwell).

Ward, A. (1993) 'The large group: the heart of the system in group care', *Groupwork*, **6**(1): 64–77

Ward, D. (ed.) (1996) *Groups and Research,* special edition of *Groupwork*, **9**(2).

Ward, D. and Mullender, A. (1991) 'Empowerment and oppression: an indissoluble pairing for contemporary social work', *Critical Social Policy*, **32**: 1–29.

Ward, H. (1995) *Looking After Children: Research into Practice* (London, HMSO).

Wardhaugh, J. and Wilding, P. (1993) 'Towards an explanation of the corruption of care', *Critical Social Policy*, **13**(1): 4–31.

Wardman, G. (1977) 'Social work: a communist view', *Marxism Today*, January, pp. 29–32.

Waterhouse, L., McGhee, J., Whyte, W., Loucks, N., Kay, H. and Stewart, R. (2000) *The Evaluation of Children's Hearings in Scotland.* vol. 3 *Children in Focus* (Edinburgh, Scottish Executive Central Research Unit).

Waterhouse, R. (2000) *Lost in Care. The Report of the Tribunal of Inquiry into the Abuse of Children in Care in the Former County Council Areas of Gwynedd and Clwyd since 1974* (London, Stationery Office).

Wearing, B. (1986) 'Feminist theory and social work', in Marchant, H. and Wearing, B. (eds) *Gender Reclaimed: Women in Social Work* (Sydney, Hale & Iremonger).

Webb, D. (1990–91a) 'Puritans and paradigms: a speculation on the form of new moralities in social work', *Social Work and Social Sciences Review*, **2**(2): 146–59.

Webb, D. (1990–91b) 'A stranger in the academy: a reply to Lena Dominelli', *Social Work and Social Sciences Review*, **2**(3): 236–41.

Webb, D. (1996) 'Regulation for radicals: the state, CCETSW and the academy', in Parton, N. (ed.) *Social Theory, Social Change and Social Work* (London, Routledge).

Webb, S. (1993) 'Women's incomes: past, present and prospects', *Fiscal Studies*, **14**(4): 14–36.

Webb, S. (1994) 'My client is subversive! Partnership and patronage in social work', *Social Work and Social Science Review* **5**(1): 5–23.

Webb, S.A. (2001) 'Some considerations on the validity of evidence-based practice in social work', *British Journal of Social Work*, **31**: 57–79.

Webb, S.A. and McBeath, G.A. (1989) 'A political critique of Kantian ethics in social work', *British Journal of Social Work*, **19**(6): 491–506.

Webb, S.A. and McBeath, G.A. (1990) 'A political critique of Kantian ethics in social work: a reply to Professor R.S. Downie', *British Journal of Social Work* **20**(1): 65–71.

Weber, M. (1947) *The Theory of Social and Economic Organization* (New York, Free Press). Reprinted in Pugh, D. (1990) *Organization Theory* (Harmondsworth, Penguin).

Webster-Stratton, C. and Herbert, M. (1994) *Troubled Families – Problem Children* (Chichester, Wiley).

Wendell, S. (1996) *The Rejected Body* (Toronto, Garamond Press).

Westwood, S. and Bhachu, P. (1988) 'Images and realities', *New Society*, 6 May.

Whetham, W.C.D. (1909) *The Family and the Nation* (London, Longman & Green).

Whitaker, D.S. (1975) 'Some conditions for effective work with groups', *British Journal of Social Work*, **5**(4): 423–39.

Whitaker, D.S. (1985) *Using Groups to Help People* (London, Tavistock/ Routledge).

Whitaker, D.S. and Archer, J.L. (1989) *Research by Social Workers: Capitalizing on Experience*, CCETSW Study 9 (London, Central Council for Education and Training in Social Work).

White, M. (1993) 'Deconstruction and therapy', in S. Gilligan and R. Price (eds) *Therapeutic Conversations* (New York, Norton).

White, M. and Epston, D. (1990) *Narrative Means to Therapeutic Ends* (New York, W.W. Norton).

White, V. (1995) 'Commonality and diversity in feminist social work', *British Journal of Social Work*, **25**: 143–56.

Wilcox, S. (1996) *Housing Review 1996/97* (York, Joseph Rowntree Foundation).

Wilkes, R. (1981) *Social Work with Undervalued Groups* (London, Tavistock Publications).

Wilkinson, R. (1996) *Unhealthy Societies: The Afflictions of Inequality* (London, Routledge).

Wilkinson, R.G. (1994) *Unfair Shares: The Effects of Widening Income Differences on the Welfare of Young Children* (Ilford, Barnardo's).

Williams, F. (1989) *Social Policy* (Oxford, Polity Press).

Willis, P. (1978) *Learning to Labour: How Working Class Lads Get Working Class Jobs* (Farnborough, Saxon House).

Wilson, A. and Beresford, P. (2000) '"Anti-oppressive practice": emancipation or appropriation?', *British Journal of Social Work*, **30**: 553–73.

Wilson, E. (1980) 'Feminism and social work', in Bailey, R. and Brake, M. (eds) *Radical Social Work and Practice*, 2nd edn (London, Edward Arnold).

Wilson, G. (1998) 'Staff and users in the postmodern organisation: modernity, postmodernity and user marginalisation', in Barry, M. and Hallett, C. (eds) *Social Exclusion and Social Work. Issues of Theory, Policy and Practice* (Lyme Regis, Russell House Publishing).

Wilson, J. (1986) *Self-help Groups: Getting Started – Keeping Going* (London, Longman).

Wilson, J. (1988) *Caring Together: Guidelines for Carers' Self-help and Support Groups* (London, King's Fund).

Wilson, J. (1995) *How to Work with Self-help Groups* (London, Arena).

Wineman, S. (1984) *The Politics of Human Services* (Montreal, Black Rose).

Winnicott, C. (1964) *Child Care and Social Work* (Hitchin, Codicote Press).

Wise, S. (1990) 'Becoming a feminist social worker', in Stanley, L. (ed.) *Feminist Praxis: Research Theory and Epistemology in Feminist Sociology* (London, Routledge).

Wise, S. (1995) 'Feminist ethics in practice', in Hugman, R. and Smith, D. (eds) *Ethical Issues in Social Work* (London, Routledge).

Wolfensberger, W. (1997) 'Major obstacles to rationality and quality of human services in contemporary society', in Adams, R. (ed.) *Crisis in the Human Services: National and International Issues*, Selected Conference Papers (Hull, University of Lincolnshire and Humberside).

Wood, K.M. (1990) 'Epistemological issues in the development of social work practice knowledge', in Videka-Sherman, L. and Reid, W.J. (eds) *Advances in Clinical Social Work Research* (Silver Spring, MD, National Association of Social Workers).

Woodroofe, K. (1962) *From Charity to Social Work in England and the United States* (London, Routledge & Kegan Paul).

Yalom, I. (1970) *The Theory and Practice of Group Psychotherapy* (New York, Basic Books).

Yates, P. (1985) Post-placement support for adoptive families of hard-to-place children. Unpublished MSc thesis, University of Edinburgh.

Yeh, C.J. and Huang, K. (1996) The collectivistic nature of ethnic identity development among Asian-American college students, *Adolescence*, **31**: 645–66.

Yelloly, M. (1980) *Social Work Theory and Psychanalysis* (London, Van Nostrand Reinhold).

Yelloly, M. and Henkel, M. (1995) *Learning and Teaching in Social Work: Towards Reflective Practice* (London, Jessica Kingsley).

Youll, P. (1996) 'Organisational or professional leadership? Managerialism and social work education', in Preston-Shoot, M. and Jackson, S. (eds)

Educating Social Workers in a Changing Policy Context (London, Whiting & Birch).

Young, N. (1977) *An Infantile Disorder? The Crisis and Decline of the New Left* (London, Routledge & Kegan Paul).

Younghusband, E. (1951) *Social Work in Britain* (London, Carnegie UK Trust).

Younghusband, E. (1970) 'Social work and social values', *Social Work Today*, **1**(4).

Yura, H. and Walsh, M.B. (1967) *The Nursing Process* (Norwalk, Appleton-Century-Crofts).

Author Index

Gelsthorpe 308 318 328
Gendreau 185
George, E. 194
George, M. 81
Geraghty 326
Geva 39
Gherardi 264
Gibbons 274
Giddens 238
Gilder 13
Gilligan 223
Ginsburg 58
Glastonbury 300
Glennerster 251 256
Goldson 315 328
Gomm 305
Gorman 181
Gould 31 32 125
Gouldner 113
Graham 38 326
Greenhorn 314
Greenfield 85
Greer 11
Gregg 269
Grimwood 80 104
Grossman 88
Groves 221
GSCC (General Social Care
    Council) 35
Guy 35
Gwynne 257

H
Hackett 147 148
Hadley 42
Hagel 276
Hagen 271 272 273
Haines 315
Hale 221
Hall 237
Hallett 272 275 277
Handler 45
Handy 83
Hanmer 5 104 219 221 222
    226
Hanvey 199
Hardiker 119 264

Harding, S. 116
Harding, T. 304
Harker 54 61
Harris, T. 178 282
Harrison, A. 90
Harrison, T.H. 333
Harrison, W.D. 128
Hart 112 119
Harwin 110
Hawkesworth 223
Hawxhurst 76
Hayman 254
Healy 124 235 237
Heap 149
Hearn 78 81 224
Heelas 238
Heineman 262
Helms 90 94
Henkel 108 147 266
Henry 93
Herbert 181
Hester 224 225
Hill, M. 60 73 185 277 281
    282 286
Hill, S. 90
Hill-Collins 227
Hills 52 54 55 268 269
Hinings 179
Hochschild 93
Hockey 290
Holdaway 316
Holland 92 235
Hollin 182 185
Hollis 32 171
Holman, B. 95 168 269
Holmans 49
Home Office 67 153 181 267
    271 309 310 312 313 314
    315 324 325
Home-Start UK 280
Hoogvelt 11 12 160
hooks 222 227
Hoopes 283
Horne 33
Horton 265
Hough 152 309
Houston 149

Subject Index